Microsoft

MW01253142

Windows 10
Step by Step

Joan Lambert
Steve Lambert

PHI Learning Private Limited
Delhi-110092
2016

This Indian Reprint—₹ 695.00
(Original U.S. Edition—₹ 2057.00)

WINDOWS 10 STEP BY STEP
by Joan Lambert and Steve Lambert

Authorized reprint from the English language edition, entitled WINDOWS 10 STEP BY STEP, 1st Edition, 9780735697959 by LAMBERT, JOAN; LAMBERT, STEVE, published by Pearson Education, Inc, publishing as Microsoft Press, Copyright © 2015 by Joan Lambert.

ISBN-978-81-203-5205-6

This book is provided "as-is" and expresses the authors' views and opinions. The views, opinions and information expressed in this book, including URL and other Internet website references, may change without notice.

Some examples depicted herein are provided for illustration only and are fictitious. No real association or connection is intended or should be inferred.

Microsoft and the trademarks listed at *http://www.microsoft.com* on the "Trademarks" webpage are trademarks of the Microsoft group of companies. All other marks are property of their respective owners.

This edition is authorised for sale in India, Pakistan, Bangladesh, Bhutan, Nepal, Sri Lanka, and the Maldives only.

The export rights of this book are vested solely with the publisher.

Published by Asoke K. Ghosh, PHI Learning Private Limited, Rimjhim House, 111, Patparganj Industrial Estate, Delhi-110092 and Printed by Raj Press, New Delhi-110012.

Contents

Introduction xi

Who this book is for xi

What this book is (and isn't) about. xi

The *Step by Step* approach xii

Download the practice files xii

     Sidebar: Adapt procedures for your environment. xiv

Ebook edition. xv

Get support and give feedback. xv

     Errata and support xv

     We want to hear from you xv

     Stay in touch xv

Part 1: The Windows 10 environment

1   **Get started using Windows 10** 3

Start a computing session. 4

     Sidebar: Use a Microsoft account or local account 4

Explore the desktop 9

Explore the taskbar. 12

     Sidebar: Hey, Cortana! 18

Explore the Start screen and Start menu 21

Give us feedback

Tell us what you think of this book and help Microsoft improve our products for you. Thank you!

http://aka.ms/tellpress

Explore computer settings 27

Update Windows system files 35

Manage content and app windows 37

    Resize, hide, and close windows 37

    Move and arrange windows 40

End a computing session 44

Skills review 46

Practice tasks 47

2   Personalize your working environment 51

Configure the Start screen and Start menu 52

    Set the Start screen size 53

    Configure Start menu content 55

Manage Start screen tiles 58

Set the desktop background and system colors 64

    Set the desktop background 65

    Set an accent color 69

Configure the taskbar 73

    Change taskbar appearance 73

    Change taskbar behavior 78

    Display and manage toolbars on the taskbar 80

Apply and manage themes 84

Skills review 91

Practice tasks 92

3   Manage folders and files 97

Understand files, folders, and libraries 98

    Folders 98

    Libraries 100

Get to know File Explorer 102

    Work with the standard ribbon tabs 105

Work with the tool tabs 109

Work with the Navigation And Search bar 111

Work with libraries 112

Change the File Explorer display options 117

Display and hide panes 117

Display different views of folders and files 118

Group folder content 122

Sort and filter folder content 124

Change folder options 126

Create and rename folders and files 129

Compress folders and files 130

Move and copy folders and files 132

Delete and recover folders and files 135

Sidebar: Recycle Bin size 137

Work with folder and file properties 138

View folder properties 138

Remove file properties 140

Find specific files 142

Windows Search 142

File Explorer Search 143

Skills review 145

Practice tasks 146

4   Work with apps and notifications 151

Locate and start apps 152

Explore built-in apps 157

Productivity and information management apps 157

Web browsers 158

Media management apps 158

Live information apps 160

Accessories 161

Utilities for geeks 162

Install Store apps 163

    Shop at the Windows Store 163

    Manage your Store account and settings. 166

    Install, reinstall, and uninstall apps. 171

Manage app shortcuts. 175

    Manage Start screen shortcuts 175

    Sidebar: Touchscreen tile management 176

    Sidebar: Manage apps from the taskbar 178

    Manage taskbar shortcuts 180

    Manage desktop shortcuts. 181

    Sidebar: Configure desktop system icons 187

Manage app startup. 188

Manage app notifications. 190

Skills review. 195

Practice tasks 196

5   Safely and efficiently browse the Internet 201

    Sidebar: About Microsoft Edge. 202

Display websites in Edge 203

Find, save, and share information. 207

Manage Edge settings 214

    Sidebar: Manage default apps. 225

    Sidebar: Anatomy of a website address 226

Configure browser security settings 228

    Protect yourself from phishing and malicious sites. 229

    Block pop-up windows 231

    Sidebar: Educate kids about online safety 233

Maintain browsing privacy 233

Troubleshoot browsing issues 235

Skills review. 239

Practice tasks 240

Part 2: Devices and resources

6   **Manage peripheral devices. 249**

Understand peripheral devices. 250

    Peripheral device terminology 250

    Install peripheral devices. 251

Locate device information 252

    Sidebar: Boost your memory. 253

Display your desktop on multiple screens 256

    Sidebar: Expand your portable computer with peripheral devices 263

Set up audio devices. 264

Change the way your mouse works. 271

Change the way your keyboard works 278

Manage printer connections 280

Skills review. 287

    Sidebar: Virtual printers. 288

Practice tasks 289

7   **Manage network and storage resources. 293**

Manage network connections. 294

    Connect to a network 294

    Sidebar: Network vs. Internet connections 296

    Display information about networks and connections 300

    Configure network connection security. 305

    Sidebar: Wireless network security 310

    Troubleshoot network connections. 312

Manage homegroup connections 316

Share files on your network 326

Skills review. 337

    Sidebar: Change the computer name 338

Practice tasks 340

Part 3: Behind the scenes

8 **Manage user accounts and settings** **345**

Understand user accounts and permissions 346

    User profiles 347

    User account permissions 348

    Family accounts 349

    User Account Control 350

Create and manage user accounts 353

    Sidebar: Manage user accounts in the Computer Management console . . 355

    Sidebar: Manage and monitor family safety settings 356

    Create and manage family user accounts 357

    Create and manage non-family user accounts 362

    Manage settings for any user account 365

Manage account pictures and passwords 369

Customize your sign-in options 375

Skills review 382

Practice tasks 383

9 **Manage computer settings** **385**

Manage date and time settings 386

Manage regional and language settings 396

    Sidebar: Install supplemental font features 403

Manage speech settings 408

Customize device display settings 413

Skills review 421

Practice tasks 422

10 Manage power and access options. 425

Configure power options 426

    Sidebar: System power settings 434

    Sidebar: Make your battery last longer. 435

Customize the lock screen 436

    Set the lock screen background 436

    Display app status information on the lock screen 440

    Sidebar: Configure a screen saver. 442

Configure Windows accessibility features 444

    High-contrast settings. 447

    Magnifier settings. 449

    Narrator and Audio Description settings 453

    Keyboard and mouse settings. 455

Skills review. 458

Practice tasks 459

11 Work more efficiently 463

Configure Quick Action buttons. 464

Get assistance from Cortana 469

    Initialize Cortana 470

    Configure Cortana settings 474

    Sidebar: Add reminders. 478

Search your computer and the web. 479

    Search storage locations and the web 480

    Manage Bing content filters. 484

    Manage File Explorer search processes 485

Specify default apps. 489

Organize apps on multiple desktops. 497

Monitor system tasks. 501

Skills review. 506

Practice tasks 507

12 Protect your computer and data 511

Configure update options 512
Configure privacy settings 515
Restore computer functionality 519
   Set and use restore points 519
   Refresh or reset your computer 522
Back up data to OneDrive 524
Back up data by using File History 530
Back up and restore your system 535
Skills review 541
   Sidebar: Two-factor authentication 542
Practice tasks 543

Appendix A: Install or upgrade to Windows 10 547
Appendix B: Keyboard shortcuts and touchscreen tips 559

Glossary 567
Index 583
About the authors 607

Give us feedback
Tell us what you think of this book and help Microsoft
improve our products for you. Thank you!
http://aka.ms/tellpress

Introduction

Welcome to the wonderful world of Windows 10! This *Step by Step* book has been designed so you can read it from the beginning to learn about Windows 10 and then build your skills as you learn to perform increasingly specialized procedures. Or, if you prefer, you can jump in wherever you need ready guidance for performing tasks. The how-to steps are delivered crisply and concisely—just the facts. You'll also find informative, full-color graphics that support the instructional content.

Who this book is for

Windows 10 Step by Step is designed for use as a learning and reference resource by home and business users of desktop and portable computers and devices running Windows 10 Home or Windows 10 Pro. The content of the book is designed to be useful for people who have previously used earlier versions of Windows and for people who are discovering Windows for the first time.

What this book is (and isn't) about

This book is about the Windows 10 operating system. Your computer's operating system is the interface between you and all the apps you might want to run, or that run automatically in the background to allow you to communicate with other computers around the world, and to protect you from those same computers.

In this book, we explain how you can use the operating system and the included tools, such as File Explorer, to access and manage the apps and data files you use in your work and play. Many useful apps come with Windows or are part of the Windows "family," such as Maps, Photos, Mail, Calendar, Groove Music, and Windows DVD Player. This book isn't about those apps, although we do mention and interact with a few of them while demonstrating how to use features of the Windows 10 operating system.

SEE ALSO For information about working with apps, see Chapter 4, "Work with apps and notifications."

The *Step by Step* approach

The book's coverage is divided into parts that represent general computer usage and management skill sets. Each part is divided into chapters that represent skill set areas, and each chapter is divided into topics that group related skills. Each topic includes expository information followed by generic procedures. At the end of the chapter, you'll find a series of practice tasks you can complete on your own by using the skills taught in the chapter. You can use the practice files that are available from this book's website to work through the practice tasks, or you can use your own files.

Download the practice files

Although you can complete the practice tasks in this book by using your own files, for your convenience we have provided practice files for many of the tasks. You can download these practice files to your computer by going to *http://aka.ms/Windows10SBS /files* and following the instructions on the webpage.

⚠ **IMPORTANT** Windows 10 is not available from the book's website. You should install that operating system before working through the procedures and practice tasks in this book. For information about installing Windows 10, see Appendix A, "Install or upgrade to Windows 10."

You can use the files that are supplied for the practice tasks to perform the tasks, and if there are changes, you can save the finished versions of each file. If you later want to repeat practice tasks, you can download the original practice files again.

 SEE ALSO For information about working with files, see Chapter 3, "Manage folders and files."

The following table lists the practice files for this book.

Chapter	Folder	File
1: Get started using Windows 10	None	None
2: Personalize your working environment	Win10SBS\Ch02	Background01.jpg through Background08.jpg
3: Manage folders and files	Win10SBS\Ch03	Files\Brochure.pptx Photos\Backgrounds\Background.jpg Photos\Backgrounds\Background03.jpg Photos\Backgrounds\Background08.jpg Photos\Lucy.jpg Photos\Lucy2.jpg Events.docx Expenses.xlsx PackingList.docx Password01.jpg through Password03.jpg Survey.docx TravelChecklist.xlsx
4: Work with apps and notifications	None	None
5: Safely and efficiently browse the Internet	None	None
6: Manage peripheral devices	None	None
7: Manage network and storage resources	Win10SBS\Ch07	Folder only
8: Manage user accounts and settings	Win10SBS\Ch08	Account01.jpg through Account05.jpg Password01.jpg through Password03.jpg
9: Manage computer settings	None	None
10: Manage power and access options	Win10SBS\Ch10	LockScreen01.jpg through Lockscreen13.jpg
11: Work more efficiently	Win10SBS\Ch11	None
12: Protect your computer and data	None	None

Adapt procedures for your environment

The instructions in this book assume that you're interacting with on-screen elements on your computer by clicking (with a mouse, touchpad, or other hardware device). If you're using a different method—for example, if your computer has a touchscreen interface and you're tapping the screen (with your finger or a stylus)—substitute the applicable tapping action when you interact with a user interface element.

 SEE ALSO For information about touchscreen interaction, see Appendix B, "Keyboard shortcuts and touchscreen tips."

Instructions in this book refer to user interface elements that you click or tap on the screen as *buttons*, and to physical buttons that you press on a keyboard as *keys*, to conform to the standard terminology that is used in documentation for these products.

Multistep procedural instructions use this format:

1. To select the paragraph that you want to format in columns, triple-click the paragraph.

2. On the **Layout** tab, in the **Page Setup** group, click the **Columns** button to display a menu of column layout options.

3. On the **Columns** menu, click **Three**.

On subsequent instances of instructions that require you to follow the same process, the instructions might be simplified in this format because the working location has already been established:

1. Select the paragraph that you want to format in columns.

2. On the **Columns** menu, click **Three**.

When the instructions tell you to enter information, you can do so by typing on a connected external keyboard, tapping an on-screen keyboard, or even speaking aloud, depending on your computer setup and your personal preferences.

Get support and give feedback

This topic provides information about getting help with this book and contacting us to provide feedback or report errors.

Errata and support

We've made every effort to ensure the accuracy of this book and its companion content. If you discover an error, please submit it to us at *http://aka.ms/Windows10SBS /errata*.

If you need to contact the Microsoft Press Support team, please send an email message to *mspinput@microsoft.com*.

For help with Microsoft software and hardware, go to *http://support.microsoft.com*.

We want to hear from you

At Microsoft Press, your satisfaction is our top priority, and your feedback our most valuable asset. Please tell us what you think of this book at *http://aka.ms/tellpress*.

The survey is short, and we read every one of your comments and ideas. Thanks in advance for your input!

Stay in touch

Let's keep the conversation going! We're on Twitter at *http://twitter.com/MicrosoftPress*.

Part 1

The Windows 10 environment

CHAPTER 1

Get started using Windows 10 3

CHAPTER 2

Personalize your working environment 51

CHAPTER 3

Manage folders and files 97

CHAPTER 4

Work with apps and notifications 151

CHAPTER 5

Safely and efficiently browse the Internet 201

Get started using Windows 10

If you're reading this book, we assume that you already have a Windows 10 computer or plan to acquire one, and want to know what to expect. This chapter will help you quickly come up to speed with the basic elements of the Windows 10 user experience and environment. Some familiar concepts have changed. We point out some of the changes from earlier versions of Windows, but concentrate on describing how things are now.

> **SEE ALSO** If you haven't yet installed Windows 10, see Appendix A, "Install or upgrade to Windows 10," for relevant information.

Windows 10 combines popular elements of Windows 7 and Windows 8 with impressive new technology. Windows 10 is designed to work not only on desktop and laptop computers, but also on smaller mobile devices such as tablets and phones. The user interface is clean and simple, and if you're an experienced Windows user, many parts of it will be familiar to you. The technical changes implemented in this version of Windows are significant, but when you're familiar with the concepts that govern the structure and navigation of the operating system, we think you'll find it to be both powerful and easy to use.

This chapter guides you through procedures related to signing in to Windows, exploring the user interface and new Settings window, updating system files, managing windows, and ending a computing session.

In this chapter

- Start a computing session
- Explore the desktop
- Explore the taskbar
- Explore the Start screen and Start menu
- Explore computer settings
- Update Windows system files
- Manage content and app windows
- End a computing session

Practice files

No practice files are necessary to complete the practice tasks in this chapter.

Start a computing session

To start a Windows 10 computing session, you sign in to Windows with a user account that is registered on that computer. Your user account can be a *Microsoft account* that connects to all the resources associated with that account, or it can be a *local account* that exists only on your computer and provides access to shared and private files on the computer.

During the process of installing Windows 10 or the first time you sign in to a new Windows 10 computer, a user configuration tool guides you through the process of setting up a computer user account. The user account can be linked to a pre-existing Microsoft account or a new Microsoft account that you create as part of the user account setup process, or it can be a local user account that exists only on one computer.

Use a Microsoft account or local account

You can choose one of two account types when signing in to Windows 10: a Microsoft account or a local account. Here is a quick overview of the two account types.

Microsoft accounts

Microsoft accounts are the current incarnation of the centrally registered accounts that were used to sign in to various Microsoft services in the past (such as Windows Live accounts and Passport accounts). A Microsoft account is a single sign-on (SSO) account that you can use to sign in to any Microsoft service, to services provided by other companies that have adopted Microsoft accounts as standard credentials, or to a computer running Windows 10, Windows 8.1, or Windows 8. To sign in with a Microsoft account, you use any email address that has been designated as a Microsoft account, and the password you specified for the account.

TIP Single sign-on isn't unique to Microsoft: Google, Facebook, and many other organizations use it. Many web services allow you to sign in by using one of the major SSO accounts, rather than requiring you to create new accounts on their sites.

You can configure any valid email address you already have as a Microsoft account or create a new email account by using one of the Microsoft webmail service–designated domains (for example, hotmail.com, live.com, msn.com, passport.com. outlook.com, or any variant for a specific country). During the process, you will create your own secure password. If you don't have a Microsoft account and would like to create one, you can do so at *https://signup.live.com/signup.aspx*.

IMPORTANT If you're signed in to any Microsoft account, you must sign out of that account before you can create a new account from that computer.

Local accounts

A local account is exactly what it sounds like: a user account that exists only on your computer. You (or someone with administrative privileges) can create multiple local accounts on one computer, and each account can sign in to that computer and access a combination of private and shared information.

Local accounts are good for children. (You can designate a local account as a child's account to add parental controls.) Local accounts are also a good choice when you don't want to link the computer to other computers that you sign in to with your Microsoft account. A local account doesn't require a password, doesn't have an associated Microsoft OneDrive storage folder, and might have only limited access to Windows apps and Microsoft Office 365 tools.

If you create a local account but later decide that you would prefer to sign in by using a Microsoft account, you can easily create a new user profile on the computer for the Microsoft account, or connect the Microsoft account to an existing local account.

SEE ALSO For more information about setting up accounts and about parental controls, see Chapter 8, "Manage user accounts and settings."

Microsoft encourages you to use a Microsoft account rather than a local account to sign in. The advantages of signing in to Windows 10 by using a Microsoft account include the following:

- You can easily share files among the other computers you sign in to by using that account because the computers have the same sign-in credentials.

- You can selectively synchronize settings such as the computer theme, web browser settings, passwords, language preferences, and Ease of Access settings among the computers you sign in to by using the same account.

- You can access other Microsoft services that require you to sign in.

- You have access to 15 gigabytes (GB) or more of free OneDrive online storage, and 30 GB or more with an Office 365 subscription.

When your computer first starts or has been idle for a while, it displays the Lock screen. As the name indicates, the Lock screen is a security layer between the world outside the computer and the information on the computer. The Lock screen displays a background picture (or a slideshow of pictures), and it can display information from some of the core Windows 10 apps, including Clock & Alarms, Weather, Store, Xbox, People, Mail, and Calendar. The Lock screen doesn't display any user account information or specific message content that you might not want to share with people who happen to walk past the computer.

The Lock screen displays current information from Windows 10 apps

Windows 10 comes with a set of attractive water-related Lock screen images. You can choose a background from among those or you can choose any picture or set of pictures stored on the computer that you want to display on this specific screen.

> **SEE ALSO** For information about specifying the image and app information that appear on the Lock screen, see "Customize the Lock screen" in Chapter 10, "Manage power and access options."

The Lock screen remains in place until you dismiss it (or the computer goes to sleep). When you dismiss the Lock screen, the Welcome screen appears. The Welcome screen displays a list of the user accounts that are registered on the computer in the lower-left corner and the image and password entry box or Sign In button for the most recent user in the center.

The Welcome screen displays links to the user accounts that are registered on the computer

> **TIP** This book contains many images of the Windows 10 user interface elements (such as the Lock screen, Welcome screen, desktop, taskbar, Start menu, and Settings window) that you'll work with while performing tasks on a computer running Windows 10. Unless we're demonstrating an alternative view of content, the screen shots shown in this book were captured on a horizontally oriented display at a screen resolution of 1920 × 1080 and a magnification of 100 percent. If your settings are different, user interface elements on your screen might not look the same as those shown in this book.

From the Welcome screen, you sign in to Windows with your user account to begin or return to your computing session.

The first time you sign in to a computer by using a new user account, Windows sets up the user account–specific folders and settings, and synchronizes settings with other computers that your Microsoft account is configured on, if you've chosen that option. While Windows goes through this process (which takes about two minutes), it displays a series of reassuring messages on the screen. At the end of this initial setup process, your personal Windows desktop appears.

 SEE ALSO For information about synchronizing system settings on multiple computers, see "Customize your sign-in options" in Chapter 8, "Manage user accounts and settings."

Depending on the processes that are configured to run when you sign in, there could be some activity, such as windows opening and closing, as various apps start. Some of these will be apps that you want to interact with—for example, you might want a communication app such as Skype or Skype for Business to start automatically. Others will be utilities that support the apps that are installed on your computer. For example, installing an app such as Adobe Acrobat or Apple iTunes also installs a utility that checks the Internet for updates to the app each time you start a new computing session. (This is usually for the purpose of increasing app security rather than adding new functionality.)

TIP Some apps, utilities, and services start automatically when any user signs in to Windows, and others run specifically when you sign in. You can review a list of apps that start automatically and remove apps from the list to conserve startup resources. For more information, see "Manage app startup" in Chapter 4, "Work with apps and notifications."

To dismiss the Lock screen

1. Use any of these methods:

   - Click a blank area of the screen.

   - Flick the screen upward by using your finger.

   - Press any key on the keyboard.

To sign in to Windows 10

1. Dismiss the Lock screen.

    If the computer has multiple user accounts, the Welcome screen displays a link to each account in the lower-left corner.

2. If your account isn't already selected, click it in the lower-left corner of the Welcome screen to display your user account picture and name in the center of the screen.

3. Do one of the following:

    -   If your account doesn't have a password, click the **Sign In** button below your account name.

    -   If your account has a password, enter the password in the box below your account name, and then press **Enter** or click the **Submit** button.

> **SEE ALSO** For information about signing in to Windows from within an existing Windows session, see "Explore the Start screen and Start menu" later in this chapter. For information about configuring and signing in by using PINs, picture passwords, and biometric recognition, see "Customize your sign-in options" in Chapter 8, "Manage user accounts and settings."

Explore the desktop

Each time you sign in to Windows, one of two user interfaces appears: the desktop or the Start screen. The default Windows 10 startup user interface is the desktop, which we discuss here.

> **TIP** Many Windows 8 users became accustomed to the clean interface provided by the Start screen in that version of Windows. You can change your settings to display the Windows 10 version of the full-screen Start screen instead of the desktop when you sign in to Windows. For more information, see "Configure the Start screen and Start menu" in Chapter 2, "Personalize your working environment."

The Windows 10 desktop is similar to the desktop in previous versions of Windows: it has a background that fills your screen, hosts Windows utilities such as the Recycle Bin, and might have app shortcuts, folders, and files stored on it. The standard Windows 10 desktop background depicts the same dramatic interpretation of the familiar Windows logo that is on the Welcome screen.

The desktop consists of a background for folders, files, apps, and shortcuts; and a taskbar that provides access to the computer content and functionality

> **TIP** When you buy a new computer, you might be surprised at how cluttered your brand-new desktop is. You can delete the desktop shortcuts to tidy it up, but that won't uninstall the apps that the shortcuts link to. Computer manufacturers or resellers frequently install trial versions of apps on a computer in hopes that you will assume you have to use those apps instead of others that are available to you. The most concerning of these is a well-known antivirus app that provides a short "free trial" and then prompts you to pay for a subscription. This app can actually interfere with the Windows Defender security system that is built into Windows 10 (for free). For information about cleaning up desktop shortcuts and uninstalling apps, see Chapter 2, "Personalize your working environment" and Chapter 4, "Work with apps and notifications."

The initial desktop background picture is set when you install Windows. If you upgrade from another version of Windows and choose to keep your personal settings, your desktop background won't change. If you purchase a computer that has Windows 10 preinstalled on it, it will probably feature a background specific to the computer manufacturer or model.

The only icon that is typically displayed by default with a clean installation is the one for the Recycle Bin, which usually appears in the upper-left corner. Apps that you install later might place (or offer to place) shortcuts on the desktop to provide a quick way to start them. You can place app shortcuts on the desktop yourself, too. Most computer manufacturers also preinstall apps from companies they have alliances with, and place shortcuts to these apps on the desktop. The appearance of your desktop might be different from the one shown in this book, but the functionality will be the same.

The Recycle Bin is a temporary storage folder for deleted files

 SEE ALSO For information about creating shortcuts on the desktop, Start screen, and taskbar, see Chapter 4, "Work with apps and notifications."

The desktop itself is really just a background for the display of items that are stored in a folder (named Desktop) that is part of your user account or in a Public Desktop folder that is shared by all users who sign in to the computer. Some people like to save files or folders to their desktops for easy access.

 SEE ALSO For information about configuring Windows to display content on two (or more) screens, see "Display your desktop on multiple screens" in Chapter 6, "Manage peripheral devices."

Explore the taskbar

The bar across the bottom of the desktop is the *Windows taskbar*. The taskbar provides access to all the apps, files, settings, and information on the computer. The fixed tools are on the left and right ends of the taskbar.

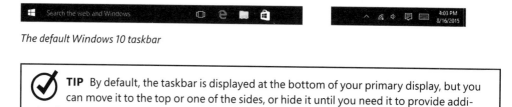

The default Windows 10 taskbar

> **TIP** By default, the taskbar is displayed at the bottom of your primary display, but you can move it to the top or one of the sides, or hide it until you need it to provide additional screen space. For more information, see Chapter 2, "Personalize your working environment."

The Windows 10 taskbar looks very similar to the taskbar in earlier versions of Windows, but there are some pleasant surprises here.

Start button   Task View button

Search box

You can search for information, settings, apps, and files from the search box

The Start button, search box, and Task View button are located at the left end of the taskbar. Each of these has an important function, as described here:

- Clicking the Start button displays the Start menu and Start screen, the primary locations from which you access apps and settings. The Start menu and Start screen both have new functionality in Windows 10. We discuss this at length in the next topic.

- Right-clicking the Start button displays the Quick Link menu of frequently accessed computer administration functions and commands.

Programs and Features

Power Options

Event Viewer

System

Device Manager

Network Connections

Disk Management

Computer Management

Command Prompt

Command Prompt (Admin)

Task Manager

Control Panel

File Explorer

Search

Run

Shut down or sign out   >

Desktop

The Quick Link menu is your fastest route to many frequently used computer management tools

> **TIP** A menu that appears when you right-click a button, file, folder, or other item is referred to as a *shortcut menu*. Most shortcut menus don't have names, but this is the Quick Link menu. You can display it by right-clicking the Start button or by pressing Win+X.

■ Entering a term in the search box displays relevant apps, files, and settings stored on your computer and, when you have an active Internet connection, relevant online information.

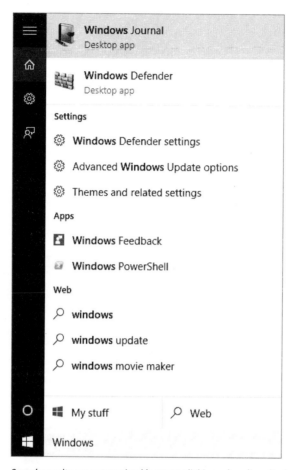

Search results are categorized by type; clicking a heading displays all results of that type

The icons to the left of the search results represent the app or system area of each result. An app icon indicates the default app for that file type; a folder indicates a folder; a gear indicates a Settings page, pane, or setting; and a control panel indicates a Control Panel setting.

> **TIP** The search box is also your interaction point with Cortana, your "personal assistant" on any Windows device. After you initially configure Cortana, the service will alert you to upcoming appointments; help you check in for flights or track packages; provide information about local restaurants, traffic conditions, and investment performance; and much more.

- The Task View button is new in Windows 10. It provides you with a large thumbnail view of all the open windows and running apps on your desktop so you can easily switch among them.

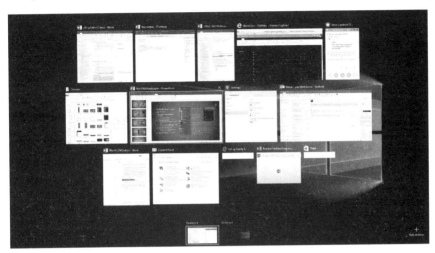

You can switch to or close windows from Task view

From Task view, you can also create virtual desktops, which are secondary instances of the Windows desktop. When you create one or more virtual desktops, you can organize the windows of running apps, files, and folders across them.

 SEE ALSO For information about virtual desktops, see "Organize apps on multiple desktops" in Chapter 11, "Work more efficiently."

The center area of the taskbar between the Task View button and the Show Hidden Icons button can display shortcut buttons and toolbars. In a default installation of Windows 10, shortcuts to the Microsoft Edge web browser, File Explorer, and the Windows Store are pinned here. You can move or delete these and pin additional items that you want quick access to.

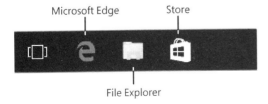

You can easily add and remove taskbar buttons

SEE ALSO For information about pinning apps to the taskbar, see "Manage app shortcuts" in Chapter 4, "Work with apps and notifications."

The right end of the taskbar is the *notification area*. The icons displayed here represent apps that run on your computer that might need to notify you of events. You can choose which apps appear in the notification area, and set them either to always be displayed or to only display an alert if something happens. You can also click or right-click notification area icons to interact with the underlying apps in various ways.

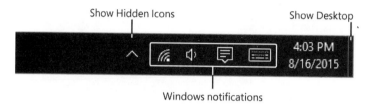

The right end of the taskbar provides access to notifications and information about system status

The notification area contains the following items:

- The Show Hidden Icons button displays a pane of notification icons that are for apps rather than for Windows functions. You can access app-management commands from these icons.

- The standard Windows notification icons provide access to network and sound settings, app and operating system notifications, and other tools. The specific icons depend on your computer configuration.

  The Action Center icon is new in Windows 10. When you have unread communications from apps (such as Microsoft Mail or Outlook), Windows, and other sources, the icon is filled, and when you have no unread notifications, it is hollow.

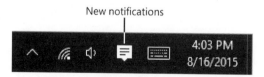

The Action Center icon is white when you have new notifications

The Action Center icon provides quick access to the Action Center. You can access messages directly from this pane, and also access many interesting settings, some of which are new in Windows 10.

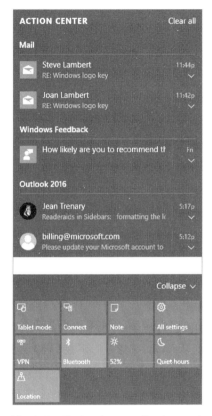

The Action Center gives you direct access to multiple communication apps and settings

- The time and date displayed on the taskbar also provide access to configure the time and date settings on your computer.

- The narrow bar at the rightmost end of the taskbar is the Show Desktop button, which you can use to hide or minimize all open windows (and thereby display the desktop).

Hey, Cortana!

Cortana is the new technology from Microsoft that is described as a "personal assistant," but is really a complex information-analysis tool that monitors your activities and communications and proactively provides you with relevant information about them. You can interact with Cortana through the taskbar search box, or if your computer or device has a microphone input you can configure your settings so that you can activate it by saying "Hey, Cortana." Configuring Cortana changes the taskbar search box prompt from "Search the web and Windows" to "Ask me anything" preceded by the Cortana symbol.

A microphone in the search box indicates that Cortana is configured for verbal input

Cortana can provide information about local restaurants and events, specific stocks you want to track, traffic, public transit options, appointments and meetings, movies, television shows, news, sports, and weather—and the list is sure to grow. You can indicate the types of information you want Cortana to provide.

The concept of being monitored can take some getting used to, but in trade you'll get proactive reminders and relevant information that Cortana locates just for you. You can ask Cortana to record notes and set reminders for you (or you can do it yourself by typing and clicking in the interface).

The same functionality is available on Windows phones and the data is available to you on any device that you sign in to with your Microsoft account.

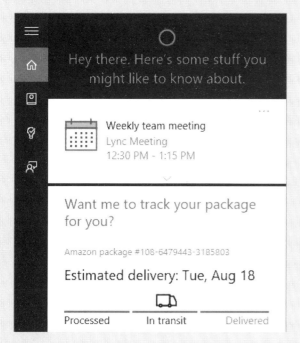

Cortana monitors your computer activity and provides useful information

SEE ALSO For more information, see "Get assistance from Cortana" in Chapter 11, "Work more efficiently."

To search for content on the computer or Internet

1. Activate the taskbar search box by doing any of the following:

   - Click the search box.

   - Press **Win+S**.

    TIP We abbreviate the Windows logo key name as "Win" in keyboard shortcuts so that it's easier to read.

   - If Cortana search has been configured (if the search box prompt says "Ask me anything") press **Win+Q**.

2. Enter the search term.

3. If necessary, refine the search results by clicking a category in the search results list.

To display the Task view of all active apps and desktops

1. Do any of the following:

   - On the taskbar, to the right of the search box, click the **Task View** button.

   - Press **Win+Tab**.

To manage windows in Task view

1. Do any of the following:

   - To close a file or app, point to the thumbnail, and then click the **Close** button (the X) in the upper-right corner.

   - To switch to a specific window, click the window thumbnail (not the window title).

   - On a touchscreen device, swipe in from the left edge of the screen.

To display app-management icons and commands

1. At the left end of the notification area of the taskbar, click the **Show hidden icons** button.

2. In the icon pane, right-click the icon of the app you want to display commands for.

To display recent, unread messages from Windows and communication apps

1. Near the right end of the taskbar, click the **Action Center** icon.

To manage messages in the Action Center

1. Do any of the following:

   - To preview message content, click the arrow to the right of the message subject.

   - To remove a message from the Action Center (but not from the messaging app), point to the message header and then click the X that appears in its upper-right corner.

   - To open a message in its app, click the message header.

 SEE ALSO For information about managing settings from the Action Center, see "Manage app notifications" in Chapter 4, "Work with apps and notifications."

To hide all open windows

1. Do any of the following:

   - To temporarily hide the windows, point to the **Show Desktop** button.

   - To minimize the windows, click the **Show Desktop** button or press **Win+D**. Use the same technique to restore the minimized windows.

 SEE ALSO For information about other techniques for minimizing, maximizing, and restoring windows, see "Manage content and app windows" later in this chapter.

Explore the Start screen and Start menu

Windows 8 replaced the previous Start menu with a Start screen that hosted app tiles, including "live tiles" that display up-to-date information from apps. Live tiles are a nifty feature, but the removal of the Start menu was a very big change. Although this change was made with the best of intentions and was well received by some people, it met with strong disapproval from other people. Windows 10 offers the best of both worlds—a combination of the traditional Start menu and the tile-based Start screen.

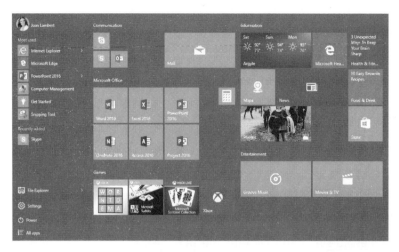

The Standard Start screen, with the Start menu on the left

 SEE ALSO For information about live tiles, see Chapter 4, "Work with apps and notifications."

You can configure the content of the Start screen however you want by adding, removing, resizing, and grouping tiles. As previously mentioned, you can opt to display a full-screen Start screen instead of the partial-screen Start screen. On the full-screen Start screen, the Start menu is minimized, but you can open it whenever you want to access its content.

The full-screen Start screen with the Start menu displayed

> **SEE ALSO** For information about adding content to the Start screen and switching to the full-screen Start screen, see "Configure the Start screen and Start menu" in Chapter 2, "Personalize your working environment."

Regardless of the Start screen configuration, the Start menu is located on the left side and contains specific content sections. As with nearly all areas of Windows 10, you have control over the content that appears on the Start screen. By default, the categories are Most Used Apps, Recently Added Apps, and user account folders. The Settings button and the All Apps button are at the bottom of the Start menu (and also available directly from the full-screen Start screen).

The Start menu with the default categories and folders

Your user account information is at the top of the Start menu and is actually a button label. Clicking the user account button displays a list of options. You can access your user account settings, lock the computer, or sign out of Windows from this menu. (You can also do all those things from other places.) If multiple user accounts are configured on your computer, they appear at the bottom of this menu, and you can switch to those accounts without signing out of your current Windows session. (For example, if your home computer has user accounts configured on it for other family members or guests, and you want to let one of those people use the computer without ending your computer session, or if you have a user account that is linked to your Microsoft account and a local user account that isn't.)

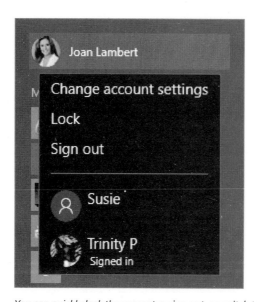

You can quickly lock the computer, sign out, or switch to another user account

If the other user account is already signed in to Windows, this is indicated by the words "Signed in" under the user account name. Switching to an account that has an active Windows session resumes that Windows session; otherwise, switching to the account starts a new Windows session. Either way, when you switch accounts Windows displays the Welcome screen, so you can either sign in to Windows with the other user account credentials (including the account password, if it has one) or sign in to the existing Windows session.

You can choose whether to display the Most Used and Recently Added sections on the Start menu, but Windows populates these sections automatically based on your computer usage and displays the section headings only when it also displays apps in those sections. Apps that you use more than others stay on the Most Used list until others take their place. Newly installed apps stay on the Recently Added list for about a day.

> ⚠️ **IMPORTANT** The purpose of the Most Used and Recently Added sections seems to be to make your life easier by providing quick access to apps that you use frequently or that you just installed. At the time of this writing, unfortunately, that purpose isn't fulfilled because the sections display only apps that are *not* pinned to the Start screen. (Apps that are pinned to the taskbar do stay on the list.) We hope that this will be remedied in the near future, perhaps even before you buy this book.

One good reason to display the Most Used Start menu section is because it provides access to jump lists. Jump lists are a marvelous time-saving feature introduced in a previous version of Windows and, happily, they're back with the Windows 10 Start menu.

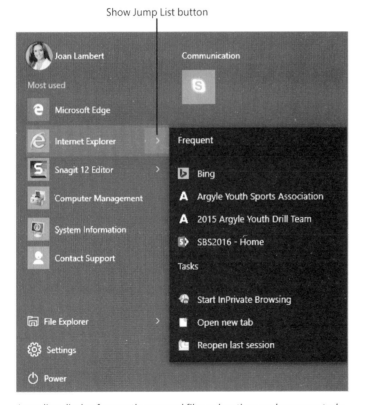

Show Jump List button

Jump lists display frequently accessed files or locations and common tasks

Different jump lists display different entries. Most display recent files or locations. The File Explorer jump list displays the entries that are pinned to the Quick Access section of the File Explorer Navigation pane, which we investigate in Chapter 3, "Manage folders and files." You can unpin items from either location.

To display the Start menu and screen (default configuration)

1. Do any of the following:

   - Click the **Start** button.

   - Press the **Windows logo key**.

   - Press **Ctrl+Esc**.

To display the Start menu on the full-screen Start screen

1. In the upper-left corner of the **Start** screen, click the menu button.

The menu button, sometimes referred to as "the hamburger menu"

To display user account controls

1. At the top of the **Start** menu, click the user account button.

To switch to another user account

1. On the **Start** menu, click the user account button, and then click the account you want to switch to.

2. On the Welcome screen, do one of the following:

   - If the account has a password, enter the password in the box below the account name, and then press **Enter** or click the **Submit** button.

   - If the account doesn't have a password, click the **Sign In** button below the account name.

To display recent files for a specific app

1. On the **Start** menu, click the **Show jump list** button to the right of the app name in the Most Used app list.

To display items you've selected for quick access

1. On the **Start** menu, click the **Show jump list** button to the right of **File Explorer**.

SEE ALSO For information about the Quick Access menu in File Explorer, see Chapter 3, "Manage folders and files."

Explore computer settings

In past versions of Windows, the various settings that controlled the behavior of the computer were available from an interface named Control Panel. Navigating through the Control Panel screens could be somewhat tricky. Control Panel still exists in Windows 10, but many of the settings have been moved from Control Panel to a much simpler interface: the Settings window. (We assume that future Windows 10 updates will result in the migration of more Control Panel content to Settings.)

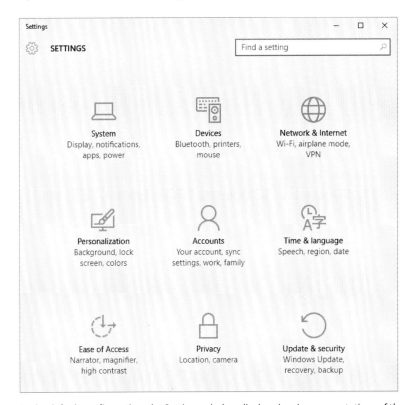

In the default configuration, the Settings window displays iconic representations of the setting categories

The Settings window is an example of the type of changes Microsoft made in Windows 10 so that the operating system can run on devices of any size, from desktop computers to smartphones. (In fact, the narrow Settings window content will look familiar to Windows phone users.) As the window width decreases, the icons become smaller and move to a list format. Regardless of the format, each category icon and name is accompanied by a short (and by no means complete) list of settings available in that category.

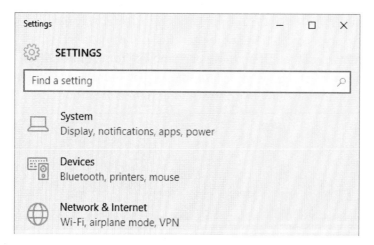

The Settings window content remains the same but its appearance changes to fit the window width

One of the benefits of the Settings window over Control Panel is that each category is only one level deep, so it's relatively easy to locate the feature or setting you want to configure. In the standard (wider) Settings window configuration, each category page displays a list of features in the left pane; clicking any feature displays the settings for that feature in the right pane.

Category   Pane list   Active pane   Search box

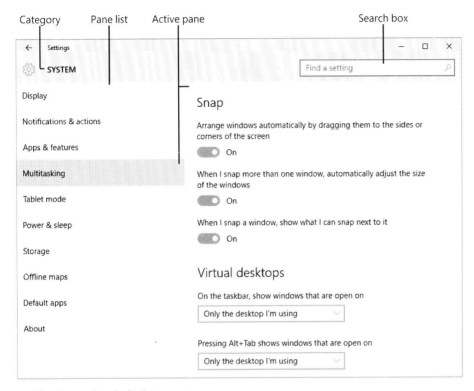

Multitasking settings in the System category

When the Settings window is narrower, clicking a category name displays only the feature list, and then clicking a feature displays that pane of settings.

The following table lists the features you can configure settings for in each of the nine categories, so you don't have to guess.

Settings category	Features included in the category
System	Display
	Notifications & actions
	Apps & features
	Multitasking
	Tablet mode
	Battery saver (mobile devices only)
	Power & sleep
	Storage
	Offline maps
	Default apps
	About (Windows and system information)
Devices	Printers & scanners
	Connected devices
	Bluetooth
	Mouse & touchpad
	Typing
	AutoPlay
Network & Internet	Wi-Fi
	Airplane mode (mobile devices only)
	Data usage
	VPN
	Dial-up
	Ethernet
	Proxy
Personalization	Background
	Colors
	Lock screen
	Themes
	Start
Accounts	Your account
	Sign-in options
	Work access
	Family & other users (or Other users)
	Sync your settings

Settings category	Features included in the category
Time & language	Date & time
	Region & language
	Speech
Ease of Access	Narrator
	Magnifier
	High contrast
	Closed captions
	Keyboard
	Mouse
	Other options
Privacy	General
	Location
	Camera
	Microphone
	Speech, inking, & typing
	Account info
	Contacts
	Calendar
	Messaging
	Radios
	Other devices
	Feedback & diagnostics
	Background apps
Update & security	Windows Update
	Windows Defender
	Backup
	Recovery
	Activation
	For developers

You can locate the configuration options for a specific feature by clicking the category and then the feature, or by searching from the Settings window search box or the taskbar search box.

> ⚠️ **IMPORTANT** At the time of this writing, the Settings window search box returns some false results that don't lead anywhere; we assume these are placeholders for configuration options that will be migrated to the Settings window with future Windows updates. In the meantime, if you don't like navigating through the categories, you can get more-dependable results from the taskbar search box.

When you configure settings in the Settings window, your changes are implemented as soon as you make them; it isn't necessary to save your changes, and it's not possible to undo your changes other than by manually reversing each change. If you ever need to identify the default settings for a feature, one way to do so is to create a new user account, switch to that user account, and then check the settings in that account.

> 🔍 **SEE ALSO** For information about creating new user accounts, see "Create and manage user accounts" in Chapter 8, "Manage user accounts and settings." For information about switching accounts, see "Explore the Start screen and Start menu" earlier in this chapter.

As previously mentioned, Control Panel still exists and you can configure many of the less frequently used settings there. The standard Control Panel configuration displays category names followed by tasks you can perform in the categories.

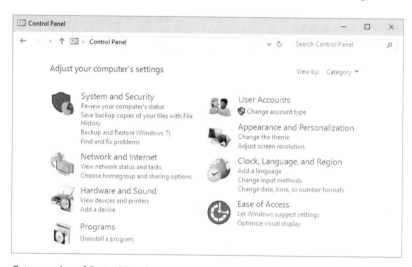

Category view of Control Panel

Alternatively, you can display features instead of categories by switching to Icon view, where you have the choice of displaying large or small icons. The content in both views is the same, but it can be much simpler to navigate through Control Panel in Icon view than in Category view. In either view, a search box is located in the upper-right corner of the window. Searching from this box returns results only from Control Panel.

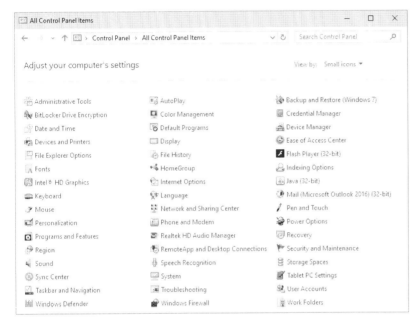

Small Icons view of Control Panel

You can access the settings in Control Panel directly (by navigating or searching in Control Panel or from the taskbar search results list), by clicking links on the Quick Link menu, and also by clicking links in the feature settings panes. Links that lead from the Settings window panes to Control Panel are located at the bottom of the panes after the settings you can configure in the pane, and are often labeled as advanced or additional settings. (For example, "Advanced sizing of text" and "Additional power settings.")

We'll work with individual settings in later chapters of this book. In this first chapter, we're just making you aware of them in case you want to investigate them on your own or need to configure something before you get to the relevant topics.

To open the Settings window

1. Do any of the following:

   - Near the bottom of the **Start** menu, click **Settings**.

   - Press **Win+I**.

   - In the taskbar search box, enter **settings**, and then in the search results list, click **Settings**.

   - Near the right end of the taskbar, click the **Action Center** icon and then, near the bottom of the **Action Center** pane, click the **All settings** button.

To display a category of settings

1. In the **Settings** window, click the category you want to display.

To display settings for a specific feature

1. From the **Settings** window, display the category page.

2. On the category page, click the feature you want to configure.

> **TIP** If the category page has two columns, the features are listed in the left column and the settings in the right.

To display the Quick Link menu

1. Do either of the following:

   - Right-click the **Start** button.

   - Press **Win+X**.

To display the Control Panel home page

1. Do any of the following:

   - On the **Quick Link** menu, click **Control Panel**.

   - In the taskbar search box, enter **control**, and then in the search results list, click **Control Panel**.

   - On the **All Apps** menu, click any index letter. In the alphabetic index, click **W**, expand the **Windows System** folder, and then click **Control Panel**.

Update Windows system files

The code behind operating systems is usually in a constant state of change. This might be to resolve internal or external issues—for example, threats from new viruses or the need to improve drivers for the devices you can connect to your computer. Microsoft has stated that Windows 10 will be the last version of Windows (a great reason to buy this book!), but the actual meaning of that statement is that the company plans to maintain and update this version of Windows for the foreseeable future rather than to immediately begin the development of a new version. This is in part a reflection of the agile software development methodology that Microsoft has embraced, which involves multiple function-specific teams completing rapid, collaborative development cycles and continually refining processes, rather than one long-term development process driven by management.

Windows 10 checks for updates during the installation process, but quite a bit of time might pass between the installation of the operating system on your computer and the time you first use it. Therefore, it's a very good idea to check for updates after you install or activate the operating system.

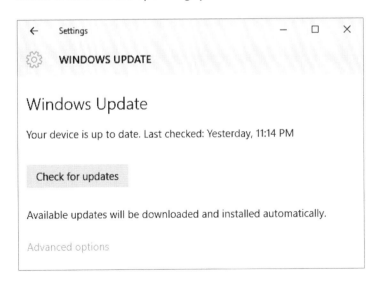

The Windows Update pane

Windows Update is part of the Update & Security category of settings. Windows Update automatically checks for, downloads, and installs updates to the operating system (including the built-in Windows Defender security software), and related files, such as device drivers, on a regular basis. If your computer is turned off or is offline when the time comes to check, you might not get an update when it first becomes available to you, but you can manually check for updates. If Windows Update locates available updates, it starts the process of downloading and installing them. Sometimes Windows Update delays certain update processes until a time that you're not using your computer. You can choose to run those processes immediately if you want to.

You have some options for the types of updates you get and the way they're delivered to your computer. For example, Windows Update can also check for updates to other Microsoft products (such as Word, Outlook, and Skype) that are installed on your computer, and can optimize the delivery of updates by downloading them to your computer through other computers that your computer is connected to by a local network or Internet connection. We delve into those options in Chapter 12, "Protect your computer and data."

To check for Windows updates

1. Open the **Settings** window, and click **Update & security**.

2. If the window is in single-pane format, click **Windows Update** to display that pane.

3. In the **Windows Update** pane, click **Check for updates**.

 TIP If the Windows Update pane indicates that updates are available to download, waiting to install, or require that you restart your computer, you can click the relevant link to start that process.

To view your update history

1. Display the **Update & security** category of settings.

2. Display the **Windows Update** pane.

3. At the bottom of the **Windows Update** pane, click **Advanced options**.

4. In the **Advanced options** pane, click **View your update history**.

Manage content and app windows

As the name of the Windows 10 operating system indicates, most of the information you view on your computer is displayed in a *window*—a rectangular content frame. (One obvious exception to that is Start screen tiles.) Files open in app windows, folders open in File Explorer windows, and operating system elements open in system windows. Regardless of the content they display, all windows share certain common characteristics and can be manipulated in the same ways.

In this topic, we discuss managing windows on the desktop.

Resize, hide, and close windows

A window can either fill the entire screen or occupy only part of the screen. You can open and close a window, move a window, and change the size of a window. (These features help us to differentiate a window from another user interface element such as a pane or dialog box.)

Windows have common features. Depending on which system or app generates the window, its controls might be or look slightly different, but in general, a window has a title bar at the top that has a title in the middle and window-sizing buttons on the right side.

The three buttons on the right end of the title bar are:

- **Minimize** Minimizing a window doesn't close the file or app in the window, but closes the window on the screen. You can reopen the window by clicking the corresponding taskbar button.

- **Maximize/Restore** When a window fills only part of the screen, maximizing it increases it to full-screen size. When a window is maximized, restoring it returns it to its previous part-screen size.

- **Close** Closing a window also closes the file or app that the window contains.

Pointing to (hovering over) the controls displays ScreenTips to help you identify them.

Word, Settings, and File Explorer windows feature the same basic controls in the upper-right corner

You can use the title bar at the top of a window or the window frame to manage the window size.

To resize a window

1. Do any of the following:

    *   To change only the window height, double-click or drag the top or bottom of the window frame.

    *   To change only the window width, drag the left or right side of the window frame.

    *   To change the window size in any direction, point to a corner of the window frame, and when the pointer changes to a diagonal arrow, drag the arrow.

TIP You cannot resize a maximized window by dragging its frame; you must first restore the window to a non-maximized state.

To maximize a window

1. Do any of the following:

   - Double-click the window title bar.

   - At the right end of the title bar, click the **Maximize** button.

   - Drag the window by its title bar to the top of the screen, and then release it.

   - Press **Win+Up Arrow** to maximize a non-snapped window.

 SEE ALSO For information about snapping windows, see the "Move and arrange windows" section of this topic.

To restore a maximized window

1. Do any of the following:

   - Double-click the window title bar.

   - At the right end of the title bar, click the **Restore** button.

   - Drag the window by its title bar away from the top of the screen, and then release it.

   - Press **Win+Up Arrow** or **Win+Down Arrow** to restore a non-snapped window.

To minimize the active window

1. Do any of the following:

   - At the right end of the title bar, click the **Minimize** button.

   - Press **Win+Down Arrow** to minimize a non-snapped window.

To minimize all windows other than the active window

1. Do any of the following:

   - Press **Win+Home**.

   - Shake (rapidly wiggle) the active window by its title bar.

To minimize all windows

1. Press **Win+M**.

To restore minimized windows

1. Do any of the following:

   - Press **Win+Shift+M**.

   - Press **Alt+Tab** to cycle through thumbnails of windows; release the **Alt** key to open the window of the selected thumbnail.

   - Press **Win+[a number from 0 to 9]** to open the first instance of the first through tenth active app on the taskbar. (The first app is the one to the right of the **Task View** button.)

To close a window

1. At the right end of the title bar, click the **Close** button.

Move and arrange windows

Some people might never open more than one window at a time. But most people have at least a few windows open at the same time, and a business computer user could easily have a dozen or more windows open on a single screen, multiple monitors, or multiple desktops.

Earlier in this chapter we looked at Task view, in which you can display a tiled view of thumbnails of all your open windows at the same time, and switch to or close individual windows. In this section, we discuss managing windows on the desktop.

You can move and arrange windows by dragging them around the screen, by using keyboard shortcuts, or by using commands on the taskbar shortcut menu.

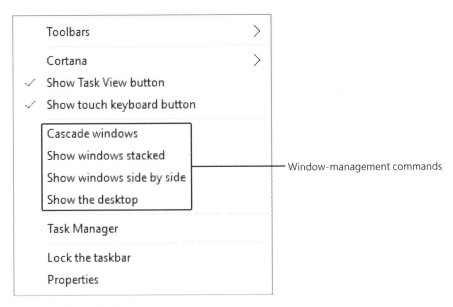

Toolbars	>
Cortana	>
✓ Show Task View button	
✓ Show touch keyboard button	

Cascade windows
Show windows stacked ————— Window-management commands
Show windows side by side
Show the desktop

Task Manager	
Lock the taskbar	
Properties	

Right-click the taskbar to display these commands

You can arrange open windows in traditional cascaded, stacked, and side-by-side arrangements or by snapping them to a half or quarter of the screen. Cascading and snapping windows also changes the window sizes.

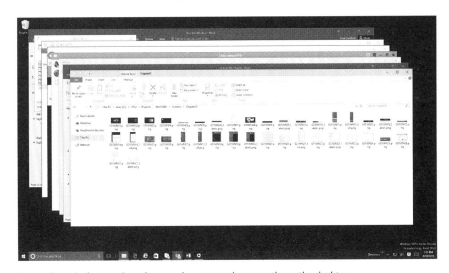

Cascading windows resizes them and arranges them neatly on the desktop

Snapping a window is a technique that sizes and positions a window to occupy the left or right portion of the screen or one corner of the screen. Snapping a window to the left or right side of the screen in Windows 10 doesn't automatically resize it at half width—if another maximum height window is docked to a screen edge, snapping a window to the opposite screen edge fills the available space.

To drag a window

1. Press and hold the window title bar by using the primary mouse button, your finger, or a stylus.

2. Move the pointing device until the contact point touches the intended destination.

To move a window

1. Do either of the following:

   - Drag the window by its title bar to the new position.

   - Press **Win+Left Arrow** or **Win+Right Arrow** to cycle the window through the left, right, and center of each screen.

To cascade all open windows

1. Right-click the taskbar.

2. On the taskbar shortcut menu, click **Cascade windows**.

To arrange all open windows in a grid

1. Right-click the taskbar.

2. On the taskbar shortcut menu, click **Show windows stacked** or **Show windows side by side**.

To restore cascaded, stacked, or side-by-side windows

1. Right-click the taskbar.

2. On the taskbar shortcut menu, click the relevant **Undo** command.

To snap a window to the left or right side of a screen

1. Do any of the following:

   - Drag the window until the pointer touches the left or right edge of the display area (the contact point will flash briefly), and then release it.

   - Activate the window, and then press **Win+Left Arrow** or **Win+Right Arrow** to cycle the window through the left, right, and center of each screen.

   > ✅ **TIP** If you have multiple monitors (as opposed to virtual desktops) pressing the right or left arrow keyboard shortcut repeatedly acts on the window on the current monitor, then moves it to the next monitor and cycles through the possibilities there. This is true whether the monitors are arranged horizontally or vertically.

2. Click the thumbnail of the window you want to display in the remaining space, or press **Esc** or click the taskbar to close the thumbnail view.

To snap a window to a quarter screen

1. Do any of the following:

   - Drag the window until the pointer touches a corner of the display area, and then release it.

   - Press **Win+Up Arrow** or **Win+Down Arrow** to snap a half-screen window to the upper or lower corner.

   - Press **Win+Left Arrow** or **Win+Right Arrow** to move a quarter-screen window to another corner.

2. Click the thumbnail of the window you want to display in the remaining space, or press **Esc** or click the taskbar to close the thumbnail view.

End a computing session

If you're going to stop working with your computer for any length of time, you can use one of these four options to leave the Windows session:

- **Lock the computer** This leaves your Windows computing session active, saves the state of any running apps and open files, and displays the Lock screen. Signing in to Windows resumes your computing session.

- **Sign out of Windows** This exits any running apps, ends your Windows computing session, and displays the Lock screen. Signing in to Windows starts a new computing session.

- **Put the computer to sleep** This leaves your Windows computing session active, saves the state of any running apps and open files, turns off the monitor, and puts the computer into a power-saving mode. When you wake the computer up, the monitor turns on, the Lock screen appears, and signing in to Windows resumes your computing session.

- **Shut down the computer** This signs all active users out of Windows, shuts down the computer processes in an orderly fashion, and turns off the computer.

You can perform these processes from the Power button on the Start menu or full-screen Start screen, or from the Quick Link menu.

You can identify the Power button in any location by its icon

The other available Power option is to restart the computer. When you do so, Windows shuts down the computer, and then starts it again. Restarting is sometimes necessary after installing an update that needs to update files that the system is using. It can also magically fix things if your computer is overtaxed with too many processes and begins to run slowly.

If apps are running when you sign out of Windows or shut down or restart the computer, Windows manages the process of exiting the apps. If files are open that have unsaved changes, Windows halts the sign-out process and prompts you to save the files. At that point, you have the option of canceling the sign-out process and returning to your Windows session.

To lock the computer

1. Display the **Start** menu.

2. At the top of the **Start** menu, click the user account button, and then click **Lock**.

Or

1. Press **Win+L**.

To sign out of Windows

1. Do any of the following:

    - Display the **Start** menu, click the user account button, and then click **Sign out**.

    - Display the **Quick Link** menu, click **Shut down or sign out**, and then click **Sign out**.

2. Respond if Windows asks whether to save unsaved changes to specific files or apps.

> **TIP** Watch the taskbar for flashing buttons that indicate an app that needs attention. Click any button to activate the app, and then provide any necessary feedback. Sometimes the notifications don't end up on top of other on-screen processes.

To put the computer to sleep

1. From within an active computing session, do either of the following:

    - Display the **Start** menu or full-screen **Start** screen. In the lower-left corner of the menu or screen, click the **Power** button, and then click **Sleep**.

    - On the **Quick Link** menu, click **Shut down or sign out**, and then click **Sleep**.

Or

1. In the lower-right corner of the Welcome screen, click the **Power** button, and then click **Sleep**.

To shut down the computer

1. From within an active computing session, do either of the following:

   - In the lower-left corner of the **Start** menu or full-screen **Start** screen, click the **Power** button, and then click **Shut down**.

   - On the **Quick Link** menu, click **Shut down or sign out**, and then click **Shut down**.

Or

1. In the lower-right corner of the Welcome screen, click the **Power** button, and then click **Shut down**.

To restart the computer

1. From within an active computing session, do either of the following:

   - In the lower-left corner of the **Start** menu or full-screen **Start** screen, click the **Power** button, and then click **Restart**.

   - On the **Quick Link** menu, click **Shut down or sign out**, and then click **Restart**.

Or

1. In the lower-right corner of the Welcome screen, click the **Power** button, and then click **Restart**.

Skills review

In this chapter, you learned how to:

- Start a computing session
- Explore the desktop
- Explore the taskbar
- Explore the Start screen and Start menu
- Explore computer settings
- Update Windows system files
- Manage content and app windows
- End a computing session

Practice tasks

No practice files are necessary to complete the practice tasks in this chapter.

Start a computing session

Perform the following tasks:

1. Start your Windows 10 computer.

2. Dismiss the Lock screen, and then sign in to Windows 10.

Explore the desktop

There are no practice tasks for this topic.

Explore the taskbar

Sign in to Windows, and then perform the following tasks:

1. From the taskbar search box, search for **desktop**. Filter the search results list to display only folders, and then open the **Desktop** folder for your user account.

2. Search for **taskbar**. Filter the search results list to display only settings. Then display the **Settings** window pane from which you can select which icons appear on the taskbar.

3. Display Task view of all active apps and desktops in your computing session. In Task view, close the **Desktop** folder window, and then open the **Settings** window.

4. Display the hidden icons in the notification area of the taskbar. Point to each icon in the window to display a ScreenTip that identifies the app. Then right-click any icon to display the available commands for that app.

5. From the notification area of the taskbar, display the Action Center.

6. If the Action Center contains messages, preview the content of a message, and then remove that message from the Action Center.

7. Hide all open windows.

Explore the Start screen and Start menu

Perform the following tasks:

1. Display the **Start** menu, and then display your user account menu.

2. From the user account menu, lock the computer. Then sign in to Windows again.

3. Display the **Start** menu. Examine the **Most Used** list for apps that display **Show jump list** buttons. Click each button to display recent files and common actions for the app.

4. Near the bottom of the **Start** menu, click the File Explorer **Show jump list** button to display the folders, locations, and items that are currently on your File Explorer **Quick Access** list.

Explore computer settings

Perform the following tasks:

1. Open the **Settings** window and display its home page.

2. Display any category of settings that interests you.

3. Within the selected category, display the settings for a specific feature.

4. Display the Control Panel home page.

5. Leave the **Settings** window and Control Panel open for later use.

Update Windows system files

Perform the following tasks:

1. Display the **Updates & security** category of settings.

2. From the **Windows Updates** pane, check for Windows updates.

3. If you have pending updates, view the details and install the updates.

4. View your update history.

Manage content and app windows

Ensure that the Settings window and Control Panel are open, and then perform the following tasks:

1. Activate the **Settings** window. Change only the width of the window so it is approximately half the width of the screen. Then drag the window to the approximate center of the screen.

2. Use the mouse or pointer to resize the **Settings** window in the following ways:

   a. Maximize the window height without changing its width.

   b. Maximize the window to fill the screen.

   c. Snap the window to the left side of the screen, and select Control Panel to fill the right side of the screen.

3. Activate Control Panel, and then use keyboard shortcuts to resize it in the following ways:

   a. Snap the window to the upper-right quadrant of the screen.

   b. Move the window to the left side of the screen.

4. Temporarily hide all the open windows to display the desktop.

5. Stack the open windows.

6. Minimize all the active windows, and then restore them.

7. Activate the **Settings** window, and then minimize all windows other than the active window.

8. Close the **Settings** window. Then activate and close Control Panel.

End a computing session

Sign in to Windows, and then perform the following tasks:

1. From the user account menu at the top of the **Start** menu, lock the computer. Then sign in to Windows again.

2. From the **Power** button at the bottom of the **Start** menu, put the computer to sleep. Then sign in to Windows again.

3. From the **Start** shortcut menu, sign out of Windows to end your computing session.

4. From the Welcome screen, restart the computer.

Personalize your working environment

In Chapter 1, "Get started using Windows 10," we looked at the Windows user interface elements that you encounter in every Windows session—the Lock screen, the Welcome screen, the desktop, the taskbar, the Start screen, and the Start menu. (The other place you'll probably spend a lot of time is in File Explorer, which we discuss at length in Chapter 3, "Manage folders and files.")

Some of the Windows user interface elements might look different on your computer from the ones we show in this book, because the colors and images might have been set by the computer manufacturer to something other than the defaults. One of the things people like to do with their Windows computers is personalize the user interface to reflect things they like and want to see rather than things that other people have decided they should see. And that is what this chapter is about!

This chapter guides you through procedures related to modifying the Start screen and Start menu, managing Start screen tiles, setting the desktop background and system colors, configuring the taskbar, and applying and managing themes.

In this chapter

- Configure the Start screen and Start menu
- Manage Start screen tiles
- Set the desktop background and system colors
- Configure the taskbar
- Apply and manage themes

Practice files

For this chapter, use the practice files from the Win10SBS\Ch02 folder. For practice file download instructions, see the introduction.

Configure the Start screen and Start menu

As mentioned in Chapter 1, "Get started using Windows 10," the Start screen that debuted in Windows 8 and the Start menu that was in Windows 7 and previous versions of Windows have been combined and are both available, all the time, in Windows 10. You have the choice of two Start screen configurations:

- A full-screen Start screen with the Start menu collapsed on the left side

- A partial-screen Start screen with the Start menu always visible on the left side

The partial-screen configuration is the default.

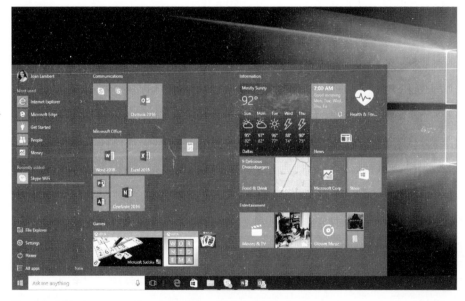

The default Start screen configuration always displays the Start menu

In either configuration, the Start menu displays predefined content, and the Start screen displays tiles. In contrast to earlier versions of Windows in which you could add shortcuts to specific apps to the Start menu, you now choose only the types of content you want Windows to display on the Start menu, and add custom content only to the Start screen.

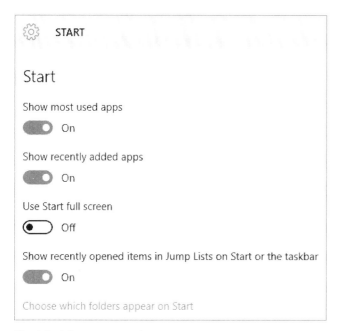

The default Start screen settings

> **TIP** In the Windows user interface, the combined Start screen and Start menu are often referred to simply as *Start*. Some documentation refers to clicking the Start button simply as *clicking Start*. Because Windows 10 has three distinct Start elements—the Start button, the Start menu, and the Start screen—we refer to each of these elements separately in this book.

Set the Start screen size

The Start menu configuration that is best for you depends on the way you work—considerations include whether you primarily interact with Windows by clicking or tapping the screen, which method you prefer to use to start apps, whether you depend on live tiles for information, whether you make use of jump lists, and how large your screen is. Your initial preference might be based solely on what you're used to and comfortable with. You can easily try out both configurations to determine which is more efficient for the way that you work.

Changing the Start menu configuration is a simple one-click process. When you turn the full-screen setting on or off, the change takes place immediately. It isn't necessary to sign out of Windows or restart your computer to implement it.

You can adjust the height and width of the partial-screen Start screen. When you make the Start screen wider or narrower, the width of the tile groups might change from three medium tiles at narrower widths to four medium tiles at wider widths.

 SEE ALSO For information about arranging tiles and tile groups on the Start screen, see the topic "Manage Start screen tiles" later in this chapter.

To switch between the default and full-screen Start screen

1. Open the **Settings** window.

2. Click **Personalization**, and then on the **Personalization** page, click **Start**.

3. In the **Start** pane, click **Use Start full screen**. Then click the **Start** button to test the setting.

To resize the partial-screen Start screen

1. Do any of the following:

   - Drag the top border of the **Start** screen up or down to increase or decrease its height.

   - Drag the right border of the **Start** screen right or left to increase or decrease its width.

To display Start screen tiles that don't fit on the partial Start screen

1. Point to the **Start** screen to display the vertical scroll bar on the right edge.

 TIP The scroll bar appears only when there are more tiles than fit on the Start screen at the current size.

2. Drag the scroll box or click the scroll bar to scroll the **Start** screen content.

Configure Start menu content

On the left side of the Start screen, the Start menu displays information that is related to users and apps. At a minimum, it displays your user account button at the top and the Power and All Apps buttons at the bottom. (The Power and All Apps buttons are also available directly from the Start screen in the full-screen configuration.)

The Start menu can also display the following lists:

- **Most Used app list** On a new Windows 10 installation, this list contains links to some standard Windows utilities, or to apps that were selected by the computer manufacturer. As you use Windows, the apps you use most often that aren't pinned to the Start screen appear in this list.

- **Recently Added app list** This list displays apps for a short time after you install them. If no apps have been installed recently, the Start menu doesn't display the Recently Added list heading.

- **Recently opened items** When this setting is turned on, you can quickly access files that you've opened with apps that support this feature (such as Microsoft Office apps) from the Start menu or taskbar.

The Windows 10 Start menu does *not* have an area in which you can pin app shortcuts—you pin these to the Start screen instead.

At the bottom of the Start menu, just above the Power button, you can display links to the following items:

- File Explorer
- The Settings window
- Your Documents, Downloads, Music, Pictures, and Videos folders
- The Homegroup and Network windows
- Your personal folder, from which you can access all your user account–specific folders and settings

The Start menu displays only File Explorer and Settings by default; you must turn on any specific folders or windows you want to display.

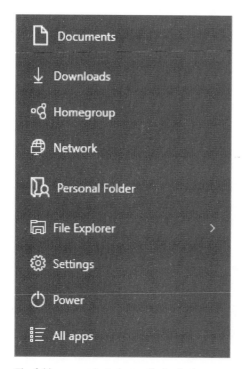

The folders you select always display in the same order

To display or hide app lists on the Start menu

1. Open the **Settings** window.

2. Click **Personalization**, and then on the **Personalization** page, click **Start**.

3. In the **Start** pane, do any of the following:

   • Click **Show most used apps** to turn off or on the Most Used list.

   • Click **Show recently added apps** to turn off or on the Recently Added list.

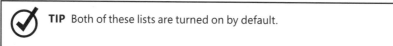 **TIP** Both of these lists are turned on by default.

4. Click the **Start** button to test the setting.

TIP Windows 10 does not have an option to specify the number of items in the Start menu lists.

To display or hide jump lists on the Start menu and taskbar

1. On the **Personalization** page of the **Settings** window, click **Start**.

2. In the **Start** pane, click **Show recently opened items in Jump Lists on Start or the taskbar** to turn jump lists on or off.

To add or remove folders on the Start menu

1. On the **Personalization** page of the **Settings** window, click **Start**.

2. At the bottom of the **Start** pane, click **Choose which folders appear on Start** to display a list of options, each with a toggle button.

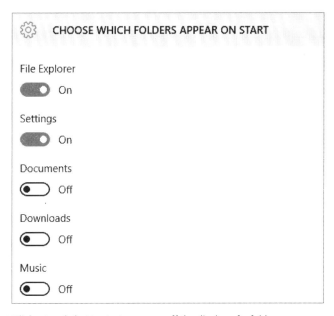

Click a toggle button to turn on or off the display of a folder

3. On the **Choose which folders appear on Start** page, set the toggle buttons for the folders that you want to appear on the Start menu to **On**, and the others to **Off**.

Manage Start screen tiles

The Start screen content (other than the Start menu) is displayed in the form of *tiles*. Each tile is actually a shortcut to something else—usually an app, but tiles can also link to other things, such as folders in File Explorer or individual songs in your Groove Music library. You can add tiles to the Windows 10 Start screen by pinning shortcuts to it, including shortcuts to apps, files, folders, web links, contact cards, songs, movies, and pictures—almost anything you want to get to quickly.

A typical Start screen configuration

Tiles are square or rectangular, and can be set to four different sizes: Small, Medium, Large, and Wide. All tiles support the Small and Medium sizes. App tiles also support the Wide and Large sizes, which are most appropriate for apps that display information (other than the app name and/or icon) on the tile that you want to see. (Of course, you can also use them if you just want a really big target to click.) When you pin an item to the Start screen, the new app tile defaults to the Medium size and appears at the bottom or far right of the Start screen.

The four Start screen tile sizes

Tiles for some Windows Store apps that provide access to frequently updated information (such as news, weather, traffic, stock market data, messages, social media network updates, and calendar events) can display and update content directly on the Start screen. These are called *live tiles*. Some apps even permit you to pin multiple live tiles that display different data to the Start screen.

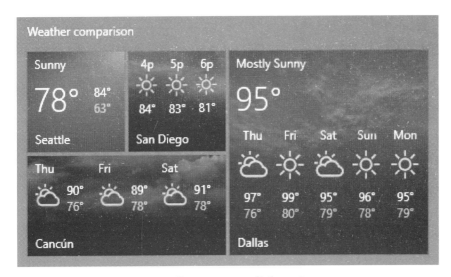

Different sizes of live tiles display different amounts of information

The content displayed on a live tile can come from an online source, such as a news service, or from a local source, such your Pictures folder. Only Medium, Large, and Wide tiles display live content; it is turned off for smaller tiles, and if the on-screen movement bothers you, you can turn off the live content for any tile. When live content is off, the tile displays the app icon and its name.

59

Tiles always align on the Start screen in a grid format. When you place tiles next to each other, they form a group, and a title bar for that group appears. You can also assign a name to the tile group. You can create additional groups of tiles by dropping them a bit further away from an existing group. After you create a group, you can easily move tiles into or out of the group, or move the entire group of tiles to a different location on the Start screen. You can organize tiles on the Start screen in whatever grouping is most logical and convenient to you—by type, by purpose, by project, alphabetically—there is no magic formula that will satisfy everyone. Fortunately, the Start screen content is easy to customize.

> **TIP** Your Start screen structure is one of the Windows settings that you can synchronize among computers that you sign in to by using your Microsoft account. For information about sychronizing settings, see "Customize your sign-in options" in Chapter 8, "Manage user accounts and settings."

Computer manufacturers place tiles on the Start screen to help you find apps and tools that you might want to use (for example, a link to the support department for the computer manufacturer, or to a free app that comes with the computer). You can remove the tiles you don't use, or just move them to one side and make them small. Removing tiles does not uninstall apps, delete folders, or otherwise affect the item that the tile links to. You can start apps from the All Apps list or locate folders in File Explorer.

> **SEE ALSO** For information about files and folders, see Chapter 3, "Manage folders and files." For information about pinning apps to the Start screen and starting apps, see Chapter 4, "Work with apps and notifications."

The procedures in this topic pertain to the mechanics of the Start screen rather than its content. For information about managing the content of the Start screen, see the "Configure the Start screen and Start menu" topic earlier in this chapter.

To move a Start screen tile

1. Click and hold the tile you want to move, and then drag it to its new location.

   > **TIP** The screen becomes shaded to indicate change when you move the tile, but until then there is no specific indicator that you're editing the screen.

Or

1. On a touchscreen device, tap and hold the tile to activate the Start screen elements for editing. The screen changes to a shaded color and the tile group title boxes are visible.

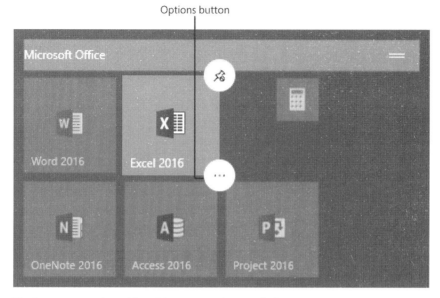

Options button

The Start screen activated for editing on a touchscreen device

2. Drag the tile to its new location.

3. Make any additional changes to the **Start** screen, and then tap an empty area of the **Start** screen to return it to its normal state.

To resize a Start screen tile

1. Do one of the following:

   • Right-click the tile, and then click **Resize**.

   • Tap and hold the tile, and then tap the **Options** button that appears in its lower-right corner.

2. Click the tile size you want (**Small**, **Medium**, **Large**, or **Wide**).

 TIP Moving or resizing a tile might change the layout of the surrounding tiles.

To add a tile to an existing tile group

1. Drag the tile to slightly overlap with an existing tile in the group you want to add it to, and then release it.

To create a new tile group

1. Drag a tile to an open space above, below, or to the side of an existing group.

2. When a shaded bar (a blank tile group title bar) appears, release the tile to create the tile group.

Creating a new tile group by dragging a song tile

To name a tile group

1. If you create a tile group by tapping and dragging a tile on a touchscreen device, the tile group title bar is active for editing when you release the tile. Tap **Name group**, and then enter the title you want to assign to the tile group.

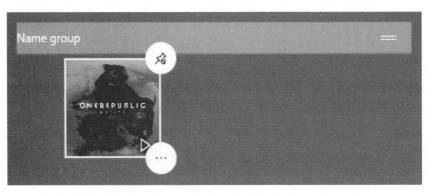

Creating a tile group on a touchscreen device

Or

1. Point to the area above the tile in a new group, or above the top row of tiles in an existing group.

2. When **Name group** appears, click it to activate it for editing.

3. Enter the title you want to assign to the tile group.

To rename a tile group

1. Point to the tile group title, and then click the title bar or the handle that appears at its right end to activate the title bar for editing.

A tile group title bar that is active for editing

2. Edit the existing title, or click the **X** at the right end of the title box to delete the existing content, and then enter the new title.

3. Press **Enter**, or click or tap away from the title box to return the Start screen to its normal state.

To move a tile group

1. Click and hold (or tap and hold) the tile group title bar, and then drag the group to its new location.

   As you drag, the group tiles collapse into the group title bar, and other groups move to make space for the group you're dragging.

2. When the group is in the location you want it, release the title bar.

Set the desktop background and system colors

You can use the options in the Personalization category of the Settings window to set the desktop background and the accent color that is used for various operating system elements, including the Start menu, taskbar, Action Center, and window title bars.

The default Windows 10 desktop background pictures

> **TIP** In addition to the changes described in this topic, you can apply a custom theme, which sets the background, color scheme, and other properties at one time. For more information, see "Apply and manage themes" later in this chapter.

Set the desktop background

Your choice of desktop background usually reflects your personal taste—what you like to see when your app windows are minimized or closed. Some people prefer simple backgrounds that don't obscure their desktop icons, some prefer photos that reflect a specific theme, and some prefer personal photos of family members, pets, or favorite places.

You can set your desktop background to any of the following:

- **A picture** You can choose one of the photos that come with Windows, or a digital image of your own. The image can be any of several file types, including BMP, GIF, JPG, PNG, TIF, and the less common DIB, JFIF, JPE, JPEG, and WDP file types.

- **A solid color** If you want to keep things simple, you can opt for a plain, colored background. You can choose from a palette of 24 colors.

Desktop background color options

- **A slideshow** You can display the contents of a folder of your choice, with the background image changing as frequently as every minute or every 10 minutes, 30 minutes, hour, six hours, or day. You can display the images in the order they appear in the folder, or in a random order.

When you select a background option, a preview of the option appears at the top of the Background pane.

When displaying an image or slideshow as your desktop background, you can specify the position of the image as follows:

- **Fill** The image is centered on the screen. The image fills the screen horizontally and vertically, and maintains its original aspect ratio. Parts of the image might overrun the left and right sides or the top and bottom edges (but not both).

- **Fit** The image is centered on the screen. The image fills the screen horizontally or vertically, and maintains its original aspect ratio. Parts of the image might not fill the left and right sides or the top and bottom edges.

- **Stretch** The image is centered on the screen. The image fills the screen horizontally and vertically, but does not maintain its original aspect ratio. No part of the image overruns the screen.

- **Tile** The image is anchored in the upper-left corner of the screen at its original size, followed by as many copies as are necessary to fill the screen. Parts of the right-most and bottom tiles might overrun the edges of the screen.

- **Center** The image is centered on the screen at its original size.

- **Span** When you have multiple monitors connected to the computer, this option stretches the image across the monitors.

When you select a picture position that doesn't fill the screen (such as Fit or Centered) the rest of the desktop is filled with the currently selected desktop background color.

 IMPORTANT At the time of this writing, the desktop background preview doesn't appear immediately when you select a new picture; there is a lag time of a few seconds. That might improve in future builds of Windows 10.

To set one desktop background image

1. Open the **Settings** window.

2. Click **Personalization**, and then on the **Personalization** page, click **Background**.

3. In the **Background** pane, click **Picture** in the **Background** list.

4. In the **Choose your picture** area, do one of the following:

    - Click a thumbnail to select a Windows 10 image or a previously selected picture.

    - Click the **Browse** button. In the **Open** dialog box, browse to and click the image you want to use. Then click the **Choose picture** button.

5. In the **Choose a fit** list, click **Fill**, **Fit**, **Stretch**, **Tile**, **Center**, or **Span** to indicate the way you want to position the image.

6. When the preview image updates to reflect your settings, make any necessary changes to configure the desktop background the way you want it.

> **IMPORTANT** If you choose the Fit or Centered option, the image will have the currently selected desktop background color behind it. If you don't like the desktop background color, change it and then reselect the desktop background image.

To display a series of desktop background images

1. Place the images you want to display into one folder.

2. Open the **Settings** window.

3. Click **Personalization**, and then on the **Personalization** page, click **Background**.

4. In the **Background** pane, expand the **Background** list, and then in the list, click **Slideshow**.

5. If you want to use a folder other than the one shown in the **Choose albums for your slideshow** area (by default, this is your Pictures folder), click the **Browse** button. In the **Select folder** dialog box, browse to and click the folder of images you want to use. Then click the **Choose this folder** button.

> **TIP** Although the area is named *Choose albums...* you can choose only one folder in the Select Folder dialog box.

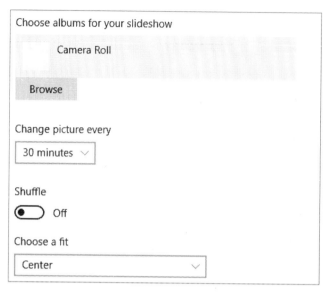

Desktop slideshow options

6. If you want to display the folder contents in a random order, set the **Shuffle** toggle button to **On**.

7. In the **Choose a fit** list, click **Fill**, **Fit**, **Stretch**, **Tile**, **Center**, or **Span** to indicate the way you want to position the images. Consider that in the slide show, image sizes might vary.

8. When the preview image updates to reflect your settings, make any necessary changes to configure the desktop background the way you want it.

To set a desktop background color

1. In the **Settings** window, click **Personalization**, and then on the **Personalization** page, click **Background**.

2. In the **Background** pane, click **Solid Color** in the **Background** list to display the color grid. An outline indicates the current color.

3. In the color grid, click the color swatch you want to use.

4. When the preview image updates to reflect your settings, make any necessary changes to configure the desktop background the way you want it.

Set an accent color

The preview at the top of the Background pane and the preview at the top of the Colors pane display the same image: a partial-screen Start screen, taskbar, and window against the currently selected background.

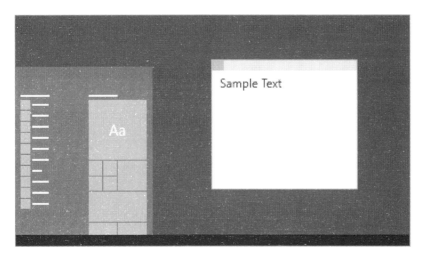

Previewing the desktop background and accent color

The colors displayed on the Start screen, taskbar, and window are controlled by the accent color settings. When selecting an accent color, you can choose from four configurations based on combinations of two settings:

- The Start screen, taskbar, tiles, and window accents can be black, or they can be shades of the accent color. If they are controlled by the accent color, tiles (on the Start screen and in the Action Center) and window accents (such as toggle buttons) are the accent color, the Start screen is a medium shade of the accent color, and the taskbar is a dark shade of the accent color.

- Windows can select an accent color based on the desktop background, or you can select an accent color. When the desktop background is any solid color, Windows selects gray as the accent color. When the desktop background is a picture, Windows selects a color from the picture.

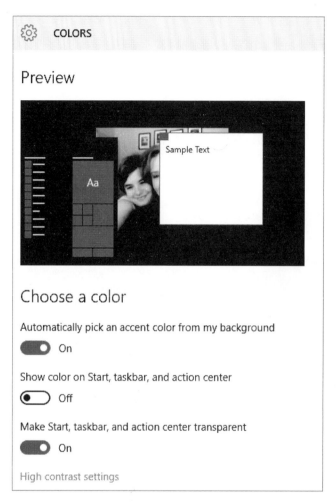

The default Colors options set an automatic accent color and transparent screens

If *you* select the accent color, you can choose from a palette of 48 standard colors.

> **TIP** When Windows selects an accent color from a background picture, the accent color grid expands to include that color in addition to the 48 standard colors, so your accent color palette might have more colors than are shown in this book.

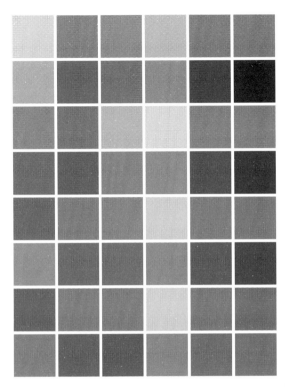

Accent color options

The final option in the Colors pane isn't related to the accent color, but it affects the same elements as the accent color. The option, which is turned on by default, makes the Start screen, taskbar, and Action Center transparent so that you can see the desktop and open windows behind them. This Windows Aero feature was introduced for windows frames and the taskbar in Windows 7, relegated to only the taskbar in Windows 8, and has returned in Windows 10. You can't control the percentage of transparency (or rather, opacity) of the user interface elements—they're either transparent or opaque—but the transparency level does seem to be slightly less in Windows 10 than in previous versions of Windows, and therefore slightly less distracting. We turned off the transparency to capture the images in this book. Try it out to find out whether you like it.

To set an accent color based on the desktop background

1. Open the **Settings** window.

2. Click **Personalization**, and then on the **Personalization** page, click **Colors**.

3. In the **Colors** pane, set the **Automatically pick an accent color...** toggle button to **On**.

> ✓ **TIP** If your desktop background is set to Slideshow and you turn on the Automatically Pick An Accent Color... setting, the accent color will change when the desktop background changes. If you like change, you'll like this combination. And if you don't, you might find it distracting.

To set a specific accent color

1. In the **Settings** window, click **Personalization**, and then on the **Personalization** page, click **Colors**.

2. In the **Colors** pane, set the **Automatically pick an accent color...** toggle button to **Off** to display the color grid. An outline indicates the current color.

3. In the color grid, click the color swatch you want to use. Windows implements the change and updates the preview image.

To display the Start menu and taskbar in color

1. In the **Settings** window, click **Personalization**, and then on the **Personalization** page, click **Colors**.

2. In the **Colors** pane, set the **Show color on Start, taskbar, and action center** toggle button to **On** to implement the change and update the preview image.

To switch between transparent and opaque user interface elements

1. In the **Settings** window, click **Personalization**, and then on the **Personalization** page, click **Colors**.

2. In the **Colors** pane, do one of the following:

   - If you want the Start screen, taskbar, and Action Center to be transparent, set the **Make Start, taskbar, and action center transparent** toggle button to **On**.

   - If you want the Start screen, taskbar, and Action Center to be opaque, set the **Make Start, taskbar, and action center transparent** toggle button to **Off**.

   Windows implements the change. This setting doesn't affect the preview image, but if your desktop background has content at the bottom of the screen, the effect might be apparent on your taskbar.

3. To check the effect of the setting, display the **Start** screen or Action Center.

Configure the taskbar

In Chapter 1, "Get started using Windows 10," we reviewed the functionality available from the taskbar. In this topic we discuss the changes you can make to the taskbar to customize it so that you can work most efficiently.

> ✓ **TIP** The most common customization of the taskbar is to add app shortcuts to it. In this topic, we discuss the functionality that is built in to the taskbar. For information about creating shortcuts on the taskbar to apps, folders, websites, and other items, see Chapter 4, "Work with apps and notifications."

Change taskbar appearance

As previously mentioned, you can move the taskbar from its default location at the bottom of the screen to any other edge of the screen. You might find it easier to move the pointer to the taskbar when it's on the side or top of the screen than when it's at the bottom of the screen. If you're working on a small screen, you might also like to have the additional vertical space that you gain by moving the taskbar to the left or right side of the screen.

Wherever you position the taskbar, the Start screen expands from the Start button

When you move the taskbar to the left or right side of the screen, it changes in the following ways:

- The width changes to accommodate the time and date, which are at the bottom of the vertical taskbar.

- The Start button is at the top of the vertical taskbar, and the Show Desktop button is at the bottom. Clicking the Start button expands the Start screen from that location.

- The search box changes to a search button. Clicking the search button expands the usual search pane.

- Buttons, icons, and taskbar toolbars rotate to a horizontal orientation, so you don't have to turn your head sideways to read them.

- Small notification area icons move side by side.

Regardless of the taskbar location, you can change the height (when horizontal) or width (when vertical) to accommodate more buttons and toolbars. Other ways to fit more onto the taskbar include the following:

- Switch to "small taskbar buttons." This change affects not only the size of the buttons, it also collapses the search interface from a rectangular input box to a button that you click to display the box, which provides significantly more space for buttons and toolbars.

- If you don't use Task view, or use a keyboard shortcut to access it, you can remove the Task View button from the taskbar.

- If you don't intend to use the on-screen keyboard, you can remove the touch keyboard button from the notification area of the taskbar.

Double-height taskbar without Task View, displaying small taskbar buttons

TIP Clicking or tapping the touch keyboard button displays an on-screen keyboard. You can click or tap keys on the keyboard to enter text as you would by using an external keyboard.

By default, you can move and resize the taskbar freely, but if you prefer you can lock the taskbar so that you don't accidentally drag the taskbar or its border. You can make changes to the taskbar only when it's unlocked.

When working with the taskbar, you can manage some of its features from the shortcut menu that appears when you right-click an empty area of the taskbar, some features from the Taskbar And Start Menu Properties dialog box, and some features in both places.

To display the taskbar shortcut menu

1. Right-click an empty area of the taskbar.

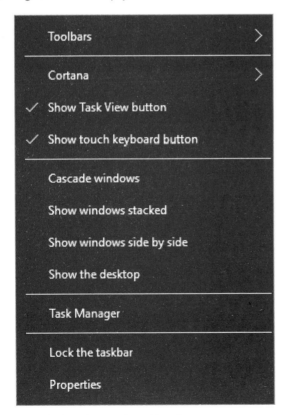

The default settings on the taskbar shortcut menu

To open the Taskbar And Start Menu Properties dialog box

1. Right-click an empty area of the taskbar, and then click **Properties**.

The default settings on the Taskbar tab of the dialog box

The Taskbar tab includes the Multiple Displays settings only when your computer has multiple displays (monitors) connected to it. We discuss the settings for multiple displays in Chapter 6, "Manage peripheral devices."

> ⚠️ **IMPORTANT** The name of the Taskbar And Start Menu Properties dialog box is left over from previous versions of Windows, in which the dialog box also had a Start menu tab from which you could manage Start menu settings. In Windows 10, you manage the Start menu and Start screen settings in the Settings window. It's possible that in a later release of the operating system, the name of this dialog box will change to more closely reflect its current content.

To prevent or allow changes to the taskbar

1. On the taskbar shortcut menu, click **Lock the taskbar**.

 TIP A check mark indicates that an option on the shortcut menu is active.

Or

1. Open the **Taskbar and Start Menu Properties** dialog box.

2. On the **Taskbar** tab, select or clear the **Lock the taskbar** check box.

3. Click **Apply** to implement the change or **OK** to implement the change and close the dialog box.

To move the taskbar

1. Do one of the following:

    *   Drag the taskbar to any edge of the screen.

         TIP The movement of the taskbar across the screen might not be apparent; instead, it might appear to jump from location to location.

    *   Right-click the taskbar, and then click **Properties**. On the **Taskbar** tab of the **Properties** dialog box, in the **Taskbar location on screen** list, click **Left**, **Right**, or **Top** (or click **Bottom** to return the taskbar to its default location).

To change the taskbar height

1. Point to the inside edge of the taskbar.

2. When the pointer changes to a double-headed arrow, drag the inside edge of the taskbar to change its height (or width, when vertical) to the size you want it. The height or width can be up to 50 percent of the screen height or width.

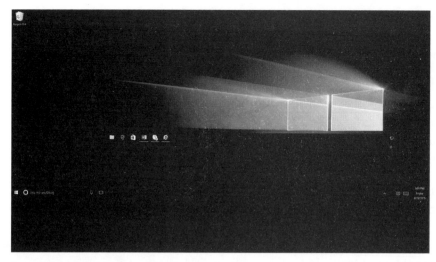

Just because you can, doesn't mean that you should...

To display small taskbar buttons

1. On the **Taskbar** tab of the **Taskbar and Start Menu Properties** dialog box, select the **Use small taskbar buttons** check box.

2. Click **Apply** or **OK**.

To hide or display the Task View button

1. On the taskbar shortcut menu, click **Show Task View button**.

To hide or display the touch keyboard button

1. On the taskbar shortcut menu, click **Show touch keyboard button**.

Change taskbar behavior

There are a few other changes you can make to the way that the taskbar functions, from the Taskbar And Start Menu Properties dialog box.

By default, each app (or each instance of an app) that you open displays a button on the taskbar. Active app buttons are differentiated from app shortcuts by a colored bar below the button. By default, multiple buttons for the same app stack on top of each other so that each app has only one button, and clicking the button displays thumb-nails of each instance of the app. If you prefer, you can display individual buttons for each instance of an app, or display individual buttons until your taskbar is full and then combine them.

If you prefer to not have the taskbar taking up space on your screen, you can hide it (on any edge of the screen) so that it appears only when you point to it. This could be convenient if you have a small screen or are simply distracted by the busyness of the taskbar.

If you find that you accidentally invoke the Peek function when your mouse pointer wanders into the corner of the screen above the Show Desktop button, you can turn off that function. Turning off Peek doesn't affect the Show Desktop function.

To hide the taskbar when it isn't active

1. Open the **Taskbar and Start Menu Properties** dialog box.

2. On the **Taskbar** tab, select the **Auto-hide the taskbar** check box.

3. Click **Apply** to implement the change or **OK** to implement the change and close the dialog box.

To change the display of multiple app taskbar buttons

1. On the **Taskbar** tab of the **Taskbar and Start Menu Properties** dialog box, click the **Taskbar buttons** list to expand it, and then click one of these options:

   - **Always combine, hide labels** (the default)

   - **Combine when taskbar is full**

   - **Never combine**

2. Click **Apply** or **OK**.

To turn the Peek function off or on

1. On the **Taskbar** tab of the **Taskbar and Start Menu Properties** dialog box, clear the **Use Peek...** check box to turn the feature off, or select the check box to turn the feature on.

2. Click **Apply** or **OK**.

Display and manage toolbars on the taskbar

Windows provides three "toolbars" that you can display on the taskbar to provide easy access to information that you'd otherwise have to open a separate app to get to. The three built-in toolbars are:

- **Address** The Address toolbar displays a browser address bar directly on the taskbar. You can perform three operations from here:

  - To start your default browser and display a website, enter a URL in the address bar and then press Enter or click the Go button.

  - To conduct a web search by using the default browser search engine, enter a search term in the address bar.

  - To start an installed app, enter the app executable name (for example, *calc* to start the Calculator, *excel* to start Microsoft Excel, or *cmd* to display the command prompt window.

  The Address toolbar retains a list of recent entries. To reopen a recent website or app or refresh a recent search, click the arrow at the right end of the address bar, and then click the entry you want.

The Address toolbar provides quick access to sites, apps, and searches

> **TIP** Notice the double-line handle to the left of the toolbar. You can drag this handle to change the space allocated to the toolbar on the taskbar.

- **Links** The Links toolbar displays information from the same source as your Internet Explorer Favorites bar. You can add and remove links (to websites, files, folders, and apps) on either bar to share those changes with the Favorites bar and Links toolbar on all computers that you sign in to by using your Microsoft account. At the time of this writing, the Links toolbar is connected to Internet Explorer and not yet connected to Edge, but that might change in later releases.

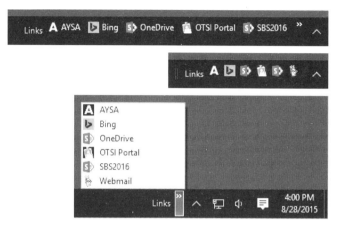

Toolbars can display names and icons on the taskbar or on a menu

> **IMPORTANT** We expect that in a future release of Windows, the Links menu will display favorites from the Microsoft Edge browser, or a shared list of favorites from both Internet Explorer and Edge.

- **Desktop** The Desktop toolbar provides quick access to the storage locations that are available in the File Explorer Navigation pane and on your desktop.

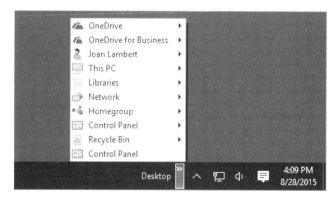

The Desktop toolbar provides easy access to shortcuts for apps, files, and folders

> **TIP** You can change the width of a toolbar on the taskbar by dragging its handle. If all the toolbar links don't fit on the taskbar, a chevron button is available at its right end. Clicking the button displays a menu of hidden links.

When you add a toolbar to the taskbar, the toolbar name appears at the left end of the toolbar, next to the toolbar handle. You can remove the name from the taskbar to save space.

In addition to displaying the built-in toolbars, you can create custom toolbars. A custom toolbar points to a folder, which can contain shortcuts to files, apps, and other folders. You can use this technique to quickly access files for a specific project, client, or process.

To display or hide a built-in toolbar on the taskbar

1. On the taskbar shortcut menu, click **Toolbars**, and then click the toolbar you want to display or hide.

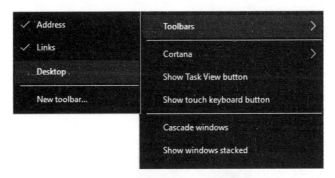

A check mark indicates that a toolbar is on the taskbar

Or

1. Open the **Taskbar and Start Menu Properties** dialog box, and then click the **Toolbars** tab.

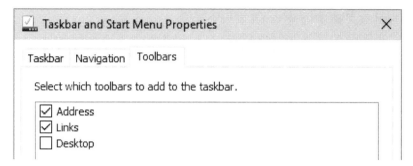

Active custom toolbars also appear in this list

2. Select the check box of each toolbar you want to display, and clear the check box of each toolbar you want to hide.

3. Click **Apply** to implement the change or **OK** to implement the change and close the dialog box.

To display a custom toolbar on the taskbar

1. Put the files and shortcuts you want to display on the custom toolbar into a folder.

 TIP Because the folder name will appear on the taskbar as the toolbar name, it's a good idea to give the folder a short name rather than a long name.

2. On the taskbar shortcut menu, click **Toolbars**, and then click **New toolbar**.

3. In the **New Toolbar – Choose a folder** window, browse to and select the folder you worked with in step 1. Then click the **Select Folder** button.

To change the width of a taskbar toolbar

1. Drag the toolbar handle (the double line to the left of the toolbar) to change the taskbar space allocated to it.

To hide or display the name of a taskbar toolbar

1. Right-click the toolbar, and then on the extended taskbar shortcut menu, click **Show title**.

To hide or display item names on a built-in or custom taskbar toolbar

1. Right-click the toolbar, and then on the extended taskbar shortcut menu, click **Show Text**.

To remove a toolbar from the taskbar

1. Do either of the following:

   - On the taskbar shortcut menu, point to **Toolbars**, and then click the toolbar you want to remove.

   - Right-click the toolbar, and then on the extended taskbar shortcut menu, click **Close toolbar**.

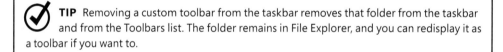 **TIP** Removing a custom toolbar from the taskbar removes that folder from the taskbar and from the Toolbars list. The folder remains in File Explorer, and you can redisplay it as a toolbar if you want to.

Apply and manage themes

Previously in this chapter, we worked with the desktop background and system colors. You can configure those elements through the Windows 10 Personalization settings, or if you prefer you can apply an entire package of personalization elements at one time by applying a *theme*. The most common elements of a theme are a desktop background image or series of images, and a corresponding system color (or colors that change with the background image). These are the same elements we worked with in "Set the desktop background and system colors" earlier in this chapter. A theme can also include custom notification sounds that play to notify you of Windows events (such as a low battery or User Account Control request for Administrator approval of a change) and app events (such as an incoming instant message, a blocked pop-up window, or a completed transaction).

Three colorful themes (Windows, Windows 10, and Flowers) and four high contrast themes (#1, #2, Black, and White) come with Windows 10. Most of the images in this book depict the "Windows" theme desktop background.

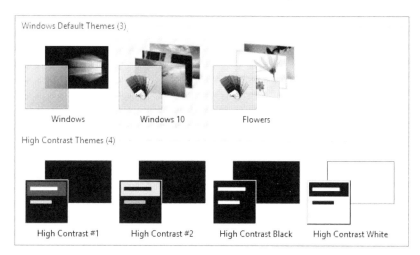

The built-in themes supplied with all Windows 10 installations

The high contrast themes increase the color contrast of text, window borders, and images on your screen to make them more visible and easier to read and identify.

> **TIP** If you use your own images as a desktop background and later want to regain access to the original "Windows" or "Windows 10" theme images, you can do so by applying that theme.

The manufacturer of your computer might also install a theme that is specific to the brand of computer you have. If you work in a managed computer environment, your company might have a corporate theme that is installed by default with the base computer image.

In addition to these theme options, thousands of themes are available online, from the Themes page of the Windows website. You can access the Themes page directly at *windows.microsoft.com/en-US/windows/themes* or from the Personalization panel that displays the themes that are already installed on your computer. The desktop backgrounds of these themes feature some breathtaking photography and creative artwork across multiple subject categories that include not only general photography (landscapes, animals, plants, people, and places) but also themes tied to specific movies or games. You could spend hours browsing through the options.

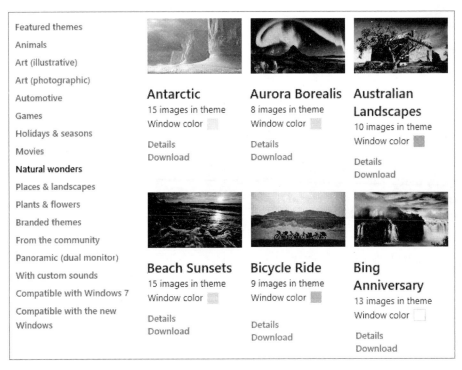

Theme categories and themes in the Natural Wonders category

 TIP Themes that include custom sounds are easy to locate by clicking With Custom Sounds in the category list.

Themes in the Panoramic category are designed to span across two screens, for people who work with a second monitor that is connected to their computer system. For panoramic themes to work as intended, both screens must have the same resolution.

 SEE ALSO For information about screen resolution, see "Display your desktop on multiple screens" in Chapter 6, "Manage peripheral devices."

Glaciers Panoramic
6 images in theme
Window color adjusts to image
Details
Download

Horizons Panoramic
7 images in theme
Window color adjusts to image
Details
Download

Majestic Mountains Panoramic
12 images in theme
Window color adjusts to image
Details
Download

Panoramic images span across monitors

Clicking any theme thumbnail displays information about the theme, including the full selection of background images and the name of the photographer if the images are attributed to an individual person. Many of the themes in the From The Community category are contributed by photographers as showcases of their work.

Theme sound description   Dual monitor preview

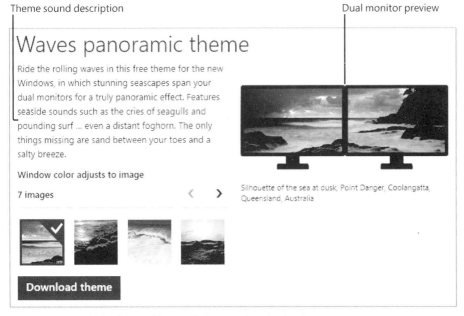

You can preview the background images before you download a theme

You can download any online theme to your computer, and then open the downloaded file to unpack the theme elements and apply the theme. The theme elements are saved in the hidden AppData\Local\Microsoft\Windows\Themes folder in your user account folder; you can access them there when you customize themes, or copy them to a more convenient location.

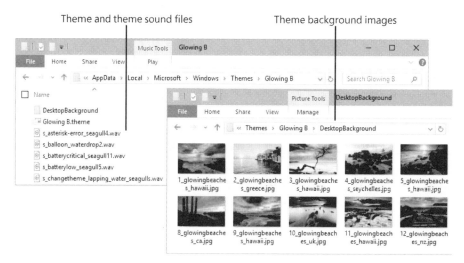

The unpacked theme files

SEE ALSO For more information about displaying hidden files and folders, see "Change the File Explorer display options" in Chapter 3, "Manage folders and files."

After you apply a theme, you can customize elements of it to suit your individual taste. For example, many themes come with multiple desktop background images, and you can choose the one that you like best, or choose a selection to display in slide show fashion. If you use your Microsoft account credentials to sign in to multiple computers, you can choose to synchronize a custom theme among all of your accounts.

Custom, downloaded, and synchronized themes

At the time of this writing, themes are ultimately managed in Control Panel, but you can also get to the theme settings through the Personalization category in the Settings window.

Any changes that you make after you apply a theme create a customized version of that theme, which is designated in the Personalization panel as Unsaved Theme. For example, you can change the system color or select a single background image from among several that come with a theme. If you like the changes you make to a theme, you can save it as a custom theme, either for your own use or for distribution to other people.

 IMPORTANT You can have only one unsaved theme at a time; until you save it, any additional changes you make will remove that specific background/color/sound combination from your themes.

To display the installed themes

1. In the **Settings** window, click **Personalization**, and then click **Themes**.

2. In the **Themes** pane, click **Theme settings** to open the **Personalization** panel.

Or

1. Open Control Panel, and then do one of the following:

    • In Category view of Control Panel, under **Appearance and Personalization**, click **Change the theme**.

    • In Large Icons view or Small Icons view of Control Panel, click **Personalization**.

To apply an installed theme

1. In the **Personalization** panel, click the theme you want to apply.

 TIP You can display the desktop background by pointing to or clicking the Show Desktop button located at the right end of the taskbar, or by pressing Win+D.

To apply a theme from the Windows website

1. In the **My Themes** section of the **Personalization** panel, click the **Get more themes online** link to display the **Themes** webpage in your default browser.

2. On the **Themes** webpage, locate the theme you want to apply.

3. Click the theme thumbnail to display the description.

4. On the theme description page, click the **Download theme** button to download the file that contains the theme elements to your Downloads folder. A notification box displays the download status.

| GlowingBeaches.themepack finished downloading. | Open | View downloads | ✕ |

Open the file to install the theme

5. When the download completes, click **Open** in the notification to unpack the theme file, add the theme to the **My Themes** section of the **Personalization** panel, and apply the theme.

> ✅ **TIP** If you close the notification without installing the theme and later want to, you can open the file from your Downloads folder. After you install the theme, you can delete the downloaded file.

To save a custom theme

1. In the **My Themes** section of the **Personalization** panel, right-click the **Unsaved Theme** thumbnail, and then do one of the following:

   - If you want to save the selected theme as a named theme in the **My Themes** section of the **Personalization** panel, click **Save theme**.

   - If you want to save the selected theme as a file that you can send to other people, click **Save theme for sharing**. Then in the **Save Theme Pack As** window, browse to the folder you want to save the Desktop Theme Pack (.deskthemepack) file in, enter a descriptive name in the **File name** box, and click the **Save** button.

To remove a theme

1. In the **My Themes** section of the **Personalization** panel, right-click the theme you want to remove, and then click **Delete theme**.

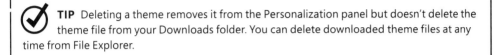 **TIP** Deleting a theme removes it from the Personalization panel but doesn't delete the theme file from your Downloads folder. You can delete downloaded theme files at any time from File Explorer.

SEE ALSO For information about synchronizing your theme among the computers associated with your Microsoft account, see "Customize your sign-in options" in Chapter 8, "Manage user accounts and settings."

Skills review

In this chapter, you learned how to:

- Configure the Start screen and Start menu

- Manage Start screen tiles

- Set the desktop background and system colors

- Configure the taskbar

- Apply and manage themes

Practice tasks

The practice files for these tasks are located in the Win10SBS\Ch02 folder.

Configure the Start screen and Start menu

Perform the following tasks:

1. Open the **Settings** window, display the Start screen personalization settings, and locate the toggle button for the full-screen **Start** screen. Set the toggle button to **On** (or leave it on if it already is).

2. Display the **Start** screen and note the organization of tiles and tile groups on the screen.

3. Display the **Start** menu on the full-screen Start screen, and observe the configuration of the menu items.

4. From the **Start** menu, return to the Start screen personalization settings. Set the toggle buttons for the Most Used app list, Recently Added app list, and jump lists to **Off**.

5. Configure the **Start** menu to display only these folders:

   - File Explorer
   - Settings
   - Documents
   - Downloads
   - Pictures
   - Network

6. Display the **Start** menu to observe the results of the changes.

7. From the **Start** menu, return to the Start screen personalization settings. Turn off the full-screen Start screen.

8. Display the partial-screen **Start** screen, and drag the corner of the screen until it is at its minimum size.

9. If a vertical scroll bar appears, scroll down to display the hidden tiles.

10. Return to the Start screen personalization settings, and implement the Start screen configuration, lists, and folders that you like best.

Manage Start screen tiles

Perform the following tasks:

1. Display the **Start** screen, and observe the configuration of the existing tiles.

2. Move a Start screen tile from an existing tile group and use it to create a new tile group. Set the tile size to the largest size it supports.

3. Move another tile into the new group, and set its size to **Small**.

4. Name the new tile group **Practice Tiles**.

5. Move the **Practice Tiles** group to the upper-left corner of the **Start** screen.

6. Rename the **Practice Tiles** group as **Favorite Apps**.

7. Arrange and resize the tiles on your Start screen to suit the way you work.

 TIP In Chapter 4, "Work with apps and notifications," you'll add more tiles to the Start screen.

Set the desktop background and system colors

Perform the following tasks:

1. Open the **Settings** window, and display the color personalization settings.

2. In the **Choose a color** section, set the three toggle buttons to **On**.

3. Return to the **Settings** window, and display the background personalization settings.

4. Set the desktop background to a solid color of your choice. Then set the desktop background to the **Background01** image located in the practice file folder. Configure the background settings to display the image in the center of the screen.

5. Minimize all open windows to show the desktop and observe the change. Notice that the background color you set in step 4 surrounds the image.

6. Return to the background personalization settings. Configure the background settings as follows:

    •   Display a slideshow of the images in the practice file folder.

    •   Display the images in a random order, with the image changing every minute.

    •   Choose the fit option that will display all the images at full-screen size without affecting the image aspect ratios.

7. Minimize all open windows to show the desktop and observe the change.

8. Expand the **Start** screen. Notice that the desktop background is visible through the Start screen and taskbar.

9. Wait for the desktop background to change. Notice that the accent color on the taskbar and other interface elements changes with the background image. Locate the source of the accent color for each new background image.

10. Return to the **Settings** window. Configure the desktop background and accent color as you want them.

Configure the taskbar

Perform the following tasks:

1. Check whether the taskbar is locked. If it is locked, unlock it.

2. Move the taskbar to the left edge of the screen.

3. Configure the taskbar to display small buttons and to hide when it isn't active.

4. When the taskbar is hidden, point to the edge of the screen to display it. Then stretch it to twice its current width.

5. Hide the **Task View** and **Touch keyboard** buttons.

6. Move the taskbar to the top of the window.

7. Display the **Desktop** toolbar on the taskbar. Hide the toolbar name and link labels. Then size the toolbar so that three icons appear on the taskbar and the rest are available on a menu at the right end of the toolbar.

8. Configure the taskbar to display large buttons, and to never combine taskbar buttons.

9. Create a custom toolbar that links to the contents of the **Ch02** practice file folder. From the toolbar, open the **Background05** image. Then open the **Background07** image. Verify that a new taskbar button appears for each image.

10. Close the **Desktop** toolbar, and remove the custom toolbar from the taskbar.

11. Configure the taskbar content the way you want it, and then lock the taskbar.

Apply and manage themes

Perform the following tasks:

1. From either the **Settings** window or Control Panel, display all the themes that are installed on your computer.

2. Apply the built-in **Flowers** theme.

3. Connect to the **Themes** webpage, and locate a theme that you like. Download and apply the theme.

4. In the **Colors** pane of the **Personalization** settings page, change the system color. Then return to the **Personalization** panel, and note that the unsaved theme reflects your changes.

5. Save the customized theme in the **My Themes** section of the **Personalization** panel as **MyCustomTheme**.

6. Remove a theme (either the theme you downloaded or your custom theme) from the **My Themes** section of the **Personalization** panel.

Manage folders and files

3

The concept of folders is one of the most basic and important things you can learn. Folders are everywhere in computing: you can organize files in folders on your computer, messages in folders in your email app, and favorite websites in folders in your Internet browser.

You use File Explorer to manage and work with the folders and files that are stored on your computer. To simplify the way that you work with files, Windows presents files in File Explorer as though the files are organized in a hierarchical storage system of folders and subfolders. In reality, files are stored on the computer's hard drive and in other locations (such as OneDrive) wherever they fit, and the storage structure that File Explorer displays is only a series of pointers to the files. This allows you to easily access files while still maintaining an organizational system.

You can organize files in folders and create virtual libraries of folders so that you can access files in multiple ways. If you forget where you stored a file, you can use the simple yet powerful search features of Windows 10 to quickly locate files and other information on your computer based on the file name, content, or type.

This chapter guides you through procedures related to getting to know File Explorer, changing the File Explorer display options, managing folders and files, working with folder and file properties, and searching for files.

In this chapter

- Understand files, folders, and libraries

- Get to know File Explorer

- Change the File Explorer display options

- Create and rename folders and files

- Compress folders and files

- Move and copy folders and files

- Delete and recover folders and files

- Work with folder and file properties

- Find specific files

Practice files

For this chapter, use the practice files from the Win10SBS\Ch03 folder. For practice file download instructions, see the introduction.

Understand files, folders, and libraries

There are many different types of files, but they all fall into these two basic categories:

- **Files used or created by apps** These include executable files (such as the Microsoft Office app files) and dynamic-link libraries (DLLs) (files used by apps to provide functionality). Some of these files might be hidden (not shown in a standard folder window view) to protect them from being inadvertently changed or deleted.

> ✓ **TIP** You can't select or delete hidden system files or the folder structure they're stored in. You can choose to display and work with hidden files, folders, and drives by clicking that option in the Folder Options dialog box, which is discussed in "Display different views of folders and files" later in this chapter.

- **Files created by you** These include documents, worksheets, graphics, text files, presentations, audio clips, video clips, and other things that you can open, look at, and change by using one or more apps.

The files that are installed with an app and those it creates for its own use are organized the way the app expects to find them, and you shouldn't move or remove them. However, you have complete control of the organization of the files you create (such as documents and worksheets), and knowing how to manage these files is essential if you want to be able to use your computer efficiently.

Folders

As with files, there are also many different types of folders, but they fall generally into two categories: folders created by Windows or apps and folders created by you to organize your files. Creating folders is covered in "Create and rename folders and files" later in this chapter.

When Windows 10 was installed on your computer, it created system folders, including these:

- **Program Files folder** Many apps install the files they need in subfolders of the Program Files folder. You might have the option to choose a different folder, but there's rarely a reason to do so. After you install an app you shouldn't move, copy, rename, or delete its folders and files; if you do, you might not be able to run or uninstall the app.

- **Users folder** For each user account on the computer, Windows also creates a user account folder in the Users folder. The user account folder contains several subfolders, which we refer to in this book as your personal folders. Some of your personal folders are visible in your user account folder; these might include Contacts, Desktop, Documents, Downloads, Favorites, Links, Music, Pictures, Saved Games, Searches, and Videos. There is also a hidden folder named AppData that contains information about your user account settings for Windows and for apps that you use. Windows creates the user account folder and its subfolders the first time a user signs in. As you work on your computer and personalize Windows, Windows saves information and settings specific to your user profile in these folders.

> **TIP** If other people have user accounts on your computer, they won't have access to the files in your Documents folder unless they have administrative rights or know your password.

In addition to the account–specific folder for each user account that is active on the computer, the Users folder also contains a Public folder, the contents of which are accessible to anyone who is logged on to the computer. The Public folder contains subfolders. Some of these are visible, such as Documents, Downloads, Music, Pictures, and Videos. Other hidden subfolders contain information about settings that are common to all user accounts on the computer. If you want to make files available to anyone who logs on to the computer, you can store them in the Public folders rather than in your personal folders.

> **TIP** To clearly differentiate your personal folders from the public folders, Windows 10 refers to your personal folders as My Documents, My Music, My Pictures, and My Videos, and to the public folders as Public Documents, Public Music, Public Pictures, and Public Videos. The default Documents, Music, Pictures, and Videos libraries include the corresponding personal and public folders. (Libraries are virtual folders that we discuss later in this topic.)

- **Windows folder** Most of the critical operating system files are stored in this folder. You can look, but unless you really know what you are doing, don't touch! Most Windows 10 users will never need to access the files in the Windows folder.

Libraries

You can display a collection of folders that you want easy access to in a *library*. Libraries are virtual folders that aren't physically present on the hard disk but that display the contents of multiple folders as though the files were stored together in one location.

The default Windows 10 installation includes six standard libraries: Camera Roll, Documents, Music, Pictures, Saved Pictures, and Videos. In previous versions of Windows, the libraries included user account folders and their corresponding Public folders, but in Windows 10 the default starting content is your user account folder.

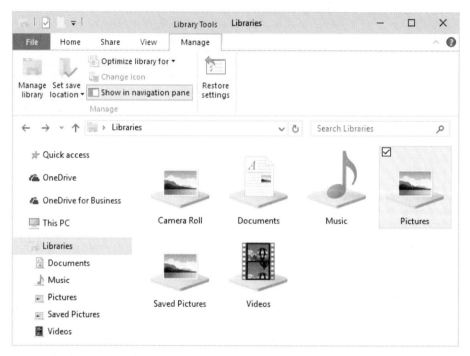

You manage libraries from the Manage tool tab

You can add folders to libraries, and some apps add folders to libraries for you when you make selections. In addition to the standard libraries, you can create your own libraries, and a folder can belong to more than one library. For example, suppose you are working on a Fall Promotion project for a client, Contoso Pharmaceuticals. If you create one library that displays all the folders of your current projects and another library that displays all the folders associated with Contoso, you can include the Fall Promotion folder in both libraries.

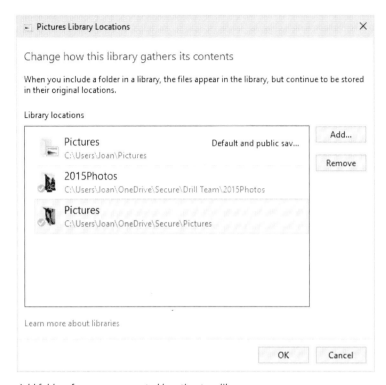

Add folders from any connected location to a library

If you don't use libraries, you can choose to not display the Libraries node at the root of the Navigation pane.

> **TIP** If you store files locally on your computer rather than in a cloud storage location such as OneDrive, we recommend that you store your private documents, spreadsheets, databases, and similar files in subfolders of your My Documents folder, and any files you want to share with other users in subfolders of the Public Documents folder. Similarly, store all your private pictures in My Pictures and those you want to share in Public Pictures; and so on for music and video files. Then include the Public folders in the libraries. When you follow this process, backing up your work is a simple matter of backing up only the libraries.

> **SEE ALSO** For more information about how to make any default or custom library available to other users or computers on your network, see "Manage homegroup connections" and "Share files on your network," both in Chapter 7, "Manage network and storage resources."

Get to know File Explorer

You view all the drives, folders, and files that are part of your computer's storage system, and those on any computers you are connected to through a network or over the Internet, in File Explorer. File Explorer can display the contents of a folder, a library of folders, or a virtual collection of items (such as the Quick Access list).

 TIP File Explorer is the current version of the tool that in versions of Windows prior to Windows 8 was called Windows Explorer.

Early versions of Windows displayed physical hard drives at the root of the file storage structure. As file management and storage practices have evolved—first to include virtual libraries of folders and now to commonly include OneDrive and other cloud storage locations—File Explorer has also evolved. At the root of the storage structure, File Explorer displays a series of conceptual organizational systems, including the following nodes:

- **Quick Access** Contains links to folders and files that you access frequently or pin here for easy access

- **This PC** Contains links to your user account-specific folders, and to the physical storage locations that are installed in or connected to your computer

- **Libraries** Contains links to virtual collections of folders, which by default are composed of the user account-specific folders and their corresponding Public folders

- **Network** Displays a representation of other computers on your local area network

- **Homegroup** Displays a representation of other computers on your local area network that are joined to the network homegroup

 SEE ALSO For information about connecting to network computers and homegroup members, see Chapter 7, "Manage network and storage resources."

 TIP In addition to storage locations, File Explorer displays the hardware devices (such as monitors, printers, and cameras) that are connected to your computer—both directly and over a network. For information about working with hardware, see Chapter 6, "Manage peripheral devices."

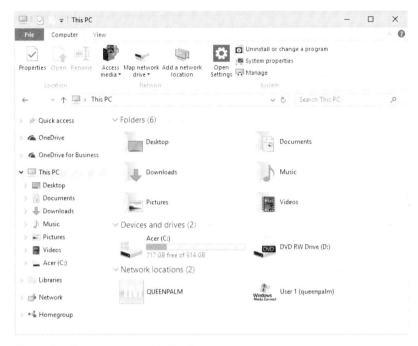

Storage locations are managed indirectly

When you connect your Windows 10 computer to OneDrive or OneDrive for Business cloud storage drives, they also appear at the root of the storage structure.

Within the This PC node, File Explorer displays the user-specific file storage folders and the storage devices that are connected to your computer. Storage locations included in This PC include hard disk drives installed in the computer and storage devices (such as CDs, DVDs, USB flash drives, and external hard drives) that are physically connected to the computer. Each storage drive that is physically connected to the computer is identified by a letter, and in some cases by a description. Your computer's primary hard drive (the one where the operating system is installed) is almost always identified by the letter C. (By tradition, the letters *A* and *B* are reserved for floppy disk drives, which have been superseded by higher-capacity storage media.) If your computer has additional built-in hard drives, they are assigned the next sequential letters, followed by any removable media drives.

> **TIP** You can't assign a specific drive letter to a local drive in File Explorer, but you can name each drive. For information, see the sidebar "Change the computer name" in Chapter 7, "Manage network and storage resources."

Navigation pane   Content pane   Ribbon   Details pane

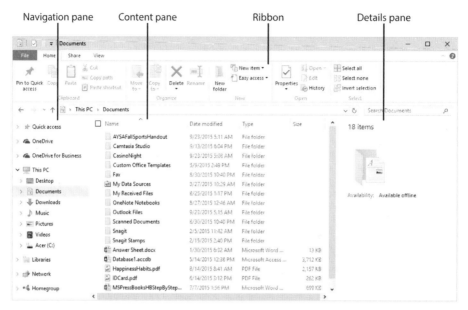

The File Explorer window layout

To explore your computer's storage system, you can use the This PC window as a convenient entry point. The devices represented in This PC are divided into groups. Internal hard disk drives (those physically installed in your computer) and external hard disk drives (those connected to your computer by a cable) are shown first, followed by internal removable storage drives (floppy disk, CD, and DVD drives) and external removable storage devices (such as USB flash drives), and then storage locations you access through a network connection. For each drive or device, the total storage space and available storage space are given, both as actual measurements and visually as a colored progress bar. The length of the progress bar indicates the portion of the total storage space that is in use. The default bar color is aqua; when less than 10 percent of the storage space on a disk or device remains available, the bar color changes to red.

The File Explorer window layout includes the following elements:

- **The ribbon** This command interface has commands organized in groups on tabs. We discuss the File menu and ribbon tabs later in this topic.

- **Navigation pane** This vertical pane is open by default on the left side of the window. It displays a hierarchical view of the physical and virtual storage structures available to the computer. You can browse to folders and files on your computer or network by clicking locations in this pane.

- **Content pane** This primary pane displays the contents of the selected folder as a textual or iconic list. You can't close the Content pane.

- **Details pane** This pane displays information about the selected folder or file.

- **Preview pane** This pane displays a preview of the file that is selected in the Content pane. The Preview pane can display the contents of image files, Microsoft Word documents, Excel workbooks, PowerPoint presentations, PDF files, and other common file types.

You can display either the Details pane or the Preview pane on the right side of the window, or you can close both. For more information, see "Change the File Explorer display options" later in this chapter.

Work with the standard ribbon tabs

The ribbon in File Explorer includes the File menu, a set of standard tabs, tabs that are displayed for specific folders, and tabs that appear only when specific types of items are selected. These context-sensitive tabs, also called tool tabs, host commands that you need only when you select an item of that type. Tool tabs are covered in the "Work with the tool tabs" section later in this topic.

The standard ribbon elements are:

- **File menu** The File menu displays commands in the left pane and a list of recently or frequently displayed folders on the right.

You can invoke commands and open specific locations from the File menu

TIP The most useful of the available commands is Change Folder And Search Options, which we work with later in this chapter.

You can pin locations to the Frequent Places list by clicking the thumbtack icon. Pinned locations stay at the top of the list.

- **Home tab** The Home tab is available when File Explorer is displaying anything other than the This PC, Network, and Homegroup nodes.

Commonly used commands are grouped on the Home tab

- **Share tab** The Share tab provides various ways for you to share a folder or file with other people. These options include sending a copy of a file to other people or sharing its location with other people who are on your network.

In addition to sharing options, the Share tab provides commands for printing, burning a file to disk, and compressing a file

 TIP The Share With list is active only when a folder is selected. You can't choose to share only one file. For information about file and folder sharing, see "Share files on your network" in Chapter 7, "Manage network and storage resources."

- **View tab** The View tab hosts the commands that you can use to customize the display of items in the File Explorer window.

Use the commands on the View tab to tailor the File Explorer window to suit your working preferences

The Home tab provides access to the most commonly used File Explorer commands. Many of them are covered in depth later in this chapter, but some deserve a quick mention, such as the following:

- **Pin to Quick access** This adds the selected folder to the Quick Access list at the top of the Navigation pane. This list is available from within apps and in File Explorer.

- **Easy access** This command displays a menu that offers various ways to make the current location more easily accessible.

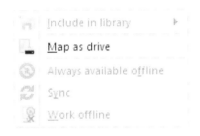

Easy access menu

- **Open and Edit** When a folder is selected in the Content pane, clicking the Open button expands the folder. The Edit button is disabled. When an editable file (such as a Word document) is selected in the Content pane, both the Open and Edit buttons open the file in the originating program (Word, in this case). The difference is that when you click the *arrow* next to Open, you get a list of all the programs known to File Explorer that can open this file type, and an option to choose a default one.

- **History** This displays the current file in the File History viewer.

> **SEE ALSO** For information about file version history, see "Back up data by using File History" in Chapter 12, "Protect your computer and data."

The View tab provides access to several commands you can use to tailor File Explorer to suit your preferences. Many of these tabs are discussed in greater detail in "Change the File Explorer display options" later in this chapter.

The following commands are the most commonly used:

- **Navigation Pane** Click this to display a list of Navigation pane features you can turn on or off, including the display of the pane itself.

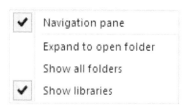

Navigation pane options

- **Preview and Details panes** You can display either one of these, but only one at a time. The active pane appears on the right side of File Explorer. When the Preview pane is active, clicking a file displays the file content in the preview pane. If the Details pane is active, clicking a file displays its icon and file information such as its size.

- **Layout commands** These commands determine whether the files are displayed as icons of various sizes or one of two types of list.

> **TIP** You can quickly switch between a detailed list and large icons view by using the icons in the lower-right corner of the File Explorer window.

- **Current view commands** Sort By allows you to select the column to sort by. You can also do this by clicking a column title. Click it again to reverse the sort. Click Group by and Add Columns to see the options for each.

- **Show/hide commands** The three check boxes in Show/Hide turn the display of their respective items on and off. You can select one or more items (files or folders) and click Hide Selected Items to mark them as hidden. Then select or clear the Hidden Items check box to display or hide them in the Content pane. To unhide the items, first show all hidden items, then select the hidden items, and click Hide Selected Items to turn it off.

> 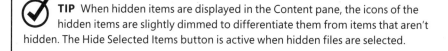 **TIP** When hidden items are displayed in the Content pane, the icons of the hidden items are slightly dimmed to differentiate them from items that aren't hidden. The Hide Selected Items button is active when hidden files are selected.

- **Options** The Options command displays the Folder Options dialog box, which we discuss in "Change the File Explorer display options," later in this chapter.

Work with the tool tabs

Tool tabs appear on the ribbon when specific storage locations are displayed or specific types of files are selected. Tool tabs are in named groups of one or more tabs. (In Windows, many groups contain only one tab.) A colored tab in the title bar displays the tool tab group name. The tool tab or tabs are below the group tab and to the right of the standard tabs. For example, when you select an image file, the Manage tool tab in the Picture Tools group appears; when you select an audio file, the Play tool tab in the Music Tools group appears; and when you select a compressed folder (a zip file), the Extract tool tab in the Compressed Folder Tools group appears.

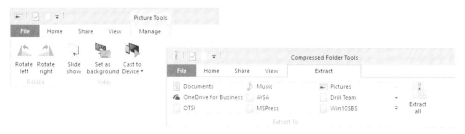

Tool tabs host commands that are specific to working with the selected type of file

 TIP The tool tabs appear when you select multiple files of the same type, but not when you select multiple types of files.

There are theoretically more than 200 tool tabs, each with its own combination of commands. The storage locations that have their own tabs include This PC, Drive, Network, Homegroup, Search, Library, and Recycle Bin. The file types that display tool tabs when you select them include ISO, ZIP, Image, Audio, Video, and Shortcut file types.

For example, when you click This PC in File Explorer, the Home and Share tabs are replaced by the Computer tab. This tab contains links to common functions and utilities that you can use to manage your computer. You can point to each command on the Computer tab to display a ScreenTip explaining its purpose.

File Explorer ribbon for This PC

> **TIP** Some of these commands open in a new window and some replace the content of File Explorer. This can be confusing. Check for a Back button in the window before clicking Close; otherwise you might close File Explorer.

When you click a hard disk drive in the Navigation pane, the Manage tool tab in the Drive Tools group appears.

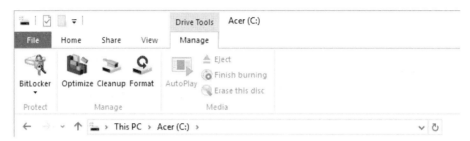

File Explorer ribbon for a disk drive

If you have a local network, you can click the icon for it in the Navigation pane. Commands appropriate to the network are displayed on the Network tab.

File Explorer ribbon for a network

Even the Recycle Bin has its own tool tab. When you double-click the desktop icon for the Recycle Bin, the Manage tab in the Recycle Bin Tools group appears on the ribbon.

File Explorer ribbon for the Recycle Bin

From this tool tab, you can empty the Recycle Bin or restore deleted items.

Work with the Navigation And Search bar

The Navigation And Search bar is displayed just below the ribbon.

Click the folder icon to display the exact path

You can use the commands on this bar to quickly navigate through the folder structure.

To the immediate right of the folder navigation arrows is the Address bar. The Address bar displays an icon and the full path to the current folder. Each item in the path has a chevron after it. If you click a chevron, the folders within that item are displayed, and you can click one to open it. You can drag the icon to another location, such as the desktop, to create a shortcut to this folder at that location. You can right-click anywhere in the Address bar to display the shortcut menu.

To the right of the Address bar are the Refresh button and the Search box. Clicking the Refresh button is the same as pressing F5: it refreshes the display. The Search box is one of those special locations that produces a tool tab. Search is discussed in more detail in "Find specific files," later in this chapter.

To start File Explorer

1. Do any of the following:

   - On the **Start** menu, click **File Explorer**.

   - On the taskbar, click the **File Explorer** button.

   - Press **Win+E**.

To display the contents of a folder in File Explorer

1. Do either of the following:

   - In the **Navigation** pane, click the folder name.

   - In the **Content** pane, double-click the folder name.

To expand or collapse a folder in the Navigation pane

1. Double-click the folder, or click the chevron to the left of the folder name.

To move through a list of recent locations

1. At the left end of the **Navigation and Search** bar, click the **Back** and **Forward** buttons.

To move directly to a location

1. In **File Explorer**, on the **Navigation and Search** bar, do either of the following:

   - Click the **Recent locations** button (the chevron at the left end of the bar, between the Forward and Up buttons) to display a menu of recent locations.

   - Click the **Previous Locations** button (the chevron at the right end of the Address box) to display a menu of previous locations.

2. Click the location you want to move to.

 TIP You can paste or enter a folder path directly into the Address bar in a dialog box to display that location.

To move up one folder in the current path

1. In File Explorer, on the **Navigation and Search** bar, click the **Up** button (the upward-pointing arrow to the left of the Address box).

Work with libraries

The Libraries folder that is optionally displayed in the File Explorer Navigation pane is more conceptual than most other folders. Rather than containing files and folders, it points to folders that might exist on your hard drive, on a USB drive, or even on a hard drive on someone else's computer on a network you can access.

 TIP You can control the display of libraries by going to the File Explorer View tab, clicking Navigation Pane, and selecting or clearing the Show Libraries check box.

Libraries are shortcuts to folders that that you can navigate to individually, but you want quicker access to. For example, the Documents library might include pointers to your private Documents folder, to the Public Documents folder, and to the Documents folder in your OneDrive folder. When you add a file to one of those folders, and it is indexed, it shows up in the Documents Library.

SEE ALSO For information about search indexes, see "Find specific files" later in this chapter, and "Search your computer and the web" in Chapter 11, "Work more efficiently."

One of the benefits of adding folders to your libraries is that the Libraries folder and all the folders it points to are included by default in File History backups.

 SEE ALSO For information about File History, see "Back up data by using File History" in Chapter 12, "Protect your computer and data."

You can add new folders to existing libraries and create new libraries.

 TIP To see what is currently included in a library, double-click the library name. This opens a list of the locations in the Content pane.

If you want to store a folder in a library so that it is backed up regularly, but you don't need to access it frequently, you can hide the folder in the library.

To display or hide libraries in the Navigation pane

1. In File Explorer, on the **View** tab, in the **Panes** group, click the **Navigation pane** button, and then click **Show libraries**.

To create a library

1. In File Explorer, display the **Libraries** node.

2. Right-click the **Libraries** node or an empty area of the **Content** pane, click **New**, and then click **Library** to create the library with its name selected for editing.

3. Enter a name for the new library, and then click **Enter**.

Projects

The icon remains neutral until you choose a content type

To add a folder to a library

1. In File Explorer, open the library. If the library doesn't contain at least one folder, it displays a button labeled Include A Folder.

2. Click the **Include a folder** button to open the Include Folder In dialog box for the library. Browse to and select the folder you want to include, and then click the **Include folder** button to add the folder to the library.

Or

1. In File Explorer, display the **Libraries** node.

2. In the **Content** pane, select the library to which you want to add a folder.

3. On the **Manage** tool tab, in the **Manage** group, click **Manage library** to open the Library Locations dialog box specific to the library.

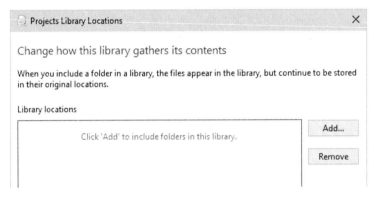

You can add folders from any connected location

4. Click the **Add** button to open the Include Folder In dialog box for the library. Browse to and select the folder you want to include, and then click the **Include folder** button to add the folder to the library. Then click **OK** to close the dialog box.

Or

1. In File Explorer, right-click the library, and then click **Properties** to display the Properties dialog box for the library.

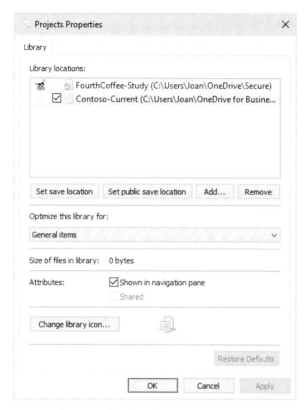

Manage all aspects of a library from the Properties dialog box

2. Under **Library locations**, click the **Add** button to open the Include Folder In dialog box for the library. Browse to and select the folder you want to include, and then click the **Include folder** button to add the folder to the library.

3. Make any other changes you want in the dialog box, and then click **Apply** or **OK**.

To optimize a folder for a type of file

1. Open the library's **Properties** dialog box.

2. In the **Optimize this library for** list, click **General items**, **Documents**, **Music**, **Pictures**, or **Videos**. Then click **Apply** or **OK**.

Or

1. In File Explorer, display the **Libraries** node.

2. Select the library you want to optimize.

3. On the **Manage** tool tab, click **Optimize library for**, and then in the list, click **General items**, **Documents**, **Music**, **Pictures**, or **Videos**.

To change the folder icon of a custom library

1. Open the library's **Properties** dialog box.

2. Click the **Change library icon** button to open the Change Icon dialog box.

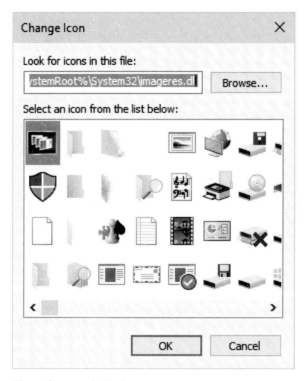

Choose from nearly 400 icons

3. Scroll the icon pane, click the icon you want to use, and click **OK**. Then in the **Properties** dialog box, click **Apply** or **OK**.

Or

1. In File Explorer, select the library you want to optimize.

2. On the **Manage** tool tab, click **Change icon**.

3. In the **Change Icon** dialog box, scroll the icon pane, click the icon you want to use, and then click **OK**.

To remove a folder from a library

1. Do any of the following:

    -   Open the library's **Properties** dialog box, click the folder, and click **Remove**. Then click **Apply** or **OK**.

    -   Open the library's **Library Locations** dialog box, click the folder, and then click **Remove**. Then click **OK**.

To hide a library in the Navigation pane

1. In the library's **Properties** dialog box, clear the **Shown in navigation pane** check box. Then click **Apply** or **OK**.

> ✓ **TIP** You can hide a folder that is in a system-created library so that the folder appears in the Content pane but not in the Navigation pane. To hide a library folder from the Navigation pane only, expand the library and right-click the folder in the Navigation pane, and then click Don't Show In Navigation Pane. To stop hiding the folder, display it in the Content pane, right-click it, and then click Show In Navigation Pane.

Change the File Explorer display options

Windows 10 offers you many ways to personalize the display of File Explorer to suit the way you work.

Display and hide panes

Each pane of the File Explorer window displays a specific type of information. You can display and hide some panes to show or hide information, or to change the amount of space available in the Content pane. For example, if your folders typically contain many files and you are adept at navigating in the Address bar, you might want to turn off the Navigation, Detail, and Preview panes so that the Content pane occupies the entire folder window.

To display or hide the Navigation pane

1. In File Explorer, on the **View** tab, in the **Panes** group, click the **Navigation pane** button.

2. Select or clear the **Navigation pane** check box to display or hide the pane.

To display or hide the Preview pane

1. Do either of the following in File Explorer:

   - Press **Alt+P**.

   - On the **View** tab, click the **Preview pane** button.

To display or hide the Details pane

1. Do either of the following in File Explorer:

   - Press **Alt+Shift+P**.

   - On the **View** tab, click the **Details pane** button.

> **TIP** You can change the width of a pane by pointing to its border, and, when the pointer changes to a double-headed arrow, dragging in the direction you want to increase or decrease its size. This technique is useful if you want to display more information in one pane without closing the other panes.

Display different views of folders and files

You use commands on the View tab to set the layout, the sort order, grouping, and columns that are displayed in the Content pane. You can choose to display a check box column (the boxes appear only when you point to or select items), file name extensions, and hidden files.

> **TIP** The Layout options that you set apply only to the current folder. The Show/Hide settings apply to all folders. You can apply some settings to all folders of the same type in the Options dialog box that is displayed when you click the Options command at the right end of the View tab.

When the Details pane is open, it displays detailed information when you select a single file. As you select more files, the Details pane displays the number of items selected, the total size of the files, and other types of information.

4 items selected

Date taken:	2/22/2005 2:27 PM ...
Tags:	Add a tag
Rating:	☆ ☆ ☆ ☆ ☆
Dimensions:	(multiple values)

Details for selected images

If you add a folder to the selection, the display changes to just the number of items selected (the folder is counted as one item, regardless of the number of subfolders and files in it) and a stack of icons.

Different views are best suited to different tasks. For example, when you are looking for a specific graphic among those stored in a folder, you might find it useful to be able to see the graphic thumbnails in the Content pane.

The available views include the following:

- **Icons** The four Icon views (Extra Large, Large, Medium, and Small) display an icon and name for each folder or file in the current folder. In all but Small Icons view, the icons display either the file type or, in the case of graphic files (including PowerPoint presentations), a representation of the file content.

- **List** This view is similar to Small Icons view in that it shows the names of the files and folders accompanied by a small icon that represents the file type. The only difference is that the items are arranged in columns instead of in rows.

- **Details** This view displays a list of files and folders, each accompanied by a small icon that represents the item type and its properties, arranged in a tabular format, with column headings. The properties shown by default for each file or folder are Name, Date Modified, Type, and Size. You can hide any of these properties, and you can display a variety of other properties that might be pertinent to specific types of files, including Author and Title.

- **Tiles** For folders, this view displays a medium-size icon and the folder name and type. For files, the icon indicates the file type and is accompanied by the file name, type, and file size.

- **Content** For folders, this view displays an icon, the folder name, and the date. For files, the icon indicates the file type and is accompanied by the file name, type, file size, and date.

> **TIP** In the Extra Large Icons, Large Icons, Medium Icons, Tiles, and Content views, folder icons display representations of the folder content depicted as pages and pictures.

To change the folder view

1. Do any of the following in File Explorer:

   - On the **View** tab, in the **Layout** group, click a layout option.

     > **TIP** If you point to one of the view layouts, the Content pane temporarily displays that layout.

   - Right-click an empty spot in the Content pane, point to **View**, and then select a view from the list.

   - In the lower-right corner of the Content pane, click the **Details** or **Large Icons** button.

> **TIP** You can optimize a folder for a specific view on the Customize tab of the folder's Properties dialog box. Doing so makes that the default view for the folder. You can select a different view at any time by using one of the techniques listed here.

To display folder content as icons

1. On the **View** tab, in the **Layout** group, click **Extra Large** icons, **Large** icons, **Medium** icons, or **Small** icons.

To display folder content as a list of items and their properties

1. On the **View** tab, in the **Layout** group, click **Details**.

To add, remove, or rearrange columns in Details view

1. In File Explorer, display the contents of the folder as a detailed list.

2. On the **View** tab, in the **Current view** group, click **Add columns**.

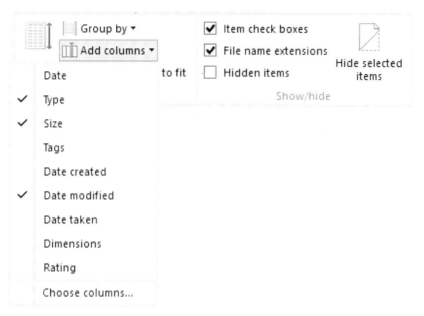

A check mark indicates that the column is already displayed in the Content pane

3. Click **Choose columns...** from the bottom of the list to open the Choose Details dialog box. If a column name has a check mark to the left of its name, it is already displayed in the Content pane.

4. Do any of the following:

   - Click a column name to add or remove its check mark, which adds or removes that column from the Content pane.

   - Select a column name, and then click the **Show** or **Hide** button to show or hide that column on the Content pane.

   - Select a column name, and then use the **Move Up** or **Move Down** button to move the column higher or lower on the list, which will also move the column to the left or right on the Content pane.

To resize a column in Details view

1. In File Explorer, point to the line between column headings, and, when the mouse pointer changes to a double-headed arrow, do any of the following:

   - Drag to the left to make the column narrower.

   - Drag to the right to make the column wider.

   - Double-click to make the column resize to fit the widest item in the column.

To automatically resize all columns to fit the widest item in the column

1. In File Explorer, display the contents of the folder as a detailed list.

2. On the **View** tab, in the **Current view** group, click **Size all columns to fit**.

To display or hide hidden items

1. In File Explorer, on the **View** tab, in the **Show/hide** group, do any of the following:

   - Select or clear the **Item check boxes** check box to turn on or off the display of check boxes when you point to or select an item.

   - Select or clear the **File name extensions** check box to show or hide each file name extension (for example: .doc).

   - Select or clear the **Hidden items** check box to show or hide hidden items.

Group folder content

By default, the folders and files in the Content pane are not grouped. They are shown as individual items that are displayed in alphabetical order by name, with the subfolders listed at the top and files below them. You can group items in any view, by any available attribute, and you can change the folder view of a folder that displays grouped items. In a library window, you can group items by author, modification date, tag, file type, or file name.

The Group By menu on the View tab displays the available grouping options.

Group by ▾	☑ Item check boxes	
Name	s ▾	☑ File name extensions
Date	mns to fit	☐ Hidden items
Type		Show/hide
Size		
Tags		
Date created		
Date modified		
Date taken		
Dimensions		
Rating		
Ascending		
Descending		
Choose columns...		

Hide selected items

You can group by any attribute, regardless of whether it is currently displayed in the window

The basic options include Name, Date modified, Type, Size, Date created, Authors, Categories, Tags, Title, and Choose Columns. You can click Choose Columns to specify the columns that are displayed in the Content pane, and then select a different one to group by.

 TIP Changing a folder's layout, type, grouping, or other attributes doesn't affect its appearance in a library. Libraries independently control the appearance of folder content.

To group files

1. On the **View** tab, in the **Current view** group, click the **Group by** button. If a column name has a dot to the left of it, items in the folder are already grouped by that column.

2. In the **Group by** list, do either of the following:

   - Click a file property to group items by that property.

   - Click **Choose columns**, and then click a file property.

Or

1. Right-click an empty area of the **Content** pane, and then click **Group b**y.

2. In the **Choose details** dialog box, select the property you want to group the files by, and then click **OK**.

To remove a file grouping

1. On the **View** tab, in the **Current view** group, click the **Group by** button, and then click **(None)** from the bottom of the list.

Sort and filter folder content

If you group folders and files, their overall arrangement changes, but within each group the sort order remains the same. You can change the order of the items in the Content pane by sorting them by any of the properties displayed in Details view.

 TIP If you choose to sort the content in ascending or descending order, the files and folders are sorted within their group.

The process and options for sorting are similar to those for grouping: you can click the Sort By command in the Current View group on the View tab, or you can right-click a blank area in the Content pane and select Sort By. Although both options are very similar, the ribbon command displays a few more options.

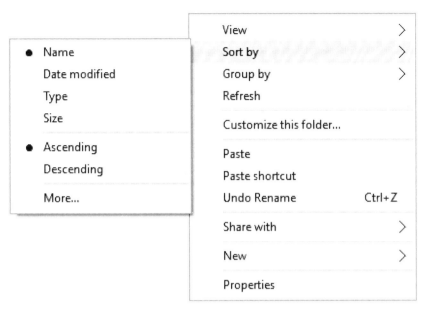

You can sort files easily in Details view

If you are viewing the folder in Details view, you can click any column header to sort the contents on that column. Click again to reverse the sort order. You can also apply filters to limit the list to only those items that satisfy one or more criteria.

To sort files

1. On the **View** tab, in the **Current view** group, click the **Sort by** button, and then do any of the following:

   - Click **Name** to sort items alphabetically by name.

   - Click **Type** to sort items alphabetically by file type, such as *Word document* or *.jpg*.

   - Click **Date** to sort items chronologically by creation date.

   - Click **Descending** to sort items in reverse alphabetical or descending numerical order.

To sort items in Details view

1. Click the column name you want to sort by.

   - Clicking the column name once sorts in alphabetical or ascending numerical order.

   - Clicking the column name a second time sorts in reverse alphabetical or descending numerical order.

   A chevron appears in the middle of the column heading to let you know the column is sorted.

To apply a filter

1. In File Explorer, display the contents of the folder as a detailed list.

2. Point to a column header until a small chevron appears at its right edge.

3. Click the chevron to display a list of items you can filter on.

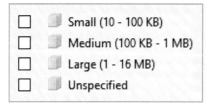

   Filter options for the Size column

4. Select a check box to show only those items in the list that match the filter.

   Each filter is applied when you click, so you can immediately see its impact.

    TIP You can repeat step 3 to apply filters from other columns to the Content pane.

5. Click outside the list to close it.

Change folder options

Most of the common folder options you might want to change are included on the File Explorer ribbon. However, some less common ones are available when you click the Options command at the right end of the View tab.

In the Folder Options dialog box, you can customize folder windows by changing settings on these two tabs:

- **General** On this tab, you can change how you browse folders, whether you click or double-click to open items, and how the Navigation pane behaves.

- **View** On this tab, you can change the default view for all folders and change specific display/hide settings. For example, on the View tab you can specify whether to show the status bar in File Explorer windows.

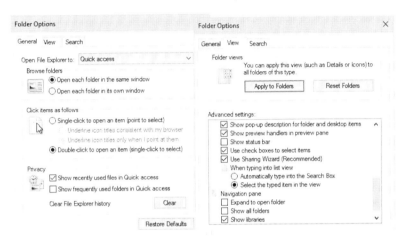

Folder Options dialog box

> **TIP** When you first start working in Windows 10, the default view for each folder is determined by its type. If you apply the current folder view to all folders of a particular type and then change your mind, you can click Reset Folders on the View tab of the Folder Options dialog box to restore the type-based default views. For information about folder types, see "Work with folder and file properties" later in this chapter.

> **TIP** In Windows 10, a new group called Quick Access was added at the top of the Navigation pane. When this is selected, the Content pane on the right displays a collection of your frequently used folders and recent files so that you can quickly return to programs, files, or locations you often need to access. These can be folders on your computer, network computers, or external hard drives.

To display the Folder Options dialog box

1. In File Explorer, do either of the following:

   - On the **File** menu, click **Change folder and search options**.

   - On the **View** tab, click the **Options** button.

To change where File Explorer opens by default

1. In the **Folder Options** dialog box, display the **General** tab.

2. Click the **Open File Explorer to** list, and then click either **Quick access** or **This PC**.

3. Click **OK**.

To change how you click to open an item

1. In the **Folder Options** dialog box, on the **General** tab, do either of the following:

   - Click **Single-click to open an item (point to select)**.

   - Click **Double-click to open an item (single-click to select)**.

2. Click **OK**.

To add a location to your Quick Access list

1. Select the folder in File Explorer, and then do either of the following:

   - On the **Home** tab, in the **Clipboard** group, click **Pin to Quick access**.

   - In the **Content** pane, right-click the folder, and then click **Pin to Quick access**.

To hide items in the Quick Access list

1. In the **Folder Options** dialog box, on the **General** tab, do either of the following:

   - Clear the **Show recently used files in Quick access** check box.

   - Clear the **Show frequently used folders in Quick access** check box.

2. Click **OK**.

Create and rename folders and files

Apps such as email readers and web browsers automatically store files in a default location, but most apps allow you to specify a storage location. You could save everything in your Documents folder, but that would soon get unwieldy. Ideally, you will use a logical system for naming and organizing folders and files so you can always find what you need.

One common approach is to store all your private files in subfolders under your Documents folder, and to store all files that you expect to share with others in subfolders under the Public Documents folder. A benefit of this approach is that Windows can automatically back up these locations to OneDrive or to an external hard drive.

You will find it much easier to locate files on your computer if they are organized in a logical manner and given names that briefly but clearly describe their contents.

To create a folder

1. In the **Content** pane of File Explorer, navigate to the location where you want to add the new folder, and on the **Home** tab, click **New Folder**.

    Or

    In the **Navigation** pane, right-click the location where you want to add the new folder, point to **New**, and click **Folder**.

    A new folder is added to the current location, with the default name *New folder* selected.

2. Enter the name you want to assign to the folder to replace the selected text.

To rename a file or folder

1. In the **Content** pane, click the folder you want to rename, and then click **Rename** on the **Home** tab.

     TIP This doesn't work in the Navigation pane. To rename a folder there, you need to right-click it and click Rename.

2. Enter the new name, and then press **Enter**.

TIP The old-fashioned manual approach to renaming a folder or file in the Content pane still works: click the file or folder to select it, then after a short pause, click it again. This selects the name so that you can enter the new one.

Compress folders and files

When you buy a computer these days, it likely comes with a hard disk that will store hundreds, if not thousands, of gigabytes (GB) of information. A gigabyte is 1 billion bytes, and a byte is a unit of information that is the equivalent of one character. Some of your files will be very small—1 to 2 kilobytes (KB), or 1000 to 2000 characters—and others might be quite large—several megabytes (MB), or several million characters. The small ones are easy to copy and move around, but large files or large groups of files are easier to copy and move from one place to another, or to send by email, if you compress them.

You can compress individual files or entire folders. The result is a compressed folder that is identified by a zipper on its folder icon.

A compressed folder

The reduction in size when you compress a file depends on the compression method and the type of file. Many modern file types, regardless of their extension, are already compressed. Microsoft Office files (the default file formats since version 2007) are actually a collection of text files (and perhaps images) that have been compressed and given a different extension. Many image file formats are already highly compressed. Therefore, compressing a folder that contains Word documents or images might have little effect on the folder size.

> **TIP** Compressing is frequently referred to as *zipping*. The term *zip file* is based on technology and devices that are proprietary to Iomega Corporation. The name *Zip* is a registered trademark of Iomega Corporation.

To view the contents of a compressed folder, you can click it in the Navigation pane or double-click it in the Content pane, just like any other folder. The Content pane then displays the files that have been compressed into the zipped folder. The Extract All Files button on the toolbar and the zipped folder icon in the Details pane indicate that you are viewing a compressed folder rather than a standard folder.

To compress a file or folder

1. In the **Content** pane, select the file, files, or folder you want to compress.

2. On the **Share** tab, click **Zip**.

   Or

   Right-click any file in the selection, click **Send To**, and then click **Compressed (Zipped) Folder** to create a compressed folder with the same name as the file you right-clicked.

3. The folder name is selected so that you can change it. Edit the name as necessary, and then press **Enter**.

To extract the files from a compressed folder

1. Right-click the compressed folder, and then click **Extract All**.

   Or

   Click the compressed folder to display its contents in the Content pane, and then, on the **Extract** tool tab, click **Extract all**.

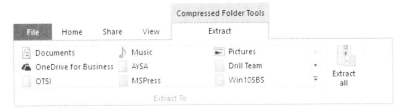

Manage compressed folders from the tool tab

The default extraction location is a new folder with the same name as the compressed folder, created in the folder that contains the compressed folder.

2. If you want to extract the files to a folder other than the one indicated in the Files Will Be Extracted To This Folder box, click **Browse** and then, in the **Select a destination** dialog box, navigate to the desired folder.

3. In the **Extract Compressed (Zipped) Folders** dialog box, click **Extract**.

> **TIP** The integration of compression into File Explorer is very useful, but there are many third-party compression programs available that have additional features and offer various other types of compression.

Move and copy folders and files

It is often necessary to move or copy folders and files from one location to another. When you move something to a new location, it is essentially deleted from the original location and copied to the new location. When you copy something to a new location, a copy remains in each location.

Before you move one or more items, you need to select them. There are various ways to select individual or multiple files in the File Explorer Content pane. When multiple files are selected, the Details pane indicates the number of items and the total size of the selection. (Because the file sizes in the Content pane are rounded up, the total in the Details pane will be more accurate.) If both folders and files are included in the selection, the Details pane indicates the number of items but not the cumulative size.

When you cut or copy a folder or file, the item is stored in a storage area called the Clipboard so that you can then paste one or more copies of it elsewhere. In addition to copying files and folders to other locations, you can also make copies of files in the original folder; when you do, File Explorer appends - *Copy* to the original file name.

When you move a folder or file by dragging it, the item is not stored on the Clipboard.

To select all the items in a folder

1. Do any of the following:

   - On the **Home** tab, in the **Select** group, click **Select All**.

   - Press **Ctrl+A**.

   - When item check boxes are shown, select the check box in the column heading area.

To select multiple contiguous items

1. Click the first item to select it, then hold down the **Shift** key and click the last item in the group you want to select.

 TIP It sometimes helps to group or sort the items to gather the ones you want to select.

To select multiple non-contiguous items

1. Do either of the following:

   - Click the first item to select it, and then hold down the **Ctrl** key and click each additional item.

   - When item check boxes are shown, select the check box next to each item you want to select.

To copy selected items to the Clipboard

1. Do any of the following:

   - On the **Home** tab, in the **Clipboard** group, click **Copy**.

   - Right-click the selection, and then click **Copy**.

   - Press **Ctrl+C**.

To cut selected items to the Clipboard

1. Do any of the following:

   - On the **Home** tab, in the **Clipboard** group, click **Cut**.

   - Right-click the selection, and then click **Cut**.

   - Press **Ctrl+X**.

To paste items from the Clipboard

1. Do any of the following:

    - On the **Home** tab, in the **Clipboard** group, click **Paste**.

    - Right-click a blank area in the folder, and then click **Paste**.

    - Press **Ctrl+V**.

To move selected items to a different folder

1. Do any of the following:

    - On the **Home** tab, in the **Organize** folder, click **Move to** and then either click the destination folder or click **Choose location** and browse to the destination folder.

    - Cut the files to the Clipboard, navigate to the new folder, and then paste the files into the folder.

    - Display the original folder and the new folder in two File Explorer windows. Use the left mouse button to drag the selected items to the new location.

    - Display the original folder and the new folder. Use the right mouse button to drag the selected items to the new location. Then click **Move Here** on the menu that appears when you release the mouse button.

To copy selected items to a different folder

1. Do any of the following:

    - On the **Home** tab, in the **Organize** folder, click **Copy to**, and then either click the destination folder or click **Choose location** and browse to the destination folder.

    - Copy the files to the Clipboard, navigate to the new folder, and then paste the files into the folder.

    - Display the original folder and the new folder. Hold down the **Ctrl** key and use the left mouse button to drag the selected items to the new location. Release the mouse button, and then release the **Ctrl** key.

    - Display the original folder and the new folder. Use the right mouse button to drag the selected items to the new location. Then click **Copy Here** on the menu that appears when you release the mouse button.

Delete and recover folders and files

Removing a file from your computer is a two-step process: You first delete the file, which moves it to the Recycle Bin—a holding area on your hard disk from which it's possible to restore an item if you realize you need it. Then you empty the Recycle Bin, which permanently erases its contents. By default, Windows prompts you to confirm the deletion of files and folders. If you prefer, you can turn off this setting.

 TIP If you aren't sure whether you will need some files, consider backing them up to a DVD, an external hard drive, or an inexpensive cloud-based storage service such as OneDrive.

There are some situations in which deleting something does not send it to the Recycle Bin. The most common are deleting from a shared network drive or an external USB drive.

You can usually recover a deleted file or folder by opening the Recycle Bin, locating the item, and restoring it. You can recover a deleted file from the Recycle Bin at any time until you empty the Recycle Bin. You can't open and work with files directly from the Recycle Bin.

You can search the contents of files in the Recycle Bin just as you can search the contents of files in other folders. If you click in the Search box when the Recycle Bin is selected, both the Search and Recycle contextual tabs are displayed. Assuming that you have deleted files listed in the Content pane, you can search for any that match the text you type in the Search box.

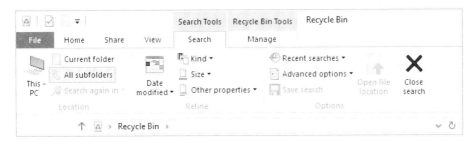

You can search the Recycle Bin

To delete an item

1. In the **Content** pane, select the file or folder.

2. Do either of the following:

   • Press the **Delete** key.

   • On the **Home** tab, in the **Organize** group, click the **Delete** button.

3. In the **Delete File** dialog box that opens, click **Yes** to confirm the deletion and send the file to the Recycle Bin.

 TIP You cannot delete a file by pressing the Backspace key.

To restore a deleted item

1. On the desktop, double-click the **Recycle Bin**.

2. Locate the file you want to restore. If it isn't at the top of the list, here are a couple of tricks:

   • Sort by Name, Original Location, Date Deleted or another column, if you know any of that information.

   • If you remember part of its name, type that into the Search box. This opens another tool tab for Search Tools.

3. When you have selected the files you want to recover, click **Restore the selected items** on the **Recycle Bin Tools** tab.

   The items should be returned to the location from which they were deleted.

To turn off confirmation when deleting items

1. On the desktop, right-click **Recycle Bin** to display the Recycle Bin Properties dialog box.

2. Clear the **Display Delete Confirmation Dialog** check box.

3. Click **OK** to apply your changes.

Recycle Bin size

The Recycle Bin is intended to be a place to temporarily store files that you think you no longer need. Keep in mind, however, that the contents of the Recycle Bin take up space on your hard disk. By default, 10 percent of a disk up to 40 GB in size is allocated to the Recycle Bin, plus 5 percent of any space over 40 GB. If your hard disk is divided into partitions, the Recycle Bin might quickly become full. For example, if the Recycle Bin is on a 10 GB partition, only 1 GB is available for deleted files.

When deleting a very large file, Windows might inform you that the file is too large to store in the Recycle Bin and that it will delete it permanently. If you're sure you won't need to recover the file, you can allow Windows to delete the file; if not, you can cancel the deletion. On a small hard disk or drive partition, you might see this "too large" message quite often.

You might need to restrict the amount of space that is used by the Recycle Bin, or you might want to instruct Windows to bypass the Recycle Bin entirely. Both of these options are available from the Recycle Bin Properties dialog box.

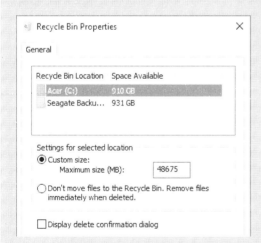

Recycle Bin properties

To manage the Recycle Bin actions, locate the Recycle Bin on the desktop, right-click it, and then click Properties. Set the maximum size as you see fit, and then click OK to apply your changes.

TIP If you want to occasionally bypass the Recycle Bin, you can do so by holding down the Shift key when you click Delete.

Work with folder and file properties

Every folder and file has certain properties that describe it or determine how it can be used. Although you can see some of these properties in Details view in File Explorer, you can see the full set by selecting that file or folder in File Explorer and clicking the Properties command on the Home tab.

The properties dialog boxes for folders and files are similar, but not identical.

View folder properties

The Properties dialog box for a folder typically has four tabs; five if version history is enabled. The tabs are:

- **General** The General tab displays the folder's name, some statistics about it, and a few attributes. You can edit the name and the attributes, though it is easier to edit the name in File Explorer.

  The Read-only attribute is the one that you will change most often. The Read-only attribute can be selected, cleared, or marked with a square box. If the attribute is selected, all the files in the folder and all the subfolders are read-only. If the attribute is cleared, all the files in the folder and all the subfolders are editable. And if the attribute is marked with a square, the folder and subfolders contain a mix of read-only and editable files.

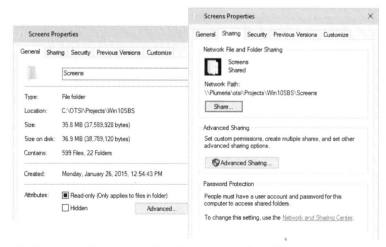

The General and Sharing tabs of a folder Properties dialog box

- **Sharing** Options on this tab control whether a folder is shared.

■ **Security** You can use the options on this tab to assign the folder's access permissions to specific users or groups.

■ **Previous Versions** If you have enabled File History in Control Panel or PC Settings, all the files in specified folders are backed up periodically. Each backup is separate, so you can view and restore a specific version. You can use this tab to review the contents of the folder after each backup.

 SEE ALSO For information about file versions and version history, see "Back up data by using File History" in Chapter 12, "Protect your computer and data."

■ **Customize** The Properties dialog box for some folder types includes a Customize tab, which has some interesting options that you can set.

Customize the appearance of a folder and its contents

• **Optimize this folder for** On this menu you can set the folder to one of five types: General, Documents, Pictures, Music, or Videos. This setting determines the file layout when you open the folder and whether a tool tab is displayed on the File Explorer ribbon when you select the folder.

• **Folder pictures** Use this setting to assign an image to be displayed for the folder in the Details pane, or when the folder appears in an icon view that is larger than Small Icons.

• **Folder icons** Use this setting to replace the default icon with one that you choose.

File Properties dialog boxes are very similar to those for folders. As with folder properties dialog boxes, the content depends on the type of file you have selected. The File Properties dialog box includes a Details tab, which isn't present in folder dialog boxes. The information on this tab varies with the file type.

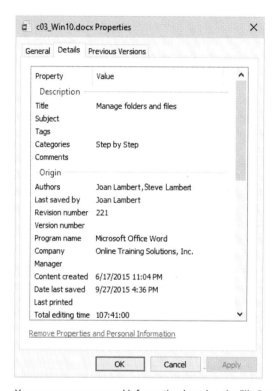

You can remove personal information by using the File Properties dialog box

Remove file properties

Clicking the Properties button on the Home tab opens the Properties dialog box for the selected item. If you click the arrow below the Properties button instead of the Properties button itself, you are presented with two options (if you have selected a folder, only the first option is enabled):

- **Properties** Clicking this option displays the properties box for the selected item and is the same as clicking the Properties button.

- **Remove Properties** Clicking this displays a dialog box in which you can choose to remove all possible properties or just selected ones. One reason to do this is to remove personal information that is stored with some file types.

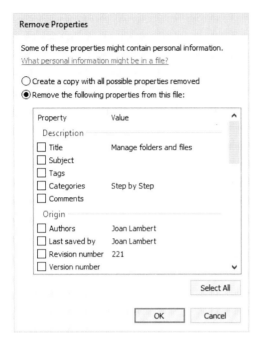

You can remove all or selected properties

Some file types contain no properties that can be removed. Others, such as Word documents, contain a long list.

 TIP The information displayed in the Remove Properties dialog box also varies depending on the type of file selected when you choose the command.

To display the Properties dialog box for a folder or file

1. In File Explorer, select the folder or file you want to display properties for.

2. Do any of the following:

   • Right-click the file or folder and then, on the shortcut menu, click **Properties**.

   • On the **Home** tab, in the **Open** group, click the **Properties** button.

   • On the **Home** tab, click the **Properties** arrow, and then click **Properties**.

To remove personal information from a file

1. In File Explorer, select the file from which you want to remove personal information.

2. Do any of the following:

   - On the **Home** tab, in the **Open** group, click the **Properties** arrow, and then click **Remove properties**.

   - In the **Open** group, click the **Properties** button to open the file's properties box, and then, on the **Details** tab click the **Remove Properties and Personal Information** link at the bottom.

   - Right-click the file and click **Properties**, and then, on the **Details** tab, click the **Remove Properties and Personal Information** link at the bottom.

3. In the **Remove Properties** dialog box, do either of the following:

   - Select **Create a copy with all possible properties removed**, and click **OK**.

   - Click **Remove the following properties from this file**, select the properties you want to remove, and click **OK**.

Find specific files

Windows 10 provides various ways to search everything from a folder on your computer to the World Wide Web, all from the taskbar search box. File Explorer provides an additional search capability that is limited to files only (that is, it doesn't return apps and web searches). The underlying search engine (Bing) is the same from all these locations, but the focus of the searches and the manner in which the results are returned varies.

Windows Search

Recent advancements in online and computer search technology have made the instant location of information and files so simple that it's easy to forget how tedious tracking down the same items would have been in the past. The search technology that is built in to Windows 10 is excellent.

Using Windows Search, you can find apps, files, messages, and message attachments on your computer. You don't need to know the name or location of the file or item you want to find; simply enter a word or phrase in the Start menu Search box to display a list of matching items, organized by type.

How does Windows Search find items so quickly? Behind the scenes, Windows Search maintains an index of all the keywords in, and associated with, the files stored on your computer—app names, common tasks, and the file names and content (when possible) of documents, audio and video recordings, images, email messages, webpages, and other data files. Windows Search automatically indexes the most common file types (such as documents, text files, and email messages) and doesn't index file types you are less likely to search (such as operating system files). It does not include the system files; such an index would be huge and would slow down the search process.

When you enter a search term, Windows looks for the term in the index instead of searching the actual files on your hard disk.

> **TIP** By default, Windows doesn't index encrypted files because a search by another computer user could reveal the encrypted data. You can add encrypted files to the search index if you first put in place a full-volume data-encryption solution, such as Windows BitLocker Drive Encryption.

> **SEE ALSO** For information about changing the file storage locations that are indexed, see "Search your computer and the web" in Chapter 11, "Work more efficiently."

File Explorer Search

File Explorer Search differs from Windows Search in that it is limited to searching for files and displays them in its own familiar interface. So when you get a results list, you can use all the usual commands on the View tab to refine the display.

You initiate a File Explorer Search from the Search box at the right end of the Navigation And Search bar. When you click in this box to enter a search term, the Search Tools tool tab appears, providing tools you can use to refine your search.

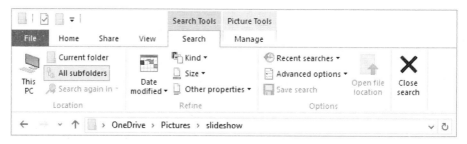

File Explorer Search tab

You can save a set of search parameters so that you can display updated results at any time. Saved searches are added to the Favorites group in File Explorer and are also available from your personal Searches folder.

To search for a file in File Explorer

1. In the upper-right corner of the File Explorer window, enter a search term in the **Search** box. As you enter the search term, Windows filters the program files, folders, and email messages stored on your computer.

To refine a File Explorer search

1. On the **Search** tool tab, in the **Refine** group, click the property by which you want to filter the search results, and then enter the criteria for the filter.

To save a search for later reference

1. On the **Search** tool tab, in the **Options** group, click the **Save search** button. The Save As dialog box displays the content of your personal Searches folder.

2. In the **Save As** dialog box, click **Save** to accept the default name and save the search in the Searches folder.

To return from the Search Results folder to the original folder

1. In the **Search Results** window, at the right end of the **Address** bar, click the **Close** button (**X**).

Skills review

In this chapter, you learned how to:

- Understand files, folders, and libraries
- Get to know File Explorer
- Change the File Explorer display options
- Create and rename folders and files
- Compress folders and files
- Move and copy folders and files
- Delete and recover folders and files
- Work with folder and file properties
- Find specific files

Practice tasks

The practice files for these tasks are located in the Win10SBS\Ch03 folder. You can save the results of the tasks in the same folder.

Understand files, folders, and libraries

There are no practice tasks for this topic.

Get to know File Explorer

Perform the following tasks:

1. Start File Explorer, and navigate to the practice file folder.

2. Open the **Ch03** folder, then open the **Photos** folder, and then open the **Backgrounds** folder.

3. Use the tools on the **Navigation and Search** bar to move up to the **Ch03** folder.

4. In the **Navigation** pane, contract all the expanded storage nodes. Then review the locations in the Navigation pane and ensure you're familiar with each.

5. In the **Navigation** pane, double-click **This PC**. Review the file storage locations that are connected to your computer.

6. On the **View** tab, display the **Navigation pane** menu. If the Navigation pane isn't already configured to display libraries, display them now.

7. Expand the **Libraries** node. Create a new library named **Win10SBS** and ensure that it appears in the Navigation pane.

8. Add the **Backgrounds** subfolder of the **Ch03\Photos** folder to the new **Win10SBS** library.

9. Optimize the **Win10SBS** library for the display of photos. Then assign an icon that you like to the library folder.

10. Hide the **Win10SBS** library from the Navigation pane. Then unhide it.

Change the File Explorer display options

Start File Explorer, and then perform the following tasks:

1. Navigate to the practice file folder and expand its contents in the **Content** pane.

2. Experiment with the settings in the **Panes** group on the **View** tab to hide and redisplay the Navigation pane.

3. Display the **Details** pane. Select a file in the **Content** pane and notice the available details. Select a different type of file, and then select multiple files, noting the details available for each.

4. Display the **Preview** pane and repeat the process in step 3. For each file that displays a preview, observe the preview content and notice the controls available in the Preview pane for scrolling or moving through the preview.

5. Resize the **Preview** pane by dragging its border.

6. Experiment with the settings in the **Layout** group on the **View** tab. Display the content of the practice file folder in each of the eight available layouts. Consider the information provided by each layout and when each would be most or least useful.

7. Display the Details view of the practice file folder content.

8. From the **Add columns** list, navigate to the longer list of columns and click **Dimensions** to add that column to the Details view.

9. Rearrange the columns in the **Content** pane so that the **Dimensions** column is immediately to the right of the **Name** column.

10. Resize all columns to fit the widest item in the column.

11. Remove the **Date Created** and **Dimensions** columns from the Details view.

12. Display item check boxes, file name extensions, and hidden items.

13. Group the items by type.

14. Sort the grouped items alphabetically by name. Then reverse the sort order.

15. Filter the items by using the **Size** filter to display only large items (1-16 MB).

16. Remove the filter, restore the default sort order, and remove the file grouping.

17. Add the **Photos** folder to your Quick Access list.

Create and rename folders and files

Display the practice file folder in File Explorer, and then perform the following tasks:

1. In the practice file folder, create a subfolder and name it **MyFiles**.

2. Rename the **MyFiles** folder as **MySBSFiles**.

3. Rename the **Events** document as **Newsletter**.

Compress folders and files

Display the practice file folder in File Explorer, and then perform the following tasks:

1. In the **Content** pane, select the three **Password** files.

2. Save the selected files to a compressed folder, and name it **PWPhotos**.

3. Extract the files from the **PWPhotos** compressed folder to the **Photos** folder.

Move and copy folders and files

Display the practice file folder in File Explorer, and then perform the following tasks:

1. Select all the items in the folder, and then release the selection.

2. Select three items that are next to each other (listed contiguously) in the folder, and then release the selection.

3. Select three items that are not next to each other in the folder, and then release the selection.

4. Copy the **Expenses** workbook to the Clipboard. Open the **Reports** folder, and paste a copy of the **Expenses** workbook in that folder.

5. Return to the **Ch03** folder. Cut the **Survey** workbook to the Clipboard, and then paste it into the **Files** subfolder.

Delete and recover folders and files

Display the practice file folder in File Explorer, and then perform the following tasks:

1. Delete the **Photos** folder and all its contents.

2. Navigate to the Recycle Bin. Then restore the **Photos** folder and all its contents.

Work with folder and file properties

Display the practice file folder in File Explorer, and then perform the following tasks:

1. Display the properties of the **Photos** folder.

2. Display the properties of one of the **Password** files.

3. Display the properties of the **Expenses** workbook. Determine whether the file is read-only. If it is, change that property.

4. Add your name as one of the properties of the **Expenses** workbook. Then use the commands in the **Remove Properties** dialog box to remove that property from the file.

Find specific files

Display the practice file folder in File Explorer, and then perform the following tasks:

1. Search for a file from the File Explorer search box by using the search term **travel**.

2. Refine the search by narrowing the results to items that are small (between 10 and 100 KB).

3. Save the search for later reference.

4. Return from the **Search Results** folder to the original folder.

Work with apps and notifications

The Windows 10 operating system provides the interface through which you communicate with your computer. When you do or create something on your computer, you're using software that runs on Windows to accomplish that task.

There are many types of apps, and you can get them from many sources. Wherever you get your apps, after you install them on your Windows 10 computer you can run them and manage access to them in the same ways.

Many apps communicate status, new activity, and other information to you in the form of *notifications*. These might pop up in the corner of your screen—to notify you of a message that has arrived or an update that is available. When these pop-up windows (sometimes called *toast popups*) appear, you can click them to open or dismiss them. In Windows 10, recent notifications are available from icons in the notification area of the taskbar, and in the Action Center that opens from that area.

This chapter guides you through procedures related to locating and starting installed apps, exploring built-in apps and accessories, installing apps from the Windows Store, and managing app shortcuts, startup options, and notifications.

In this chapter

- Locate and start apps
- Explore built-in apps
- Install Store apps
- Manage app shortcuts
- Manage app startup
- Manage app notifications

Practice files

No practice files are necessary to complete the practice tasks in this chapter.

Locate and start apps

At the time of this writing, software programs that install components on a computer or mobile device that runs Windows are divided into two groups: desktop apps and Store apps. Store apps are those that you download and install on your Windows 10 computer, phone, or mobile device from the Windows Store, which is called simply Store. (Somewhat confusingly, Store itself is an app.) In general, Store apps have a smaller installation footprint than desktop apps and aren't as powerful.

When you purchase a new computer, it's likely that the computer will have a variety of apps installed on it by the computer manufacturer. These apps generally fall into the following categories:

- Apps provided by Microsoft with the Windows operating system. These are installed with Windows 10 regardless of whether you upgrade to this version of the operating system or have a clean installation.

- Apps that are specific to the management of the hardware elements of your computer. These are usually related to hardware support and firmware update functions.

- Free full or trial versions of third-party apps. Software companies often allow computer manufacturers to provide full or limited-use versions of apps with their computers as a way to add value to the package. You're usually required to register your information with the software company to use the app, and they can then offer you updates and upgrades over time. This is a win-win for the hardware and software manufacturers, and sometimes for you.

You can start an app by clicking it on the All Apps menu, or by clicking a shortcut to the app that is in another location. Most commonly, shortcuts are on the Start screen, the desktop, or the taskbar.

 TIP You can also start an app by locating and running the app executable file, but that isn't the intended interface for most apps that you'll work with.

The All Apps menu provides access to most of the apps and utilities that are installed on your computer. These include apps that are installed as part of Windows 10, by the computer manufacturer, and by you. The All Apps menu is integrated into the Start menu and also available directly from the full-screen Start screen.

The All Apps menu displays apps in alphabetical order

The All Apps menu opens in the space otherwise occupied by the Start menu. It provides an alphabetical listing of apps, separated by index letters. You can scroll through the menu manually or click any index letter to display a menu from which you can jump directly to recently added apps; apps with names that begin with a symbol, a number, or a specific letter; or Windows utilities. This is a nice improvement over the All Programs menu that was available in earlier versions of Windows.

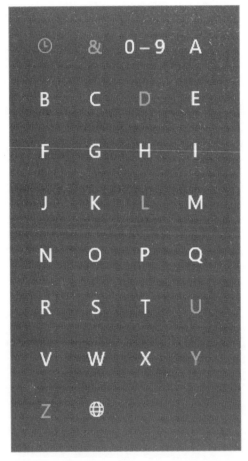

Dimmed index letters have no menu entries

Most apps are listed on the All Apps menu by name, but some are in folders and therefore don't appear on the menu where you might expect them to. This is one reason why it's almost always faster to locate an app by entering the first few letters of its name in the search box, and start it from the search results list.

Some apps are organized on the All Apps menu in folders

To display the All Apps menu

1. Do either of the following:

   • In the lower-left corner of the **Start** menu or **Start** screen, click the **All Apps** button.

   • Display the **Start** menu, and then press **Up Arrow, Enter**.

    TIP There is no keyboard shortcut to directly open the All Apps menu, but you can move around the Start menu by pressing the arrow keys.

To return from the All Apps menu to the Start menu

1. At the bottom of the **All Apps** menu, click the **Back** button.

To scroll the All Apps menu to apps beginning with a specific letter

1. On the **All Apps** menu, click any index letter to display the alphanumeric index.

2. In the index, click any letter or symbol to jump to those entries on the menu.

 TIP The clock symbol represents recently installed apps. The globe symbol represents Windows utilities.

To locate and start a specific app

1. Enter the app name in the taskbar search box.

2. In the search results, click the app name, or click the **Apps** heading and then click the app name in the filtered results pane.

To start an app

1. Do any of the following:

   - On the **All Apps** menu or **Start** menu, click the app name.

   - On the **Start** screen, click the app tile.

   - On the taskbar, click the app button, or right-click the button and then click the app name.

 TIP On a touchscreen device, press and release instead of right-clicking. For more information about touchscreen interaction, see Appendix B, "Keyboard shortcuts and touchscreen tips."

TIP If you experience problems with a desktop app, it might be necessary to run the app with elevated permissions so you can resolve the issue. To do so, right-click the app and then click Run As Administrator. The Run As Administrator command is available only for desktop apps. It is not available for Store apps.

Explore built-in apps

Windows 10 includes many fun and functional apps. Some of these apps are part of Windows and others are powered by MSN or Bing. It is not the purpose of this book to teach you how to use those apps. We do preview some of the more useful apps and work with them in the practice tasks, but you should definitely explore them further on your own.

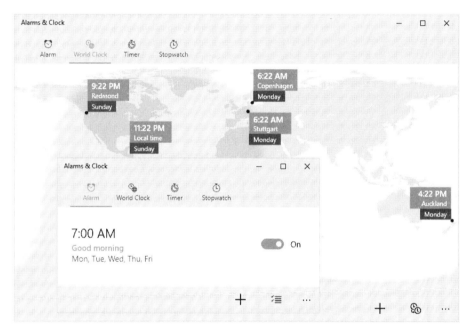

The Alarms & Clock app includes a world time map, timer, and stopwatch

Productivity and information management apps

The many and varied Microsoft apps that you can use on a day-to-day basis to get things done have been brought together under the Windows umbrella. Although they have simple names and are free, they're quite fully featured and updated on a regular basis. These apps include Alarms & Clock, Calculator, Calendar, Mail, and Maps.

Other apps that fall loosely into the productivity category but have more specialized purposes include Scan and Voice Recorder.

The apps draw information from many sources and are designed to be useful both on your desktop and on the go.

The Maps app coordinates with all devices you sign in to by using your Microsoft account

Web browsers

Microsoft Edge and Internet Explorer are both installed with Windows 10. We discuss working in these browsers (primarily Edge, because it's new in Windows 10) in detail in Chapter 5, "Safely and efficiently browse the Internet."

Media management apps

The Movies & TV and Music apps provide access to online media. The branding of the site behind these apps has changed several times over the years. Movies & TV provides access to video content you've purchased or rented from the Store or from one of Microsoft's earlier video outlets, such as Xbox, and to video files stored on your computer or on a local or online storage location. Similarly, Music (officially branded *Groove Music*) provides access to music that you own or have licensed the rights to through the Store or one of its predecessors (Xbox Music and Zune). You can configure these apps to link to multiple media storage locations.

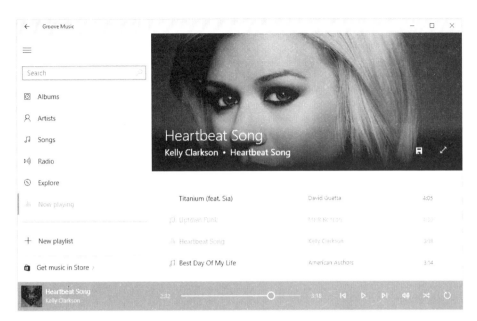

You can find, play, and manage recorded music in the Music app

Windows 10 also includes Windows Media Player, which has been around for quite a while now. You can use this app to play and manage media files, and to manage the transfer of media to discs. It doesn't interface directly with the Store, but it's a dependable media manager.

The full-fledged Windows Media Center app is not part of the initial release of Windows 10, but Microsoft advises that they'll provide a DVD playback app called Windows DVD Player after the first official Windows 10 update. This will be very convenient for consumers who have generally had to rely on third-party apps installed by original equipment manufacturers (OEMs) or from the web for this purpose.

If your computer or device has a built-in camera, you can take pictures by using the Camera app.

The Photos app is a convenient and easy-to-use app in which you can efficiently manage and enhance pictures. The app tracks pictures stored in multiple locations (including your OneDrive) and automatically catalogs photos by date. You can organize photos in albums, and edit and enhance them in various ways, and share them through apps that provide that functionality. The Photos app also provides a shortcut to setting a photo as your desktop background or lock screen image.

Live information apps

The information apps are frequently featured on Start screen tiles in new or updated installations of Windows. They all have live tile functionality, although they might not show anything specific or pertinent until you configure them. When their live tiles are turned on (as they are by default), these apps can provide interesting and timely updates about things that are happening in the world around you, courtesy of Bing or MSN. The apps include Food & Drink, Health & Fitness, Money, News, Sports, and Weather.

> **TIP** Having the latest headlines constantly available can be quite distracting. If you don't want to see the headlines, but still want to have easy access to the information, you can turn off the live tile content for individual apps.

The information apps provide general information but also allow you to identify information that is specific to you and pin that information to the Start screen. For example, you can track a specific stock in Money, or pin a specific person's contact information in People.

Information at your fingertips on the Start screen

Accessories

Along with the shiny new Store apps, Windows 10 comes with several useful desktop apps that have been around for a long time and perform a lot of useful functions. (For that reason, they're frequently referred to as *utilities*.) These apps (and others) are available from the Windows Accessories folder on the All Apps menu:

- **Math Input Panel** You can use Math Input Panel, which was originally designed for tablet PC users, to convert simple and complex mathematic equations to text.

- **Notepad** You can use this simple text editor to edit unformatted documents or HTML files.

- **Paint** You can use this simple (but freshly updated) graphics app to produce drawings in a variety of graphics formats (including .bmp, .gif, .jpg, .png, and .tif) and to save screen images captured by using the Print Screen utility.

- **Sticky Notes** You can use this app to attach electronic notes to your computer desktop in the same way you'd stick the paper version of a sticky note to your physical desktop.

- **Snipping Tool** You can use this tool to capture an image of a screen area and then annotate it with handwritten notes, save it as an .html, .png, .gif, or .jpg file, and send it by email.

- **Windows Fax and Scan** You can use this desktop app to send and receive faxes through an analog phone line and a modem, or through a fax server. If a scanner is connected to your computer, you can also use Windows Fax And Scan to scan text documents and graphics to your computer as digital files that you can then send as faxes or email message attachments. The Scan app that also comes with Windows 10 is a more modern Store app that does the same thing.

- **Windows Journal** You can use this tool, which was originally designed for tablet PC users, to record handwritten notes, typed information, and pictures.

- **WordPad** You can use this word-processing app to work with documents that include rich text formatting and character and paragraph styles.

Other tried and true accessories include Character Map, Remote Desktop Connection, Steps Recorder, and XPS Viewer.

> **✓ TIP** Like the Portable Document Format (PDF), the XML Paper Specification (XPS) format allows a file to be saved in such a way that it can be viewed but not changed without the use of special software. Windows 10 comes with the XPS Viewer, in which you can view XPS files, and with the software that is required to create XPS files from any app you can print from. Simply open the file in its originating app, display the Print dialog box, specify the Microsoft XPS Document Writer as the printer, and click Print. When prompted, save the file with the name and in the location you want.

Utilities for geeks

Experienced computer users who want to be able to run apps and manage their computers in traditional ways might find the following utilities useful:

- **Windows PowerShell** With a text-based interface similar to that of Command Prompt, Windows PowerShell provides command-line tools that can be used to automate administrative tasks. Windows 10 also includes PowerShell ISE (Integrated Scripting Environment), which substantially extends the Windows PowerShell user interface.

- **Command Prompt** The Windows 10 Command Prompt (cmd.exe) is the latest in a progression of command-line interpreters in the tradition of MS-DOS and command.com. You can use it to run many DOS and Windows command-line utilities. Windows 10 has enhanced the user interface in a number of ways, including the ability to use standard keyboard shortcuts to copy and paste text.

> **✓ TIP** As software development models and installation footprints have changed, so has terminology. At one time, there were only software applications, which were called *programs*. With the development of small-footprint mobile technology came apps. Over time, different types of apps were referenced as desktop apps, Windows apps, modern apps, gadgets, and other terms. In this book, unless there's a specific reason to differentiate among app types, we simply refer to programs in both categories as *apps*.

Install Store apps

Windows 10 works across multiple form factors (desktop, laptop, tablet, and phone), which has two notable effects. First, the simplified Windows user interface adapts gracefully to different screen sizes; and second, developers can more easily create (and support) apps that provide the same user experience on multiple devices. As the relentless rush to become constantly connected, more mobile, and less tied to desktop computers continues, these changes benefit both the software companies and the software users.

You can install software on a Windows 10 computer from multiple locations. In the past, the most common installation source was a CD or DVD, but software distribution has rapidly moved toward an online installation model. You can purchase or subscribe to software and install it on your computer or device immediately.

Thousands of apps (and games, music, movies, and television programs) that are specifically designed and optimized for use on Windows 10 are available from the Store, many for free. You can also purchase and install apps from websites or use the old-fashioned method and install them from CDs or DVDs.

Shop at the Windows Store

The Store was first introduced in Windows 8. It has been substantially updated in Windows 10 and changes frequently. This chapter includes some images for guidance, but it's quite possible that by the time you read this book, the Store interface will be different from what we depict in this book. In this section, we give an overview of the Store and describe Store functionality that we think is likely to stay in place over time.

You access the Store by starting the Store app, which is installed by default and can't be uninstalled (though it can be unpinned from your Start menu if you don't want it there).

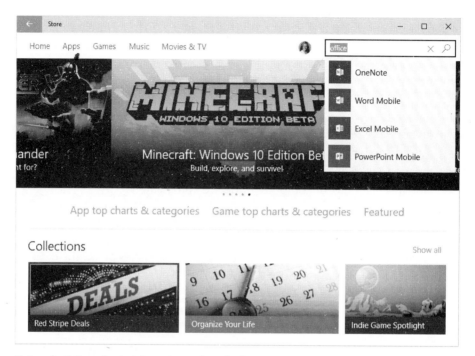

Get productivity and entertainment apps from the Store

From the home page of the Store you can search for specific apps, search by category, or browse through collections of apps such as the most popular free or paid apps or games, new music or movies, top-selling television shows, or various collections of apps that are related by a common feature (such as music, zombies, or productivity).

If you know the app, or the type of app, that you're looking for, the simplest method of finding it is to enter the name or descriptive information into the search box located in the upper-right corner of the Store window. Generally, the more text you enter into the search box, the more you limit the search results. For example, at the time of this writing, the search term *cards* returns 112 apps, 170 games, 199 albums, 2,000 songs, 15 movies, and 11 television shows. The search term *flash cards* returns only two results, both of which are math flash card apps.

TIP At the time of this writing, the Store search engine doesn't support Boolean search restrictions such as AND, OR, or wildcards.

Regardless of your choice of navigation method, the Store presents consistent information, including app tile, name, rating, and price for each app.

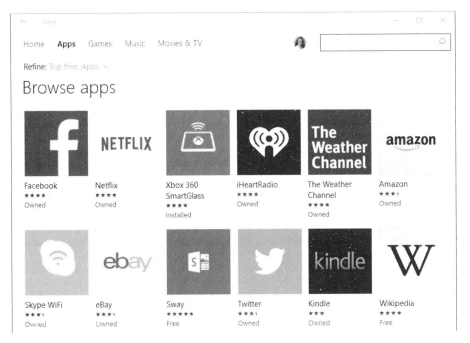

Typical app representations when browsing the Store

Most Windows apps are classified as Free, and many of them are. Some app developers accept donations. Some apps are free only for a trial period, or require that you purchase an upgrade or accompanying service to unlock the really useful functionality. Because there are variations of "free," it's a good idea to read the details before you actually install an app. You can click any app tile for more information.

Some of the useful details provided for apps in the Store include these:

- Screenshots of the app user interface

- Ratings and reviews that can be filtered by device type

- Feature lists

- The publisher's name, website, support site, and privacy policy

- Hardware and storage space requirements

- Category and age rating

- Supported processors and languages

- The number of devices you can install the app on

- The access permissions the app requires, which might include permission to use your location, access your Internet connection, access your local network, act as a server, read data from other apps, use your device's camera, record audio, and more

To start the Store app

1. On the **Start** menu, click **All Apps**.

2. On the **All Apps** menu, click any index letter, and then click **S**.

3. In the list of apps that have names beginning with *S*, click **Store**.

Manage your Store account and settings

The Store is linked to your Microsoft account. Information about business that you've transacted when signed in to a site or service with that account is stored with your account information. Transactions include those for free and paid apps, services, and subscriptions through entities such as the Store app, the online Microsoft Store, Xbox Live, Groove Music, Bing Rewards, Office 365, and OneDrive.

You can manage your Store settings from within the Store app, and you can also link from the Store account menu directly to specific areas of your online Microsoft account information.

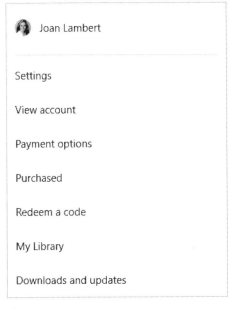

 Joan Lambert

Settings

View account

Payment options

Purchased

Redeem a code

My Library

Downloads and updates

The Store account menu

IMPORTANT To use the Store, you must be signed in with a Microsoft account, or your local user account must be associated with a Microsoft account.

At the time of this writing, the only settings you can configure are whether to auto-matically update apps and activate live tiles. The Settings window in the Store is similar to the pages of the Settings window in Windows 10. A toggle button controls each of the settings.

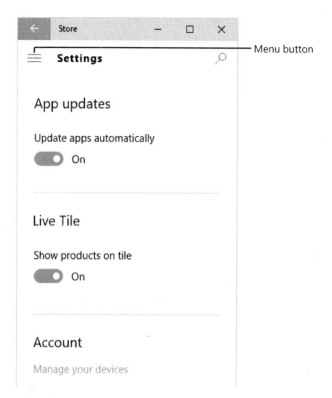

Menu button

When the window is narrow, the menu button appears

> **TIP** When you narrow the Store app window, a menu button appears in the upper-left corner. Clicking the menu button displays all the menu items that usually appear on the Store menu bar and all the items that usually appear on the Store account menu.

Clicking any link other than Settings, My Library, or Downloads And Updates on the Store account menu starts or opens your default browser and displays information from your Microsoft account. You must sign in to your account (if you haven't already), and reconfirm your credentials when accessing pages that contain financial information. The following table describes the actions you can take from these pages that are relevant to Store purchases.

Menu item (page)	Description
View account (Home)	Review recent purchases and your devices. Browse from here to any other account information.
Payment options (Payment Options)	Add, edit, and remove payment options that are linked to your account. Valid forms of payment include PayPal accounts, credit cards (Visa, MasterCard, American Express, and Discover), physical and digital gift cards, and Microsoft account credit that is added from a Bitcoin digital wallet.
	You can remove only payment options that aren't associated with an active subscription. (If you want to remove a payment option that's assigned to a subscription, you must first assign a different form of payment to the subscription.)
Purchased (Purchase History)	Display the date, description, form of payment, and amount for transactions that are associated with your Microsoft account.
	You can display up to one year of purchases at a time.
Redeem a code (Redeem Your Code or Gift Card)	Enter a gift card number or promotional code on this page to add credit to your Microsoft account. If your Microsoft account has a credit balance, Store purchases use the credit first and then charge only the difference to your selected payment option.

 SEE ALSO For more information about Microsoft accounts, see the sidebar "Use a Microsoft account or local account" in Chapter 1, "Get started using Windows 10."

You can go directly to a specific page of your account information from the Store account menu, or navigate among the pages within the browser window. When you install an app or game from the Store on any Windows 10 device, you own that app and can install it on up to 10 devices. If you want to install the same app on another device, you can locate the app in your list of apps and install it from there.

To turn off automatic app updates

1. Start the Store app.

2. On the menu bar, click your user account picture to display a menu of options.

User account picture

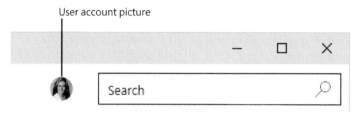

Access your Store and Microsoft account settings from the Store

3. On your account menu, click **Settings** to display the Settings pane for the Store app.

4. In the **Settings** pane, set the **Update apps automatically** toggle button to **Off** to immediately implement the change.

To access your Microsoft account settings from the Store

1. From the Store menu bar, display your user account menu, and then do any of the following:

   - To display the home page of your Microsoft account, click **View account**.

   - To display the Payment Options page, click **Payment options**.

   - To display the Purchase History page, click **Purchased**.

   - To display the gift card/promotional code–entry interface, click **Redeem a code**.

 TIP All these links display a page of the Microsoft account management website, and you can move to any other page of the website from there.

Install, reinstall, and uninstall apps

Most apps are free. When you purchase an app that isn't free and doesn't include a free trial, you select a payment method on the Payment & Billing section of your Microsoft account. Most require only a one-time payment, but some are managed on a subscription basis, and until you cancel the subscription, the payment option that you select is charged each month.

The Store tracks all the apps, games, music, movies, and television episodes that you purchase. From your library, you can display information about the items you've purchased, and you can install, reinstall, and share those items.

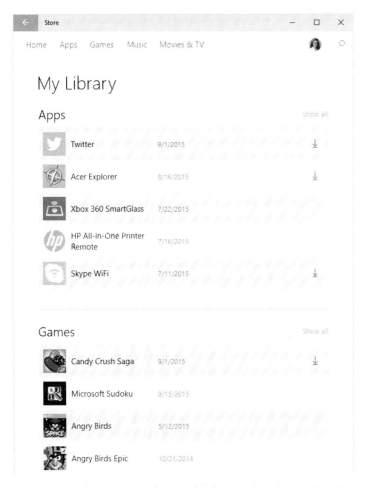

My Library displays recent purchases and links to the Your Apps or Your Games page

The My Library page displays recent purchases that you made when signed in with your Microsoft account, on any device, in order from most recent to least recent. Clicking the Show All link adjacent to any category heading displays all the items of that type that are installed on any device that is associated with your Microsoft account. Depending on your installation history, the entries on the Your Apps and Your Games pages might be divided into sections that are titled "Works on this device" and "Doesn't work on this device." For example, when you're in the Store on your Windows 10 computer, Windows phone apps that were developed for versions of Windows Mobile earlier than Windows 10 appear in the "Doesn't work" list because they won't run on your Windows 10 computer.

You can start (launch) an app or game from your library if it's already installed on your computer. Apps and games that work on your Windows 10 computer and aren't already installed on it have an Install icon on the right side.

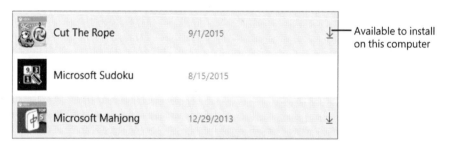

The app and games lists indicate whether you can install each on the current computer

When you click the icon, the Store app checks your current installations to make sure that you haven't exceeded the 10-device limit. It then assigns one of your 10 device licenses to the app, downloads the app, and installs it. During that process, the app appears on the Downloads And Updates page, which is an interim staging location for apps and updates that are pending installation on your computer. By default, Store apps automatically download and install updates. If you would prefer to approve updates, you can turn off the automatic update option and manage the updates from this page. When an app or update is ready for installation, the installation icon appears on the Store menu bar, next to your user account icon.

Apps or updates ready to install

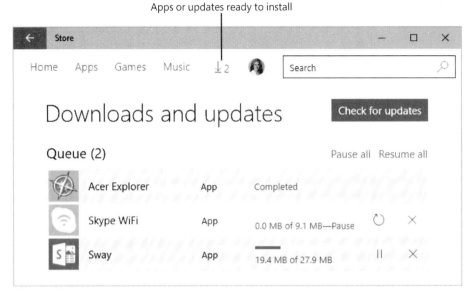

You can monitor and manage downloads

To install an app or game for the first time

1. In the Store, search for or browse to the app or game you want to install.

2. Click the app or game thumbnail to display its information page.

3. On the information page, below the description, click the button labeled either **Free** or with the price of the app or game.

4. If you selected an app or game that requires a purchase, enter your Microsoft account password when prompted to do so. Then select a payment option and approve the purchase to install the app and add it to the All Apps menu.

To display your purchased and installed apps and games

1. From the Store menu bar, display your user account menu, and then click **My Library**.

2. By default, the My Library pane displays recently installed apps and games. To display *all* apps or games, do either of the following:

    *   Click the **Show All** link to the right of the **Apps** heading to display the Your Apps pane.

    *   Click the **Show All** link to the right of the **Games** heading to display the Your Games pane.

To install a purchased app or game on a different computer

1. On the computer where you want to install the app or game, start the Store app.

2. From the menu bar, display your user account menu, and then click **My Library**.

3. If the app or game you want to install doesn't appear in this pane, display the **Your Apps** or **Your Games** pane.

4. Locate the app or game, and click the **Install** icon on the right side of its entry.

 IMPORTANT If there is no Install icon, then the app is already installed on or incompatible with the current device.

You can monitor the installation process from the Downloads And Updates pane.

To manage downloads and updates

1. From the Store menu bar, display your user account menu, and then click **Downloads and Updates**.

2. In the **Queue** area of the **Downloads and Updates** pane, do any of the following:

    *   Click the **Check for updates** button to search for any available updates that haven't yet been registered on your computer.

    *   Click an available update to download and install it.

    *   Click the **Pause** or **Restart** button near the right end of an in-process update to pause or restart the process.

    *   Click the **Close** button at the right end of an in-process update to remove the update from the queue.

To uninstall a Store app

1. Locate the app on the **All Apps** menu.

2. Right-click the app, and then click **Uninstall**.

 IMPORTANT Some apps (such as Calculator, Calendar, and Camera) can't be uninstalled, and the Uninstall option doesn't appear on the shortcut menu.

Manage app shortcuts

Installing a Store app or desktop app adds it to the All Apps menu, and you can start the app by locating it on the menu and clicking it. If you plan to use the app often, you can save time by creating a shortcut to the app in a more convenient location. You can create app shortcuts in these locations:

- On the Start screen, where the shortcut is a tile

- On the taskbar, where the shortcut is a button

- On the desktop, where the shortcut is indicated by an arrow on the icon

- In a folder, where the shortcut is indicated by an arrow on the item

Manage Start screen shortcuts

As we mention in Chapter 2, "Personalize your working environment," all Start screen tiles are actually shortcuts to files and folders that are stored elsewhere. You can pin any Store app or desktop app to the Start screen. To start an app from the Start screen shortcut, simply click the tile.

All Start screen tiles are actually shortcuts

By default, pinning an app to the Start screen creates a Medium tile. Start screen tiles that link to desktop apps can be Small or Medium; Start screen tiles that link to Store apps can be Small, Medium, Wide, or Large.

 SEE ALSO   For information about changing the size and location of tiles, see "Manage Start screen tiles" in Chapter 2, "Personalize your working environment."

Many Store apps are configured to display live tile content (but not all apps that are configured for it have live tile content available at this time). If a Start screen tile links to an app that is configured for live tile content, the tile shortcut menu includes the command Turn Live Tile On or Turn Live Tile Off, depending on the current setting. You can turn on live tile content for an app at any tile size, but only Medium, Wide, and Large tiles can display live content.

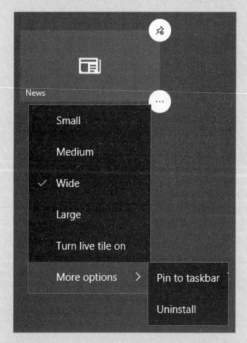

Touchscreen tile management

If you're working on a touchscreen device, you can display the equivalent of the tile shortcut menu commands by pressing and holding a tile until the Unpin and Options buttons appear.

Press and hold a tile to activate its commands

Tapping the Options (...) button displays the available tile sizes and live content options for the active tile. Tapping More Options displays the available app management commands for the active tile. The commands available for a tile depend on the app that it links to and the current state of the tile.

To create an app shortcut on the Start screen

1. Do either of the following:

   - Locate the app on the **All Apps** menu or on the **Start** menu.

   - In File Explorer, navigate to the app executable file.

2. On the menu or in File Explorer, right-click the app or its executable file, and then click **Pin to Start**.

To display or hide live content on an app tile

1. On the **Start** screen, right-click the tile, and then click **Turn live tile on** or **Turn live tile off**.

Or

1. On a touchscreen device, press and hold the tile until the Unpin and Options buttons appear on the tile to indicate that it is active for editing.

2. In the lower-right corner of the tile, tap the **Options (…)** button to display the options.

3. Tap **Turn live tile on** or **Turn live tile off**.

 TIP There might be a short delay after you turn on live tile content while Windows connects to the app source to fetch and then display the current content.

To remove an app shortcut from the Start screen

1. Do either of the following:

   - On the **Start** screen, right-click the app tile, and then click **Unpin from Start**.

   - On the **All Apps** menu or **Start** menu, right-click the app and then click **Unpin from Start**.

Or

1. On a touchscreen device, press and hold the tile until it becomes active for editing.

2. In the upper-right corner of the tile, tap the **Unpin** button.

Manage apps from the taskbar

You can start or switch to a pinned or running app by clicking its taskbar button. If you prefer to use a keyboard shortcut, you can start or switch to any of the first 10 apps in the taskbar button area by pressing Win+n, where n is a number from 0 through 9 (with 0 representing 10).

When an app is running, a thick underline appears below the app icon. A color variation on the bar indicates when multiple instances of an app are running.

Pointing to (hovering over) an active taskbar button displays thumbnails of each instance of the app. You can switch to a specific app window by clicking its thumbnail. You can close an app window by pointing to its thumbnail, and then clicking the Close button (the X) that appears in the upper-right corner.

Manage running apps from the taskbar

Right-clicking a taskbar button (or dragging the button up slightly above the taskbar) displays a jump list and a shortcut menu. Depending on the app, the jump list displays tasks that are related to the app or files that were recently opened in that app.

You can right-click files on the jump list to display additional commands. The taskbar button shortcut menu typically displays commands for starting or quitting the app and pinning or unpinning the app.

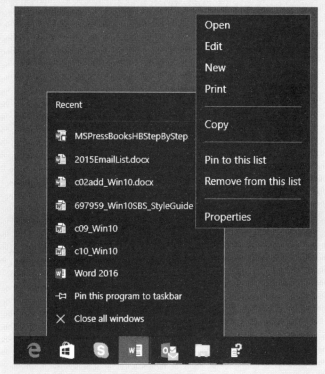

A jump list and file shortcut menu

You can manually pin items to a jump list by dragging files or folders of the appropriate type to the taskbar button. For example, you can drop a Word document on the Word icon, or drop a folder on the File Explorer icon, to pin the document or folder to the relevant jump list.

Manage taskbar shortcuts

Because the taskbar is always available from the desktop, it can be much faster to access app, file, and folder shortcuts that are on the taskbar than it is to access them on the Start screen. You can pin any Store app or desktop app to the taskbar. Taskbar shortcuts look like buttons. To start an app from the taskbar shortcut, simply click the button.

App shortcut

Running apps

App shortcuts display only icons until the app is active

On the taskbar, you can arrange shortcuts and active app buttons by dragging them into the order you want. You can change the size of all the taskbar buttons at one time, but you can't change the size of individual taskbar buttons.

 SEE ALSO For information about changing the size of taskbar buttons, see "Configure the taskbar" in Chapter 2, "Personalize your working environment."

To create an app shortcut on the taskbar

1. Do either of the following:

   - Locate the app on the **All Apps** menu, on the **Start** menu, or on the **Start** screen.

   - In File Explorer, navigate to the app's executable file.

2. Right-click the app, the app tile, or the app executable file, and then click **Pin to taskbar**.

Or

1. On a touchscreen device, press and hold the Start screen tile until it becomes active for editing.

2. In the lower-right corner of the tile, tap the **Options** button, tap **More Options**, and then tap **Pin to taskbar**.

To create a taskbar shortcut for a currently running app

1. On the taskbar, right-click the app button, and then click **Pin this program to taskbar**.

To move an app shortcut on the taskbar

1. Drag the taskbar button left or right to its new location.

To remove an app shortcut from the taskbar

1. Right-click the taskbar button, and then click **Unpin this program from taskbar**.

Manage desktop shortcuts

Traditionally, many desktop app installation processes create app shortcuts on the desktop. There is no interface to "pin" an app to the desktop, but you can easily create a desktop shortcut to any app. You can also create shortcuts to webpages, files, and folders, or save files and folders directly on the desktop. Items on the desktop are represented by icons, usually of the app that opens them. A shortcut is differentiated from an item that is stored directly on the desktop by an arrow in the lower-left corner of the icon.

Arrows indicate shortcuts on the desktop

By default, desktop icons are created at a Medium size and aligned to a grid that helps to maintain a bit of order. You can change the icon size to Small or Large.

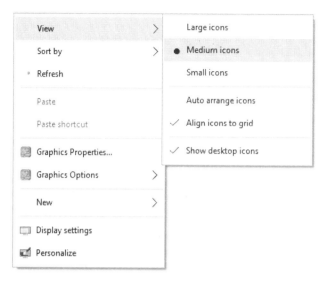

You can automatically resize and arrange desktop icons

If you want to organize (or disorganize) icons without using the grid, you can turn off grid alignment, and then drag items to whatever desktop position you want.

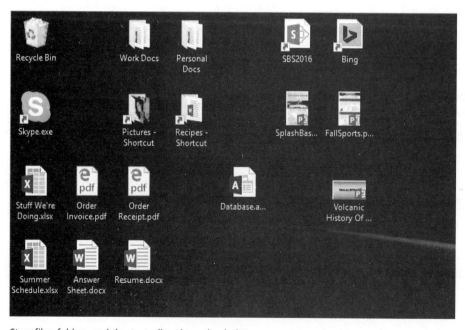

Store files, folders, and shortcuts directly on the desktop

Some people like to organize their active files, folders, and apps on the desktop so they have everything they need in one place. You can organize content on the desktop manually, in whatever order you want, or you can have Windows manage the order for you. When you turn on the Auto Arrange Icons feature, Windows moves all desktop icons so they line up from the upper-left corner of the screen in the order (from top to bottom and then left to right) that you specify on the Sort By submenu.

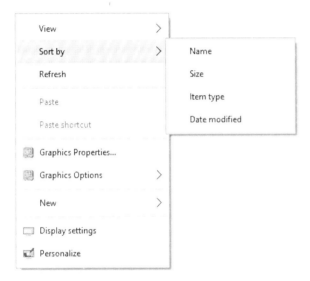

Automatic desktop icon arrangement options

The desktop content is actually stored in a folder—or rather, in two folders. In addition to system icons (such as the Recycle Bin), your desktop displays content from two locations:

- Content that is specific to your user account and displayed on only *your* desktop is stored in the *C:\Users\[user account name]\Desktop* folder.

- Content that is displayed for all users of the computer is stored in the *C:\Users \Public\Public Desktop* folder.

If you want your desktop to appear totally clean, you can hide the desktop icons without affecting the content of the Desktop folders.

You can open either folder in File Explorer to display a different view of the shortcuts, folders, and files on the desktop.

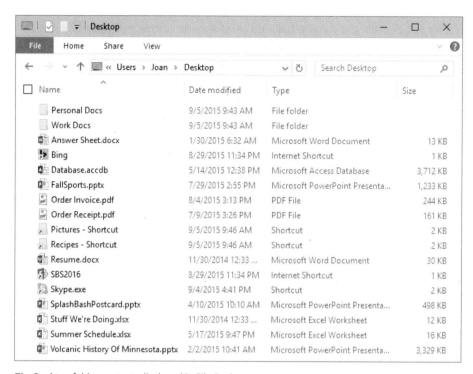

The Desktop folder contents displayed in File Explorer

To create an app shortcut on the desktop

 TIP The first procedure option works only for desktop apps; the second procedure option works for any app.

1. Right-click the app on the **All Apps** menu or **Start** menu, or the app tile on the **Start** screen, and then click **Open file location** to open the Start Menu\Programs folder. This folder contains shortcuts to all the installed apps that are available from these locations.

2. Do either of the following to create the desktop shortcut:

- Right-click and drag the shortcut from the **Start Menu\Programs** folder to the desktop, and then click **Copy** on the menu that appears after you release the shortcut.

- Right-click the app, click **Create shortcut**, and then in the **Shortcut** dialog box that appears, click **Yes**.

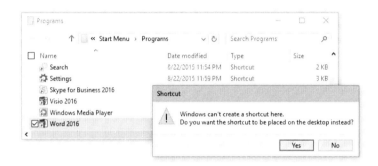

Use this method to avoid accidentally removing the shortcut from the Start menu

Or

1. Right-click an empty area of the desktop, click **New**, and then click **Shortcut**.

2. In the **Create Shortcut** dialog box, enter or browse to the location of the app executable file. Then click **Next**. Then enter a name for the shortcut, and click **Finish**.

 TIP Use the same processes to create app shortcuts in File Explorer that you do to create app shortcuts on the desktop.

To arrange desktop icons

1. Do any of the following:

   - Drag icons to any location on the desktop to snap them to the nearest grid location.

   - If you want to force icons into the grid positions from top to bottom and left to right, right-click the desktop, click **View**, and then click **Auto arrange icons**.

   - If you want to permit less-precise arrangements, right-click the desktop, click **View**, and then turn off the **Auto arrange icons** and **Align icons to grid** options.

   - If you want Windows to set the order for you, right-click the desktop, click **Sort by**, and then click the order you want: **Name**, **Size**, **Item type**, or **Date modified**.

To set the size of desktop icons

1. Right-click the desktop, click **View**, and then click **Large icons**, **Medium icons**, or **Small icons**.

To hide or display desktop icons

1. Right-click the desktop, click **View**, and then click **Show desktop icons**.

To remove an app shortcut from the desktop

1. Right-click the shortcut, and then click **Delete**.

> **IMPORTANT** An arrow in the lower-left corner of the icon indicates that the icon represents a shortcut to a file or folder rather than an actual file or folder. Deleting a shortcut does not delete the file or folder the shortcut links to. Deleting a file or folder icon that doesn't have a shortcut arrow deletes the file or folder. If you do this accidently, you can retrieve the file or folder from the Recycle Bin.

Configure desktop system icons

The default desktop displays the Recycle Bin. You can configure the display of this and four other system icons—Computer, Control Panel, Network, and your user account folder—in the Desktop Icon Settings window. If you want to get creative, you can personalize the system folders by assigning non-standard icons to them.

Display or change the appearance of desktop system icons

To access the desktop icon settings, open the Settings window, click Personalization, and click Themes. Then in the Related Settings area of the Themes pane, click Desktop Icon Settings.

Manage app startup

Many apps and services start automatically when Windows starts. This can be very helpful, but it can also add unnecessary overhead to your computer's startup tasks, and slow down the process. Not all the background processes that apps run are necessary to perform every time you start your computer. It's worth your time to periodically review and refine the items that start automatically. You can identify and manage the startup of many of these apps in Task Manager.

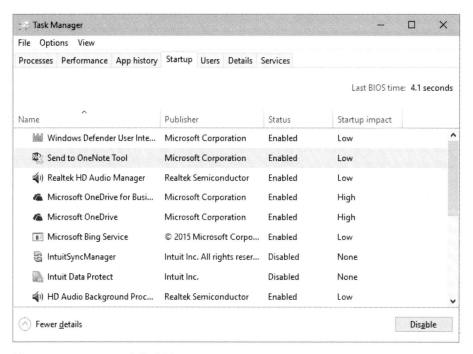

Manage startup processes in Task Manager

You can sort items on the Startup tab by any column. The Startup Impact column indicates the level of delay caused by each item.

> **SEE ALSO** For more information about Task Manager, see "Monitor system tasks" in Chapter 11, "Work more efficiently."

There are two groups of apps that Task Manager doesn't manage startup for—Store apps and apps that start automatically because they're identified in the Startup folder that is specific to your user account. If you always use a specific app and want it to start automatically with Windows, you can put a shortcut to it in this folder.

To identify apps and services that start automatically

1. Start Task Manager by doing either of the following:

   - Right-click a blank area of the taskbar, and then click **Task Manager**.

   - Press **Ctrl+Shift+Esc**.

2. If **More details** is displayed in the lower-left corner of Task Manager, click it to display a tabbed window, and then click the **Startup** tab.

To prevent an app or service from starting automatically

1. On the **Startup** tab of Task Manager, click the app or service, and then click the **Disable** button.

To automatically start an app when Windows starts

1. In File Explorer, navigate to **C:\Users\[your account name]\AppData\Roaming \Microsoft\Windows\Start Menu\Programs\Startup**. Windows 10 automatically starts apps by using the shortcuts in this folder.

> **TIP** A quicker way to open the Startup folder in File Explorer is to press Win+R to open the Run box, enter *shell:startup*, and then press Enter.

2. Drag the app from the **All Apps** menu or **Start** menu to the **Startup** folder. Release the app after the word *Link* appears next to the app icon.

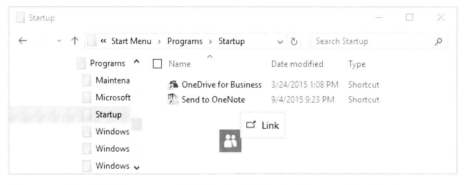

Drag an app from the All Apps menu to the Startup folder to start the app automatically

The next time you restart Windows, your app will start automatically.

> **TIP** The apps you add to the Startup folder don't appear on the Task Manager Startup tab, so you can't disable them there.

Manage app notifications

A notification is a short message that is generated when an event happens in an installed app. Not all apps generate notifications; the app developer determines whether notifications will be issued and for which events.

When an event issues a notification, it might play a sound and briefly display a banner in the lower-right corner of your screen. You can point to the notification banner to keep it visible, click the banner to display pertinent information (if available) in the app that generated it, or click the Close button that appears in its upper-right corner to dismiss it. The notification is also stored in the Action Center.

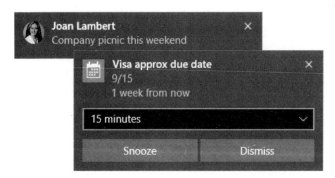

Typical notification banners

You might or might not notice notifications when they appear, but the Action Center icon on the taskbar changes color to indicate that you have unread notifications. You can open the Action Center to display and process the notifications.

 SEE ALSO For more information about the Action Center, see "Explore the taskbar" in Chapter 1, "Get started using Windows 10."

You manage these three aspects of notifications in the Notifications & Actions pane of the Settings window:

- The general behavior of notifications

- Which apps generate notifications

- The specific types of notifications each app generates

You manage the general behavior of notifications in the Notifications section of the Notifications & Actions pane. In this section, you can turn on or off the display of Windows system notifications and of app notifications; the display of notifications, alarms, reminders, and incoming calls on the lock screen; and whether Windows automatically hides notifications when you're sharing your screen in an online presentation.

Notifications

Show me tips about Windows

⬤⚪ On

Show app notifications

⬤⚪ On

Show notifications on the lock screen

⬤⚪ On

Show alarms, reminders and incoming VOIP calls on the lock screen

⬤⚪ On

Hide notifications while presenting

⚫⚪ Off

The default notification settings

The options to display Windows notifications and app notifications are fairly general. In early builds of Windows 10, many users found that turning on Windows tips caused Windows to proactively check system settings so often that it slowed down their systems. The issue seems to be resolved at the time of this writing, but if your computer seems slow you could experiment with this setting.

After the notification settings, there is a list of all the apps installed on the computer that are configured to generate notifications.

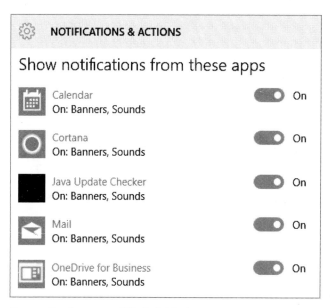

Turn notifications on or off for individual apps

You can turn notifications on or off for each individual app. Clicking an app name displays toggle buttons for the two types of notifications that the app can generate—banners and sounds. By default, these are both on for all apps, but if you want to individually turn off sound or banners for specific apps, you can do so.

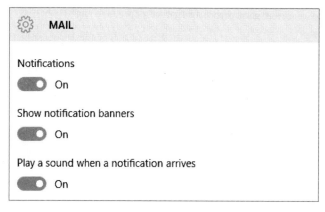

Specify the types of notifications each app generates

> **TIP** If you leave the Notifications toggle button set to On and turn off banners and sounds, the app generates notifications and delivers them to the Action Center for you to review at your leisure.

You can temporarily disable all banners and sounds by using the 'Quiet Hours fea- ture. When Quiet Hours is turned on, the Action Center icon changes to indicate that notifications are not active.

Quiet Hours is on

A Do Not Disturb symbol indicates Quiet Hours

> **IMPORTANT** When the Quiet Hours feature first debuted, you could configure it to turn on and off automatically at specific times. For example, you could set your quiet hours to be from 10:00 P.M. to 6:00 A.M. so you wouldn't be disturbed by notifications from a Windows 10 computer or device during the night. At the time of this writing, the Quiet Hours options have been reduced to On and Off, so it's basically just a quick way to turn off notifica- tions. We're hopeful that the timing aspect of this feature will be restored in later releases of Windows.

Notifications are still available in the Action Center when Quiet Hours is turned on. The Action Center icon changes to a filled white icon when notifications are available.

> **TIP** You can also add a few apps to the lock screen and they will show very basic noti- fications. For more information about this, see "Customize the lock screen" in Chapter 10, "Manage power and access options."

To open the Action Center

1. Do either of the following:

   • In the notification area of the taskbar, click the **Action Center** icon.

   • Press **Win+A**.

To limit system notifications

1. In the **Settings** window, click **System**, and then click **Notifications & actions**.

2. In the **Notifications** area of the **Notifications & actions** pane, set the **Show me tips about Windows** toggle button to **Off**.

To turn off all notifications for an app

1. Display the **Notifications & actions** pane.

2. In the **Show notifications from these apps** list, locate the app, and then set the toggle button for the app to **Off**.

To turn off banners or audio notifications for an app

1. Display the **Notifications & actions** pane.

2. In the **Show notifications from these apps** list, click the app that you want to configure notifications for.

3. In the pane that is specific to the app, do either of the following:

    -   To turn off notification banners, set the **Show notification banners** toggle button to **Off**.

    -   To turn off audio notifications, set the **Play a sound when a notification arrives** toggle button to **Off**.

4. In the upper-left corner of the pane, click the **Back** arrow to return to the app list and check the settings.

You can configure apps to send notifications directly to the Action Center

To temporarily turn off banner and audio notifications

1. Do either of the following:

    -   In the notification area of the taskbar, right-click the **Action Center** icon, and then click **Turn on quiet hours**.

    -   Open the Action Center, expand the **Quick actions** section if necessary, and then click the **Quiet Hours** button.

Skills review

In this chapter, you learned how to:

- Locate and start apps
- Explore built-in apps
- Install Store apps
- Manage app shortcuts
- Manage app startup
- Manage app notifications

Practice tasks

No practice files are necessary to complete the practice tasks in this chapter.

Locate and start apps

Perform the following tasks:

1. From the **Start** screen, display the **All Apps** menu.

2. Manually scroll the menu to display apps that begin with the letter **G**. Along the way, notice the apps that are installed on your computer.

3. Display the alphabetic index of the **All Apps** menu. From the index, jump to the apps that begin with the letter **M**.

4. From the **All Apps** menu, start the Maps app.

5. In the taskbar search box, enter **weather**. Locate and start the Weather app.

6. Leave both apps running for the next task.

Explore built-in apps

Start the Maps and Weather apps, and then perform the following tasks:

1. Switch to the Maps app.

2. Enter your address in the search box. If the app locates an address match, click the address to display it on the map.

3. On the button bar in the right pane, click the **Views** button to display the available views of the location.

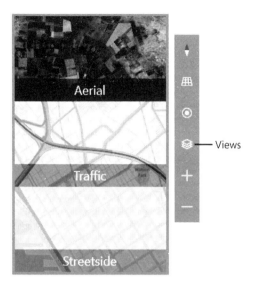
Views

Display different aspects of the map location to provide helpful information

4. Display each of the available views of the map. Experiment with zooming in and out in each view, and note the details that are available in each view.

5. Switch to the Weather app. In the search box, enter the name of the nearest large city to you. Experiment to find out what types of information are available in this app.

6. On the **All Apps** menu, scroll to the **W** section. Open and browse the contents of the folders in that section to familiarize yourself with the apps, accessories, and utilities that are available.

7. Exit all the running apps.

Install Store apps

Perform the following tasks:

1. Start the Store app.

2. Locate a free app that interests you, and install it. Then locate another free app that you don't want to keep and install that, too.

3. Display your library of recent apps and games, and then display the list of apps associated with your account.

4. In the **Your Apps** pane, look for an app that has an Install icon. If you find one, install the app on your computer.

5. From the Store, display your Microsoft account information. Locate your list of purchases and identify the apps you installed in steps 2 and 4.

6. If you've had a Microsoft account for a while, identify the first year for which your account has a record of transactions.

7. On the **All Apps** menu, locate the apps that you installed in step 2. Uninstall one or both of the apps.

Manage app shortcuts

Perform the following tasks:

1. On the **All Apps** menu, identify two apps that are not yet pinned to the Start screen or to the taskbar.

2. Pin the first app to the **Start** screen, and then locate its Start screen tile. Right-click the tile, and then examine the shortcut menu to determine whether the app supports live tile content. Then start the first app from the **Start** screen.

3. Pin the second app to the taskbar, and then locate its taskbar button. Right-click the taskbar button to examine the shortcut menu options for the app. Then start the app from the taskbar.

4. On the taskbar, locate the button of the first app. Move the button to the right end of the taskbar button area. Then pin the running app to the taskbar.

5. From the **All Apps** menu, open the **Start Menu\Programs** folder. From the folder, create a desktop shortcut to any app.

6. Experiment with arranging and ordering the icons on your desktop.

7. Open the **Desktop** folder associated with your user account, and locate the shortcut you created in step 5. Start the app from the **Desktop** folder.

8. Exit all the running apps.

9. Delete any of the shortcuts you created in this exercise that you think you won't use in the future.

Manage app startup

Perform the following tasks:

1. Start **Task Manager**, and display the **Startup** tab.

2. Sort the apps and services by their impact on the computer startup time.

3. For each item that has a **High** startup impact, look at the available information to determine what the item does.

4. Sort the apps and services by publisher.

5. Identify any app publishers in the list who you aren't familiar with. Examine the startup impact of the items associated with each unfamiliar publisher.

6. Sort the list by status. Look for any items that are already disabled from starting automatically.

7. Select one app that starts automatically, and take note of its name. Disable the app and wait for it to change status. Then enable it for automatic startup again.

8. Open the **Startup** folder associated with your user account. Add a shortcut to the Maps app to the folder so that Maps starts automatically the next time you start your computer.

Manage app notifications

Perform the following tasks:

1. Open the Action Center and examine any current notifications.

2. In the **Settings** window, display the **Notifications & actions** pane. Review your current notification settings.

3. Review the list of apps installed on your computer that can generate notifications.

4. Display the notification options for the Calendar app. Turn off audio notifications for Calendar. Then return to the list of apps and note the change.

5. Review and modify the notification settings to meet your needs.

6. Turn on the **Quiet Hours** feature and note that the Action Center icon changes. Then turn off **Quiet Hours**.

Safely and efficiently browse the Internet

There are businesses and government agencies that totally isolate their computers from any direct connection to the public Internet, for security and privacy reasons. But for the average person, Internet access is one of the primary reasons for having a computer.

Many apps connect to the Internet without any external input, but the primary method for individuals to interact on the Internet is through an Internet browser.

Microsoft Edge, which was released with Windows 10, is a new browser designed from the ground up for speed and agility. It offers many interesting and useful features, and Microsoft has announced (or hinted at) many improvements that will be released in future updates.

Internet Explorer also ships with Windows 10, and Edge hands off the heavy lifting to it gracefully whenever necessary. Microsoft released the first version of Internet Explorer in 1995, and it enjoyed the majority of the market share for many years. Regardless of the browser that you use to access the Internet, there are many common experiences when browsing the Internet.

This chapter guides you through procedures for displaying websites in Edge; finding, saving, and sharing information; managing Edge settings; configuring browser security settings; maintaining browsing privacy; and troubleshooting browsing issues.

In this chapter

- Display websites in Edge
- Find, save, and share information
- Manage Edge settings
- Configure browser security settings
- Maintain browsing privacy
- Troubleshoot browsing issues

Practice files

No practice files are necessary to complete the practice tasks in this chapter.

About Microsoft Edge

Microsoft Edge is a *universal app*, which means it will run on many different devices—not only on your computer, but also on tablets, phones, Xbox gaming systems, HoloLens headsets, and Surface Hub devices. This is a bigger deal than it might sound like—universal apps have only recently become an achievable reality. The benefit for app developers is that they can learn one coding system, create only one version of each app, sell it to consumers on multiple platforms, and provide support for only one source code project. The benefit to consumers is that they can purchase one app that is of better quality and use it across multiple platforms. (Imagine having to purchase an Angry Birds game only once, that you could play on your computer and your phone and your tablet, with your progress following you across all the devices.) Universal apps are a win-win situation for everyone.

Edge is installed as part of the Windows 10 operating system and is automatically set as the default browser. This means that you can use any browser you want, but when you click a link in an app, it automatically opens in Edge. From what we've seen so far, Edge will become a really good browser. It's reasonably fast, reasonably secure, has a sleek interface, and features some cool tools. The version released with Windows 10 is still a little rough around the edges, but there's a lot to like about it.

If you updated your computer from another version of Windows to Windows 10, any browsers you had installed on your system are still installed and available for use. Internet Explorer is also available; it's hidden in the Windows Accessories folder on the All Apps menu, but if you want to use it (or any other browser) you can create a Start menu or taskbar shortcut.

SEE ALSO For information about creating app shortcuts, see "Manage app shortcuts" in Chapter 4, "Work with apps and notifications."

IMPORTANT At the time of this writing, some Edge features are still in development, so we provide general information about this new browser, and more specific information about Internet use and safety.

Display websites in Edge

The Edge user interface is simple and clean. The browser was designed to be secure, but also to provide a minimal interface with relatively few distractions.

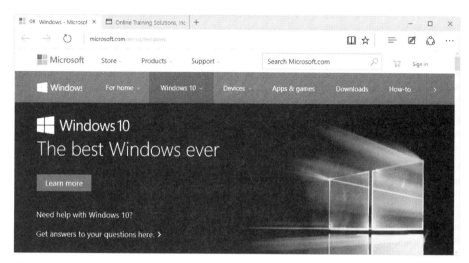

The Windows 10 website displayed in Edge

Edge has a tabbed browser interface so you can display multiple webpages in one window. When Edge starts, it displays either the Start page, a new tab, the most recent tab set, or a home page (or pages) that you specify. New tabs display your choice of a blank page, links to the websites that you frequently visit, or website links and newsfeed content.

The Edge controls are on a simple toolbar below the page tabs.

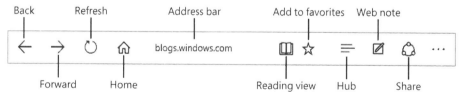

The address bar is visible only when you point to or click it

In addition to the standard browser view experience, Edge supports playing audio in the background of webpages (for example, the sound of birds shown in the Bing background image) and has a Reading view that hides the distracting elements and displays the current webpage as it might appear in an ebook reader, so you can concentrate on the content.

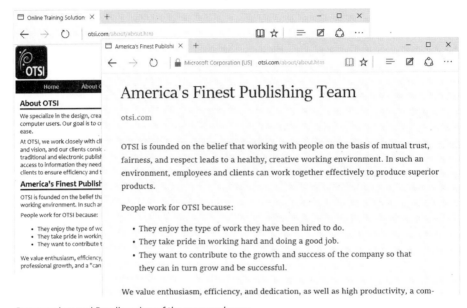

Browser view and Reading view of the same webpage

 TIP When Edge displays a webpage that doesn't support Reading view, the Reading View toolbar button is dimmed.

Reading view becomes available only after Edge loads all the webpage content, including advertisements. Reading view is available only for some webpages because it displays primarily text content. It doesn't display all the content on the page—and the standards by which it chooses content aren't entirely clear. It isn't available for website home pages, online commerce sites, or webpages that don't contain much text.

TIP If you own a website that doesn't display well in Reading view, check this webpage to see possible causes, or to learn how to prevent it from being opened in Reading view: *msdn.microsoft.com/en-us/library/Mt203633(v=VS.85).aspx.*

To start Edge

1. Do either of the following:

- On the taskbar, click the **Edge** button (labeled with an **e**).

Windows 10 installs the Edge button on the taskbar to the right of the Task View button

- On the **Start** menu, click **All apps**. On the **All apps** menu, scroll to and click **Microsoft Edge**.

To open a new browser tab

1. Do either of the following:

- At the top of the Edge window, to the right of the rightmost tab, click the **New tab** button (+).

Edge supports audio content on webpages

- Press **Ctrl+T**.

To display a webpage

1. Do any of the following:

- On a blank tab, enter a URL into the **Search or enter web address** box, and then press **Enter** or click the **Go** button (the arrow) at the right end of the box.

You can search for a page or enter its URL

- On a tab that is displaying a webpage, click the URL to activate the Address bar. Type a URL into the **Address** bar, and then press **Enter**.

- Enter a search term into the **Search or enter web address** box or activate the **Address** bar and enter the search term there, and then press **Enter**. On the search results page, click the webpage you want to display.

To display webpages on separate Edge tabs

1. Right-click a link, and then click **Open in new tab**.

2. Right-click a tab, and then click **Duplicate tab**.

To display webpages in separate Edge windows

1. Do any of the following:

   - Right-click a link, and then click **Open in new window**.

   - Drag an existing tab away from the original Edge window to display it in its own window.

   - Right-click a tab, and then click **Move to new window**.

   - On the **More actions (...)** menu, click **New window**.

   - On the **More actions** menu, click **New InPrivate window**.

To move between webpages visited on a tab

1. At the left end of the active tab toolbar, click the **Back** button or **Forward** button.

To refresh the display of a webpage

1. Do either of the following:

   - At the left end of the active tab toolbar, click the **Refresh** button.

   - Press **F5**.

To switch the display of a webpage to and from Reading view

1. When the **Reading view** button is active, click it.

 TIP You can configure the Reading view background color and type size. For more information, see "Manage Edge settings" later in this chapter.

Find, save, and share information

A web search for specific information sometimes leads to webpages that contain a lot of content. It can be difficult to locate the information you're looking for on the webpage. You can quickly highlight all instances of a search term on the current webpage, and scroll to spot them or cycle through them in order.

After you find the information you're looking for, you can annotate (draw and write on) a snapshot of the webpage by using the Web Notes tool, and then save or share the annotated webpage.

You can share webpages or their content with other people, or save them for your own reference. You can easily keep track of and return to sites of ongoing interest. If you think you will want to return to a site frequently, you can add it to your list of favorites. If you just don't have time to read the site now, but want to do so later, you can add it to your reading list. The reading list is primarily intended for short term storage of articles rather than long term storage of online resource sites.

The Share pane displays the apps you can use to share the webpage

You can share a screenshot of the webpage, or you can send, post, or save information from the webpage and a link to the webpage. Your sharing options depend on the apps that are installed on your computer and the user account that you're signed in to Windows with. Some common options include the Mail and Reading List apps.

> **TIP** The Reading List app is a Store app in which you can collect content from multiple sources that you want to read later. The Edge browser also has a reading list in which you can store links to webpages that you want to go back and read later.

You can pin specific websites to the Start screen or taskbar so that you can easily access them.

To find text on a webpage

1. Display the webpage in Edge or Internet Explorer.

2. Press **Ctrl+F** to display the Find toolbar.

Search a page for content

3. Enter your search term in the search box.

   As you enter the search string, every instance of matching text on the webpage is highlighted. The number of instances found on the page appears to the right of the search box.

4. After you enter the search term (or as much as is necessary to return a manageable number of results), you can scroll through the page content to review the highlighted instances of the search term, or press the Next or Previous buttons to move among the results.

5. To further restrict the search, click the **Options** button on the **Find on page** toolbar, and then click **Match whole word** or **Match case**.

To annotate a webpage

1. On the Edge toolbar, click the **Make a Web Note** button. Edge converts the page to a screenshot and displays an annotation toolbar at the top of the page.

The Web Note toolbar

2. Click the buttons on the toolbar to activate any of the following functions:

- Drag the image

- Draw with a pen

- Highlight

- Erase

- Add a typed note

- Clip part of the image

- Save

- Share

- Exit

To share the current webpage

1. On the Edge toolbar, click the **Share** button to open the Share pane on the right side of your screen.

2. The name of the page you're sharing appears below the Share heading. Click the chevron next to the page name to display additional sharing options.

You can share the page or a screenshot of the page

3. In the list, click the sharing method you want to use. The pane updates to display the apps that support that method.

4. In the **Share** pane, click the app you want to use to share the webpage, and then provide any information that is specific to the app.

To save a webpage to the Reading List app

1. On the Edge toolbar, click the **Share** button.

2. In the **Share** pane, click **Reading List app** to open the Reading List App pane containing a description of the webpage content.

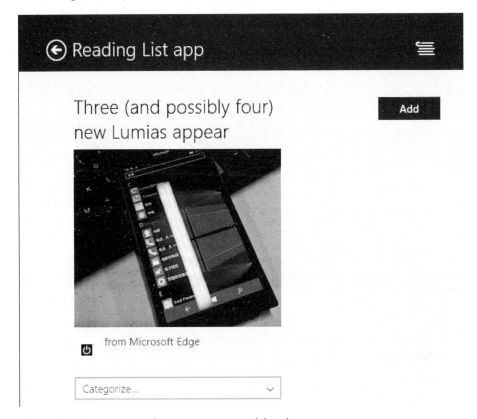

The Reading List app saves webpages so you can read them later

3. In the **Categorize** list below the webpage content, you can select an existing category or quickly create a new one.

4. Click the **Add** button to add the webpage to the Reading List app.

To save a webpage to the Edge favorites list or reading list

1. In the Edge window, at the right end of the **Address** bar, click the **Add to favorites or reading list** button (the star), or press **Ctrl+D**.

2. At the top of the pane, click either **Favorites** or **Reading list** to select the list you want to save the webpage to.

3. Edit the name that will be displayed in the list, if you want to.

4. If you're saving the webpage to your favorites list, select a storage folder.

5. Click **Add** to save the webpage to the selected list.

To display your Edge favorites list, reading list, browsing history, or file downloads

1. On the Edge toolbar, click the **Hub** button (marked with three horizontal lines) to display the Hub pane.

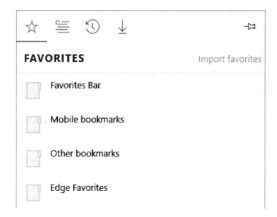

Clicking the Hub icon displays buttons for Favorites, Reading List, History, and Downloads

2. At the top of the **Hub** pane, click the **Favorites**, **Reading list**, **History**, or **Downloads** icon to display that list.

 TIP You can pin the Hub pane to the browser window so that it stays open, by clicking the pushpin icon in the upper-right corner of the pane.

To read articles from the reading list

1. Click the **Hub** icon on the address bar.

2. Click the **Reading list** icon.

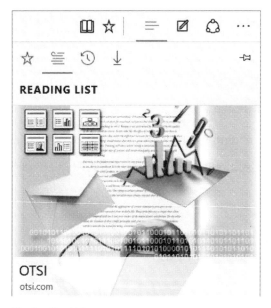

The Reading List pane

3. Click the article you want to read.

   The article is displayed in the current tab.

To pin a site to the Start screen

1. Start Edge, and connect to the site.

2. In the Edge window, click the **More actions** button, and then on the **More actions** menu, click **Pin to Start**.

To pin a site to the taskbar

1. Start Internet Explorer, and connect to the site.

> **IMPORTANT** At the time of this writing, you can't pin Edge shortcuts to the taskbar.

2. At the left end of the **Address** bar, a site icon precedes the URL. Drag the icon to the taskbar to create a taskbar shortcut to the site.

To print the current webpage

1. In the Edge window, on the **More actions** menu, click **Print** to preview the page in the **Print** dialog box.

Preview the page as it will be printed, and configure the print settings

2. In the **Printer** list, click the printer or app you want to print to.

3. Configure any additional print settings, and then click **Print**.

Manage Edge settings

All browsers provide a way to set options and default behavior. The settings in Edge are well organized and for the most part fairly simple. You manage Edge settings from the More Actions menu that expands from the upper-right corner of the browser window.

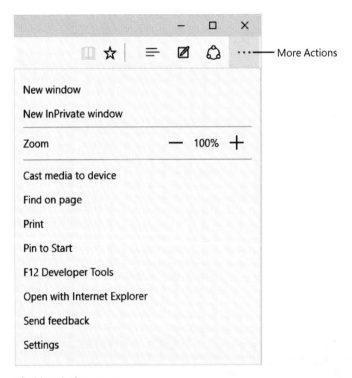

The More Actions menu

Edge has far fewer settings than Internet Explorer, which in part makes it much easier to configure. The settings panes are quite bland and don't currently have icons to visually differentiate between settings, so it can be slightly difficult to locate specific settings.

You configure most of the Edge settings in the Settings pane and the Advanced Settings pane. We don't cover configuration processes for *all* the individual settings in this section, but they're easy to locate and most have simple On/Off toggle buttons.

You can specify the page or pages that Edge displays when it starts, and you can specify, to some extent, the content of new tabs that you open. The options include:

- A blank page, which displays only a search box

- Top sites, which displays up to eight tiles that link to sites that you visit most frequently

- Top sites and suggested content, which displays site tiles and news feeds

To display the More Actions menu

1. In the upper-right corner of the Edge window, below the **Close** button (the **X**), click the **More actions** button (...).

To set or change your home page or starting content

1. In the Edge window, on the **More actions** menu, click **Settings**.

2. In the **Open with** section, do one of the following:

   - Click **Start page** to display news feeds from MSN.

   - Click **New tab page** to display a new tab showing either a blank page, your frequently visited sites, or sites and suggested content.

   > **SEE ALSO** For information about setting the content for new tabs, see the procedure "To specify the content of new tabs" later in this topic.

   - Click **Previous pages** to display the tabs that were open when you last closed Edge.

   - Click **A specific page or pages** to specify one or more home pages.

3. If you choose to specify a home page or pages, click the list below that option to display the home page options.

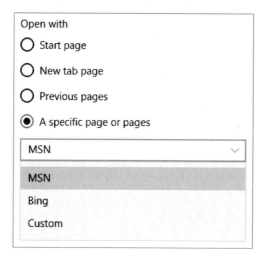

Setting a home page or pages

In the list, click one of the available options, or click **Custom** to display the current home page options, and then do any of the following:

- To remove a webpage from the home page set, click the **X** at its right edge.

- To add a webpage to the home page set, enter the URL or one of the following in the box, and then click the **Add** button.

  - about:start to display the Edge Start page

  - about:blank to display a blank page

> **TIP** If you set a home page or home pages, display the Home button on the Edge toolbar so you can return to your home page by clicking the button. To display the button, set the Show The Home Button toggle button at the top of the Advanced Settings pane to On.

Home page tabs appear in Edge in the same order as in the list

4. When you finish, close and reopen Edge to display your selected starting configuration.

To specify the content of new tabs

1. In the Edge window, on the **More actions** menu, click **Settings**.

2. In the **Settings** pane, click the **Open new tabs with** list to display the basic options.

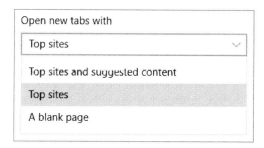

The "suggested content" is a newsfeed

3. In the **Open new tabs with** list, click the content you want Edge to display on a new tab. Then test the setting by opening a new tab.

To customize your suggested content (news feed)

1. Set the new tab content to **Top sites and suggested content** (referred to in some places as **Top sites and my news feed**).

2. Open a new tab in Edge.

3. At the right end of the **Top sites** heading, click **Customize** to display your suggested sites/news feed customization options.

4. In the **Choose your favorite topics** section, click one or more of the topics to select it.

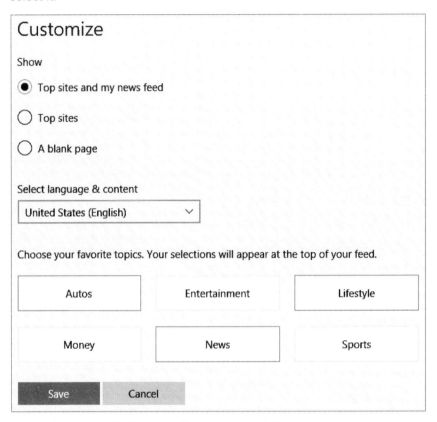

You can choose the topics that appear first in your news feed

5. Click **Save** to apply your changes.

To change your default Edge search engine

1. In the Edge window, on the **More actions** menu, click **Settings**.

2. In the **Settings** pane, click the **View advanced settings** button.

3. In the **Advanced settings** pane, click the **Search in the address bar with** list to display the search engine options.

The list contains previously selected search engines

4. Do any of the following:

   - If the list includes the search engine you want to use, click the search engine.

   - If the list doesn't include the search engine you want to use, click **<Add new>** to display additional search engines.

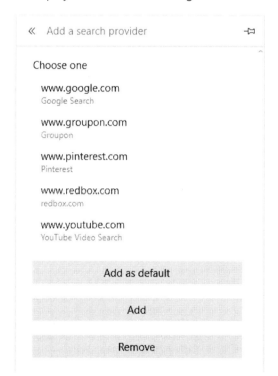

Some of the available search engines

   - If the **Add a search provider** pane doesn't include the search engine you want to use, return to the Edge window, browse to the search engine website to make it available in the pane, and start over at step 1.

To save and manage passwords and form entries

1. In the Edge window, on the **More actions** menu, click **Settings**.

2. In the **Settings** pane, click the **View advanced settings** button. Then scroll to the **Privacy and services** section.

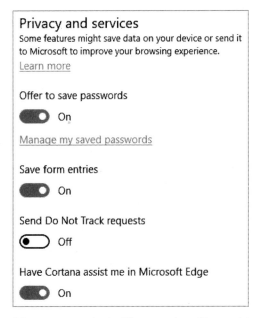

Edge can save and auto-fill passwords and form entries

3. Do any of the following:

   - To save and auto-fill passwords that you enter in password boxes in the Edge browser, set the **Offer to save passwords** toggle button to **On**.

     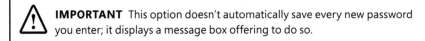

     ⚠️ **IMPORTANT** This option doesn't automatically save every new password you enter; it displays a message box offering to do so.

   - To stop saving passwords, set the **Offer to save passwords** toggle button to **Off**.

- To review the sites that you've saved passwords for, click **Manage my saved passwords** to open the Manage Passwords pane.

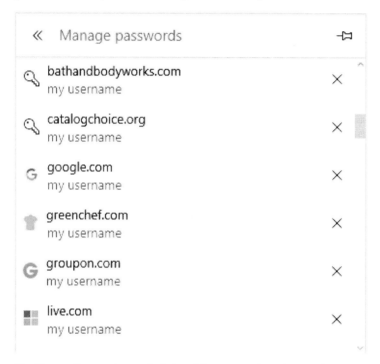

The Manage Passwords pane includes all the passwords you've saved

Click any website to display and edit the saved user name and password, or click the X at the right edge of any password to delete it.

- To save form entries that you enter in the Edge browser (so the browser can automatically enter them for you in other forms), set the **Save form entries** toggle button to **On**.

- To stop saving form entries, set the **Save form entries** toggle button to **Off**.

> ⚠️ **IMPORTANT** The information you save will be used to automatically fill forms in the future. This is convenient, but might also be a security risk. Some less-than-scrupulous websites add hidden form fields to collect information that you don't know you're providing.

To delete saved information

1. In the Edge window, on the **More actions** menu, click **Settings**.

2. In the **Clear browsing data** section of the **Settings** pane, click the **Choose what to clear** button to display the types of data you can clear.

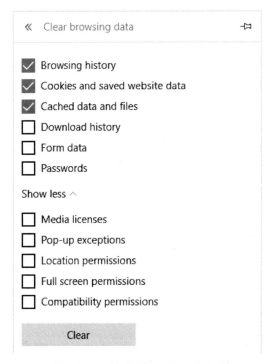

You can clear any category of browsing data

3. In the **Clear browsing data** pane, select the check boxes of the types of browsing data you want to purge. Then click the **Clear** button.

 IMPORTANT Clearing a browsing data category doesn't stop Edge from collecting data; you must turn off data collection separately.

 TIP Another interesting password management tool is Credential Manager, which you can open from an Icons view of Control Panel.

To configure your Reading view settings

1. In the Edge window, on the **More actions** menu, click **Settings**. The Reading view settings are in the **Reading** section at the bottom of the **Settings** pane.

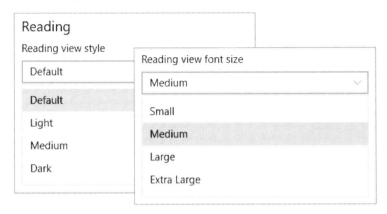

You can choose the color scheme and font size for Reading view

2. In the **Reading** section, click the **Reading view style** list, and then click the style you want.

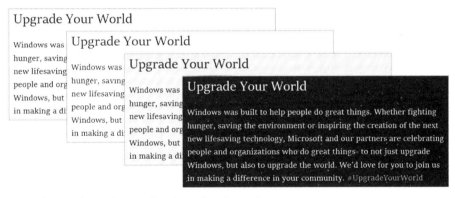

The Default, Light, Medium, and Dark Reading view styles

3. Click the **Reading view font size** list, and then click the font size you want. The actual font size will vary between monitors based on your screen resolution.

To import your Favorites list from another browser to Edge

1. In the Edge window, on the **More actions** menu, click **Settings**.

2. In the **Settings** pane, set the **Show the favorites bar** toggle button to **On**.

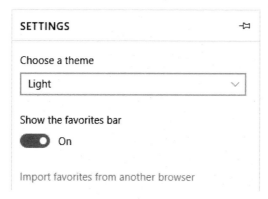

Display the favorites bar if you're importing favorites bar entries

3. Click the **Import favorites from another browser** link to display a list of installed browsers that have saved favorites.

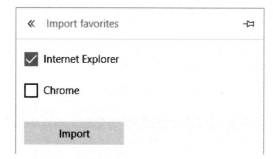

Only browsers that have favorites saved are available

4. Select the check box for each browser you want to import favorites from, and then click the **Import** button.

Manage default apps

If you give Edge a try and find that it isn't going to work for you, you can change the default browser to any other that you have installed or can install from the Store. Internet Explorer is preinstalled, and we assume you know where to find and how to install any other browser that is your personal preference.

Windows has designated default email, maps, music player, photo viewer, video player, and web browser apps. You manage the default apps in Windows Settings. To change your default browser (or any other default app), follow these steps:

1. If necessary, install the browser on your computer. If the Settings window was open during the installation, close and reopen it to make sure it finds the newly installed browser.

2. In the **Settings** window, click **System**, and then click **Default apps** to display the current default apps.

3. In the **Web browser** section, click the name of the current default browser to display a list of all the installed browsers.

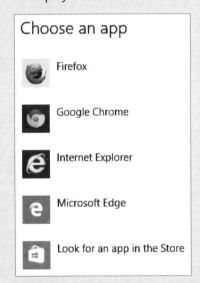

Choose an app

    Firefox

    Google Chrome

    Internet Explorer

    Microsoft Edge

    Look for an app in the Store

You can select an installed browser or install one from the Store

4. In the **Choose an app** list, click the browser you want to designate as the default. Windows implements the change immediately.

Anatomy of a website address

The words, letters, numbers, and symbols that appear in the Address bar of your web browser window when you connect to a website or webpage might look like a logical address or like a bunch of nonsense. Even when you connect to a simple website address such as *http://www.microsoft.com*, the Address box contents change to include additional information about the specific page displayed. Every character has a specific purpose. Here's a breakdown of a typical webpage address and a description of what each part does. The webpage address is *http://movies.msn.com/showtimes/today.aspx?zip=76226*.

Protocol	Sub-domain	Domain name	Folder	Page	Query
http	movies	msn.com	showtimes	today.aspx	?zip='76226'

The *protocol* tells your web browser what type of connection to make to the destination site. The most common protocol is *http* (Hypertext Transfer Protocol, the protocol that delivers information over the World Wide Web). Another common web protocol is *https* (HTTP over a secure connection). In a URL, the protocol is followed by a colon and two forward slashes (://).

TIP There are dozens of protocols for many different types of communication, including Internet connections, email delivery, file sharing, local and remote network connections, and a plethora of others. Some of the more familiar protocols include ADSL, DHCP, DNS, FTP, HTTPS, IMAP, IP, ISDN, POP3, SMTP, SOAP, TCP, and Telnet.

The *domain name* is the base address of the site. The top-level domain (TLD), such as *.com*, is part of the domain name. Each domain name is purchased and registered by an organization or individual and is assigned to an Internet Protocol (IP) address representing the location of the site content on a server. Domain names and IP addresses are managed by ICANN (the Internet Corporation for Assigned Names and Numbers), a nonprofit corporation based in California. Although ICANN is an American corporation, it manages Internet-related tasks worldwide in cooperation with international agencies.

When you go to a website, your computer connects to the Internet to find out the IP address currently assigned to the domain name. Then it connects to the server located at that IP address and displays the content located on that server.

Because the alphabetic domain name leads to the less-obvious IP address, the domain name is sometimes referred to as a *friendly name*.

If an address includes a *subdomain*, it points to a specific site, usually one of a group of sites presented under the umbrella of one domain name. The sites represented by the subdomains don't need to be of the same type and don't need to reside in the same location. For example, Contoso Corporation might have the registered domain name contoso.com. The company's public website might be located at http://www.contoso.com. The company might also have the following subdomains:

- *sharepoint* that connects to its collaboration site at http://sharepoint.contoso.com

- *mail* that connects to its web email server at http://mail.contoso.com

- *shopping* that connects to a secure online shopping cart application at https://shopping.contoso.com

A *folder name* indicates the location in the website structure of the page on the screen. In the same way that you store files within a logical folder structure on your hard drive, a website administrator might arrange files in a logical structure within the site. Single forward slashes (/) separate folders from other address elements, in the same way that single backward slashes (\) separate folders in the File Explorer Address bar.

The *page name* represents the specific file containing the content and code that generates the information displayed on the screen. The page name includes a file name extension indicating the file type. Common page name extensions include .htm for HTML files containing static content, and .aspx for Active Server Pages (ASP pages) displaying dynamic content gathered from a database or other source within a framework governed by code in the file.

An HTML page name might include a bookmark, preceded by a pound sign (#), indicating a specific location in a file. An ASP page name might include a query, preceded by a question mark (?), indicating the search term that generated the page content. In the example given at the beginning of this sidebar, the query *?zip=76226* is intended to return show times for movies playing in the geographical area identified by the ZIP Code 76226.

When you connect to a simple website address, Internet Explorer uses the protocol to establish the communication method, connects to the server hosting the domain or subdomain, and then displays the page designated by the website administrator as the home page for the site.

> ✓ **TIP** Top-level domains (TLDs) are governed by an international organization. Each TLD has a specific meaning: generic TLDs (such as .com and .net) are available to anyone, sponsored TLDs (such as .edu, .gov, and .travel) belong to private agencies or organizations, and two-letter country code TLDs are intended to represent the country or region of origin or use of a site's content. Country code TLDs are frequently used for other purposes, however; for example, the TLD .am is assigned to Armenia, and .fm is assigned to the Federated States of Micronesia, but many radio stations have website addresses ending in these TLDs.

Configure browser security settings

It is difficult (at least for some people) to imagine how we would survive without constant access to the Internet. The Internet has become a primary source of information and services. But it is often difficult to know whether the information is accurate and the services are benign: there are a lot of people who use the Internet to try to steal information from other people, or damage their computers, through malicious attacks on computer systems.

The security of the Edge and Internet Explorer browsers is constantly monitored and managed by Microsoft. Windows Defender updates are released frequently to safeguard your computer against newly discovered threats, or source code issues through which someone who really wants to could exploit the browser. There are bad people who launch malicious attacks, and good people who fix problems; between those two groups, there are people who have the challenging job of finding potential problems before the bad guys do, so the good guys can fix them. All these people are smart and dedicated to playing their roles in the threat life cyle.

Malware can present itself in many forms—you can find it, or it can find you. Some of the problems that the browser can guard against include:

- Unsafe websites that are phishing websites or that contain malicious software.

- Pop-up windows that display false information and links to malicious software. These frequently are crafted to look like Windows warning messages.

Taking care of Edge and Internet Explorer is the responsibility of Microsoft. Protection generally lags slightly behind the threat, so there is no guarantee that Microsoft or any other company can protect you from all threats. Being aware while browsing the Internet is the responsibility of each individual. In this topic we discuss measures that you can take to be safe and secure while browsing the Internet.

Protect yourself from phishing and malicious sites

One of the special security features of both Edge and Internet Explorer is Microsoft SmartScreen Filter. It runs in the background of your browsing session and monitors websites, webpages, and downloads for known issues or suspicious content. If Smart-Screen Filter identifies (or suspects) a security problem, it handles it in one of these ways:

- If you visit a website that has been reported as an unsafe website, SmartScreen Filter blocks the website and informs you.

- If you visit a webpage that has characteristics that might indicate a security risk, SmartScreen Filter displays a warning page. If you know that the webpage content is safe, you can provide feedback and continue to the webpage.

- If you download an app that is known to be unsafe, SmartScreen Filter blocks the file download and informs you.

- If you download an app that isn't known to be unsafe, but also hasn't been downloaded by many people, SmartScreen Filter displays a warning. If you trust the website and app publisher, then you can continue with the download.

SmartScreen Filter is on by default in Edge and in Internet Explorer. The only management option in Edge is whether it is on or off. In Internet Explorer, you can manually check a website against the current list of known phishing sites, and you can report sites that you suspect are unsafe.

You manage SmartScreen Filter settings for each browser independently. You can also turn on SmartScreen Filter for Store apps that pass URLs, from the Privacy page of the Settings window.

To turn SmartScreen Filter on or off

1. In the Edge window, on the **More actions** menu, click **Settings**.

2. In the **Settings** pane, click the **View advanced settings** button.

3. At the bottom of the **Advanced settings** pane, set the **Help protect me for malicious sites and downloads with SmartScreen Filter** toggle button to **On** or **Off**.

Or

1. In the Internet Explorer window, on the **Tools** menu, click **Safety**, and then click **Turn on SmartScreen Filter** or **Turn off SmartScreen Filter**.

2. In the **Microsoft SmartScreen Filter** dialog box, click the option you want, and then click **OK**.

To manually check a website against the list of known unsafe websites

1. In the Internet Explorer window, on the **Tools** menu, click **Safety**, and then click **Check this website**.

2. If the **SmartScreen Filter** dialog box opens, click **OK**.

To report an unsafe website to Microsoft

1. In the Internet Explorer window, on the **Tools** menu, click **Safety**, and then click **Report this website**.

2. On the **Report a website** page, verify that the URL shown in the **Website you are reporting** section is that of the website you want to report.

3. Select any of the following check boxes:

   • I think this is a phishing website

   • I think this website contains malicious software

4. At the bottom of the page, enter the characters from the image into the box to verify that you are a person rather than a computer. Then click the **Submit** button.

Block pop-up windows

Pop-up windows (or just *pop-ups*) are secondary web browser windows that open in front of (or sometimes behind) the window you're working in when you display a website or click an advertising link. The content of these windows might be informational—for example, a new window might open when you click a link for more information or when you sign in to a secure site—or in some cases might be irritating or malicious—for example, when browsing the Internet for information you might display a page that causes several advertisements to pop up behind it. However, pop-ups frequently display annoying advertisements, adware (fake warning messages containing links to product sites), spyware (malicious software that can collect personal information from your computer), or other types of content you did not invite and probably don't want.

If a suspicious pop-up does open, it's best to not click any buttons in it; instead, you can usually close the window from Task view, from the taskbar, or from Task Manager. You can also configure your browser to block pop-up windows from opening. When a site does try to display a pop-up, the browser alerts you and you can choose to provide a one-time or permanent exception for that site. If you later change your mind, you can review and remove specific exceptions in Internet Explorer, or clear all the exceptions in Edge.

To block pop-up windows

1. In the Edge window, on the **More actions** menu, click **Settings**.

2. In the **Settings** pane, click the **View advanced settings** button.

3. In the **Advanced settings** pane, set the **Block pop-ups** toggle button to **On**.

Or

1. In the Internet Explorer window, on the **Tools** menu, click **Internet Options**.

2. On the **Privacy** tab of the **Internet Options** dialog box, select the **Turn on Pop-up Blocker** check box. Then click **OK** to apply the change.

To clear pop-up window exceptions that you've granted

1. In the Edge window, on the **More actions** menu, click **Settings**.

2. In the **Clear browsing data** section of the **Settings** pane, click the **Choose what to clear** button.

3. Display all the options in the **Clear browsing data** pane, and select the **Pop-up exceptions** check box. Then click the **Clear** button.

Or

1. In the Internet Explorer window, on the **Tools** menu, click **Internet Options**, and then click the **Privacy** tab.

2. In the **Pop-up Blocker** section, click the **Settings** button to display the Pop-up Blocker Settings dialog box.

You can configure exceptions and notifications, and choose a blocking level

3. Do either of the following:

    *   To clear all exceptions, click the **Remove all** button.

    *   To clear the exception for a specific site, click the site in the **Allowed sites** list, and then click the **Remove** button.

4. Click **Close**, and then click **OK** to apply the change.

Educate kids about online safety

In November 1998, the U.S. Congress passed the Children's Online Privacy Protection Act (COPPA), which requires that operators of US-based online services or websites obtain parental consent before collecting, using, disclosing, or displaying the personal information of children under the age of 13. COPPA went into effect on April 21, 2000 and is governed by regulations established by the Federal Trade Commission.

Many children have Internet access at home, at school, and at friends' houses. On their own computers, you can protect children from exposure to objectionable content by setting up their user accounts as Child accounts and configuring the Family Safety settings at age-appropriate levels. However, it's important to proactively educate children about online safety and computer security.

The Federal Trade Commission provides helpful information for parents and teachers about computer security, mobile phones, social networks, virtual worlds, texting, video games, parental controls, and COPPA at *consumer.ftc.gov /topics/kids-online-safety*.

Maintain browsing privacy

Internet browsers keep track of the websites you visit so that you can return quickly to them from your browsing history list. They also track the credentials you sign in to websites and services with, so they can resupply them to the site without bothering you. This can cause conflicts if you have multiple user names for the same site—for example, if you have two different Microsoft accounts, or two different Office 365 accounts.

Some sites temporarily save credentials and other information that you provide, in session variables that expire after some period of time. To ensure that your information isn't available to other people who connect to the site from the same computer, take care to sign out of secure sites instead of just closing the browser window.

You can restrict Edge or Internet Explorer from tracking your browsing and credentials by using an InPrivate browsing session. This opens a separate browser window that doesn't carry forward any credentials that are currently in use. The browsing that you do in this window is not tracked—the pages and sites do not appear in your browsing history, and temporary files and cookies are not saved on your computer.

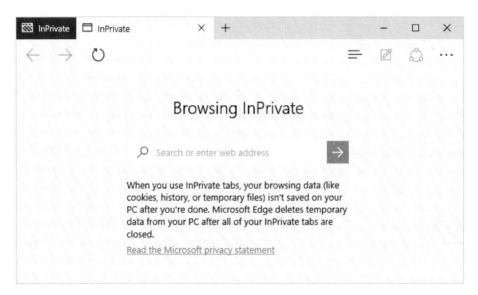

InPrivate browsing sessions are compartmentalized from other sessions

The InPrivate browsing session lasts only as long as the window is open. Any browsing that you do in other browser windows is recorded as usual.

You can increase the security of an InPrivate browsing session by disabling toolbars and extensions in those sessions. This setting is turned on by default in Edge and in Internet Explorer, but can be modified in Internet Explorer, so it's a good idea to check it.

To start an InPrivate browsing session

1. Do any of the following:

   - In the Edge window, on the **More actions** menu, click **New InPrivate window**.

   - In the Internet Explorer window, on the **Tools** menu, click **InPrivate Browsing**.

   - In either browser, press **Ctrl+Shift+P**.

To disable toolbars and extensions in InPrivate browsing sessions

1. In the Internet Explorer window, on the **Tools** menu, click **Internet Options**, and then click the **Privacy** tab.

2. In the **InPrivate** section, select the **Disable toolbars and extensions when InPrivate browsing starts** check box. Then click **Apply** or **OK**.

Troubleshoot browsing issues

If Edge is unable to support site requirements, it displays a link so that you can switch to Internet Explorer. If you think Edge is having difficulty with a site, you can switch to the other browser from directly within Edge, or you can have Edge act as though it's a different browser (emulate the browser), even one that doesn't usually run on your computer or device. Edge and Internet Explorer can emulate many different browsers, not only those installed on your computer.

Edge and Internet Explorer can emulate many browsers and platforms

Some sites, particularly those that run add-ins, still have compatibility issues with Internet Explorer 11 (the current version at the time of this writing). If you experience difficulty with a site that you're displaying in Internet Explorer—for example, if you click a button on a site and nothing happens—switching to Compatibility view will often fix the problem.

If you have difficulty navigating a webpage by using the mouse, you can use caret browsing instead. Caret browsing enables you to use standard navigation keys on your keyboard—Home, End, Page Up, Page Down, and the arrow keys—to select text and move around on a webpage. The concept of caret browsing has been available for years. Like many things associated with accessibility, it can be useful to almost anyone.

You can turn on caret browsing for the current browser tab or you can simply turn it on.

To switch the display of a site from Edge to Internet Explorer

1. In the Edge window, on the **More actions** menu, click **Open with Internet Explorer**.

To emulate a different browser

1. In the Edge window, on the **More actions** menu, click **F12 Developer Tools**.

2. In the **F12 Developer Tools** window, click the **Emulation** tab.

 TIP You can move the F12 Developer Tools window away from the browser window so you can watch the content change.

3. In the **User agent string** list, click the browser (or browser and platform, if appropriate) that you want Edge to emulate.

Or

1. In the Internet Explorer window, on the **Tools** menu, click **F12 Developer Tools**.

2. In the **F12 Developer Tools** pane, click the **Emulation** tab.

3. In the **User agent string** list, click the browser (or browser and platform, if appropriate) that you want Internet Explorer to emulate.

 TIP Watch the webpage as you select a browser to emulate. The page will refresh and might look a little or a lot different, depending on your selection.

To display a site in Compatibility view

1. In the Internet Explorer window, on the **Tools** menu, click **Compatibility View settings**. The Compatibility View Settings dialog box opens with the current site prefilled in the Add This Website box.

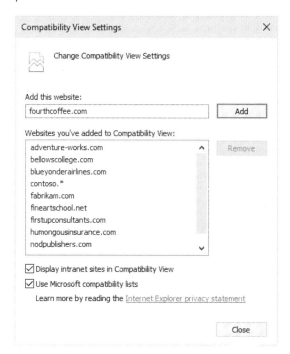

Regardless of what you enter, Compatibility view retains only the domain name and extension

2. To add the current website, click the **Add** button.

3. To add another website, enter the domain name in the **Add this website** box, and then click the **Add** button.

 TIP You can use an asterisk (*) as a wildcard character—for example, to represent any top-level domain.

4. When you finish adding websites, click **Close** to close the dialog box and implement your changes.

To turn on caret browsing for all tabs

1. In the Edge window, on the **More actions** menu, click **Settings**.

2. In the **Settings** pane, click the **View advanced settings** button.

3. In the **Advanced settings** pane, set the **Always use caret browsing** toggle button to **On**.

Or

1. In the Internet Explorer window, on the **Tools** menu, click **Internet Options**.

2. On the **Advanced** tab of the **Internet Options** dialog box, select the **Enable Caret Browsing for new windows and tabs** check box. Then click **Apply** or **OK** to apply the change.

To use caret browsing

1. Click or tap in a text area on the webpage to set the initial insertion point.

2. Do any of the following:

    - Press the arrow keys to move the insertion point one character or line at a time.

    - Press the **Home, End, Page Up**, and **Page Dow**n keys to move greater distances.

    - Hold down the **Ctrl** key and press **Home** or **End** to move to the beginning or end of the page.

    - Hold down the **Shift** key and press the navigation keys to select text.

To turn caret browsing on or off for the current tab

1. Press **F7**.

 TIP If caret browsing is turned on for all tabs in the browser settings, you can't turn it off for a tab.

Skills review

In this chapter, you learned how to:

- Display websites in Edge

- Find, save, and share information

- Manage Edge settings

- Configure browser security settings

- Maintain browsing privacy

- Troubleshoot browsing issues

Practice tasks

No practice files are necessary to complete the practice tasks in this chapter.

Display websites in Edge

Perform the following tasks:

1. Start Edge and display the **bing.com/news** site. Click an article title on the page to display an article. Notice whether the article opens in the same tab or in a new tab.

2. If the article opened in the same tab, the Back button is now available. Click the **Back** button to return to the first page, and the Forward button becomes available. Click the **Forward** button to return to the new article.

 TIP If the article opened in a new tab, try the Back and Forward buttons later, when the Back button is available.

3. In the new article, right-click a link, and then click **Open in new tab**. Right-click another link, and then click **Open in new window**. Note the differing results.

   You now have two Edge windows open. The first window has at least two page tabs, and the second window has one page tab.

4. Arrange the Edge windows side by side, and drag one tab from the first window to the second window, to move the page between windows.

5. In either window, to the right of the rightmost tab, click the **New tab** button to open a new tab. Note the content of the tab, which will be one of the following:

   - A "blank" page that displays a search box

   - A page that displays eight squares, some or all of which might contain tiles that represent websites

   - A page that displays eight site tile spaces and news articles

   In a later exercise, you'll configure this page to display different content.

6. Click near the top of the new tab, between the **Refresh** and **Reading view** buttons, to activate the Address bar.

7. On the Edge toolbar, in the **Address** bar, enter **windows 10** to display a list of search suggestions (and possibly sites, if you've visited any Windows 10 sites). Enter **microsoft** after your existing search term to further refine the search term list.

8. Click the highlighted search term directly below the Address bar to search for the phrase as you entered it, and to display a page of search results.

9. On the Edge toolbar, to the right of the **Address** bar, notice the **Reading view** button. Note whether the button is active (with a dark outline) or inactive (with a pale outline).

10. On the search results page, locate the result that represents the Windows page of the Microsoft website. Click the link to display the Windows home page.

11. On the Edge toolbar, note whether the **Reading view** button is active. If the button isn't active, click a link to display another page until you find one that does support Reading view.

12. On the Edge toolbar, click the **Reading view** button to display the current page in Reading view. Note the background color of the page.

    In a later exercise, you'll change the Reading view color scheme.

13. Scroll the page to determine the content that is displayed in Reading view.

14. Click the **Reading view** button again to return to the standard view of the page. Locate the information from Reading view on the page and note the page elements that Reading view did not display.

15. Close the browser windows, clicking the option to close all tabs when prompted to do so.

Find, save, and share information

Perform the following tasks:

1. Start the Edge browser and display the website of your company, your school, an organization you belong to, or another organization whose website content you're familiar with. (If you can't think of another website, display the Windows website at **windows.microsoft.com**.)

2. Press **Ctrl+F** to display the Find toolbar. In the search box, start entering a word or phrase that appears multiple times on the page. As you enter each character, notice that the number of results changes.

3. On the **Options** menu, click **Match whole word** to include only search results that aren't part of other words. Note whether the number of results changes. Then click **Match whole word** again to remove the filter.

4. On the **Options** menu, click **Match case** to include only search results that have the same letter casing that you entered. Note whether the number of results changes. Then click **Match case** again to remove the filter.

5. On the **Find** toolbar, click the **Next result** button (the greater than symbol) to display the first search result. Press **Next result** again to display the second search result. Then scroll the page and notice that all search results are highlighted.

6. On the Edge toolbar, click the **Make a Web Note** button to display the annotation toolbar. Point to each of the buttons on the toolbar to display the button name.

7. On the annotation toolbar, click the **Pen** button. Use the pen tool to circle something on the page, and then to underline something else.

8. On the annotation toolbar, click the **Add a typed note** button. Click the webpage next to the circle you drew in step 7, and then enter **Good idea!** in the note window that appears.

9. On the annotation toolbar, click the **Eraser** button. Then swipe anywhere on the underline you drew in step 7 to erase it. Notice that swiping anywhere on the line erases the entire line.

10. Experiment with other annotation techniques. When you finish, click the **Share** button near the right end of the annotation toolbar to display the Share pane and the apps you can use to share the webpage.

11. Near the top of the **Share** pane, click the webpage name and then click **Screen-shot** to display the apps you can use to share a screenshot of the webpage.

12. Share either the webpage or a screenshot of the webpage by using one of the available options.

13. Exit the annotation toolbar.

14. On the Edge toolbar, click the **Add to favorites or reading list** button. Save the current webpage to the Edge reading list.

15. On the Edge toolbar, click the **Hub** button. In the **Hub** pane, display your reading list, and then display your browsing history. Review the **Today** list in your browsing history.

16. From the **More options** menu, pin the current webpage to the Start screen. Then close the browser window and locate the Start menu tile for the webpage.

Manage Edge settings

Perform the following tasks:

1. Start the Edge browser and display the **Settings** pane.

2. In the **Settings** pane, set your home page to either **MSN**, **Bing**, or **Custom**. If you choose Custom, specify a webpage of your choice.

3. Without closing the **Settings** pane, display the **Open new tabs with** list, and then click a tab content option. (Choose something different from the content you noted in step 5 of the first practice task.)

4. Display the **Advanced settings** pane, turn on the display of the Home button, and then configure the Home button to display the same page you designated as your home page. (Use **msn.com** for MSN or **bing.com** for Bing.)

5. Click anywhere on the webpage to close the Advanced Settings pane. Then on the Edge toolbar, click the **Refresh** button to update the Home button settings.

6. Click the **Home** button and verify that it displays the home page you chose in step 2.

7. Click the **New tab** button, and verify that it displays the content you chose in step 3.

8. Display the **Settings** pane and locate the **Reading** section. In the **Reading view style** list, click a style option. (Choose something different from the style you noted in step 12 of the first practice task.)

9. Return to the webpage and display it in Reading view to verify the style change.

10. Follow the procedure for importing your Favorites list from another browser into Edge. If another browser is available, import those favorites into Edge. Then display the **Hub** pane and verify that your Edge favorites list includes the imported entries.

11. Close the browser window.

Configure browser security settings

Perform the following tasks:

1. Start the Edge browser and display the **Advanced Settings** pane.

2. Near the top of the **Advanced settings** pane, verify that the option to block pop-ups is turned on.

3. Locate the **Privacy & service**s section of the pane. Review and consider the settings you can configure. At the bottom of the section, verify that the option to use SmartScreen filter is turned on.

4. Perform any other procedures from the "Configure browser security settings" topic of this chapter that interest you. When you finish, close the browser windows.

Maintain browsing privacy

Perform the following tasks:

1. Start the Edge browser and display any website that you sign in to by using credentials. (If you can't think of another website, display your OneDrive site at **onedrive.live.com**.) Sign in to the website.

2. Open a new tab and display the same website you chose in step 1. Notice that it recognizes your credentials and signs you in.

3. From the **More actions** menu, open a new InPrivate browsing window. In the InPrivate window, display the same website you chose in step 1. Notice that it doesn't automatically sign you in.

4. Close the browser windows.

Troubleshoot browsing issues

Perform the following tasks:

1. Start the Edge browser and display any website.

2. From the **More actions** menu, display the **F12 Developer Tools** window. Move or resize the window so you can see the website.

3. On the **Emulation** tab, choose a different browser to emulate. Notice any differences in the display of the website.

4. Choose a browser that is on a different platform, and notice differences in the display of the website.

5. Close the **F12 Developer Tools** window, and then close the browser window.

Part 2

Devices and resources

CHAPTER 6

Manage peripheral devices. 249

CHAPTER 7

Manage network and storage resources 291

Manage peripheral devices

6

If your computer is a desktop computer, you'll need to connect a few peripheral hardware devices—such as a monitor, a keyboard, and a mouse—to it before you can use it. Other common peripheral devices are printers, speakers, scanners, fax machines, external storage drives, and external media drives such as DVD drives. Depending on your interests and how you use your computer, you might also use devices such as a microphone, webcam, fingerprint reader, joystick, touchpad, or drawing tablet. The point of all these devices, of course, is to make your computing experience more productive, more enjoyable, and (hopefully) simpler.

Many people now use laptop computers as their primary computer at home or at work. Laptops have the basic peripherals built in, but you can also connect an external monitor, keyboard, mouse, and other peripherals to your laptop to make it feel more like a desktop environment.

In this chapter, you'll work with a computer's most common external devices—the monitor, mouse, keyboard, printer, speakers, and microphone. In the process, you'll learn about plug-and-play devices, device drivers, and ports.

This chapter guides you through procedures related to installing peripheral devices, locating device information, displaying your desktop on multiple screens, setting up audio devices, changing the way your mouse and keyboard work, and managing printer connections.

In this chapter

- Understand peripheral devices
- Locate device information
- Display your desktop on multiple screens
- Set up audio devices
- Change the way your mouse works
- Change the way your keyboard works
- Manage printer connections

Practice files

No practice files are necessary to complete the practice tasks in this chapter.

Understand peripheral devices

Peripheral devices are things that you can add to your computer to extend its functionality or power, or to serve as an interface between it and human users. There are two general types of peripheral devices:

- **Internal** You install these inside your computer's case and are likely to consider them part of the computer. Internal devices can come in the form of an expansion card, or a new hard disk drive or DVD drive. For example, you might install an additional video card to improve your computer's graphics capabilities or support multiple monitors.

- **External** You attach these to your computer by connecting them to ports on the outside of your computer's case.

Peripheral device terminology

Ports are outlets in your computer's case through which various types of information can pass. Ports come in many shapes and sizes, each designed for a specific purpose. A typical modern computer has a VGA or HDMI port to which you can connect a monitor, an Ethernet port to which you can connect a network cable, and several USB ports to which you can connect a variety of devices. The computer might also support wireless connections through Wi-Fi, Bluetooth, and radio waves (typically used for wireless keyboards and mice).

An older computer might have a DVI monitor port, PS/2 keyboard and mouse ports, a parallel printer port, or an IEEE 1394 port to which you can connect high-speed devices such as digital video cameras. But you probably won't be running Windows 10 on one of these computers.

If you find that you don't have enough ports to connect all the devices you want to use with your computer, you don't have to limit your device choices. Here are three options for expanding your connection capacity:

- **Install extra ports** You can purchase an expansion card with more ports. After turning off your desktop computer and removing its cover, you insert the card into one of the available expansion slots. When you turn the power back on, Windows 10 detects and installs the new ports.

- **Use a hub** You can connect a single multiport hub to your computer and then connect multiple devices to the hub, enabling all the devices to share that single connection. Hubs are available for network, USB, and other connection types.

- **Use more wireless devices** A wireless version of almost every external peripheral you might want to use is now available. You can connect to a printer, scanner, fax, keyboard, mouse, or hard drive without using a cable. You can listen to audio and use a microphone without plugging anything into your computer.

Install peripheral devices

Installing a new peripheral device is usually easy and intuitive, because most of these devices are now *plug and play*. Plug and play quite literally means that you can connect devices to the computer and begin using them. Plug-and-play devices include printers, external hard drives, flash drives, fingerprint readers, smart card readers, cameras, and many others.

When you connect a device to your computer, Windows 10 identifies the device and searches through its database of device drivers to locate the appropriate driver for the device.

Device drivers are files that let Windows communicate with your device. Drivers can be specific to an individual device or to a family of devices (such as all HP LaserJet printers), and they are often specific to a certain version of Windows.

Windows 10 doesn't automatically support all devices (no operating system does). Sometimes old hardware is simply incompatible, or the manufacturer hasn't chosen to provide an updated Windows 10 driver. You can check the compatibility of your current devices or one you are thinking about buying by going to *www.microsoft.com /en-us/windows/compatibility/CompatCenter/Home*.

If Windows 10 doesn't have a current driver for your particular device, it asks you to provide the driver. You might have the driver on an installation disc provided by the device manufacturer. Alternatively, Windows can search the Internet for the driver, or you can visit the device manufacturer's website.

> ✓ **TIP** If your device is on the list of compatible devices at *www.microsoft.com/en-us /windows/compatibility/CompatCenter/Home*, allowing Windows 10 to search for the drivers online is almost always the fastest and easiest way to get them.

Some devices come with software you can install to take full advantage of their capabilities. For example, you might connect an all-in-one printer/scanner/fax/copy machine to your computer and be able to print, fax, and copy without installing additional software. However, to be able to scan documents to electronic files, you might need to install the software provided with the device.

Locate device information

You can display information about the devices that are connected to your computer from the Devices page of the Settings window. On this page, Windows 10 displays information about printers, scanners, projectors, the mouse or touchpad, the keyboard, Bluetooth and USB devices, and other devices that are connected to the computer.

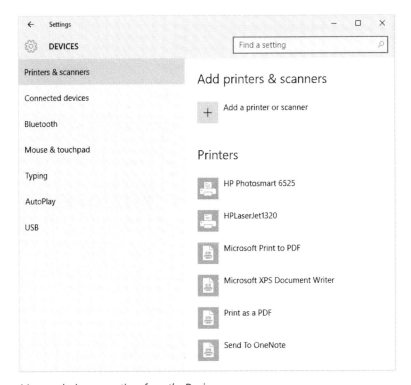

Manage device connections from the Devices page

The information that is available from this page is specific to the hardware and peripheral devices that are connected to your computer either directly or through a network.

> **SEE ALSO** Monitor connections are managed from the System page of the Settings window. For information about monitors, see "Customize device display settings" in Chapter 9, "Manage computer settings," and "Display your desktop on multiple screens" later in this chapter.

Boost your memory

If you want to upgrade your computer's memory, you don't necessarily have to physically install additional RAM in your computer case. The Windows ReadyBoost feature enables your Windows 10 computer to use a qualifying USB flash drive as a memory-expansion device.

For best performance, you should use a USB drive (also referred to as a USB stick or thumb drive) with available space of at least double the amount of memory that is installed in your computer, and preferably four times as much memory. You can use up to eight flash memory devices synchronously (with a total of up to 256 gigabytes [GB] of memory) on one computer—if you have enough ports.

ReadyBoost is easy to use. Insert the USB drive in a USB port, right-click the drive in File Explorer, and click Properties. On the ReadyBoost tab of the Properties dialog box, Windows suggests the amount of flash drive memory you can dedicate to ReadyBoost, and you select the amount you want to use.

When ReadyBoost is enabled, Windows 10 creates a file named ReadyBoost. sfcache in the root of the flash memory device.

TIP To use more than 4 GB on a single flash drive, you need to format it with the NTFS file system.

If one or more solid-state drives (SSDs) are connected to your computer, ReadyBoost might be unavailable, because some solid state drives are faster than flash memory devices and are unlikely to benefit from ReadyBoost.

You can add devices to your system by clicking the Add button at the top of the appropriate settings pane and following the steps described in the wizard to install the compatible device drivers on your computer. You can remove the connection to a device by clicking it in the list and then clicking Remove Device. Doing so doesn't delete the device's drivers from your computer, so if you add the device again later, the process is a bit simpler.

Adding or removing a device means more than just that the device is physically connected or wirelessly available; it means that Windows has confirmed that the drivers
are correct and it can communicate with the device. What you are really adding it to is
the list of available devices that are displayed when you choose to do something that
requires a device. For example, when the Print dialog box is displayed, all the available
printers are listed so you can choose the one you want. When you remove a device,
you are really just removing it from that list.

When a device isn't working properly, you can get information about the device and
its drivers, and often troubleshoot the problem, from the Device Manager window.

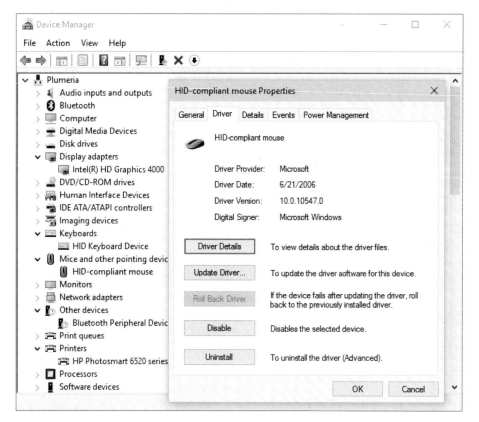

Information about the internal and external devices installed on your computer is available from the
Device Manager window

You can double-click any device to display its Properties dialog box, in which you can
explore detailed information about any device.

You can also display information about the hardware, software, and components that form your computer system, in the System Information window.

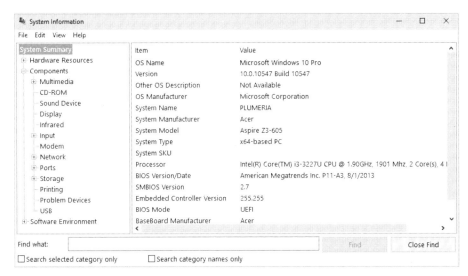

You can search System Information for specific components

To display the Settings window

1. Click the **Start** button, and then click **Settings** on the menu.

> ✓ **TIP** When the Settings window opens, its icon is displayed on the taskbar. To make it easier to open this window in the future, you can right-click that icon and click Pin This Program To Taskbar.

To display information about installed devices

1. Do either of the following to start Device Manager:

   • Right-click the **Start** button and then, on the **Quick Link** menu, click **Device Manager**.

   • In the **Settings** window, click **Devices**. At the bottom of the **Printers & Scanners** pane, click **Device Manager**.

> ✓ **TIP** There are various ways to do almost everything in Windows 10. We try to introduce different approaches in these procedures. Always feel free to explore each approach more fully on your own.

2. In the **Device Manager** window, expand any category to display the devices in that category that are installed on your computer.

3. To display information about a specific device, double-click the device (or right-click the device, and then click **Properties**).

 IMPORTANT Don't change any of the settings unless you have the experience necessary to anticipate the consequences of the change.

To display information about hardware, software, and components

1. Enter **system** in the taskbar search box and then, in the search results, click the **System Information** desktop app.

2. In the **System Information** window, expand any category to display information about the system components that are installed on your computer.

Display your desktop on multiple screens

A basic computer system includes one monitor that displays your Windows desktop. This is sufficient for many computing experiences. However, in some situations, you might find it convenient, or even necessary, to extend your desktop across multiple monitors or duplicate your desktop on a secondary display (such as a monitor or video projector screen). You can easily add one, two, or more monitors or other display devices to your computer system.

To connect multiple display devices to your Windows 10 computer, your computer must have an adequate number of ports, which can be provided by multiple video cards, a multiport video card, or USB ports. Windows 10 also supports Miracast—a wireless technology you can use to project a screen image from your Windows 10 device to a monitor, projector, or other device that also supports Miracast. Miracast uses a peer-to-peer wireless connection, based on Wi-Fi Direct (WiDi) technology. Miracast does not require a wireless network or use your network bandwidth.

IMPORTANT WiDi is an Intel product and requires Intel or compatible graphic and network cards. To check your system for compatibility, you can install the Intel WiDi Update Tool from *supportkb.intel.com/wireless/wireless-display/templates/selfservice/intelwidi/#portal/1026/article/16168*.

You can connect as many display devices as you have ports available. You connect the display to the computer by using a cable with the appropriate port connectors on it, or, if you are using Miracast, wirelessly. If you don't have a cable with connectors that match the available ports, you can use an adapter to match the cable connector type to the port type.

When you physically connect a secondary display device to your computer, Windows 10 detects the device and, if your computer system already has the necessary drivers, automatically extends the desktop to the newly connected display device.

After connecting the display device, you can change the way Windows displays information on the devices. Options include:

- **Duplicate these displays** The same content appears on both displays. This is useful when you are giving a presentation and are not facing the screen (for example, when standing at a podium facing an audience) or want to have a closer view of the content you're displaying.

- **Extend these displays** Your desktop expands to cover both displays. The Windows Taskbar appears only on the screen you designate as the primary display.

- **Show desktop only on** Content appears only on the selected display. This is useful if you are working on a portable computer that is connected to a second, larger display.

When you are working on a computer that is connected to two display devices, Windows designates one as the primary display and the other as the secondary display. The Welcome screen and taskbar automatically appear on the primary display, as do most application windows when they first open. You can set the taskbar to appear on one or all displays, and drag selected windows between displays. You configure these settings separately, from the Taskbar And Start Menu Properties dialog box.

By default, Monitor 2 appears to the right of Monitor 1. When you move the mouse pointer horizontally from screen to screen, it should leave the right edge of the left screen and enter the left edge of the right screen at vertically the same point. If your monitors are not physically the same size, are set to different screen resolutions, or are not placed level with each other, you can change the alignment of the displays so that the pointer moves cleanly between them.

To display the Display pane

1. Do either of the following:

   - In the **Settings** window, click **System**, and then click **Display**.

   - Right-click an empty area of the desktop, and then click **Display settings**.

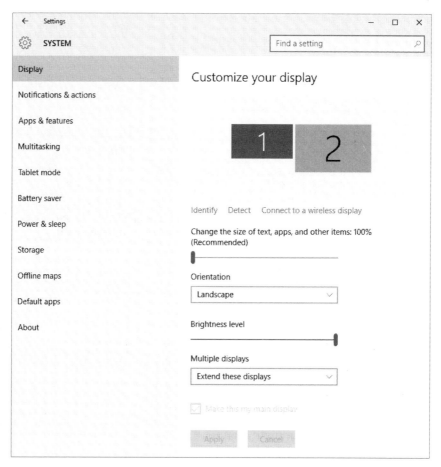

The Display pane provides options for customizing information displayed across screens

TIP If a technical problem involving the connection between your computer and one monitor occurs when your desktop is extended across two or more monitors, you might find yourself in the situation of having windows open on the inactive monitor. To retrieve a hidden window, press Alt+Tab until the window you want to move is selected in the on-screen display, and then press Shift+Win+Right Arrow (or Left Arrow) to move the active window to the next monitor.

To extend or duplicate your desktop across multiple displays

1. In the **Display** pane, select an option from the **Multiple displays** list (which is available only if a second display is connected), and then click **Apply**.

 TIP If you later want to change the Multiple Display settings, you can do so quickly by pressing Win+P. A panel slides out from the right side of your main display, offering the same options to extend or duplicate the display.

To ascertain which screen is the primary display

1. In the **Settings** window, click **System**, and then click **Display**.

2. Click **Identify** to display the numbers from the monitor icons on the screens that they represent.

To change which screen is designated as the primary display

1. In the **Display** pane, click the secondary display.

2. Select the **Make this my main display** check box, and then click **Apply**.

To adjust the relative position of the displays

1. In the **Display** pane, drag the rectangle representing Monitor 2 to the location you want it to be in relation to Monitor 1. Try to align the monitor rectangles so that the arrangement resembles the way your physical displays are aligned.

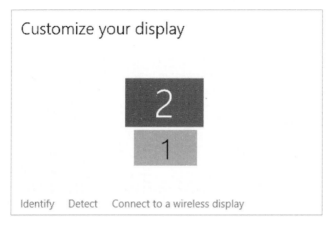

The preview area of the Screen Resolution window

2. Click **Apply**.

 TIP After rearranging the monitor icons, you can judge whether the monitors are appropriately aligned by moving the pointer between the screens. Ideally, the pointer will remain on the same horizontal or vertical plane when you do so.

 SEE ALSO For information about changing monitor resolution and increasing the size of on-screen elements, see Chapter 10, "Manage power and access options."

To extend your screen to a TV or monitor by using a WiDi connection

1. Make sure the remote screen is turned on and the dongle is connected (if applicable).

2. In the **Settings** window, click **System**, and then click **Display**.

3. Below the preview of the current display, click **Connect To A Wireless Display**.

4. A pane slides out from the right side of your screen and displays a list of wireless display and audio devices within range. Double-click the device you want to connect to.

The Connect pane slides out from the right side of your screen

5. Follow any directions displayed on your screen or on the remote screen.

   The remote screen displays a message telling you that it is connecting to the computer. After a while, the connection is made and the desktop is wirelessly extended to that monitor.

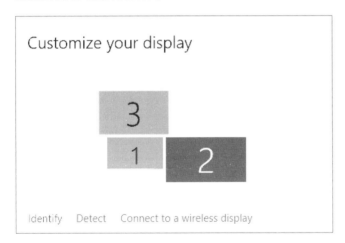

The wireless display is added to the preview area as display 3

> **✓ TIP** Wireless screen extensions are not made automatically, so they are a bit more effort to initially establish and need to be reestablished each time you restart your computer. (Wired connections are restored with the previous settings each time you restart). After setting up the connection, you can customize the display settings.

To specify the position of the taskbar on multiple displays

1. Right-click an empty area of the taskbar, and then click **Properties**. When you have multiple screens connected to your computer, the Taskbar tab of the Taskbar And Start Menu Properties dialog box includes a Multiple Displays section.

You can choose where to display taskbar buttons when you use multiple screens

2. In the **Multiple displays** section, do any of the following:

   - If you want to extend the taskbar across the screens, select the **Show taskbar on all displays** check box.

   - In the **Show taskbar buttons on** list, click the location where you want to display the working taskbar content.

3. Click **Apply** or **OK** to implement any changes.

Expand your portable computer with peripheral devices

Portable computers (such as laptops, notebooks, and tablets, are useful when you want to be able to move around with your computer—from room to room, from work to home, or from city to city.

Although portable computers can offer fast computing and large-capacity hard disks, you might have to deal with a smaller monitor, a smaller keyboard, and a touchpad or stylus instead of a standard mouse. Many "ultra-portable" notebooks don't have internal CD or DVD drives.

Although carrying a full-size monitor, keyboard, and mouse when you travel with your portable computer is not always convenient, adding full-size peripherals is a great way to improve your computing experience when you're using your portable computer in your office or at home. If you use a portable computer so that you have a seamless transition between work and home, you can set up a monitor, keyboard, and mouse at each location for a relatively small sum of money. You then have the best of both worlds—mobile computing and a full-size setup.

Instead of connecting your hardware devices to your portable computer through a USB port or wirelessly, you could connect the devices to a docking station or USB hub, and then connect your computer to that whenever you want to use the devices.

When you attach an external monitor to your portable computer, you might at first see the same display on both monitors, or the display might appear only on the portable computer's monitor. To change which monitor displays your desktop, use the techniques described in "To change which screen is designated as the primary display" earlier in this topic.

Set up audio devices

Computers are no longer devices used primarily to produce traditional business documents such as letters, reports, and worksheets. You can use your computer for multimedia activities such as listening to music, watching movies, or playing games, and you can create sound-enhanced documents such as presentations and videos. Even if you're not likely to work with these types of files, your productivity might be diminished if you cannot hear the sound effects used by Windows 10 to alert you to events such as the arrival of email messages. And you'll need speakers and a microphone if you want to participate in video conferences or use your computer to place telephone calls.

Most computers are equipped with sound cards, and many have built-in speakers so that you can listen to music and other audio, and microphones so you can communicate through the computer. Some monitors come with built-in speakers, and you can also set up external speakers. Or, if you want to listen to audio output privately, you can connect headphones directly to your computer.

If you want to use external audio input and output devices, you can connect them to your computer either through the audio jacks, through USB ports, or through Bluetooth or wireless connections. USB-connected microphones generally produce cleaner audio because the processing is done externally to the PC, so the sound isn't subject to as much electronic interference. This is particularly important in text-to-speech conversion.

Desktop computers have audio output jacks (usually found on the back of the computer case) and might also have dedicated headphone jacks (either on the front or on the back of the case). Laptop computers have headphone jacks and microphone jacks, or on rare occasions one jack that handles both output and input.

 TIP The audio output jack might be indicated by a small speaker icon, an arrow symbol, or the words Audio or Audio/Out.

On desktop computer cases that feature standard component color-coding, the audio output jack is light green, the headphone jack is light orange, and the audio input jack is pink. This color-coding simplifies the process of locating the correct jacks. Some audio device connection cables are color-coded to match.

With the rapid evolution of Internet-based communications, digital video, and speech-to-text technologies, microphones are being used more commonly with business and home computer systems. Microphones come in a variety of types, such as the following:

- Freestanding microphones

- Headset microphones with built-in headphones that allow more private communication and consistent recording quality

- Boom microphones with a single headset speaker

If you will be recording a lot of speech or using the Windows Speech Recognition feature, consider investing in a good-quality microphone. To get the highest quality sound, it's critical that you choose the type of microphone that fits your needs. Headset and boom microphones maintain a constant distance between the microphone and your mouth, which helps to maintain a more consistent sound level than a stationary microphone.

The Speech Recognition feature in Windows 10 includes a fairly good speech recognition engine. After you set up speech recognition, you can use it to control your computer and enter text into most applications where you would normally type it. Windows 10 also features Cortana, a service that is designed to be your new digital assistant and can respond to your voice instructions.

SEE ALSO For information about configuring your Windows 10 computer for speech recognition, see "Manage speech settings" in Chapter 9, "Manage computer settings."

When you connect an audio device to your Windows 10 computer, a notification might appear briefly and then be stored with other notifications in the Action Center.

A notification might appear when you connect or remove an analog audio device

To switch between audio playback devices

1. In the notification area of the taskbar, right-click the **Sound** icon (labeled with a speaker), and then click **Playback devices** to display the Playback tab of the Sound dialog box.

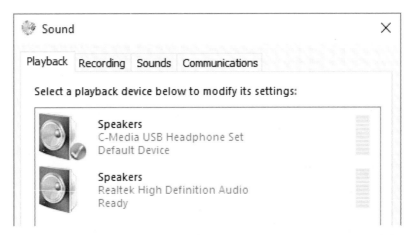

On the Playback tab of the Sound dialog box, you can access speakers to manage their settings

2. Click the speakers, headphones, or other playback device you want to use, and then click **Set Default**.

To manage audio playback device settings

1. On the **Playback** tab of the **Sound** dialog box, click the device you want to manage, and then click **Properties** to display settings that you can configure manually.

Or

1. On the **Playback** tab of the **Sound** dialog box, click the device you want to manage, and then click **Configure** to start the Speaker Setup wizard.

 TIP A configuration appears twice in the list if the audio channel has multiple speaker-arrangement options.

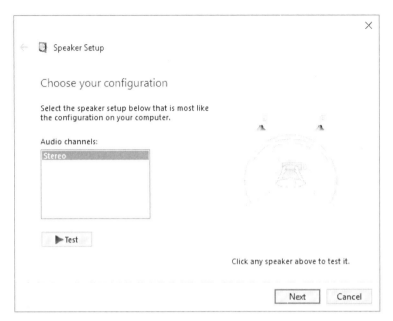

Choose a speaker configuration and test the output

2. On the **Choose your configuration** page, select the appropriate audio channel, and click **Test**. Then click each speaker in the speaker setup diagram.

   An image representing sound waves appears next to each speaker as the wizard plays a sound through that speaker. If a sound is not audible each time the sound waves appear, or if the sound plays through a speaker other than the one indicated in the wizard, verify that the speakers are properly connected and test again.

3. Click **Next** to display the **Select full-range speakers** page.

4. In some configurations, the front left and right speakers, or the surround speakers, are full-range speakers that produce the entire audio range and include a subwoofer unit to enhance bass output. If your speaker configuration includes full-range speakers, select the check box for those speakers. Then click **Next**.

5. On the **Configuration complete** page, click **Finish**, and then click **OK** to close the **Sound** dialog box.

To switch between audio recording devices

1. In the notification area of the taskbar, right-click the **Sound** icon, and then click **Recording devices** to display the Recording tab of the **Sound** dialog box.

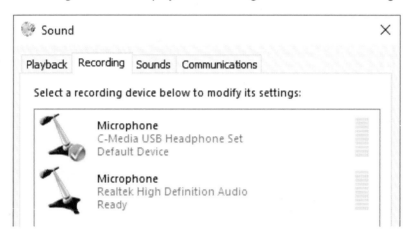

The Recording tab of the Sound dialog box displays any sound input devices connected to your computer

2. Click the microphone, headset, or other recording device you want to use, and then click **Set Default**.

To manage audio playback device settings

1. On the **Playback** tab of the **Sound** dialog box, click the device you want to manage, and then click **Properties** to display settings that you can configure manually.

Or

1. On the **Playback** tab of the **Sound** dialog box, click the device you want to manage, and then click **Configure** to open the Speech Recognition window of Control Panel.

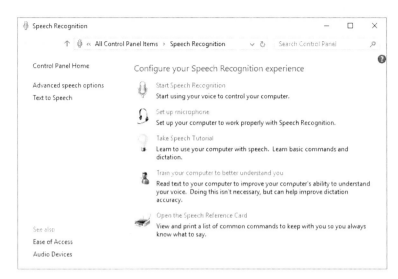

From the Speech Recognition window, you can configure Windows 10 to accept and recognize audio input

2. In the **Speech Recognition** window, click **Set up microphone** to start the Microphone Setup wizard.

The Microphone Setup wizard guides the process of setting up a microphone

3. Select the type of microphone you are using, and then click **Next**.

4. On the **Set up your microphone** page, follow the instructions to correctly position the microphone, and then click **Next**.

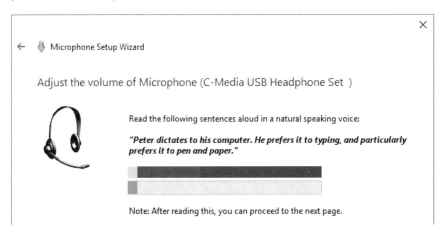

You dictate a passage to adjust the microphone settings to your natural speaking volume

5. On the **Adjust the volume** page, read the microphone test paragraph aloud in your normal speaking voice. Or, just for fun, you might try singing a couple of lines from your favorite song! Any audio input delivered at the volume you'll usually use when using the microphone will work.

As you speak (or sing), the volume gauge moves in response to your voice.

> ✓ **TIP** If the volume gauge does not move, your microphone might be incorrectly connected, malfunctioning, or incompatible with your computer. If this happens, hold the microphone close to your mouth and speak loudly—if the recording meter moves slightly, the connection is good, and the problem is compatibility between your microphone and your computer. You might be able to solve this problem by downloading new device drivers from the microphone manufacturer's website, or it might be simpler to replace the microphone.

6. When you finish reading the paragraph, click **Next**.

If the wizard didn't gauge the input to be of the necessary quality for regular use, it displays a message and gives you the opportunity to return to the Adjust The Volume page and repeat the input sample.

7. If it seems necessary to repeat the input sample, do so. When you're satisfied with the results, click **Next** on each page until the wizard confirms that the microphone is set up. On the last page of the wizard, click **Finish**.

Change the way your mouse works

In the beginning, a computer mouse consisted of a shell with one clickable button and a rubber ball on the bottom that correlated your mouse movements with a pointer on the screen. Nowadays, mice come in many shapes and sizes, employing a variety of functions, buttons, wheels, and connection methods.

Windows 10 offers enhanced wheel support that allows for smooth vertical scrolling and, on some mice, horizontal scrolling. Check the manufacturer's documentation to see whether your mouse can take advantage of this technology. Even if it can't, you can still customize your mouse settings in various ways to optimize the way it works with Windows.

 TIP If you have a fairly fancy mouse, it might come with software you can install that extends its functionality beyond what the Settings window or Control Panel offer.

You can change the function performed by each of the buttons and of the wheel, if your mouse has one, in addition to the appearance of the pointer in its various states, and its functionality. If you want, you can allow the appearance of the mouse pointer in Windows 10 to be controlled by the visual theme.

 IMPORTANT Some mice and keyboards include custom management interfaces that augment or override the Windows settings.

To set basic button and wheel options

1. In the **Settings** window, click **Devices**, and then click **Mouse & touchpad**.

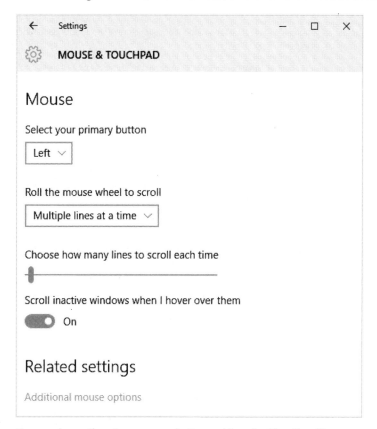

You can change the primary mouse button and the wheel functionality

2. Configure any of the following settings:

- To specify the normal functionality of the mouse buttons, in the **Select your primary button** area, select **Left** or **Right**.

  If you select Right, you would click the right mouse button to select an item and click the left one to display a shortcut menu.

   TIP This setting is useful if you are left-handed, if you have injured your right hand, or if you want to switch mousing hands to decrease wrist strain.

- To set the distance scrolled when you move the scroll wheel, from the **Roll the mouse wheel to scroll** list, select either **Multiple lines at a time** or **One screen**. When you select Multiple Lines At A Time, you can specify how many lines to scroll at a time by dragging the slider.

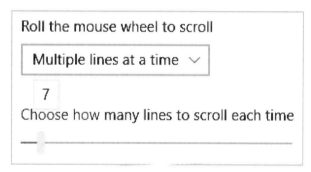

Set the number of lines to scroll at a time

  Dragging the slider displays the number of lines in a small box above the slider. This number is approximate and varies depending on where the text is and how it is formatted.

- To scroll an inactive window when you point to it, set the **Scroll inactive windows...** toggle button to **On**.

To change additional mouse button settings

1. At the bottom of the **Mouse & touchpad** page, click **Additional mouse options** to open the **Mouse Properties** dialog box with the **Buttons** tab active.

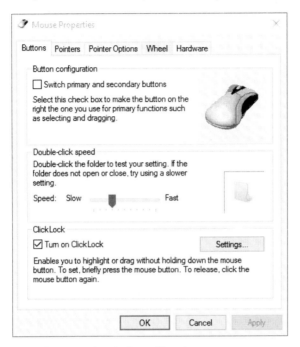

Mouse button settings in Control Panel

2. Do any of the following:

    - Test the speed at which Windows registers a double-click. Then, if necessary, in the **Double-click speed** area, drag the **Speed** slider to adjust the speed. (If you have changed the default primary button, use the right mouse button to double-click the folder and to drag the slider.)

    - To drag without holding down the mouse button, in the **ClickLock** area, select the **Turn on ClickLock** check box.

3. Click **Apply** to apply the changes but leave the dialog box open, or **OK** to apply the changes and close the **Mouse Properties** dialog box.

To change how the entire set of mouse pointers looks

1. In the **Mouse Properties** dialog box, click the **Pointers** tab.

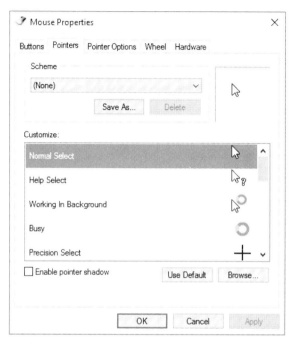

On the Pointers tab, you can change the pointer scheme, in addition to the pointer icon used to indicate individual functions

2. In the **Scheme** list, select a different scheme to display the set of pointers associated with that scheme.

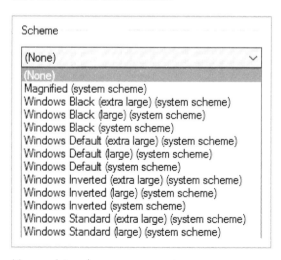

Mouse pointer schemes

3. Click **Apply** to apply the changes and keep the dialog box open, or **OK** to apply the changes and close the Mouse Properties dialog box.

To change an individual pointer icon

1. In the **Mouse Properties** dialog box, display the **Pointers** tab.

2. In the **Customize** list, click any pointer icon, and then click **Browse**.

    The Browse dialog box opens with the contents of the Cursors folder displayed.
    (*Cursor* is another name for pointer.)

3. In the **Browse** dialog box, double-click any pointer icon to replace the one you
    selected in the Customize list.

    > **TIP** You can restore the selected pointer to the default for the original scheme
    > at any time by clicking Use Default.

4. If you want to add a shadow to your pointers, select the **Enable pointer shadow**
    check box.

5. Click **Apply** to apply the changes and keep the dialog box open, or **OK** to apply
    the changes and close the Mouse Properties dialog box.

To change how the mouse pointer works

1. In the **Mouse Properties** dialog box, click the **Pointer Options** tab.

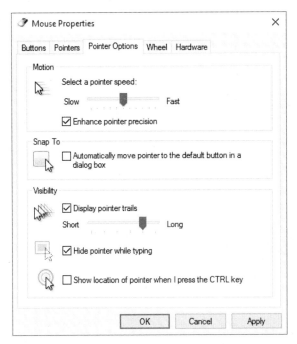

On the Pointer Options tab, you can set the speed, movement, and visibility of the pointer

2. Make any of the following changes:

    *   To change the pointer speed, in the **Motion** section, drag the slider.

    *   To speed up dialog-box operations, in the **Snap To** section, select the **Automatically move pointer to the default button in a dialog box** check box.

    *   To make the pointer more visible on the screen, in the **Visibility** section, select or clear any of the three check boxes.

3. Click **Apply** to apply the changes and keep the dialog box open, or **OK** to apply the changes and close the Mouse Properties dialog box.

To change how the mouse wheel works

1. In the **Mouse Properties** dialog box, click the **Wheel** tab.

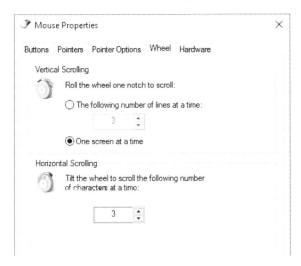

On the Wheel tab, you can adjust vertical and horizontal scrolling

Here you can set the scroll distance just as you can in the Settings window. If you set this in either location, the change is reflected in the other location the next time you open it.

2. To control how much of the screen scrolls with each click of the mouse wheel, in the **Vertical Scrolling** section, do either of the following:

    *   Click **The following number of lines at a time,** and then enter or use the arrows to select the number of lines you want to scroll.

    *   Click **One screen at a time**.

TIP You can move forward and backward between visited webpages by holding down the Shift key and then scrolling the wheel.

3. If your mouse supports horizontal scrolling, in the **Tilt the wheel to scroll the following number of characters at a time** box, enter or select the number of characters you want to scroll horizontally when you tilt the mouse wheel to the left or right.

4. Click **Apply** to apply the changes and keep the dialog box open, or **OK** to apply the changes and close the Mouse Properties dialog box.

Change the way your keyboard works

Regardless of the type of keyboard you have, all keyboards work in the same general way: Pressing each key or key combination generates a unique key code that tells the computer what to do. Pressing a key or key combination that gives a command always carries out that command.

You can change the keystrokes that Windows receives from a keyboard to those of another language. In Chapter 9, "Manage computer settings," we review procedures for installing languages and switching among installed keyboards.

In the Typing pane of the Devices page of Settings you can change settings that control the following text input features:

- **Spelling** Choose whether to automatically correct misspelled words and highlight misspelled words.

- **Typing** Show text suggestions as you type, add a space when you insert suggested text, and add a period after when you insert two spaces.

- **Touch keyboard** Play key sounds as you type, capitalize the first letter of each sentence, turn on All Caps when you double-tap the Shift key, add the standard keyboard layout as a touch keyboard option, and automatically show the touch keyboard in windowed apps when there is no keyboard attached to your device.

You can configure options on the Speed tab of the Keyboard Properties dialog box, which is accessible from Control Panel or search, to change the speed at which you must press and release a key to input a single character.

To configure text input settings

1. Open the **Settings** window.

2. In the **Settings** window, click **Devices**, and then click **Typing** to display spelling, typing, and touch keyboard options.

3. Set each toggle button to **On** or **Off** to configure the settings as you want them.

To change the key repeat delay and rate

1. Display an Icons view of Control Panel, and then click **Keyboard** to open the Keyboard Properties dialog box.

A blinking cursor in the lower-left corner models the current cursor repeat rate

2. To adjust how long you can hold down a key before Windows repeats its character, drag the **Repeat Delay** slider.

3. To adjust the rate at which Windows repeats a character while you hold down its key, drag the **Repeat Rate** slider.

> **TIP** You can test the Repeat Delay and Repeat Rate settings in the box at the bottom of the Character Repeat area.

4. To adjust how fast the cursor blinks, drag the **Cursor Blink Rate** slider.

5. Click **Apply** or **OK**.

Manage printer connections

In previous editions of this book, we provided many pages of information about connecting printers to your computer and connecting your computer to printers. The good news is that modern printer connections are incredibly simple to complete.

If you have only one computer and one printer, you can connect them directly, by using a physical cable, or over a network. When you do, Windows searches for the printer driver. If you have an installation disc for your printer, you can install the printer drivers from the disc. However, the installation disc might contain out-of-date drivers. The more dependable option is to have Windows download the current list of printers that are supported by the drivers that are available through Windows Update. You can choose your printer in the list and immediately install the latest driver. Printer driver discs frequently include printer management apps that provide an interface to information about your printer; you can also get that information by entering the IP address and port the printer is connected to into a browser window.

You can manage installed printers from several locations. The Printers & Scanners pane of the Devices settings page is one. More information is available from the Devices And Printers window; this is currently the best place to manage printer settings.

Your network might include one or more printers that are connected directly to the network through a wired or wireless network connection. These printers are called *network printers*. Network printers aren't connected to any computer and are available on the network whenever they are turned on.

> **SEE ALSO** For information about sharing printers and other resources with a home-group, see "Share files on your network" in Chapter 7, "Manage network and storage resources."

To install a local plug-and-play printer

1. In the **Settings** window, click **Devices**, and then click **Printers & scanners** to display the Add Printers & Scanners page. The Printers section displays a list of the currently installed printers.

Physical printers, virtual printers (those that print to a file rather than on paper), print services, and fax services appear in the Printers area of the Printers & Scanners page

2. Connect the printer to the appropriate port on your computer.

3. If necessary, connect the printer to a power outlet, and then turn it on.

    Windows 10 locates and installs the appropriate device driver while displaying a progress bar in the Printers area. If the printer appears in the Printers area of the Printers & Scanners page, your printer is installed and ready to use.

 IMPORTANT If the printer wasn't recognized or the drivers weren't properly installed, continue with the next procedure.

To manually install a local printer

1. In the **Settings** window, click **Devices**.

2. In the **Printers & scanners** pane of the **Devices** page, click **Add a printer or scanner**. Windows searches for any available printers that aren't yet installed on your computer.

Available printers are listed, along with a link to manually search for the printer to add

3. If the list includes the printer that you want to install, click it. Windows will install the printer as described in step 3 of the "To install a local plug-and-play printer" procedure earlier in this topic.

4. If the search didn't locate the printer you want to add, click **The printer that I want isn't listed** to start the Add Printer wizard.

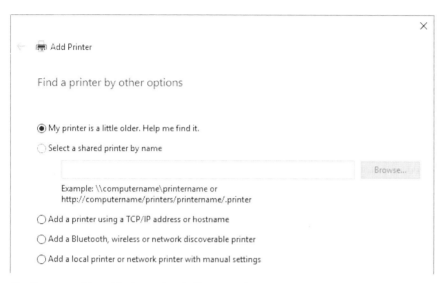

The first page of the Add Printer wizard offers several options

> **TIP** A printer that is connected directly to your computer is called a *local printer*. A printer that is available to you through your network is called a *remote printer*.

5. On the first page of the **Add Printer** wizard, click **Add a local printer or network printer with manual settings**, and then click **Next**.

6. On the **Choose a printer port** page, select the port to which your printer is connected from the **Use an existing port** list. If the printer is connected to a USB port but did not automatically install, choose **USB001 (Virtual printer port for USB)**. Then click **Next** to display the Install The Printer Driver page.

> ⚠ **IMPORTANT** It's likely that the correct port will already be selected. If not, the installation instructions from your printer manufacturer will tell you which port you should use. Some manufacturers supply helpful drawings to guide you.

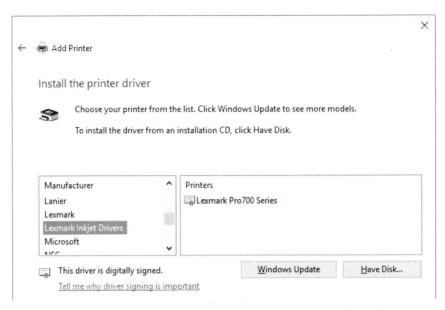

With the Add Printer wizard, you can choose a non–plug-and-play printer from a list, let Windows Update refresh the list, or install it from the manufacturer's disc

7. If your printer model is listed, select it.

   Or

   Click **Windows Update**. Windows Update retrieves the current set of Windows 10 printer drivers from its online database and updates the Manufacturer and Printers lists. There are a lot of printer drivers, so this process can take a couple of minutes. In the updated list, select your printer.

8. Click **Next** to display the Type A Printer Name page.

> ⚠ **IMPORTANT** The Printers list is actually a list of drivers, rather than printers. Many printer drivers support multiple printers, and the supported printers might not all be in the Printers list. If the list doesn't include your specific printer model, select a model with a similar name. Alternatively, download the necessary drivers from the manufacturer's website, return to the Install The Printer Driver page, and click Have Disk to install the printer manually.

9. On the **Type a printer name** page, change the printer name if you want to, or accept the suggested name. Then click **Next**.

A progress bar indicates the status of the driver installation. When the installation is complete, the Printer Sharing page appears.

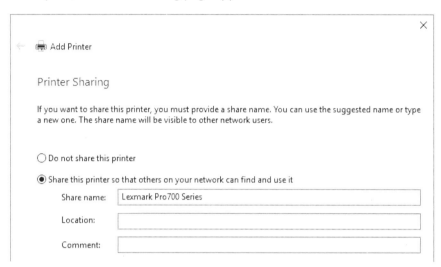

During the setup process, the Add Printer wizard gives you the option of sharing the printer

10. On the **Printer Sharing** page, click **Do not share this printer**. Then click **Next**.

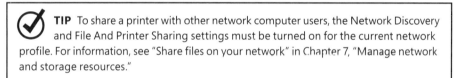

TIP To share a printer with other network computer users, the Network Discovery and File And Printer Sharing settings must be turned on for the current network profile. For information, see "Share files on your network" in Chapter 7, "Manage network and storage resources."

The Add Printer wizard confirms that you've successfully added the printer. If you chose to share the printer, it is now available to other network computer users.

11. On the last page of the **Add Printer** wizard, click **Print a test page**.

Your printer might require an additional step or two here to print the page. After Windows 10 sends the test page to the printer, a confirmation message box appears.

12. In the confirmation message box, click **Close**. Then in the **Add Printer** wizard, click **Finish**.

An icon for the newly installed, local printer appears in the Printers area of the Printers & Scanners window.

To open information about printer status

1. Display the **Printers & Scanners** page of the **Settings** window, and, at the bottom of the page, click **Devices and printers**.

2. In the **Devices and Printers** window, click the icon for your printer.

   The device window for the printer displays information about the printer status and related tasks.

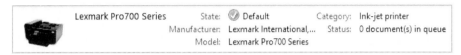

You can display status information in the Devices And Printers window

To manage printer settings

1. In the **Devices and Printers** window, double-click the printer icon to open a window that contains printer-specific configuration options.

You can manage printer settings in the printer window

To disconnect a device from your computer

1. In the **Settings** window, click **Devices**, and then click the category of device that you want to disconnect to display that category's pane.

2. In the pane, locate the device. Click the device, and then click the **Remove device** button that appears.

Or

1. In the notification area of the taskbar, click the **Show Hidden Icons** button.

2. Click the **Safely Remove Hardware and Eject Media** icon (labeled with a check mark in a green circle on a USB connector), and then click the device you want to remove.

    You can now physically disconnect the device without leaving any stray information or open ports behind, or damaging the device.

Skills review

In this chapter, you learned how to:

- Understand peripheral devices
- Locate device information
- Display your desktop on multiple screens
- Set up audio devices
- Change the way your mouse works
- Change the way your keyboard works
- Manage printer connections

Virtual printers

Some apps install printer drivers that you can use to "print" content to their default file type. Most notably, virtual printer drivers allow you to print to a PDF file, a text file, an XPS file, or Microsoft OneNote. When you install an app that has this capability, it usually automatically installs the appropriate driver and adds the virtual printer to the printer list.

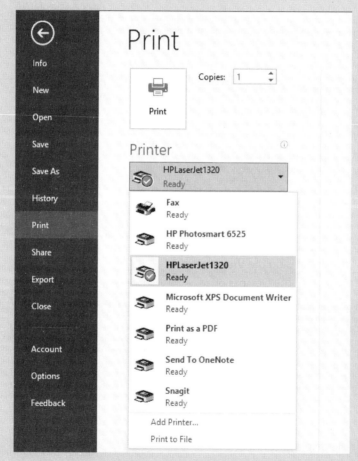

Six virtual printers and two real printers in the Word printer list

You can print to a virtual printer just as you do to a real printer. Virtual printers are available in apps in the same locations as other printers.

Practice tasks

No practice files are necessary to complete the practice tasks in this chapter.

Understand peripheral devices

There are no practice tasks for this topic.

Locate device information

Perform the following tasks:

1. Open the **Settings** window and display the **Device** category page. Review each pane of the page. Identify the devices that you can currently configure from this page.

2. Open **Device Manager**, and familiarize yourself with the categories of installed devices. Then do any of the following:

   • If any device displays a warning symbol, open its **Properties** dialog box and on the **Driver** tab, click the **Update Driver** button to search for a new device driver.

   • Click each of the options on the **View** menu to display other ways of locating devices. Then return to the Devices By Type view.

3. If you want to, open the **System Information** window to locate technical information about the hardware, software, and components in your computer system.

Display your desktop on multiple screens

Perform the following tasks:

1. If you have multiple displays connected to your computer, do any of the following:

   • In the **Settings** window, click **System**, and then click **Display**. From the **Display** pane, identify the monitors by number.

   • If you want to, change the screen that is designated as the primary display.

- Experiment with extending and duplicating the display. Consider the circumstances under which you might want to use each of these settings.

- If your desktop is extended across displays, adjust the relative position of the displays, and then move the cursor across the displays and notice the effect.

- Open the **Taskbar and Start Menu Properties** dialog box, and try each of the taskbar settings for multiple displays. Choose the one you like best, and then click **OK**.

Set up audio devices

Perform the following tasks:

1. Open the **Sound** dialog box.

2. Configure the settings for the playback device you want to use, manually or by using the wizard.

3. Configure the settings for the recording device you want to use, manually or by using the wizard.

Change the way your mouse works

Perform the following tasks:

1. In the **Settings** window, click **Devices**, and then click **Mouse & touchpad**. Review the settings that you can manage in this pane, and configure them as you want them.

2. At the bottom of the **Mouse & touchpad** pane, click **Additional mouse options**. In the **Mouse Properties** dialog box, review the settings that you can manage, and configure them the way you want them. Then click **Apply**.

3. Compare and contrast the settings in the **Mouse & touchpad** pane with those in the **Mouse Properties** dialog box. Then close the dialog box.

Change the way your keyboard works

Perform the following tasks:

1. In the **Settings** window, click **Devices**, and then click **Typing**. Review the settings that you can manage in this pane, and configure them as you want them.

2. From Control Panel (or taskbar search), open the **Keyboard Properties** dialog box. Review the settings that you can manage in the dialog box, and configure them the way you want them. Then click **Apply**.

3. Compare and contrast the settings in the **Typing** pane with those in the **Keyboard Properties** dialog box. Then close the dialog box.

Manage printer connections

Perform the following tasks:

1. Open the **Devices and Printers** window, and review the devices that are available in the window.

2. If you have a printer installed, double-click the printer icon to display printer-specific configuration options. Review the available options and configure them the way you want them. Then close the window.

Manage network and storage resources

In the early days of Microsoft, Bill Gates envisioned a future with "a computer on every desk and in every home." Today, the business world couldn't function without computers, and terms such as "information worker" have popped up to describe people who spend most of the day working on computers. Computers make it possible for an increasing number of people to successfully run small businesses with large presences, to maximize productivity by working from home, to have learning resources at their fingertips (literally), and to stay connected to information all the time, from any location.

As more apps become available as online services, an Internet connection is increasingly important to the computing experience. Your computer connects to the Internet through a network that provides and safeguards the connection. Windows 10 uses network connection security profiles to govern the way your computer interacts with other computers and devices on the network. On a local network, you can connect directly to other computers or manage the connection through a homegroup—a password-protected security group that defines the sharing of specific information and devices with other homegroup member computers.

This chapter guides you through procedures related to managing network connections, managing homegroup connections, and sharing files on your network.

In this chapter

- Manage network connections
- Manage homegroup connections
- Share files on your network

Practice files

For this chapter, use the Win10SBS\Ch07 practice files folder. For practice file download instructions, see the introduction.

Manage network connections

A network is a group of computers that communicate with each other through a wired or wireless connection. A network can be as small as two computers or as large as the Internet. In the context of this book, we primarily use the term network to mean the connection between computers in one physical location that are connected to each other, and to the Internet, through a network router.

> ⚠ **IMPORTANT** This chapter assumes that you are connecting to an existing, functioning network. This chapter does not include instructions for setting up or configuring networking hardware. When setting up a network infrastructure, be sure to follow the instructions provided by the hardware manufacturer.

Connect to a network

If your computer is a desktop computer, you'll probably connect it to only one network: your home or office network. However, you might connect a laptop computer or mobile devices to networks in many locations for the purpose of connecting to the Internet: at home, at work, at a friend's or relative's house, at a public library, at a coffee shop—some highway rest areas even offer free Internet access! You can't connect a computer directly to the Internet, so wherever you want to connect to the Internet you will first need to connect to a network.

Connecting your computer to a network requires two things:

- Your computer must have an active network adapter. This is usually in the form of a network interface card that is part of the internal workings of the computer, but you can purchase external network adapters that connect to a USB port on your computer. A network adapter can be for a wired network or a wireless network. Many laptop and desktop computers have both. If a computer has a wired network adapter, it has an external Ethernet port that the cable connector fits into. This looks a bit like a wide telephone cable port.

- The environment you're in must have a network. This could be a wired network that you connect to directly or through a switch box, a wireless network that you connect to through a router, or a wireless network connection that you share from a phone or other device that connects to a cellular network.

If your computer has an enabled network adapter, whether or not it is actively connected to a network, a connection icon appears in the notification area at the right end of the Windows Taskbar. The connection icon indicates whether your network adapter is an Ethernet adapter or a wireless adapter.

The connection icon indicates the adapter type and connection status

The bars on the wireless connection icon indicate the strength of the wireless network signal that the computer is currently connected to. When the computer is configured for a connection but not connected to a network, different versions of the basic network connection icon indicate the network status, as follows:

- A white starburst indicates that a connection is available.

- A white X on a red background indicates that no network is available.

Clicking the network connection icon displays information about the current network connection status and any available networks.

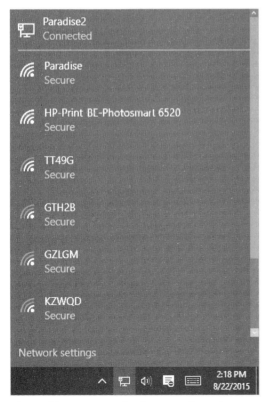

The scroll bar appears only when you point to the pane

Each network connection has a name; it might be a generic name provided by the network router or a specific name assigned by the network owner. The icon to the left of the network name indicates the connection type and, for wireless connections, the signal strength. The word or words below the network name provide additional information about the network.

Right-clicking the connection icon in the notification area displays a shortcut menu of commands that you can use to open the Network And Sharing Center and diagnose network connection problems.

When you physically connect your computer to a network by using an Ethernet cable, Windows 10 automatically creates the network connection. To connect to a wireless network for the first time, you need to make the connection.

Network vs. Internet connections

Connecting a computer to a network does not automatically connect the computer to the Internet; it connects the computer to the network router or hub that sits between the computer and the Internet. Additional action might be necessary to connect to the Internet.

For example, when you connect to a corporate network, it might scan the security settings on your computer and require that you install updates before it permits a connection. When this happens, the connection will be noted as Limited, and you must disconnect from the connection, perform the required action, and then reconnect.

When connecting to a free, pay-per-use, or subscription-based public network (such as one at an airport, restaurant, coffee shop, library, or hotel), you might have immediate Internet access. Frequently, though, you will be required to provide information, credentials, or payment in order to connect from the public network to the Internet. You might be prompted to provide this information when the connection is established. If you connect to a network but then find that you can't connect to the Internet, start a new instance of the web browser to display the organization's connection page, and then provide the required information. (It might be necessary to refresh the page to force the display of the gateway page.)

The purpose of connecting a computer to a network is usually to connect beyond the network to the Internet, but it might also be for the purpose of accessing devices (such as printers) or information (such as files) on other computers that are connected to the same network. On a computer running Windows 10, connecting a computer to a network doesn't automatically allow users to access folders on other computers on the network. If you want to do so, you must first turn on network discovery. The network discovery feature enables the computer to "see and be seen by" other computers on the network that also have this feature turned on. Simply turning on network discovery doesn't automatically expose the information stored on your computer to other computers; you configure the sharing of specific folders and of Public folders individually on each computer. This helps to ensure that you don't accidentally share information that you don't want to.

 SEE ALSO For information about sharing folders and Public folders, see "Share files on your network" later in this chapter.

To connect to an available wired network

1. Plug one end of an Ethernet cable into the port on the network router or a switch box that is connected to the router.

2. Plug the other end of the cable into the Ethernet port on your computer.

To connect to an available wireless network

1. In the notification area of the taskbar, click the wireless connection icon to display a list of available connections.

2. In the connection list, click the network you want to connect to.

Connection options

3. If you want the computer to automatically connect to this network when it's available, select the **Connect automatically** check box.

> **TIP** Automatic connection is appropriate when connecting to a home network or another network that you trust. It works less well when connecting to a public network that has a gateway access page. If your computer establishes a connection, it might appear that you have Internet access when you actually don't. And you might not realize that you don't have a connection until you notice a dozen unsent messages in your email outbox.

4. Click the **Connect** button. If the network prompts you to enter credentials or a password (such as a WEP encryption key or WPA password) do so.

> **TIP** Wired Equivalent Privacy (WEP), Wi-Fi Protected Access (WPA), and Wi-Fi Protected Access II (WPA2) are security protocols that govern the credentials passed from a computer to a wireless network when establishing a connection. WPA2 is the most current of these.

To turn on network discovery

1. Open File Explorer.

2. In the **Navigation** pane, click **Network**. If network discovery is turned off, Windows displays this information on a banner below the ribbon.

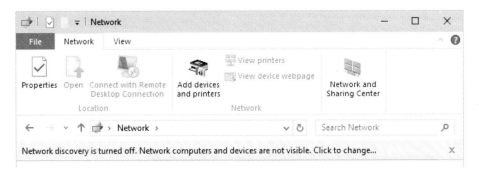

The Network list is empty until you turn on network discovery

3. Click the banner to display the Network Discovery And File Sharing message box. Because Windows 10 automatically designates new connections as Public networks, you must specify whether to permit network discovery on all Public networks.

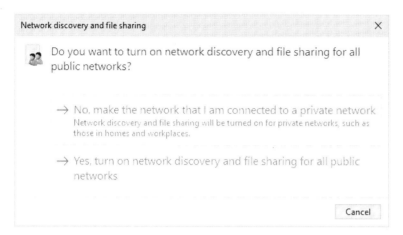

You can quickly turn on network discovery from File Explorer

> ⚠️ **IMPORTANT** You almost certainly do NOT want to click the Yes option in this dialog box. Doing so would keep the network connection Public and allow computers on other Public network connections to gain access to your computer.

4. Unless you specifically want to allow computers on Public networks to connect to your computer, click **No, make the network that I am connected to a private network** to change the network connection type to Private and turn on network sharing.

To disconnect from a wired network

1. Do either of the following:

   - Remove the cable from the Ethernet port on your computer or from the network connection point.

   - Disable the network adapter.

   > 🔍 **SEE ALSO** For information about disabling network adapters, see "Troubleshoot network connections" later in this topic.

To disconnect from a wireless network

1. In the notification area of the taskbar, click the wireless connection icon.

2. At the top of the list of network connections, click the network that is designated as Connected.

Disconnecting from a wireless network

3. Click the **Disconnect** button.

> **TIP** Unless you're connecting to a wireless network that is accessing the Internet over a cellular network, moving out of range of the network broadcast will automatically disconnect you.

Display information about networks and connections

After you connect to a network, you can display information such as which computers, printers, and other devices are connected to it. In File Explorer, the Network window displays the devices on your network that the current Public or Private security profile settings allow the computer to detect, and the devices that support the network infra-structure, such as the network router.

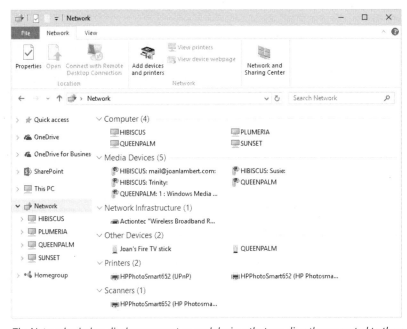

The Network window displays computers and devices that are directly connected to the network

TIP Your Network window will show the devices on your network rather than those shown in the images in this book.

From the Network window, you can access information and devices in different ways. For example:

- In the Computer list, double-click a computer to display the folders that are shared with you on that computer. Right-click a computer to display the shortcut menu, which has options for displaying content or starting a Remote Desktop Connection session.

   SEE ALSO For information about sharing files and folders on a network, see "Share files on your network" later in this chapter.

- In the Media Devices list, double-click a device to display the default media interface for that device, which might be Windows Media Player or a proprietary app for the operating system that is installed on the device.

- In the Network Infrastructure list, double-click a router to display its web management interface in your default web browser.

- In the Other Devices list, double-click a device to display properties such as the manufacturer, model, webpage, serial number, media access control (MAC) address, GUID, and IP address.

- In the Printers or Scanners list, double-click a device to display its web management interface, if it has one, in your default web browser.

Most of the device shortcut menus include options for displaying device webpages or properties. You can change the display of devices in the Network window from the View tab. In Details view, you can display properties such as the discovery method, MAC address, and IP address.

 SEE ALSO For more information about working with File Explorer views, see "Change the File Explorer display options" in Chapter 3, "Manage folders and files."

In Control Panel, the Network And Sharing Center displays information about the network (or networks) your computer is connected to, and the Internet status of each connection.

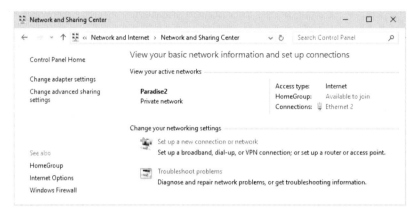

The Network And Sharing Center has links to tools you can use to manage network connections

Beyond the general network connection information, you can also display useful information about the connection speed and the data transfer to and from the computer. Each connection is linked to a network adapter, so you display the connection information by displaying the adapter information.

The speed varies with the signal quality, but also depends on other factors

New information sources in Windows 10 include information about the amount of data transfer by each app on the computer in the past 30 days.

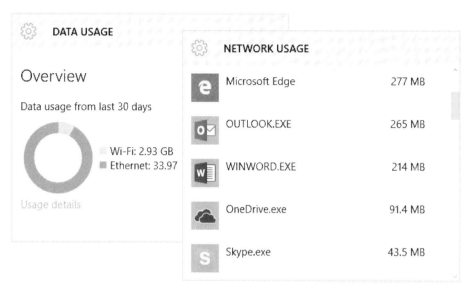

The Network Usage pane shows usage by individual apps and by the operating system

To display network device information in the Network window

1. Start File Explorer.

2. In the **Navigation** pane, click **Network**.

 TIP If network discovery is off, an error message appears when you click Network. For information about this, see "Configure network connection security" later in this topic.

To display network connection information in the Network And Sharing Center

1. Do any of the following:

    *   In the notification area of the taskbar, right-click the network icon, and then click **Open Network and Sharing center**.

    *   In the network connections pane, click **Network settings**. Scroll to the bottom of the pane that opens, and then click **Network and Sharing Center**.

    *   Open Control Panel in Category view. In the **Network and Internet** category, click **View network status and tasks**.

    *   Open Control Panel in Icons view, and then click **Network and Sharing Center**.

To display the status of all network adapters in the Network Connections window

1. Right-click the **Start** button, and then on the **Quick Links** menu, click **Network Connections**.

Or

1. Open the Network And Sharing Center.

2. In the left pane of the Network And Sharing Center, click **Change adapter settings**.

Or

1. Open the **Settings** window.

2. Display the **Network & Internet** category, and then either the **Wi-Fi** pane or the **Ethernet** pane.

3. Scroll to the bottom of the pane. In the **Related settings** section, click **Change adapter options** to open the **Network Connections** window.

To display network connection speed and data transfer information

1. Open the Network And Sharing Center.

2. In the **View your active networks** section, to the right of **Connections**, click the network adapter name.

Or

1. Open the **Network Connections** window.

2. Do one of the following:

   - Double-click the network adapter you want to display information for.

   - Click the network adapter to activate the toolbar buttons. Then, on the toolbar, click **View status of this connection**.

 TIP If the Network Connections window isn't wide enough to display all the buttons related to a selected adapter on the toolbar, chevrons appear at the right end of the toolbar. Click the chevrons to display the remaining commands.

To display data usage by app

1. In the **Settings** window, click **Network & Internet**.

2. Click **Data usage** to display the total amount of data transferred in the past 30 days, broken down by connection type.

3. In the **Data usage** pane, click **Usage details** to display the amount of data transferred by each app.

Configure network connection security

Each time you connect your computer to a network that you haven't previously connected to, Windows 10 associates the network connection with one of two security profiles, Private or Public, and then assigns the security settings configured for that profile to the network connection.

 TIP Previous versions of Windows prompted you to designate whether the network was at work, at home, or in a public place for the purpose of configuring appropriate security settings for the environment. Windows 10 has only Private and Public network security profiles.

The network security profiles include the following settings:

- **Network discovery** Determines whether the computer can see and be seen by other computers connected to the network.

- **File and printer sharing** Determines whether network users can access folders and printers that you configure for sharing from the computer.

- **HomeGroup connections** Determines whether user account credentials are necessary to connect to computers that are joined to your homegroup. Available only for the Private network security profile.

- **Public folder sharing** Determines whether network users can access files that are stored in the Public account folders on your computer.

- **Media streaming** Determines whether network users can access music, videos, and pictures that are stored in your media library.

- **File sharing connections** Determines the security requirements for devices that connect to your computer's file sharing connections.

- **Password-protected sharing** Determines whether shared files are available to any network user or only to those users with user accounts on your computer.

You can review and configure the settings for the individual security profiles and the security settings that apply to all network connections in the Advanced Sharing

Settings window. The window has three sections of settings: Private, Guest Or Public, and All Networks. You can expand or hide each section separately.

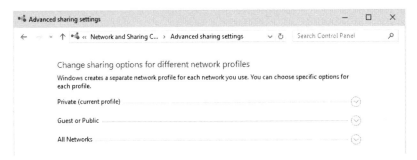

You can configure the settings for each network profile

The settings that are applied to all network connections are available in the All Networks section at the bottom of the window. These include settings for sharing Public folders, streaming media, protecting file-sharing connections, and specifying the type of credentials that are required to access the computer from another computer on the network.

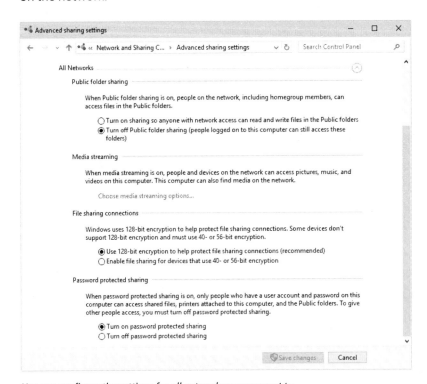

You can configure the settings for all networks you connect to

The settings that are applied to Guest or Public networks are intended for the types of networks that you might connect to in a public place, such as an airport or coffee shop, only for the purpose of connecting your computer to the Internet. You don't have a need to access information on other computers that are connected to a Public network, and it isn't a good idea to allow those other computers to access information on your computer. When you connect to any network that you don't explicitly trust, configure the connection as a Public network to protect your privacy.

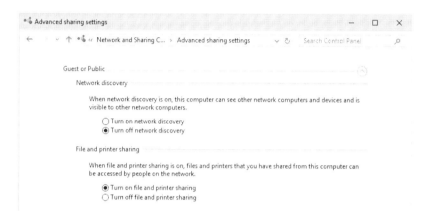

The Public network profile connects your computer to the network without exposing it to other network users

Windows 10 assumes that every network you connect to is Public until you tell it otherwise. Before you can access network resources from or on the computer, over the network, you must either change the network connection type from Public to Private, and turn on network discovery or create a homegroup.

 SEE ALSO For more information about homegroups, see "Manage homegroup connections" later in this chapter.

The settings that are applied to Private networks are intended for networks such as the network in your home or small business. If you connect computers and devices that only you use and control to the network and want to share information among the computers (for example, if you want to insert a picture stored on one computer into a document you're creating on a different computer) then the Private network security profile is the one for you.

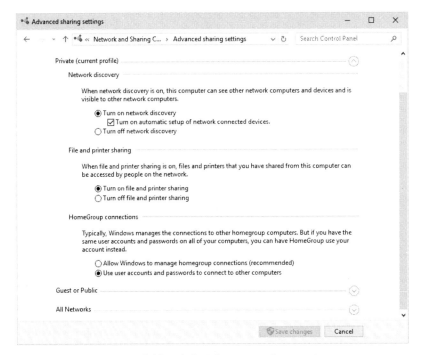

Homegroup settings are available only for Private network connections

If you share your network credentials with people who visit your home so that they can connect their laptops or mobile devices to the Internet through your network, be aware that assigning the Private network security profile to a computer will expose any information you choose to share from that computer with anyone you provide the network credentials to, should they choose to look for it.

 SEE ALSO For more information about sharing network resources with other people, see the sidebar "Wireless network security" later in this topic.

The Private network security profile connects your computer to the network and configures the network profile to include network discovery, file and printer sharing, Public folder sharing, media streaming, and password-protected sharing. Your computer is visible to other computers on the network. You don't necessarily have permission to access these computers or devices, but you know they're connected to the network, and other network members know that your computer is also connected.

> **TIP** If you're running Windows 10 on a computer in an enterprise environment, the computer and its network settings are likely managed by the IT department, and you won't have to concern yourself with these settings. You're more likely to encounter this situation when connecting a laptop computer or mobile device to a network, or if you have multiple computers on a home network.

You can change the settings for the Private security profile, the Public security profile, or all connections. When you do so, Windows automatically applies the new settings to all network connections.

Network discovery is controlled by the network security profile—it is off for Public networks and on for Private networks. In the Settings window, you can change the security profile for a specific network that you're connected to. The heading and text that precede the toggle button don't explain this clearly, but the toggle button changes the security profile rather than simply turning network discovery on or off.

 WI-FI 2

Find devices and content

Allow your PC to be discoverable by other PCs and devices on this network. We recommend turning this on for private networks at home or work, but turning it off for public networks to help keep your stuff safe.

 On

Change a network from Public to Private

> **TIP** At the time of this writing, most of the network configuration controls are in Control Panel, but we expect that, as updates to the operating system are released, more controls will move to the Settings window.

There will be instances in which you want to change the security profile that is assigned to a specific network connection. For example, if you connect to a wireless network at a friend's house and want to allow your friend to copy files from your computer over the network, you can change the network connection from Public to Private. (And when you finish, you can change it back so that the next time you connect to the network, your shared folders are protected.)

Wireless network security

If you have a wireless network router, it is important that you secure the network properly to prevent unauthorized users from connecting to it and gaining access to the computers on your network.

When you set up your wireless router, be sure to follow the instructions that come with it. For the initial setup, you'll usually be required to connect the router directly to a computer (by using an Ethernet cable) and run a setup program. After the router is set up, you can usually connect to it wirelessly by using its IP address on your network. During the setup process, you can do several things to increase the security of your wireless network, such as:

- Change the administrative password from the default password shared by all routers of that type to a unique, strong password. (Some manufacturers use the same password for all routers and some use blank passwords.)

- Secure the network with an appropriate level of encryption. Establish a WEP key or WPA password to prevent unauthorized users from connecting to your wireless network.

Your router configuration might offer multiple levels of WEP encryption, controlled by the length of the WEP key. A 10-character WEP key provides 64-bit encryption, and a 26-character key provides 128-bit encryption.

WPA encryption is a far more secure encryption standard than WEP encryption. If you have a gigabit network router (which transmits data at 1,000 kilobytes per second (KBps), as opposed to the standard 100 KBps), you should use WPA encryption. WPA encryption supports gigabit data transmission; WEP encryption does not.

When creating a security key or password, use a combination of letters and numbers that you can remember—for example, a series of birthdays, or your street address. If the key is particularly long or difficult, you might want to keep a printed copy of it handy for when visitors want to connect their mobile computers to your wireless network. Better yet, set up a Guest network that is isolated from the network that you connect your computers to. Guests can then access the Internet without also being able to locate or attempt to access the computers on your regular network.

To open the Advanced Sharing Settings window

1. Open the Network And Sharing Center.

2. In the left pane, click **Change advanced sharing settings**.

Or

1. Open the **Settings** window.

2. Display the **Network & Internet** category, and then display either the **Wi-Fi** pane or the **Ethernet** pane.

3. Scroll to the bottom of the pane. In the **Related settings** section, click **Change advanced sharing options** to open the **Network Connections** window.

To identify the security profile assigned to the current connection

1. Open the **Advanced Sharing Settings** window.

2. Review the three security profile headings. The phrase *current profile* appears in parentheses after the name of the active security profile.

To display or hide settings for a specific security profile

1. Click the chevron at the right end of the security profile heading.

The chevron reverses direction when the profile is expanded

To modify the settings for a network security profile

1. Open the **Advanced Sharing Settings** window.

2. Expand the security profile that you want to change.

3. Make your changes and then, at the bottom of the window, click the **Save changes** button. If you're signed in with a standard user account, Windows prompts you to provide administrative credentials.

4. If the **User Account Control** dialog box opens, select an administrative user account and enter its password, or have the person who owns the account do it for you.

To change the security profile assigned to a network connection

1. Open the **Settings** window.

2. Display the **Network & Internet** category, and then display the pane for the adapter that you want to configure.

3. Scroll to the bottom of the pane, and then click **Advanced options**.

4. In the **Find devices and content** section of the pane, click the toggle button to turn the setting on or off.

> **TIP** Computers running Windows 10 can easily coexist on a network with computers running earlier versions of Windows. Other computers and devices on the network do not affect the available network security profiles or their settings. However, network security profiles and homegroups aren't available on a computer running a version of Windows earlier than Windows 7.

Troubleshoot network connections

A network of any size includes several components that affect the network connection. Your network might include one or more wired routers, wireless routers, hubs, or switches. These hardware devices, the cables that connect them, and the external connection to your Internet service provider (ISP) can all develop problems or entirely quit functioning. A large organization usually has one or more network technicians (if not an entire IT department) who maintain the organization's hardware and keep the internal and external network connections running smoothly. In a small to medium organization, or in a household, it helps if you know enough about your network to be able to function as your own network technician. In this book, we provide information specifically about managing the network connections on a Windows 10 computer.

As mentioned earlier in this topic, the network adapter is the hardware on your computer's end of a network connection. A computer typically has one or two network adapters. You can monitor and manage network adapters and their current connections from the Network Connections window of Control Panel. This window displays connectivity information for each network adapter and for each dial-up or virtual private network (VPN) connection on your computer. A red X on an adapter icon indicates that the adapter is disabled or disconnected.

Select an adapter to display the applicable commands on the toolbar

If you experience connectivity issues, fixing them can be as simple as resetting the adapter.

When you experience a network or Internet connection problem, first determine whether the problem occurs only on your computer, or also on other computers on your network. You can frequently resolve connection issues by taking one of these simple actions:

- If the problem occurs on only one computer, reset the network adapter or restart the computer.

- If computers can connect to the network but not to the Internet, restart the router that connects your network to your ISP.

When you experience a connection problem beyond these simple issues, either when connecting to the Internet or when connecting to another computer on your network, you can use one of the handy troubleshooting tools included with Windows 10. These troubleshooting tools (referred to as *Troubleshooters*) can help you identify and resolve problems. Troubleshooters are available from Control Panel. Links to specific categories of Troubleshooters are available in the locations you're likely to be working when you experience problems.

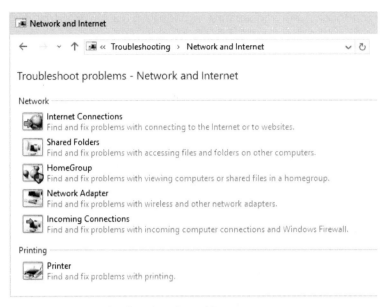

Troubleshooters can identify and resolve problems

> ⚠️ **IMPORTANT** The following procedures require administrative permission.

To disable a network adapter

1. Open the **Network Connections** window.

2. Click the adapter you want to disable.

3. On the toolbar, click **Disable this network device**. The icon and words that represent the disabled adapter change from color to grayscale, and the word *Disabled* appears below the adapter name.

A disabled network adapter

To enable a network adapter

1. In the **Network Connections** window, click the adapter you want to enable.

2. On the toolbar, click **Enable this network device**. The icon and words that represent the disabled adapter change from grayscale to color. If the adapter is configured to automatically connect to a network, it does so.

To reset a network adapter

1. In the **Network Connections** window, disable the adapter.

2. After the process of disabling the adapter completes, enable the adapter.

To display network troubleshooting tools

1. Open the Network And Sharing Center.

2. At the bottom of the right pane, click the **Troubleshoot problems** link to display the **Troubleshoot problems – Network and Internet** page of Control Panel.

To run a Troubleshooter

1. On the relevant **Troubleshoot problems** page, click the Troubleshooter you want to run, and then click **Next**. The Troubleshooter starts, scans your system, and then leads you through a diagnostic process.

   If the Troubleshooter finds an issue, it applies known fixes for the problem and reports its progress.

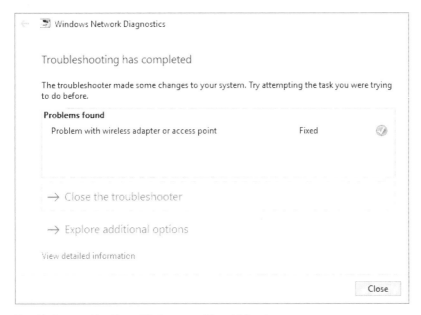

Troubleshooters identify and fix issues or offer additional resources

If the Troubleshooter doesn't identify any specific issues, it offers you the option to explore additional options.

2. Click **Close the troubleshooter** to quit the process, or click **Explore additional options** to display a list of pertinent resources.

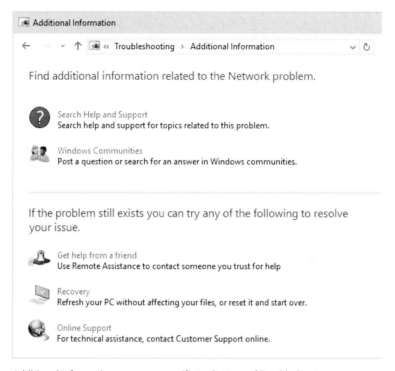

Additional Information pages are specific to the type of Troubleshooter

Manage homegroup connections

When your computer is connected to a Private network, computer users can connect to resources on other computers either through the network or through a homegroup. You can think of a homegroup as a private network that allows secure access to specific resources, such as files and printers, stored on the computers that are joined to it. Only one homegroup can exist on a local network; it exists as long as it has at least one member. (If your environment has multiple networks, each can have one homegroup.) The homegroup doesn't have a name, a designated administrator, or a management interface.

TIP Homegroups were introduced in Windows 7 and are not accessible to computers running earlier versions of Windows or a non-Windows operating system.

When a homegroup exists on a Private network, other computers on that network can join the homegroup. The only information you need to join the homegroup is the homegroup password, which Windows generates randomly when the homegroup is created. If the homegroup password isn't readily available, it's quite simple to locate.

You can change the random password to something that is easier to remember

If you want to change the password, it's best to do so immediately after you create the homegroup because changing the password immediately disconnects any computers that joined by using the original password. Alternatively, you can have Windows validate your identity when joining multiple computers to the homegroup by using your user account credentials.

You can create and manage homegroup connections from two separate places:

- The HomeGroup window of Control Panel, which displays commands as links

- The Homegroup node in File Explorer, which displays commands on a ribbon

You can create or join a computer to a homegroup when signed in with a Standard or Administrator user account. When you start the process of connecting a computer to a homegroup, Windows 10 tells you whether a homegroup already exists on the network.

Homegroup membership is on a per-computer basis, not a per-user basis. (In other words, the computer joins the homegroup, not the user.) When any user of a computer that has multiple user accounts joins the computer to a homegroup, the computer is joined to the homegroup on behalf of all its users. However, each user has control over the resources that he or she shares with other homegroup members.

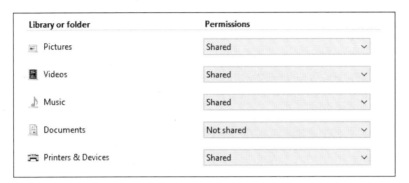

By default, all libraries other than the Documents library are selected for sharing

> **SEE ALSO** For information about libraries, see "Understand files, folders, and libraries" in Chapter 3, "Manage folders and files." For information about changing the resources shared with your homegroup, see "Share files on your network" later in this chapter.

On a multiple-user computer, if another user joins your computer to a homegroup, it doesn't share any of your user account folders. You can specify your homegroup resource sharing settings at any time from either homegroup window. When another user has shared the computer, a message appears in the homegroup window.

Each user sets individual sharing settings

The only resource sharing setting that is common to all user accounts of a home-group member computer is the Printers & Devices setting, which controls access to the Devices And Printers folder. When any user shares or excludes this folder from the shared homegroup resources, the printer is shared or excluded on behalf of the computer rather than the user.

If at any time you decide that you no longer want to share resources with other home-group members, you can remove your computer from the homegroup with no adverse effects. It is not necessary to disconnect from the network. If you have any problems with the homegroup, Windows 10 has a built-in troubleshooting tool that can help you to diagnose and fix homegroup problems.

 SEE ALSO For more information about Troubleshooters, see "Troubleshoot network connections" earlier in this chapter.

To open the Homegroup window in File Explorer

1. In the **Navigation** pane of File Explorer, click the **Homegroup** node. If a home-group already exists on the network, the window contains a **Join now** button. If no homegroup exists, the window contains a **Create a homegroup** button.

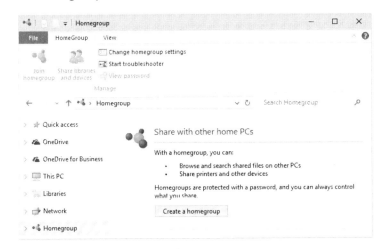

The Homegroup window in File Explorer

To open the HomeGroup window of Control Panel

1. Do any of the following:

    - In Category view of Control Panel, under **Network and Internet**, click **Choose homegroup and sharing options**.

    - In Large Icons view or Small Icons view of Control Panel, click **Homegroup**.

    - In File Explorer, right-click the **Homegroup** node, and then click **Change HomeGroup settings**.

    - In File Explorer, open the **Homegroup** window. Then on the **HomeGroup** tab, click **Change homegroup settings**.

If a homegroup already exists on the network, the window contains a Join now button. If no homegroup exists, the window contains a Create a homegroup button.

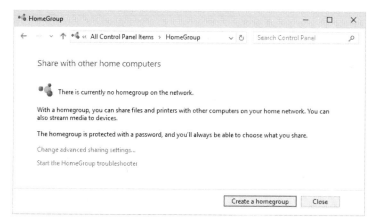

The HomeGroup window of Control Panel

To create a homegroup

1. Open the **HomeGroup** window of Control Panel or the **Homegroup** window in File Explorer.

2. Click the **Create a homegroup** button to start the **Create a Homegroup** wizard. On the first page of the wizard, click **Next**.

3. On the **Share with other homegroup members** page of the wizard, do the following for each folder or library:

   • If you want to share the resource, click **Shared** in the **Permissions** list adjacent to it.

   • If you want to keep the resource private, click **Not shared** in the **Permissions** list adjacent to it.

    SEE ALSO For information about changing the resources you've shared through a homegroup, see "Share files on your network" later in this chapter.

4. Click **Next** to create the homegroup and display the homegroup password.

5. If you want to print the password, do the following:

   a. On the **Use this password to add other computers to your homegroup** page of the wizard, click **Print password and instructions**.

b. On the **View and print your homegroup password** page of the wizard, click the **Print this page** button.

c. In the **Print** dialog box, select a printer, and then click **Print**.

6. If you don't want to print the password, manually record it in a convenient location (write it down or save a screen clipping in OneNote).

7. Click **Finish** to display your homegroup resource sharing settings and options for working with the homegroup.

To display the password for an existing homegroup

1. Sign in to any computer that is joined to the homegroup.

> **TIP** You might have to ask another person to sign in to a computer that is connected to the homegroup and retrieve the password for you.

2. Do any of the following:

    *   Open the **HomeGroup** window of Control Panel, and then click the **View or print the homegroup password** link.

    *   In File Explorer, right-click the **Homegroup** node, and then click **View the HomeGroup password**.

    *   In File Explorer, open the **Homegroup** window. Then on the **HomeGroup** tab, click the **View password** button.

> ⚠ **IMPORTANT** You can perform the following procedure only if you have multiple computers on a Private network and a homegroup has been created from another computer on the network.

To discard the password requirement for a homegroup

1. Open the Network And Sharing Center.

2. In the left pane, click **Change advanced sharing settings**.

3. In the **Advanced sharing settings** window, expand the **Private** security profile.

4. In the **HomeGroup connections** section of the profile, click **Use user accounts and passwords to connect to other computers**.

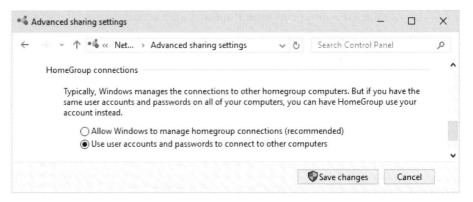

Change the default homegroup password settings only if necessary

5. Click **Save changes**, and then sign out of Windows to apply your changes to the homegroup.

To join a computer to an existing homegroup

1. If you haven't already joined a computer to the homegroup when logged in with the current user account, obtain the homegroup password.

 TIP The homegroup doesn't require an existing user to enter the password when joining additional computers to the homegroup.

2. Do either of the following:

   - Open the **HomeGroup** window of Control Panel.

   - Open the **Homegroup** window in File Explorer.

3. Click the **Join now** button to start the **Join a Homegroup** wizard. On the first page of the wizard, click **Next**.

4. On the **Share with other homegroup members** page, designate each folder or library as **Shared** or **Not shared**, and then click **Next**.

 SEE ALSO For information about changing the resources you've shared through a homegroup, see "Share files on your network" later in this chapter.

5. If the wizard displays the **Type the homegroup password** page, enter the password you obtained in step 1, and then click **Next**.

6. On the **You have joined the homegroup** page of the wizard, click **Finish**.

To connect to homegroup resources

1. In the **Navigation** pane of File Explorer, expand the **Homegroup** node to display the user accounts that have shared resources through the homegroup.

2. Expand each user account to display the computers or devices the user has shared resources from.

3. Expand each computer or device to display the specific shared folders, libraries, and devices. Devices that are offline or sleeping aren't shown.

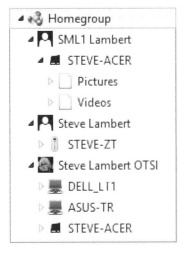

Directory of Homegroup users and computers

4. Click any user account, device, or shared item to display its contents in File Explorer.

To disconnect all other computers from a homegroup

1. Change the homegroup password.

To change a homegroup password

1. In the **HomeGroup** window of Control Panel, in the **Other homegroup actions** section, click **Change the password** to start the **Change your Homegroup Password** wizard. If you're logged in as a Standard user, provide the credentials of an Administrator account when prompted to do so.

> **TIP** You can't change the password from the Homegroup window in File Explorer.

2. On the **Changing the homegroup password will disconnect everyone** page of the wizard, read and heed the warning. Then when you've prepared the homegroup-joined computers, click **Change the password**.

3. On the **Type a new password for your homegroup** page of the wizard, enter the new password (or accept the new randomly generated password), and then click **Next**.

4. On the **Your homegroup password was successfully changed** page of the wizard, click **Finish**.

To reconnect computers to a homegroup after changing the password

1. On each computer, display the **HomeGroup** window of Control Panel or the **Homegroup** window in File Explorer.

2. Click the **Type new password** button to start the **Update Your Homegroup Password** wizard.

3. Enter the new password, click **Next**, and then click **Finish**.

To remove a computer from a homegroup

1. Open the Network And Sharing Center.

2. In the **Change your networking settings** section, click **Choose homegroup and sharing options**.

TIP The Choose Homegroup And Sharing Options link is available only when the computer is joined to a homegroup.

3. In the **HomeGroup** window of Control Panel, click **Leave the homegroup** to start the **Leave the Homegroup** wizard.

4. On the first page of the wizard, click **Leave the homegroup**.

5. When the wizard confirms that the computer has successfully been removed from the homegroup, click **Finish**.

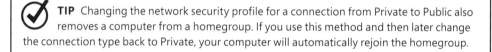 **TIP** Changing the network security profile for a connection from Private to Public also removes a computer from a homegroup. If you use this method and then later change the connection type back to Private, your computer will automatically rejoin the homegroup.

To delete a homegroup

1. Remove each member computer from the homegroup.

To run the HomeGroup troubleshooter

1. Do any of the following:

   - Open the **HomeGroup** window of Control Panel and then, in the **Other homegroup actions** section, click the **Start the HomeGroup trouble-shooter** link.

   - In File Explorer, right-click the **Homegroup** node, and then click **Start the HomeGroup troubleshooter**.

   - In File Explorer, open the **Homegroup** window. Then on the **HomeGroup** tab, click the **Start troubleshooter** button.

Share files on your network

If you have more than one computer in your organization, you might find it convenient to share files and file storage locations with other people on your network. And if you have more than one computer in your household, you might want to share resources with family members, whether or not your computer is joined to a homegroup. For example, you might:

- Share project-related files with specific team members.

- From your laptop computer, work on a file that is stored on your desktop computer.

- Share household management documents with your family members.

- Collect all your family photos in one place by having all your family members save their digital photos to a shared external hard drive.

There are several ways to share files with users (including yourself) who are logged on to other computers in your network. To share files by using any of these methods, you must first make sure network discovery and file and printer sharing are turned on so that your computer and any resources you choose to share are visible to other network computers and devices. Network discovery and file and printer sharing are turned on by default for Private network connections.

> **TIP** When network discovery is on, your computer is visible in the Navigation pane of File Explorer and in the Network window. When file and printer sharing is on, any resources you choose to share from the computer are also visible in the Network window.

You can configure file sharing options only when network discovery, file sharing, and printer sharing are turned on.

When you share a folder, you can specify the people (in the form of user accounts or groups of users) you are sharing the folder with and what each person (or group) can do with the folder contents. The permission level options are:

- **Read** The user can open a file from the shared folder but cannot save any changes to the file in the shared folder.

- **Read/Write** The user can open and edit a file and save changes to the file in the shared folder.

The default permission level is Read. If you want to allow a network user or group of users to modify shared files, you must explicitly assign the Read/Write permission level.

 TIP Files and printers that you share are available only when your computer is on, and not when it is in Sleep mode.

Files that you store in the Public folders (Public Documents, Public Downloads, Public Music, Public Pictures, and Public Videos) are accessible to any user logged on to your computer. If you choose to share the Public folders on your computer with other computers on your network, their contents are visible to any user connected to your network. Public folder sharing with other network computer users is turned on by default for Private and Public network connections.

If you frequently connect to public networks, consider carefully whether you want to share the contents of your computer's Public folders with strangers. If not, you can easily turn off this feature to safeguard your privacy.

When your computer is a member of a homegroup, you can share files with other homegroup members while still keeping the files hidden from computers that aren't homegroup members. (Remember that computers, rather than users, are the home-group members.) When you first create or join your computer to a homegroup, you have the option of sharing the built-in Documents, Pictures, Music, and/or Videos libraries. The choices you make at that time are not binding; you can change the library selections at any time. You can add or remove libraries from the shared home-group resources at any time. Files that you store in a library that you share with your homegroup, whether in your personal folders or the Public folders, are accessible to any user logged on to a computer that is a member of the homegroup.

Regardless of whether your computer is a member of a homegroup, you can share a folder, or a built-in or custom library with users of other computers on your network. You can control access to the shared folder or library by specifying the user accounts or groups of users who can access the shared resource and assigning a specific level of access for each user account or group.

You can share an entire storage drive—either a disk drive that is built in to your computer, or an internal or external storage device such as a freestanding storage disk or a USB flash drive. For example, you might share an internal hard disk drive on which you store only project-related resources with all the computers on your work network so that your co-workers have access to them, or you might share an external hard disk drive with all the computers on your home network so that all your family members can save digital photos in one place for safekeeping.

To configure your computer to share files with other network computer users

1. Open the Network And Sharing Center.

2. In the left pane, click **Change advanced sharing settings**.

3. In the **Advanced sharing settings** window, expand the **Private** profile, and then do the following:

   • In the **Network discovery** section, click **Turn on network discovery**.

   • In the **File and printer sharing** section, click **Turn on file and printer sharing**.

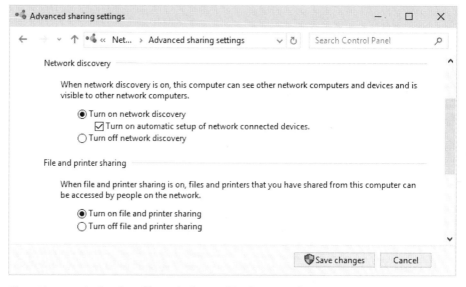

The settings required to share files and printers with other network computer users

4. At the bottom of the **Advanced sharing settings** window, click **Save changes**. (If you didn't make any changes, click **Cancel**.)

To prevent network users from accessing your Public folders

1. In the left pane of the Network And Sharing Center, click **Change advanced sharing settings**.

2. In the **Advanced Sharing Settings** window, expand the **All Networks** profile.

3. In the **Public folder sharing** section of the profile, click **Turn off Public folder sharing**.

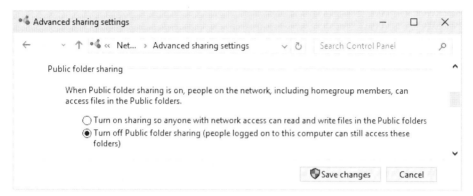

With this setting off, the Public account folders on your computer can be accessed only from your computer, and not from the network

4. At the bottom of the **Advanced Sharing Settings** window, click **Save changes**.

> **SEE ALSO** For more information about Public folders, see Chapter 3, "Manage folders and files." For information about the Network And Sharing Center, see the "Connect to a network" section in the topic "Manage network connections" earlier in this chapter.

To change the resources that you're sharing with a homegroup

1. Do either of the following to start the **Change Homegroup Sharing Settings** wizard:

   - Display the **HomeGroup** window of Control Panel, and then click **Change what you're sharing with the homegroup**.

   - Display the **Homegroup** window in File Explorer. On the **HomeGroup** tab, click the **Share libraries and devices** button.

2. On the **Share with other homegroup members** page of the wizard, do the following for each folder or library, and then click **Next**:

   - If you want to share the resource, click **Shared** in the **Permissions** list adjacent to it.

   - If you want to keep the resource private, click **Not shared** in the **Permissions** list adjacent to it.

3. On the **Your sharing settings have been updated** page of the wizard, click **Finish**.

> **SEE ALSO** For more information about homegroups, see "Manage homegroup connections" earlier in this chapter.

> ✓ **TIP** Custom libraries that you create on your computer aren't among those listed in the wizard. You can share a custom library by following the procedure for sharing individual folders and libraries.

To share a folder or library through a homegroup

1. Do one of the following to display a menu of user accounts on network-connected computers, and other sharing options:

   - In File Explorer, right-click the folder or library you want to share, and then click **Share with**.

Sharing options from the folder shortcut menu

TIP The Share With arrow points to the right, but the Share With menu always opens to the left.

- In File Explorer, display the folder or library you want to share. On the **Share** tab, click the **More** button at the bottom of the **Share with** gallery scroll bar.

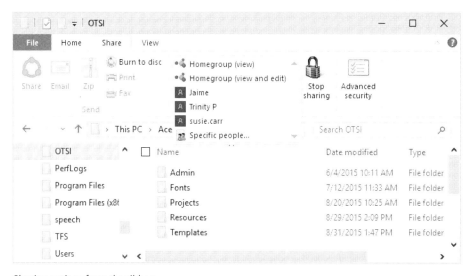

Sharing options from the ribbon

 TIP If the computer is not joined to a homegroup, the Share With menu has a Create Or Join A Homegroup option instead of the Homegroup options.

2. In the **Share with** gallery, do one of the following to select the level of access that users of homegroup-joined computers will have to the folder:

- To allow homegroup users to display the folder and open (but not edit) files stored in the folder, click **Homegroup (view)**.

- To allow homegroup users to edit files stored in the folder, click **Homegroup (view and edit)**.

If the folder you share that requires administrator permission to access, or contains a subfolder that requires administrator permissions, Windows prompts you to confirm that you want to share the restricted items.

To share these items, Windows requires your permission. If you click No, selected items won't be shared.

🛡 Yes, share the items.

→ No, don't share the items.

Restricted items are shared only if you give explicit permission

3. In the **File Sharing** dialog box, do one of the following:

    *   To share the folder and all its contents, click **Yes, share the items**.

    *   To share only the unrestricted items in the folder, click **No, don't share the items**.

    *   To cancel the sharing process so you can review the restricted items, click the **Cancel** button.

To share a folder or library with one person

1. Display the **Share with** menu for the folder, and then click the user account name or email address of the person you want to share the folder with.

To share a folder or library with everyone on your network

1. Display the **Share with** menu for the folder, and then click **Specific people...** to open the **File Sharing** window.

2. In the **File Sharing** window, click the chevron at the right end of the empty box to display a list that includes of people and groups you can share the folder with.

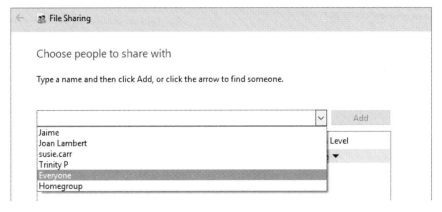

Share the folder with a specific person or group

3. In the list, click **Everyone**. Then click the **Add** button.

4. If you want to allow network users to edit files stored in the folder, click the arrow in the **Permission Level** column adjacent to **Everyone**, and then click **Read/Write**.

5. In the **File Sharing** window, click the **Share** button. After sharing the folder, the window displays the shared folder's information.

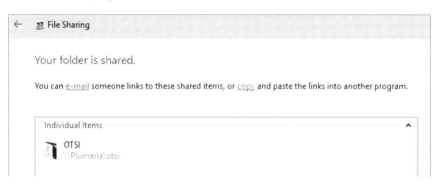

You can quickly share a link to the folder with other people

 TIP When you select a shared file or folder in File Explorer, the Details pane displays a list of the people or groups the folder is shared with.

To stop sharing a folder or library

1. Do one of the following:

    -   In File Explorer, right-click the folder, click **Share with**, and then click **Stop sharing**.

    -   In File Explorer, display the folder or library you want to stop sharing. On the **Share** tab, in the **Share with** group, click the **Stop sharing** button.

To make shared resources available to people who don't have user accounts on your computer

1. In the left pane of the Network And Sharing Center, click **Change advanced sharing settings**.

2. In the **Advanced sharing settings** window, expand the **All Networks** profile.

3. In the **Password protected sharing** section, click **Turn off password protected sharing**.

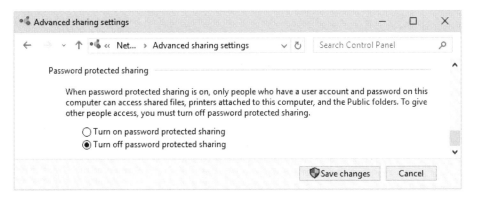

Turn this setting off to allow any network user to access your shared files and printers

4. At the bottom of the **Advanced Sharing Settings** window, click the **Save changes** button.

> **TIP** If you collaborate with a team of people on a document, working with the document in a shared folder entails the risk of one person overwriting another person's changes, even if you restrict access to the folder. To eliminate this risk, you need to use a system with version control. If your organization uses SharePoint, you can store the document in a document library so that only one person at a time can check out and work on the document.

To share a drive

1. In File Explorer, do one of the following:

   - Display the drive you want to share. On the **Share** tab, in the **Share with** gallery, click **Advanced sharing....**

   - Right-click the drive you want to share, and then click **Properties**.

   - Right-click the drive you want to share, click **Share with**, and then click **Advanced sharing....**

Sharing options for a drive

 TIP Remember that if the shared drive is removable, it is shared only until it is removed.

2. In the **Properties** dialog box for the drive, click the **Sharing** tab, and then click the **Advanced Sharing** button. If Windows prompts you to enter administrator credentials, do so.

3. In the **Advanced Sharing** dialog box, select the **Share this folder** check box.

4. The **Share name** box displays the drive letter of the drive you're sharing. If you want to replace the drive letter with a more user-friendly name to distinguish it from other network drives, enter the name in this box.

You can identify a shared drive by its drive letter or you can assign it a name

5. Click the **Permissions** button to display the share permissions for the drive.

6. If the group or user name you want to share with is not listed in the **Group or user names** box, click the **Add** button, and then do the following:

   a. In the **Select Users or Groups** dialog box, enter the name of the user account, group, or computer you want to share the drive with, and then click the **Check Names** button.

You can enter multiple names, separated by semicolons

> **TIP** To display a list of valid users and groups, click the Advanced button and then, in the secondary Select Users Or Groups dialog box that opens, click Find Now.

   b. After Windows indicates a valid name by underlining it, click **OK** to return to the **Permissions** dialog box.

7. In the **Group or user names** box, select the user account or group you want to share the drive with.

8. In the **Permissions for** list, select the check boxes of the permission levels you want to grant to the user account or group.

You can set the permission level for each user account or group

9. In the **Permissions** dialog box, click **Apply** to apply the selected permissions.

10. Click **OK** in the **Permissions** dialog box and in the **Advanced Sharing** dialog box. Then close the drive's **Properties** dialog box.

Skills review

In this chapter, you learned how to:

- Manage network connections
- Manage homegroup connections
- Share files on your network

Change the computer name

When your computer was initially set up by the original equipment manufacturer (OEM) it was assigned a default name, probably based on its make or model. Our Windows 10 test computers, along with thousands of others, were named *acer*. When network discovery is turned on, the computer name is displayed to other network users. On your computer, the name is displayed in the System panel and in the System category of settings.

During the process of installing or upgrading to Windows 10, the installation wizard might suggest another name, perhaps one based on your account name, such as *Steve-PC*.

The name isn't really important, as long as it is unique within your local network. However, you might want to assign a name that makes it easier for you and other network users to identify it—such as *OfficePC*, *GuestLaptop*, *BetaTest*, or *GamingPC*—or that follows a themed naming convention you have for your network—such as *Hibiscus*, *Plumeria*, and *QueenPalm* on a network named *Paradise*.

IMPORTANT You must be signed in with an Administrator account to rename your computer.

To rename your computer, follow these steps:

1. In the **Settings** window, click **System**, and then click **About**. The About pane displays your current computer name, organization association, operating system version and product ID, and hardware information.

About your computer

2. In the **About** pane, below your current computer name, click the **Rename PC** button to open the **Rename your PC** dialog box.

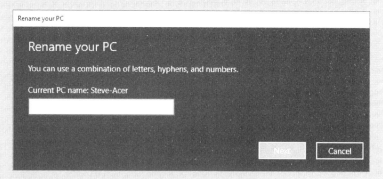

Rename your PC

3. In the input box below your current computer name, enter the new name. The name can include uppercase and lowercase letters, numbers (0-9), and hyphens, but no other symbols. Then click **Next**.

    IMPORTANT Clicking *Next* irrevocably commits you to the name change. You can't change the name again until after you restart the computer.

    After a short process, the dialog box displays a restart notice. You can restart the computer now or later; the name change takes effect after the restart.

Practice tasks

The practice file for these tasks is the Win10SBS\Ch07 folder. Some of the practice tasks require that you have access to and any credentials required for a network connection.

Manage network connections

Complete the following tasks:

1. In the notification area of the taskbar, point to the network icon to display information about your current network connection status.

2. Click the network icon to display a list of available networks.

3. If your computer is not currently connected to a network and one is available, click that network name, and connect to it.

4. Right-click the network icon, and then click **Network and Sharing Center**.

5. In the **Network and Sharing Center**, review the information about your active network connection.

6. Click the connection name to display its status. Notice the information about the connection speed, duration, and activity. Then close the **Status** dialog box.

7. In the left pane, click **Change adapter settings** to display the network adapters available on your computer. Notice the adapter types that are available and whether each is enabled, disabled, or connected.

8. Click any adapter to select it. Notice the toolbar buttons that become active. Note that you can enable or disable the adapters and diagnose, rename, or change the settings of the current connection.

9. Return to the **Network and Sharing Center**. In the left pane, click **Change advanced sharing settings** to display the sharing options for the different network profiles.

10. Note the type of network that your computer is currently connected to. Review the settings for that network security profile.

11. Return to the **Network and Sharing Center**. Click the **Troubleshoot problems** link to display the network troubleshooting tools. Run any troubleshooter that interests you.

12. On the **Start** menu, click **Settings** to open the Settings window. Click the **Network & Internet** category, and then display the **Data usage** pane.

13. Review the historical information about data transfers by connection type.

14. In the **Data usage** pane, click **Usage details** to display the amount of data transferred by each app.

15. When you finish, close the open windows.

Manage homegroup connections

Complete the following tasks:

1. Open the **HomeGroup** window of Control Panel.

2. Determine whether your computer is currently part of a homegroup. If it isn't, determine whether a homegroup is available to join.

3. If your computer is not connected to a homegroup, do either of the following:

   - If no homegroup is available, create a homegroup.

   - If a homegroup is available, join the homegroup.

   Or

   If your computer is connected to a homegroup, do any of the following that interest you:

   - Display the homegroup password.

   - Display the homegroup resources in File Explorer.

   - Disconnect from the homegroup.

Share files on your network

Complete the following tasks:

1. Display the **Network and Sharing Center**, and then open the **Advanced sharing settings** window.

2. Review the **Private** network security profile settings, and verify that network discovery and file and printer sharing are turned on, so that your computer can detect and connect to other computers on private networks.

3. In the **Advanced Sharing Settings** window, expand the **All Networks** profile.

4. In the **Public folder sharing** section of the profile, turn on or off the sharing of Public folders from your computer. (Choose the option you want.)

5. Save your changes and close the **Advanced sharing settings** window.

6. Start File Explorer and locate the practice file folder for this book.

7. Click the **Ch07** folder to select it. On the **Share** tab, notice your options for sharing the folder with other people. If you want to, follow the procedure for sharing the folder with everyone on your network.

8. If you have access to another computer on the network, verify that the folder is available from that computer.

9. On your computer, stop sharing the **Ch07** folder.

10. When you're done, close the File Explorer window.

Part 3

Behind the scenes

CHAPTER 8
Manage user accounts and settings 345

CHAPTER 9
Manage computer settings 385

CHAPTER 10
Manage power and access options 425

CHAPTER 11
Work more efficiently 463

CHAPTER 12
Protect your computer and data 511

Manage user accounts and settings

Computers have become an integral part of our lives. We store personal and business information on them, and use them to access financial and social information online. That information might be protected by a password, but the password could easily be accessible to any other person who is using your computer. To protect your privacy and the integrity of your information, it is important to control who can sign in to your computer or tablet, and what they can do when they're signed in.

Computer access is managed through user accounts. Each individual user of a computer, regardless of age, should sign in with his or her own account. Each user account has access to a private file storage area and user interface customizations, and to a shared public file storage area. Accounts designated as Child accounts have additional safeguards that are designed to protect them from content that isn't age appropriate.

When you sign in to your computer, you have a myriad of options available for doing so. User accounts can be protected by passwords, but users can choose alternative sign-in credentials such as PINs, picture passwords, and biometric identification.

This chapter guides you through procedures related to creating and managing user accounts, managing account pictures and passwords, and customizing your sign-in options.

In this chapter

- Understand user accounts and permissions

- Create and manage user accounts

- Manage account pictures and passwords

- Customize your sign-in options

Practice files

For this chapter, use the practice files from the Win10SBS\Ch08 folder. For practice file download instructions, see the introduction.

Understand user accounts and permissions

Windows 10 requires at least one user account. You specify that account when you're completing the installation processes, or the first time the computer starts after Windows 10 has been installed. Windows 10 designates this first account as an administrator account so that the account can be used to manage the computer. It isn't possible to sign on to the computer without a user account.

There are a lot of uses of the word "user" and "account" in this book, and particularly in this chapter. Here's a summary of the uses of those terms:

- A *user* is the person who is using the computer.

- A *user account* is an account that a person uses to sign in to a computer.

Each user account is either:

- A *Microsoft account*, which is any email address that has been registered with the Microsoft account service

- A *local account* that exists only on a single computer and is not associated with a specific email address

You can use your Microsoft account to sign in to multiple computers, websites, and services by using the same email address and password. Signing in with your Microsoft account credentials allows you to share settings and files among all your devices. Any device you sign in to with this account can have access to the same settings and information. Signing in with a local account places limits on the applications you can purchase or download from the Store, and might limit your access to OneDrive. Because almost any email account can also be set up to be a Microsoft account, it's a good idea to take advantage of the extra benefits that allows.

Every user account is also classified as either:

- An *Administrator account*

- A *Standard User account*

This classification provides a specific level of permission to manage system actions on the computer. We explain what each of these types of accounts can do in the next section of this topic.

A user account can also be one of the following:

- A *Child account* that is monitored by using Family Safety

- An *Adult account* that can manage Family Safety settings for Child accounts

These are optional designations that make the user account holder part of your family group. We explain family safety in the sidebar "Manage and monitor family safety settings" later in this chapter.

 IMPORTANT The information in this chapter applies to computer user accounts (sometimes referred to as local user accounts) and not to network domain user accounts.

User profiles

Windows provides the ability to share one computer among multiple users, or for one user to have multiple accounts for different purposes. To do this, each user account (whether a Microsoft account or a local account) is associated with a user profile that describes the way the computer environment (the user interface) looks and operates for that user. This information includes simple things such as the desktop background, desktop content, and Windows color scheme. It also includes personal and confidential information, such as saved passwords and your Internet browsing history.

Each user profile includes a personal folder that is not generally accessible by other people who are using the computer, in which you can store documents, pictures, media, and other files that you want to keep private.

The Windows 10 system of user profiles allows more than one person to use the same computer while providing the following safeguards:

- **Each user's information is stored separately** You prevent Standard Users from reading or altering your documents, pictures, music, and other files by storing them in subfolders that are automatically set up within your user account folder. For example, if you manage your family's financial records on a home computer that your children use to do their homework, the children log in with separate accounts and don't have access to confidential information or the ability to change your files. Administrators can access all user accounts.

- **Each user's working environment is protected** You can personalize your environment in various ways, without worrying about other people making changes to your personal settings.

- **Each user's app usage is unique** Each user runs separate instances of each app on the computer. For example, you can set up Outlook to connect to your accounts, and other computer users can set up Outlook to connect to their accounts, but they cannot also connect to your accounts. Each user's data is stored and managed separately.

User account permissions

The system actions that a user can perform are governed by the type of account he or she signs in with. An administrator account has higher-level permissions than a standard user account, which means that an administrator account owner can perform tasks on your computer that a standard user account owner cannot.

Standard user account credentials allow a user to do things that affect only his or her account, including:

- Change or remove the password.

- Change the user account picture.

- Change the theme and desktop settings.

- View files stored in his or her personal folders and files in the Public folders.

Administrator account credentials are necessary to do things such as:

- Create, change, and delete accounts.

- Change settings that affect all of the computer's users.

- Change security-related settings.

- Install and remove apps.

- Access system files and files in other user account profiles.

Tasks that require administrator permission are indicated in windows and dialog boxes by a Windows security icon.

User Accounts
🛡 Change account type

The Windows security icon is shaped like a shield

If you have an administrator account—even if you're the only person who will be using your computer—it's a good idea to create and use a standard user account for your day-to-day computing. There is a much higher risk of serious damage to a computer system if malware infiltrates your computer (or a malicious person gains control of it) when you're signed in as an administrator than there is when you're signed in as a standard user. Through an administrator account, the person or app has access to all system files and settings, whereas a standard user account doesn't have access to certain functions that can permanently damage the system.

Family accounts

Many children use computers for educational or entertainment purposes. Each child should have a unique Microsoft account that you designate as a Child account. For each Child account, you (and other adults you designate as family members) can do the following:

- Monitor web browsing history, app use, and game use.

- Block websites that contain adult content, or allow young children to visit only specific websites.

- Restrict the usage of apps and games to only those that meet specific age ratings.

- Monitor screen time, and restrict computer usage to only specific times or to a specific number of hours per day.

- Manage payment options and monitor purchases in the Windows Store and Xbox Store.

You can monitor children's activity on every computer or device they sign in to with their Microsoft accounts.

You can check on your child's recent computer usage on the Family page of your Microsoft account website (at *account.microsoft.com*) at any time, and you can opt to receive weekly reports summarizing your child's computer use.

> **SEE ALSO** For more information about monitoring and managing children's computer activity, see the sidebar "Manage and monitor family safety settings" later in this chapter.

User Account Control

User Account Control (UAC) protects your computer from changes to Windows system settings by requiring that an administrator expressly permit certain types of changes. Each area of the Windows interface that requires administrator permission is labeled with a security icon. When you attempt to access or change protected Windows settings, a User Account Control dialog box appears, asking for confirmation that Windows should continue the operation.

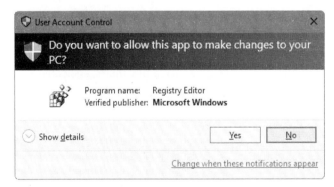

The User Account Control message box varies depending on your account and the action

If you're signed in with an administrator account, you can simply click the Yes button to continue the operation. If you're signed in with a standard user account, the message box displays a list of the administrator accounts on the computer. To continue the operation, you click one of the administrator accounts, enter its password in the box that appears, and then click Yes.

TIP If an administrator account doesn't have an associated password, you can continue the operation by simply clicking that account and then clicking Yes. This is one of the reasons that it's important that each administrator account on the computer has a password.

Windows doesn't save the credentials you enter in the User Account Control message box; they are valid for this operation only. Anyone who doesn't have access to administrator credentials can't perform the operation, which effectively prevents non-administrators from making changes you haven't authorized.

UAC has four levels of control. Only the first two are available when you're signed in with a standard user account, even if you have access to administrator credentials:

- **Always notify me** This is the default setting for a Standard User account. When a user or app initiates a change that requires administrator credentials, the desktop dims and the User Account Control message box opens. You must respond to the message box before you can take any other action.

- **Notify me only when apps try to make changes to my computer** This is the default setting for an Administrator account. When an app initiates a change that requires administrator credentials, the desktop dims and the User Account Control message box opens. You must respond to the dialog box before you can continue.

- **Notify me only when apps try to make changes to my computer (do not dim my desktop)** When an app initiates a restricted action, the User Account Control message box opens. The restricted action will not be performed until you respond to the dialog box, but you can perform other tasks while the message box is open.

- **Never notify me** This is the equivalent of turning off UAC. Any user or app can make any changes to the computer without restriction.

With the default setting, Windows 10 prompts for administrator credentials when a user or app initiates an action that will modify system files. There's not a lot of reason to change the User Account Control setting, but you can.

To change the User Account Control setting

1. On the taskbar or in the **Settings** window, enter **UAC** in the search box and then, in the search results list, click **User Account Control Settings**.

> **TIP** The security icon to the left of the command indicates that administrator credentials are required to complete this operation.

The User Account Control Settings window opens.

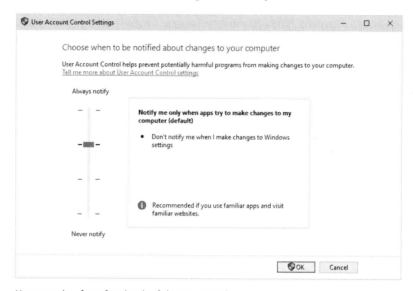

You can select from four levels of change control

2. Click above or below the slider, or drag it, to set UAC to the level you want, and then click **OK**.

3. In the **User Account Control** message box that appears, enter administrator credentials if necessary, and then click **OK**.

> **TIP** You must be signed in with an administrator account to select either of the two lowest settings. If you select the Never Notify setting, you must restart your computer to complete the process of turning off UAC.

Create and manage user accounts

An administrator can give other people access to the computer in one of three ways:

- Create a user account that is linked to an existing Microsoft account.

- Create a user account that is linked to an email address, and register that account as a Microsoft account.

- Create a local account that isn't linked to a Microsoft account.

Every user account has an associated user account name and can have a user account picture and a password. Any user can change the following details for his or her account:

- **Account name** You can change the display name that appears on the Welcome screen and Start menu.

- **Account picture** You can change the picture that identifies you on the Welcome screen and Start menu.

- **Password** You can create or change the password.

If you have administrator credentials, you can change these properties for any user account. You can also change the account type from Administrator to Standard User (provided that at least one Administrator account remains on the computer) or vice versa.

You create computer accounts and designate permission levels from the Family & Other Users pane of the Accounts category page of the Settings window.

> ⚠️ **IMPORTANT** All types of user accounts are visible in the Family & Other Users pane. However, the processes for managing family accounts and non-family accounts differ, so we cover them separately in the following sections to avoid confusion.

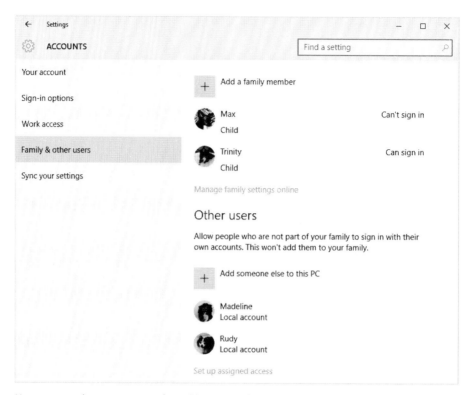

You manage other user accounts from this pane, so the lists don't include your account

Only administrators can create user accounts—if you're signed in with a standard user account, you don't have the option to do so. When you create a user account, you must designate whether the user is part of your family group.

When you first add a user account, it is identified in lists by its email address or by the name you give it. You can change the user account name (and delete user accounts) from the Users node of the Computer Management console.

If a person is not going to sign in to a specific computer again, it's a good idea to delete his or her user account. This will clean up the user account lists and recover the hard-drive space that is used by that user's data. If you don't want to delete the user account data, you can disable the account instead of deleting it.

Manage user accounts in the Computer Management console

Some user account management tasks can be completed from the Family & Other Users settings pane, but others must be performed in the Users node of the Computer Management console.

Some aspects of user accounts can't be managed from the Settings window

To open the Computer Management console, do any of the following:

- Right-click the **Start** button, and then click **Computer Management**.

- On the **Start** menu, click **All Apps**. In the **All Apps** list, expand the **Windows Administrative Tools** folder, and then click **Computer Management**.

- Enter **computer management** in the taskbar search box, and then in the **Apps** section of the search results list, click **Computer Management**.

To open the Users node, follow these steps in the left pane of the console:

1. Expand the **System Tools** folder.

2. Expand the **Local Users and Groups** folder.

3. Click the **Users** folder.

Manage and monitor family safety settings

Microsoft Family Safety is an impressive system for safeguarding against young family members accidentally accessing inappropriate content on the Internet. It allows you to place restrictions on their computer usage and provides you with reports that you can use to spot problems. Family Safety was introduced with Windows 7, and has evolved with each version of Windows. If you've used it in the past, it's a good idea to revisit it now to make sure the settings are up to date for the way your children use the computer.

Originally, Family Safety was an app through which you could register specific computer user accounts. It was necessary to register a child on each computer he or she used, and Family Safety reported separately on each local account. Since then, Family Safety has evolved into an online service that can monitor your child's activity on each device he or she signs into that is running Windows.

The key to the successful use of Family Safety is for each child to sign in to Windows 10 computers and devices with his or her own Microsoft account, and for parents to designate the account as a Child account. Family Safety monitors and reports on the websites children visit, the apps they use, the games they play, and the time they spend signed in to the computer.

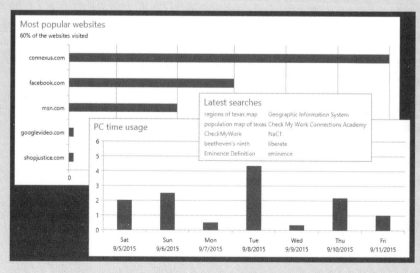

You can drill down on statistics in a family safety report

You can review usage and modify settings on the Family page of your Microsoft Account site, or directly through *familysafety.microsoft.com*, and opt to receive weekly activity reports by email. From the Family page, you can choose to block or allow specific websites or content by rating so that children have access to only age-appropriate information.

Create and manage family user accounts

You can designate a user account as belonging to a family member. When you do, the account is added to your family group. Adults in the family group can manage family safety settings online.

For the safety of your children, all family user accounts must be associated with Microsoft accounts. You can't create a local account in the Your Family group, or an account linked to an email address that isn't yet registered as a Microsoft account.

 IMPORTANT You must sign in to the computer with an administrator account to perform any of the following procedures.

To create a family user account

1. In the **Settings** window, click **Accounts**, and then click **Family & other users**.

2. In the **Family & other users** settings pane, click **Add a family member** to start the wizard.

3. On the **Add a child or an adult** page, click **Add a child** or **Add an adult**, and then enter the person's Microsoft account address in the **Enter the email address** box. If the person doesn't have an email address, or has an email address that isn't yet registered as a Microsoft account, click **This person doesn't have an email address**, and then skip to the procedure "To create or register a Microsoft account" in the "Manage settings for any user account" section of this topic.

4. After you enter the email address, click **Next**. The wizard searches the Microsoft account database for the email address.

5. If the email account is already registered as a Microsoft account, click **Confirm** on the **Add this person?** page to add the person to your family group and create a user account for him or her on the computer.

   Or

   If the email account isn't already registered as a Microsoft account, the wizard displays a warning.

   ## Add a child or an adult?

   Enter the email address of the person you want to add. If they use Windows, Office, Outlook.com, OneDrive, Skype, or Xbox, enter the email address they use to sign in.

   ○ Add a child

   ● Add an adult

   　Adults will be able to manage requests and change kids' settings

joan@fourthcoffee.com

   Looks like this isn't a Microsoft account. Try another email or sign up for a new one.

   The person I want to add doesn't have an email address

   Every family account must be linked to a valid Microsoft account

   If the warning appears, do either of the following:

   • Enter a registered email address, click **Next**, and then click **Confirm** to create the account.

   • Click **sign up for a new one**, and then skip to the procedure "To create or register a Microsoft account" in the "Manage settings for any user account" section of this topic.

6. When you register an adult family account, the person receives an email message and must click a link in the message and then sign in to his or her Microsoft account to confirm membership in the family group.

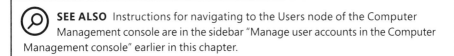

The recipient must sign in to accept the invitation

Until the family membership is confirmed, the person can sign in to the computer but the account status is shown as *Adult, Pending*.

To change the display name of a family user account

1. Display the **Users** node of the **Computer Management** console.

   > 🔍 **SEE ALSO** Instructions for navigating to the Users node of the Computer Management console are in the sidebar "Manage user accounts in the Computer Management console" earlier in this chapter.

2. Do any of the following:

   - To change the full name that appears in the user account lists, double-click the account name to open the **Properties** dialog box. Then enter or update the name in the **Full name** box, and click **Apply** or **OK** to make the change.

You can change the display name of a family user account to use something other than that person's email address

- To change the short name by which Windows identifies the account, right-click the account name in the **Users** list, and click **Rename** to activate the name for editing. Then enter the short name you want, and press **Enter** to complete the change.

To disable a family user account

1. On the **Accounts** page of the **Settings** window, click **Family & other users**.

2. In the **Family** section of the **Family & other users** pane, click the account you want to disable to display your options for managing the account.

If the user is a family member, you have an option to block the account

3. On the account tile, click **Block**. Windows displays a confirmation request.

4. In the **Block this person from signing in?** box, click **Block**.

To enable a disabled family user account

1. On the **Accounts** page of the **Settings** window, click **Family & other users**.

2. In the **Family** section of the **Family & other users** pane, click the account you want to enable to display your options for managing the account.

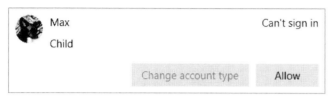

Max
Child   Can't sign in

Change account type   Allow

The dimmed Change Account Type button is a quick indicator that an account has been disabled

3. On the account tile, click **Allow**. Windows displays a confirmation request.

4. In the **Allow this person to sign in?** box, click **Allow**.

To delete a family user account

1. Ensure that the user has moved or copied personal files from the user account folders and uninstalled or deactivated any apps that require this to free up the user license.

> **IMPORTANT** To preserve any files that are saved in the user account folders, back up the folder C:\Users\[UserName] (where [UserName] is the account name of the user).

2. Display the **Users** node of the **Computer Management** console.

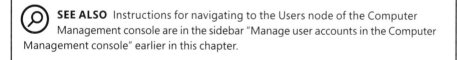

> **SEE ALSO** Instructions for navigating to the Users node of the Computer Management console are in the sidebar "Manage user accounts in the Computer Management console" earlier in this chapter.

3. Right-click the user account you want to delete, and then click **Delete**. A message box displays a warning.

It's hard to accidentally delete a user account

4. In the message box, click **Yes** to delete the account and all its files.

Create and manage non-family user accounts

Accounts in the Other Users group are not associated with your family safety group. These accounts can certainly belong to members of your family, but they can't be part of your family safety settings group. Local computer accounts can be created only in the Other Users group.

 IMPORTANT You must sign in to the computer with an administrator account to perform any of the following procedures.

To create a non-family user account that is linked to an existing Microsoft account

1. In the **Settings** window, click **Accounts**, and then click **Family & other users**.

2. In the **Other users** section of the pane, click **Add someone else to this PC** to start the wizard.

3. On the **How will this person sign in?** page, enter the Microsoft account address in the **Email or phone** box, and then click **Next**.

    The wizard confirms that the email address is a registered Microsoft account.

The user must provide a Microsoft account password to sign in

4. Click **Finish** to complete the process.

To create a local user account

1. On the **Accounts** page of the **Settings** window, click **Family & other users**.

2. In the **Other users** section of the pane, click **Add someone else to this PC** to start the wizard.

3. At the bottom of the **How will this person sign in?** page, click **The person I want to add doesn't have an email address**.

4. At the bottom of the **Let's create your account** page, click **Add a user without a Microsoft account** to get to the interface for creating a local account.

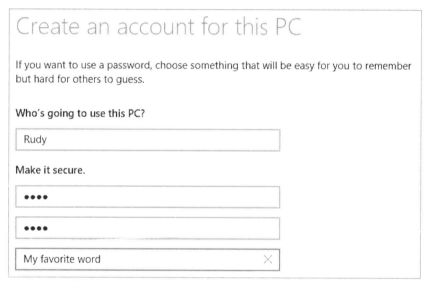

The password hint appears on the Welcome page if you can't remember your password

5. Enter a user name. If you don't want to create a password for the local account, leave the rest of the boxes blank. Otherwise, enter the password (two times) and an optional password hint. Then click **Next** to create the account.

> ⚠ **IMPORTANT** If you don't implement a password, anyone can sign in to your computer by selecting your user account and then clicking Sign In. Your data is especially vulnerable if you travel with your computer or use it in a public place.

To disable a non-family user account

1. Display the **Users** node of the **Computer Management** console.

   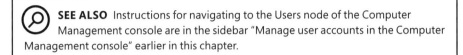

   > **SEE ALSO** Instructions for navigating to the Users node of the Computer Management console are in the sidebar "Manage user accounts in the Computer Management console" earlier in this chapter.

2. Double-click the account you want to disable.

3. In the **Properties** dialog box, select the **Account is disabled** check box. Then click **OK**.

To enable a disabled non-family user account

1. Display the **Users** node of the **Computer Management** console.

2. Double-click the account you want to enable.

3. In the **Properties** dialog box, clear the **Account is disabled** check box. Then click **OK**.

To delete a non-family user account

1. Ensure that the user has moved or copied personal files from the user account folders and uninstalled or deactivated any apps that require this to free up the user license.

   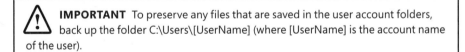

   > **IMPORTANT** To preserve any files that are saved in the user account folders, back up the folder C:\Users\[UserName] (where [UserName] is the account name of the user).

2. Display the **Settings** window, click **Accounts**, and then click **Family & other users**.

3. In the **Other users** section of the **Family & other users** pane, click the account you want to delete, to display your options for managing the account.

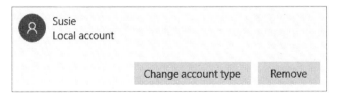

You can remove non-family accounts directly from the Family & Other Users pane

4. On the account tile, click **Remove**. Windows displays a confirmation request.

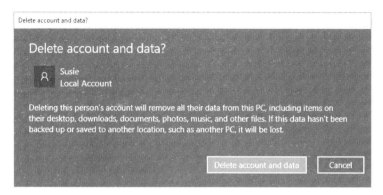

You must confirm that you understand you're deleting data

5. In the message box, click **Delete account and data**.

Windows deletes the account and then returns to the Other Users pane.

Manage settings for any user account

Windows 10 has two built-in accounts, Administrator and Guest, which don't have passwords assigned. When Windows creates the first user-specific administrator account, it disables the default Administrator account. The Guest account is inactive by default (and disabled on computers that are part of a domain.) You can activate the Guest account to give someone temporary, limited access to your computer without having to create a user account for that person.

Another method of giving someone limited access is to restrict the account so that it can access only one app. Access restriction works only with Store apps that are already installed on your computer.

When creating a family or non-family user account, if you don't supply an email address, the wizard displays a page on which you can create a new outlook.com email address or register an existing email address as a Microsoft account. The email address that you provide will receive a confirmation email message and must respond to it to activate the account.

Let's create an account

Windows, Office, Outlook.com, OneDrive, Skype, Xbox. They're all better and more personal when they sign in with their Microsoft account. Learn more

Joan	Lambert

✓ After you sign up, we'll send you a message with a link to verify this user name.

joan@fourthcoffee.com

Get a new email address

••••••••

United States ⌄

July ⌄	31 ⌄	1979 ⌄

It's simple to register an email address as a Microsoft account

To activate the built-in Guest account

1. Display the **Users** node of the **Computer Management** console.

2. Double-click the disabled **Guest** account.

3. In the **Properties** dialog box, clear the **Account is disabled** check box, and then click **Apply** or **OK**.

To grant administrative permissions to an account

1. In the **Settings** window, click **Accounts**, and then click **Family & other users**.

2. Click the account you want to modify, to display your options. Then click **Change account type**.

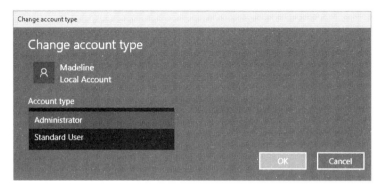

Any account can be an Administrator account

3. In the **Account type** list, click **Administrator**. Then click **OK**.

To revoke administrative permissions

1. In the **Accounts** category of settings, display the **Family & other users** pane.

2. Click the account, and then click **Change account type**.

3. In the **Account type** list, click **Standard User**. Then click **OK**.

To restrict an account to one Store app

1. In the **Accounts** category of settings, display the **Family & other users** pane.

2. At the bottom of the pane, click **Set up assigned access**.

3. In the **Choose which account will have assigned access** area, click **Choose an account** (or, if the pane already displays a restricted account, click the account).

4. In the **Choose which app this account can access** area, click **Choose an app** (or click the currently selected app) and then in the **Choose an app** pane, click the app you want to assign (or click **Don't start an app when the account is signed in** to remove the assigned access).

Choose which account will have assigned access

 Rudy

Choose which app this account can access

 Weather

You can restrict a user account to a specific Store app

5. Restart the computer to complete the access assignment process.

> **TIP** When you sign in to Windows 10 with an assigned access account, you have access only to the assigned app. To sign out of an assigned access account, press Ctrl+Alt+Del.

To create or register a Microsoft account

1. On the **Let's create an account** page, provide the requested information, and then click **Next**.

2. If you want to, clear the check boxes permitting Microsoft to send and track information for marketing purposes. Then click **Next**.

3. On the final page of the wizard, click **Finish**.

To switch from a Microsoft account to a local account

1. In the **Settings** window, click **Account**, and then click **Your account**.

2. In the **Your account** settings pane, click **Sign in with a local account instead**.

3. In the **Switch to a local account** window, enter your Microsoft account password to confirm your identity, and then click **Next**.

4. Provide a user account name for the local account. If you don't want to use a password, leave the rest of the entries blank. Otherwise, fill in the password and password hint entries.

5. Click **Next**, and then click **Sign out and finish**.

To connect a local account to a Microsoft account

1. Display the **Your account** settings pane, and click **Sign in with a Microsoft account instead**.

2. On the **Make it yours** page, enter the email address and password of your Microsoft account, and then click **Sign In**.

3. On the **Enter your old password one last time** page, enter the password of the local user account that you're connecting to your Microsoft account. (If the local user account didn't have a password, leave this box blank.) Then click Next.

4. Enter your local account password to confirm your identity, and then click **Next**.

5. Enter your Microsoft account email address, and then click **Next**.

   A code will be sent to that email address, or you can open the list below the question about how you want to get the code, and choose to receive it in a text message. After you receive the code, return to this process and enter it in the box provided. Then click **Finish**.

   > ✓ **TIP** The verification code arrives quickly and is valid for only a short time, so check your email or text messages for the code and finish the account creation process promptly. If the code expires before you complete the process, you can click the Back button on the code page and request another code.

6. Click **Sign out and finish** to return to your profile, where you can add an account picture to the local account.

Manage account pictures and passwords

As previously discussed, you can sign in to Windows 10 by using a Microsoft account or a local account.

Each user account has an associated user account picture that is shown on the Welcome screen, at the top of the Start menu, on app and browser window title bars when you're signed in, and in other places. If you sign in to Windows with your Microsoft account credentials, Windows displays the user account picture that is associated with that account. If you sign in by using a local account, you can associate a picture with that account on that computer. Until you associate a picture with either type of account, the computer account displays a placeholder account picture (a head-and-shoulders icon) wherever the account picture would usually appear.

Clicking your user account button displays all active user accounts

You can easily add or change an account picture, regardless of whether you're signed in with a Microsoft account or a local account, on any computer you sign in to.

Previous versions of Windows provided many standard user account picture options, depicting a variety of animals, sports, and interests. Windows 10 doesn't provide any account pictures, but does offer the option of taking a picture if your computer has a webcam. You can use .bmp, .gif, .jpg, or .png files as user account pictures. The original image can be any size or shape, but Windows 10 displays the user account picture as a circle, so when selecting a picture, keep in mind that it will be cropped to a square and then have its corners cut off.

> ⚠️ **IMPORTANT** The change from square to circular user account pictures has met with strong opposition from Windows 10 and Windows 10 mobile users, in part because of the corners being cut off the pictures, but also because the circular icons don't tile neatly on the screen. Perhaps by the time you read this book, square pictures will be the default, or at least an option.

All Microsoft accounts have passwords. If you sign in to Windows or any website with your Microsoft account credentials, you use the same password wherever you sign in. (The user account name and password, together, are referred to as *credentials*.) Local accounts can have or not have passwords. If you don't store or access personal information on your computer, a password is not essential. However, it's never a bad idea to have a password. You can add a password (and an optional password hint) to a local account or change the password, and you can change your Microsoft password. Changing your Microsoft account password changes it across all computers, sites, and services.

If you're going to take the trouble to protect your user account with a password, choose one that no one is likely to guess. A strong password is at least eight characters long, does not contain words that might be in the dictionary or names, and contains at least one uppercase character, one lowercase character, one number, and one punctuation mark.

> ⚠️ **IMPORTANT** If you change your Microsoft account password and then sign in to a computer that hasn't been able to connect to the Microsoft account database since before you changed the password, the computer won't be able to verify your new password and will prompt you to sign in with the last password you used on that computer.

When you assign a password to a local user account, you can also save a password hint. Windows displays the password hint on the Welcome screen after you enter an incorrect password.

Each computer user manages his or her own account picture and password. The information in this section assumes that you're working with your own account.

To display the Your Account settings pane

1. Do either of the following:

   - At the top of the **Start** menu, click your user account button, and then click **Change account settings**.

   - In the **Settings** window, click **Accounts**, and then click **Your account**.

The content of the Your Account pane varies based on whether you're signed in with a Microsoft account or a local user account, and what pictures have been associated with the account on the computer.

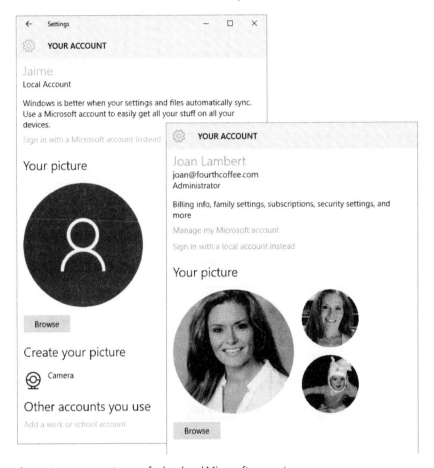

Account management panes for local and Microsoft accounts

To set or change your user account picture

1. If you plan to use an existing picture, consider reviewing and editing the photo before proceeding, to ensure that it displays well in the available space.

2. Display the **Your account** settings pane.

3. Do one of the following:

   - If you want to select a previously used image, click the image in the **Your picture** section.

   - If you want to select an image that isn't shown in the **Your picture** section, click the **Browse** button. Then in the **Open** dialog box, locate and select the image you want to use, and click the **Choose picture** button.

   > ⚠ **IMPORTANT** At the time of this writing, you can't modify the portion of the photo that Windows selects. Windows users have been requesting this feature, so perhaps by the time you read this book it will be possible to modify the selection.

   - If you want to capture an image, in the **Create your picture** section, click the **Camera** button. (If Windows Camera prompts you to permit it to access your location, click **Yes** or **No**.) Adjust the camera, yourself, and your background as necessary, and then click the camera icon to take the picture.

To set or change your Microsoft account picture

1. Display the **Your account** settings pane.

2. Click **Manage my Microsoft account** to display your Microsoft Account home page.

3. Click **Your info** on the menu bar, or click your account picture.

4. On the **Your info** page, do one of the following:

   - To initially set the picture, click **New picture**.

   - To change the existing picture, click **Change picture**, and then on the next page, click the **New picture** button.

5. In the **Open** dialog box, locate and select the picture you want to use, and then click **Open**.

6. On the **Your info** page, drag any of the picture handles to resize the circle, and drag the circle to change the part of the picture that is displayed. The crosshairs mark the center of the picture.

To add a local user account password

1. In the **Settings** window, click **Accounts**, and then click **Sign-in options**.

2. In the **Password** section, click **Add**.

3. On the **Create a password** page, enter and reenter the password you want to use. Enter a password hint if you want to be able to display one from the Welcome page, and then click **Next**.

4. Click **Finish**.

To change a local user account password

1. In the **Settings** window, click **Accounts**, and then click **Sign-in options**.

2. In the **Password** section, click **Change**.

3. On the **Change your password** page, enter your current password, and then click **Next**.

4. On the second **Change your password** page, enter and reenter the password you want to use. Enter a password hint if you want to be able to display one from the Welcome page, and then click **Next**.

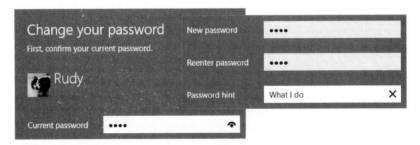

There are no reuse restrictions on local passwords

5. On the final **Change your password** page, click **Finish**.

To change a Microsoft account password

1. Display the **Sign-in options** settings page.

2. In the **Password** section, click **Change**.

3. On the **Please reenter your password** page that displays your Microsoft account name, enter the current password for the Microsoft account, and then click **Sign in**.

4. On the **Change your Microsoft account password** page, enter your current password and then enter and reenter the new password.

> ⚠ **IMPORTANT** The new password must be one that you haven't used before. The password reset system will not permit you to enter a password that you've used previously.

If you're uncertain whether you entered the password correctly, press and hold the eye icon at the right end of the input box to temporarily display the password.

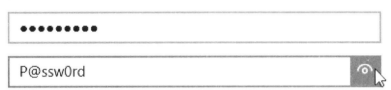

Hold down the eye icon to display the password

5. When you're satisfied with the new password, click **Next**.

6. On the page confirming the password change, click **Finish**.

In addition to the onscreen confirmation, Microsoft sends a confirmation email message to your Microsoft account email address and to any email addresses that you provided as secondary contacts for the Microsoft account.

Customize your sign-in options

Each user manages the password and sign-in options for his or her account. This topic addresses actions you can take for your user account, not for other people's user accounts.

If (and only if) your sign-in account has a password, you can create alternative sign-in options on each computer you log in to. These sign-in options include the following:

- **Personal identification number (PIN)** A number (at least four digits long) that you enter in place of your password.

- **Picture password** An image of your choice on which you perform a specific combination of gestures. Windows divides the picture into a 100x100 grid and looks for your selected gesture pattern in the appropriate grid coordinates. You can perform the gestures directly on a touchscreen or by using a mouse.

> ⚠️ **IMPORTANT** Some critics say that a picture password isn't very secure because people generally do the obvious thing on any picture. For example, on a picture of a person, people tap the eyes and draw a line across the mouth. When you set up a gesture-based password, try to do something less obvious.

- **Windows Hello** Biometric identification through a fingerprint, facial, or iris recognition. This feature is available only on computers that have biometric identification hardware such as a built-in or external fingerprint reader.

After you set up a PIN or picture password sign-in option, the Welcome page changes to offer your new option by default. There is also a Sign-In Options link on the page, so if you forget your PIN or the specific gestures of your picture password, you can sign in at any time by using your password.

In addition to controlling sign-in options, each user who signs in with Microsoft account credentials can choose whether to synchronize settings across all the computers he or she signs in to with those credentials. This is a very cool feature after you have it set up the way you want it and get used to it. You can synchronize the following groups of settings:

- **Theme** Desktop background, colors, and sounds

- **Web browser settings** Favorite sites and recent searches

- **Passwords** Passwords that you've saved for specific websites

- **Language preferences** Installed language packs, regional date and time settings, and keyboard language

- **Ease of Access settings** Narrator and other accessibility tools

- **Other Windows settings** Your Start screen configuration and various other settings that we haven't found a clear description of

When you have a fingerprint reader or other biometric hardware installed on your computer, the Sign-In Options settings pane includes the Windows Hello category. At the time of this writing, you must create a PIN before you can configure a Windows Hello authentication method.

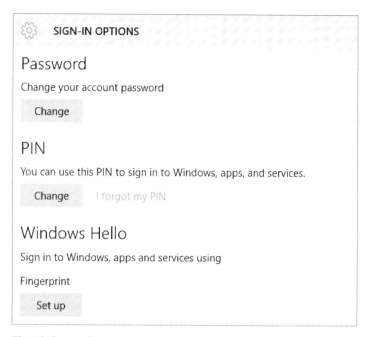

The Windows Hello category lists the biometric readers that are installed on your computer

 IMPORTANT At the time of this writing, biometric readers aren't very common on personal and business computers, but we expect that as new hardware is developed specifically for Windows 10, that will change. We've documented the current procedures for setting up a fingerprint password, but the Windows Hello procedures might change along with the hardware.

When you have multiple sign-in options configured for your account, the Welcome screen displays the most recently configured sign-in option by default. You can switch to a different sign-in option from the Welcome screen.

 IMPORTANT You can perform the following procedures only for your own account (or the account that is currently logged in).

To create a PIN

1. Open the **Settings** window, click **Accounts**, and then click **Sign-in options**.

2. In the **Sign-in options** settings pane, in the **PIN** section, click the **Add** button.

3. In the **Please reenter your password** window, enter the password for your account, and then click **Sign in** to open the **Set up a PIN** window.

4. Enter a personal identification number that is at least four digits long in the **New PIN** and **Confirm PIN** boxes.

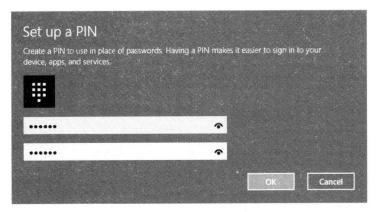

You can click the eye icons to check your entries

5. In the **Set up a PIN** window, click **OK** to create your PIN and make the PIN sign-in option available from the Welcome screen.

To change a PIN

1. In the **Sign-in options** settings pane, in the **PIN** section, click the **Change** button.

2. In the **PIN** box, enter your current PIN to validate your credentials.

3. Enter the new personal identification number (at least four digits long) in the **New PIN** and **Confirm PIN** boxes, and then click **OK**.

To configure Windows Hello fingerprint authentication

1. Create a PIN.

2. In the **Sign-in options** settings pane, in the **Windows Hello** section, click the **Add** button to start the Windows Hello setup wizard, and then click **Get started**.

 TIP The Windows Hello heading appears only if your computer system includes a compatible biometric reader.

3. Swipe any finger across the fingerprint reader, from the first joint to the fingertip. Keep the finger flat and steady as you swipe.

After the reader detects a usable fingerprint reading, it prompts you to swipe the same finger again, until it gets about four good readings.

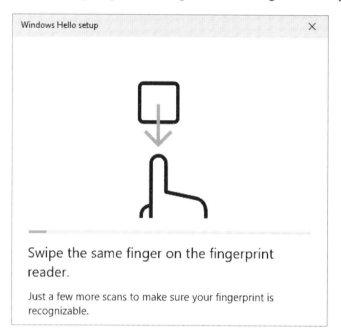

You must confirm the authentication method multiple times

4. After Windows registers the fingerprint, you can immediately add another fingerprint by clicking **Add another** and repeating step 3.

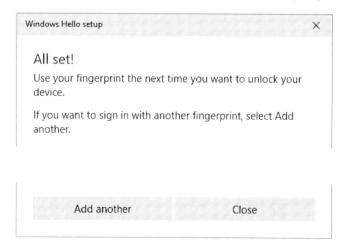

You can store multiple fingerprints and sign in with any one

To create a picture password

1. In the **Sign-in options** pane, in the **Picture password** section, click the **Add** button to start the Picture Password wizard. The wizard has a background picture of purple flowers in a field of green.

2. In the **Create a picture password** dialog box, enter your account password, and then click **OK** to verify your identity.

3. The wizard demonstrates the three permissible gestures against the floral background. After you're familiar with the gestures, click the **Choose picture** button.

4. In the **Open** dialog box, browse to and select the picture you want to use, and then click **Open** to replace the wizard background picture. Drag the picture to adjust it in the available space, and then click **Use this picture**.

5. Decide on a combination of three taps, lines, and circles you'll be able to consistently remember, and then perform them on the picture. The wizard changes the number in the left pane as you perform each gesture.

Choose a picture that includes objects you can use to correctly position your gestures

6. Repeat the three gestures when the wizard prompts you to do so, and then click the **Finish** button.

To change authentication methods on the Welcome screen

1. On the Welcome screen displaying your user account name, click the **Sign-in options** link to display an icon for each sign-in method you have configured.

2. Click the icon for the sign-in method you want to use.

To configure setting synchronization across computers

1. In the **Settings** window, click **Account**, and then click **Sync your settings**.

2. In the **Sync your settings** pane, set the **Sync settings** toggle button to **On** to activate synchronization on this computer.

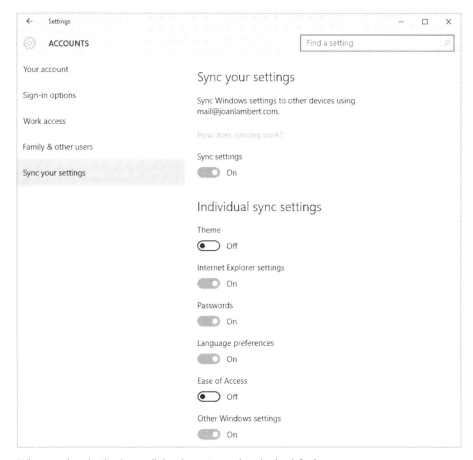

When synchronization is on, all the elements synchronize by default

3. Consider the computers that you sign in to with the current Microsoft account credentials. The in the **Individual sync settings** section, do the following:

- Set the toggle button to **On** for each setting that you want to synchronize to and from this computer.

- Set the toggle button to **Off** for each setting that you want to maintain independently on this computer.

Skills review

In this chapter, you learned how to:

- Understand user accounts and permissions

- Create and manage user accounts

- Manage account pictures and passwords

- Customize your sign-in options

Practice tasks

The practice files for these tasks are located in the Win10SBS\Ch08 folder.

Understand user accounts and permissions

There are no practice tasks for this topic.

Create and manage user accounts

Display the Family & Other Accounts settings pane, and then perform the following tasks:

1. Create a local user account with the name **Duke** that is not part of your family group.

2. Disable the account and verify that it no longer appears in the Family & Other Accounts settings pane.

3. Activate the built-in **Guest** account.

4. Enable the **Duke** account for use in the next practice task.

5. Verify that the **Duke** and **Guest** accounts appear in the Family & Other Accounts settings pane.

6. Check the permissions for the **Duke** account, and make sure that it is a **Standard User** account.

Manage account pictures and passwords

Perform the following tasks:

1. From the user account menu at the top of the **Start** menu, switch to the **Duke** account, and sign in to the computer.

2. Open the **Settings** window, click **Accounts**, and then click **Your account** to display Duke's account information.

3. Add an account picture to Duke's account. Choose one of the **Account** pictures in the practice files folder.

4. Add a password to Duke's account.

5. Lock the computer, and sign in as Duke, using the password.

Customize your sign-in options

Perform the following tasks:

1. Sign in using the Duke account you created in the preceding task, or if you want to configure your own sign-in options, sign in using your account.

2. Open the **Settings** window, click **Accounts**, and then click **Sign-in options** to display the sign-in options that are available for the account.

3. Create a PIN that you can use instead of the current password to sign in to the computer.

4. Lock the computer.

5. Dismiss the lock screen, and then sign in by using the PIN.

6. If your computer has a biometric identification system that is compatible with Windows Hello, create a Windows Hello sign-in authentication. Then lock the computer, dismiss the lock screen, and sign in by using Windows Hello.

7. Create a picture password that you can use to sign in to the computer. Use one of the **Password** pictures in the practice file folder.

8. Lock the computer.

9. Dismiss the lock screen. On the Welcome screen, click the **Sign-in options** link and notice the icons that represent the available authentication methods.

10. Sign in by using the picture password. If you want to, change the picture password to use a picture of your own.

11. Display the **Sync your settings** pane. Review the elements that you can synchronize among computers and consider which of these would be useful or not useful. (If you're signed in as Duke, you won't be able to modify the sync settings because it is a local account.)

12. If you have a Microsoft account and want to modify the sync settings for that account, sign in using your own account, return to the **Sync your settings** pane, and modify the settings to fit your needs.

Manage computer settings

In Windows 10, the management of computer settings is gradually migrating from the more complex Control Panel to the seemingly simple Settings window. This migration supports the development of Windows 10 as a cross-platform system that operates equally gracefully on large and small display screens. The Settings window organizes function-specific pages into nine categories that, due to the simplification of the category titles, aren't always self-explanatory. The organization is not entirely different from that in Windows 8.1, Windows 7, and earlier versions of Windows, but it's different enough that users of any previous version of Windows are likely to need a bit of time to get used to it. Users should check the Settings window first; if the setting isn't there, a link to its location in Control Panel will most likely be provided.

> ✓ **TIP** We assume that settings will continue to migrate through Windows updates until the Settings window is the primary interface for managing settings for a desktop or mobile device.

In previous chapters, we worked with user interface settings. In this chapter, we work with settings that control the underlying behavior of the computer.

This chapter guides you through procedures related to managing date and time settings, regional and language settings, and speech settings, and for customizing the display of on-screen content.

In this chapter

- Manage date and time settings
- Manage regional and language settings
- Manage speech settings
- Customize device display settings

Practice files

No practice files are necessary to complete the practice tasks in this chapter.

Manage date and time settings

Your computer system has an internal clock that keeps track of the date and time (down to time increments as small as nanoseconds), even when the computer is turned off. By default, Windows 10 displays this system date and time in the notification area at the right end of the taskbar, and most of us refer to that information frequently.

The taskbar clock doesn't display the time down to the nanosecond. But programmatically, when a system tool or app captures the time or a time duration, it will typically be accurate to between 1 millisecond and 100 nanoseconds, depending on the hardware platform and the programming language. This accuracy can be very important in some cases. Communication and calendaring software coordinates with the internal clock to keep us on time and on task, but more importantly, system tools and apps use that clock to monitor and manage events on your computer.

To help keep the date and time that are used in your computer accurate, the clock is set to automatically synchronize with an Internet time server every seven days. Internet-based time servers transmit the current Coordinated Universal Time to your computer. This time is known as *UTC*, an acronym based on a compromise between the English and French terms. UTC is a standard that is based on International Atomic Time that corresponds to the time at the Royal Observatory in Greenwich, England. UTC is within one second of Greenwich Mean Time (GMT). If your computer isn't located in the UTC/GMT time zone, you need to change the time zone setting so that your computer displays the correct time. If your computer is in a region that participates in daylight saving time, you also need to indicate that fact, so that your computer adjusts from standard time to daylight saving time and back again on the appropriate days.

 TIP If your computer is connected to a network domain, the domain server synchronizes with the time server, and your computer synchronizes with the domain server.

When you install Windows 10, it prompts you to select a time zone. If you move or travel with your computer, you can easily change the time zone. If you want to keep track of the time in a different time zone, you can configure Windows to display up to three clocks; for example, if you work in a regional office, you might want to keep track of the time at your company headquarters. The taskbar displays the primary clock. You can display additional clocks in a ScreenTip or in the calendar pane.

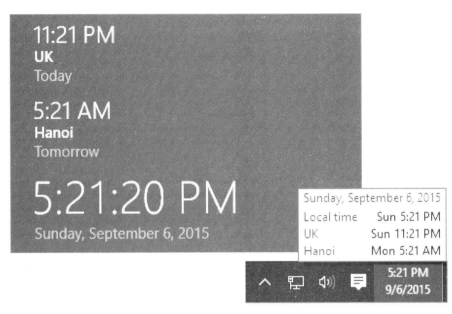

Quickly check the time, day, and date in other locations

If you need to display time in more than three locations, you can do so on the World Clock page of the built-in Alarms & Clock app.

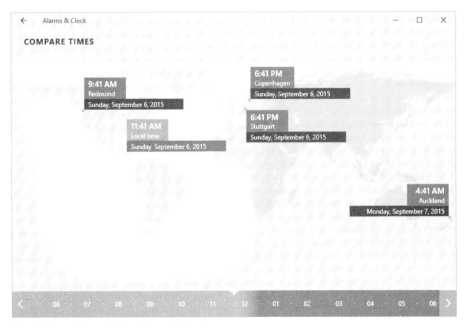

Watch the world turn in the Alarms & Clock app

You can manage the date, time, time zone, daylight saving time, and date and time formats in the Date & Time pane of the Settings window.

The Date & Time pane

To display the current time and date

1. The taskbar displays the time and the date. To display additional information, do either of the following:

   • Point to the time or date to display the day of the week, the month, the day, and the year.

   • Click the time or date to display the calendar for the current month, which includes the current day and date, and the time to the second.

Your First Day Of Week setting determines the first column

To display the Date & Time settings pane

1. Do either of the following:

   - From the taskbar, display the calendar, and then at the bottom of the calendar, click **Date and time settings**.

   - In the **Settings** window, click **Time & language** and then click **Date & time**.

To manually set the system date and time

1. Display the **Date & time** settings pane.

2. To stop the computer from synchronizing with a time server, set the **Set time automatically** toggle button to **Off**.

3. Click the **Change** button to display the Change Date And Time pane.

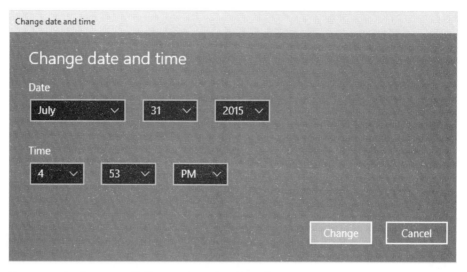

You can set the time manually if you can't synchronize with a server

4. In the **Change date and time** pane, set the date and time as you want them,
    and then click **Change** to apply your changes.

To synchronize with an Internet time server

1. Open Control Panel, and then do either of the following to open the Date And
    Time dialog box:

    -   In Category view, click **Clock, Language, and Region**, and then click **Date
        and Time**.

    -   In Small Icons or Large Icons view, click **Date and Time**.

2. In the **Date and Time** dialog box, click the **Internet Time** tab, and then click the
    Change settings button to open the Internet Time Settings dialog box.

3. Select the **Synchronize with an Internet time server** check box, and then click
    the **Server** list to display the available servers.

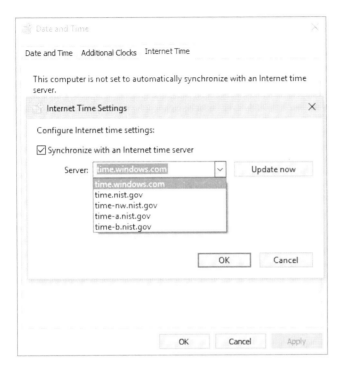

Time server options

> **TIP** There are five Internet time servers available in the Server list. The default server is time.windows.com, which is maintained by Microsoft. The four servers with *nist* in their names are maintained by the National Institute of Standards and Technology (NIST) at various locations around the United States. The time.nist.gov server is at the National Center for Atmospheric Research in Boulder, Colorado; time-nw.nist.gov is at Microsoft in Redmond, Washington; and time-a.nist.gov and time-b.nist.gov are at NIST in Gaithersburg, Maryland.

4. In the **Server** list, click the server you want to synchronize with, and then click the **Update now** button to try to connect to the server and update your system time. A message below the server list lets you know whether the clock was successfully synchronized.

TIP If the synchronization fails, and you have an active Internet connection, click Update Now again to resubmit the synchronization request to the server.

5. After the clock successfully synchronizes, click **OK** in the **Internet Time Settings** dialog box, and again in the **Date and Time** dialog box.

To change the time zone

1. Display the **Date & time** settings pane.

2. Click the **Time zone** list to display a list of the time zones. Notice that there are multiple time zone descriptions per time zone.

(UTC+09:30) Adelaide

(UTC+09:30) Darwin

(UTC+10:00) Brisbane

(UTC+10:00) Canberra, Melbourne, Sydney

(UTC+10:00) Guam, Port Moresby

(UTC+10:00) Hobart

(UTC+10:00) Magadan

(UTC+10:00) Vladivostok, Magadan (RTZ 9)

(UTC+11:00) Chokurdakh (RTZ 10)

Choose any entry that matches your UTC variance; the description doesn't matter

3. In the **Time zone** list, click any time zone that matches your region's variance from UTC. Then check the taskbar clock to confirm that the system time has changed.

4. If your region participates in daylight saving time, set the **Adjust for daylight saving time automatically** toggle button to **On**.

To change date and time formats

1. Display the **Date & time** settings pane. The Formats area displays the current settings for the first day of the week, short date, long date, short time, and long time.

2. In the **Formats** area, click **Change date and time formats** to display the Change Date And Time Formats pane.

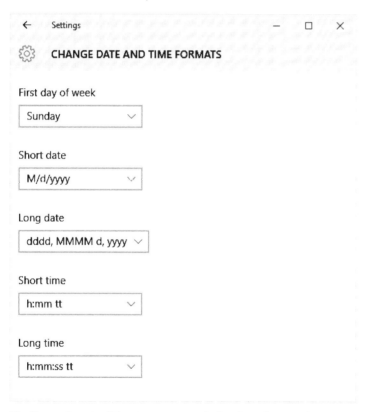

The Change Date And Time Formats pane displays lists of options for each setting

The First Day Of Week options, which control the display of weekly and monthly calendars, are simply the days of the week. The other lists use abbreviations to represent different expressions of the month, day, year, hour, minute, second, and 12-hour time notation.

Short date

M/d/yyyy

M/d/yy

MM/dd/yy

MM/dd/yyyy

yy/MM/dd

yyyy-MM-dd

dd-MMM-yy

Abbreviations represent numeric and alphabetic versions of time and date elements

3. In the **Change date and time formats** pane, click the setting you want to use for the first day of the week, the short and long date expressions, and the short and long time expressions.

   Changes to the Short Time and Short Date are immediately reflected on the taskbar. Changes to the Long Date are reflected in the ScreenTip that appears when you point to the taskbar time or date.

SEE ALSO For information about changing date and time formats to those of a specific region or language, see "Manage regional and language settings" later in this chapter.

To configure Windows to display multiple clocks

1. Display the **Date & time** settings pane. At the bottom of the pane, click **Add clocks for different time zones** to display the Additional Clocks tab of the Date and Time dialog box.

2. For each additional clock you want to display, select the **Show this clock** check box, select a time zone in the corresponding list, and then enter a display name to identify the time on calendars.

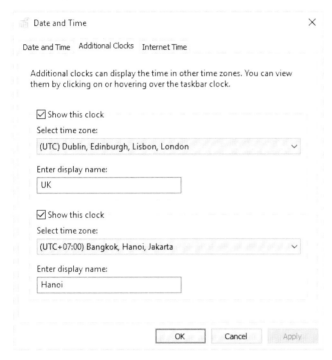

Keep track of the time where your clients or friends are

3. Click **OK** in the **Date and Time** dialog box to implement your changes.

To display secondary clocks

1. Do either of the following:

   • Point to the taskbar clock to display the additional clocks in a ScreenTip.

   • Click the taskbar clock to display the calendar pane with the information for the additional time zones at the top.

Manage regional and language settings

Windows 10 was initially released in 190 countries/regions and 111 languages. At the time of this writing, the operating system is "fully localized" in 39 location-specific language variations, shown in the following table.

Arabic (Saudi Arabia)	Bulgarian (Bulgaria)	Chinese (Simplified, China)
Chinese (Hong Kong)	Chinese (Traditional, Taiwan)	Croatian (Croatia)
Czech (Czech Republic)	Danish (Denmark)	Dutch (Netherlands)
English (United Kingdom)	English (United States)	Estonian (Estonia)
Finnish (Finland)	French (France)	French (Canada)
German (Germany)	Greek (Greece)	Hebrew (Israel)
Hungarian (Hungary)	Italian (Italy)	Japanese (Japan)
Korean (Korea)	Latvian (Latvia)	Lithuanian (Lithuania)
Norwegian, Bokmål (Norway)	Polish (Poland)	Portuguese (Brazil)
Portuguese (Portugal)	Romanian (Romania)	Russian (Russia)
Serbian (Latin, Serbia)	Slovak (Slovakia)	Slovenian (Slovenia)
Spanish (Spain, International Sort)	Spanish (Mexico)	Swedish (Sweden)
Thai (Thailand)	Turkish (Turkey)	Ukrainian (Ukraine)

Regional variations of these languages are available as Language Interface Packs, which provide a translated version of the most widely used dialog boxes, menu items, and help content.

The Windows display language is used by the operating system to label user interface elements (such as settings and button names). When you upgrade to Windows 10, the default Windows display language stays the same as before the upgrade. If you want or need to work with features in a language other than the current Windows display language, you can change the system language, switch between languages, or simply install the other language to make its features available on your computer. Other apps can check the system language and use features that are installed with the language. For example, installing a language that uses characters other than those in the default language installs fonts that support those characters, and you can use those fonts when creating documents in Microsoft Word. Windows and installed apps fetch content based on your region and language settings.

> ⚠ **IMPORTANT** At the time of this writing, the interactive Cortana service is available in seven countries/regions—US, China, UK, France, Germany, Italy, and Spain—but can translate phrases in 40 languages. When the system language is set to one that Cortana doesn't speak, the feature is automatically disabled. The standard search feature is available when Cortana isn't. Cortana support is indicated in the Manage Optional Features pane of the System page of the Settings window.

Installing a language makes the keyboard layout for that language available. If you connect a physical keyboard with the layout and character set that is typically used with that language, switching the keyboard language enters the correct characters when you press the keys. If you don't have a physical keyboard that is configured for a language, switching the keyboard language makes your existing keyboard function as though it were labeled in that language. It also makes the on-screen keyboard available in that language.

> ✓ **TIP** To display the touch keyboard icon on the taskbar, right-click or press and hold a blank area of the taskbar, and then click Show Touch Keyboard Button. Although this is called the touch keyboard, you can also use your mouse to click the keys.

You can manage the country or region of record and the system language in the Region & Language pane of the Settings window.

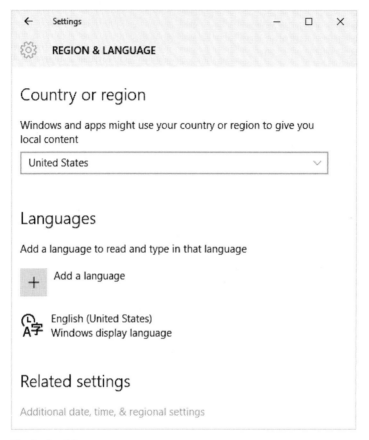

The Region & Language pane

To display the Region & Language settings pane

1. In the **Settings** window, click **Time & language** and then click **Region & language**.

To specify your country or region for local content

1. Display the **Region & language** settings pane.

2. Click the **Country or region** list, and then click the location you want Windows and installed apps to consider your home location.

> ✓ **TIP** Many websites discern your location based on the IP address of your Internet connection. The location you select in the Region & Language pane does not affect the location that is conveyed by the IP address.

To install an additional system language

1. Display the **Region & language** settings pane. The Languages area displays the currently installed languages. (There is only one until you add a language.)

2. In the **Languages** area, click **Add a language** to display the list of languages you can install. The name of each language is shown in that language and in your current system language.

Windows offers a dazzling array of system languages

TIP At the time of this writing, 141 languages, plus dialects, are available. Unlike most panes, the Add A Language pane scrolls sideways to accommodate the list.

3. Scroll the list and click the language you want to install. If Windows has multiple dialects of that language available, click the dialect you want.

Some languages offer multiple location-specific options

Windows displays a notification and installs the language from Windows Update, or adds the language to the language list and notifies you that you need to install a language pack.

Windows allows you to work with multiple alphabets

To install a language pack

1. In the **Languages** area of the **Region & language** settings pane, click a language that has an available language pack.

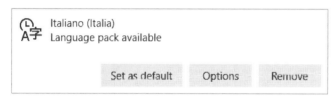

Clicking a language displays additional options

2. In the pane that expands, click **Options** to display the Language Options pane.

3. At the top of the **Language options** pane, in the **Download language pack** area, click the **Download** button to download and then install the language pack.

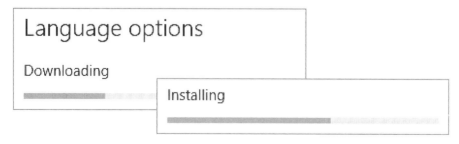

Downloading and installing the language pack is a quick process

To configure language options

 TIP The options available for each language vary.

1. In the **Languages** area of the **Region & language** settings pane, click a language and then, in the pane that expands, click **Options** to display the Language Options pane.

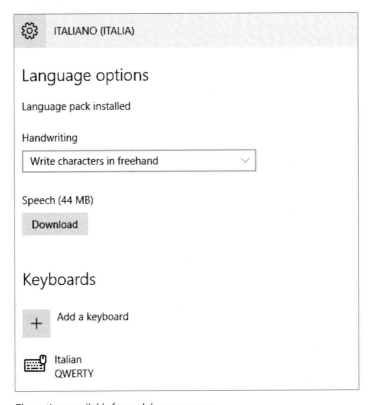

The options available for each language vary

2. Peruse the available options and download or configure any you want to use.

 TIP You can install a keyboard in any language, not only the language displayed at the top of the pane, from the Language Options pane.

Install supplemental font features

Some system languages include enhanced language-specific features such as spelling, text prediction, alphabet-specific fonts, handwriting recognition, optical character recognition, speech recognition, text-to-speech, and Cortana support. When you install a system language that includes supplemental features such as these, you will have to restart your computer to complete the installation of these features.

If Windows displays a banner asking for help, clicking the banner opens the Apps & Features pane.

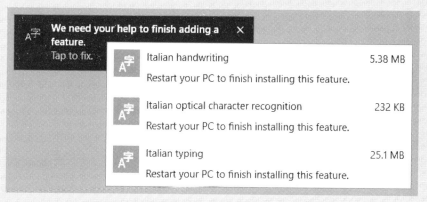

Supplemental font features require a restart

At this point, Windows doesn't indicate what help it needs, but if you recently installed a font, click the Manage Optional Features link at the top of the pane to check there for features that need your attention.

To complete the installation, you need to restart your computer. You can do that at any time, but the optional language features won't function correctly until you do. The restart process might take longer than usual if the extra font features are complex.

To change the Windows display language

1. In the **Languages** area of the **Region & language** settings pane, click a language that is not labeled *Windows display language* and then, in the pane that expands, click **Set as default**.

The change takes effect immediately in some system areas

2. Sign out of Windows, and then sign back in to completely implement the display language change.

To remove a system language

1. In the **Languages** area of the **Region & language** settings pane, click the language you want to remove and then, in the pane that expands, click **Remove**.

To change the keyboard language

1. Install the system language of the keyboard you want to use.

2. On the taskbar, to the left of the clock, click the keyboard language button to expand the available keyboard list.

ENG   English (United States)
        US keyboard

ﭘﺐ   Punjabi (Arabic)
        Urdu keyboard

ITA   Italian (Italy)
        Italian keyboard

⚙   Language preferences

                            11:15 PM
∧ 🖥 🔊 📋 ENG   9/6/2015

Alternative language keyboards are available from the taskbar

Or

1. Press **Win+Spacebar** to cycle through the installed keyboard languages.

To change date and time formats to those of a specific region

1. Display the **Date & time** settings pane.

2. In the **Related settings** area, click **Additional date, time, & regional settings** to display the Clock, Language, And Region category of Control Panel.

3. In the **Region** category, click **Change date, time, or number formats** to display the Formats tab of the Region dialog box. The default format is *Match Windows display language.*

4. Click the **Format** list, and then click the language and country or region that you want to use for the standard date and time formats.

You can use date and time formats for a country or region that doesn't use your default language

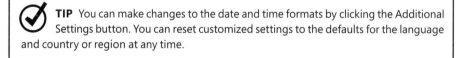

TIP You can make changes to the date and time formats by clicking the Additional Settings button. You can reset customized settings to the defaults for the language and country or region at any time.

5. In the **Region** dialog box, click **OK** to apply your changes and close the dialog box.

To copy regional settings to Windows system screens and new user accounts

1. Display the **Region** dialog box, and then click the **Administrative** tab.

2. In the **Welcome screen and new user accounts** section of the tab, click the **Copy settings** button to display the current settings.

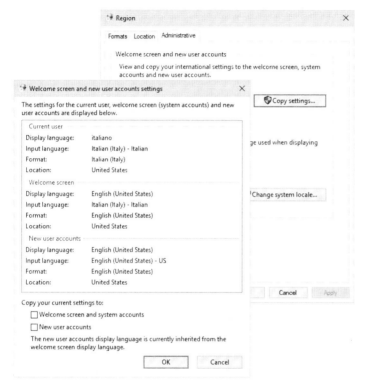

Copy regional settings to new user accounts on your computer

3. At the bottom of the **Welcome screen and new user accounts settings** dialog box, select one or both check boxes to specify the settings that you want to change. Then click **OK**.

4. Restart the computer to implement the changes.

Manage speech settings

Many people talk to their computers, but the time has finally come when doing so represents more of an efficiency than an eccentricity. If your Windows 10 computer is configured to run one of the system languages that supports speech recognition, you can now accomplish even more by speaking to your computer, through the Cortana user interface. You can also configure your computer to respond to verbal commands, and you can dictate content into apps.

> **TIP** At the time of this writing, speech recognition is available for only the following languages: English (United States and United Kingdom), French, German, Japanese, Mandarin (Chinese Simplified and Chinese Traditional), and Spanish.

You can make the best use of speech recognition if you have a good-quality microphone. Most computers and devices have built-in microphones, but you can also purchase reasonably priced headset microphones that maintain a constant distance between the microphone and your mouth, and block out external distractions. They also tend to pick up fewer keyboard and mouse noises than built-in microphones that are close to those interface elements.

As you interact with Cortana, Windows 10 uses a feature called *Getting to know you* that monitors your spoken, handwritten, and typed input in addition to your messages and appointments. From this information, Cortana can make adjustments to the speech recognition patterns and can also serve up content that is pertinent to the things it detects happening in your life. *Getting to know you* is on by default and is required to use Cortana. If you're not using Cortana, you can turn off *Getting to know you* in the Windows 10 privacy settings.

> **SEE ALSO** For more information about Cortana, see "Get assistance from Cortana" in Chapter 11, "Work more efficiently."

Your computer can talk back to you, too. By using text-to-speech technology, it can read printed content to you, or provide verbal cues for the visual aspects of the user interface (for example, reading button labels or dialog box options to you). Windows 10 has two default voices—a female voice identified as Zira (pronounced something like "Sarah") and a male voice identified as Mark. Other voices might be available on your computer or device.

Under the best of conditions, this technology is amazing, and seems almost like arti-ficial intelligence. Under the worst of conditions, it is at least mildly funny. Between those extremes it can range from mildly useful to mildly annoying.

You can manage the speech language, text-to-speech, and microphone settings in the Speech pane of the Settings window, and turn the Getting To Know You feature off or on from the Privacy settings page.

To display the Speech settings pane

1. In the **Settings** window, click **Time & language**, and then click **Speech**.

To configure the computer to recognize your speaking voice

1. Display the **Speech** settings pane.

2. In the **Speech language** section, click the **Choose the language...** list, and then click the language that you speak and want the computer to recognize.

> ✓ **TIP** The list includes only the system languages that are installed on your computer that support speech recognition. To make one of these languages available that isn't your default, you must first install the language pack. For more information, see "Manage regional and language settings" earlier in this chapter.

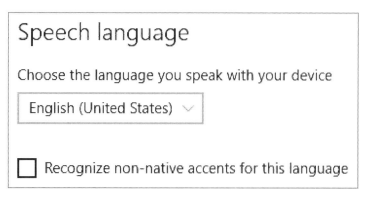

Speech language

Choose the language you speak with your device

| English (United States) ∨ |

☐ Recognize non-native accents for this language

The Speech Language section of the Speech pane

3. To give the computer the best chance of understanding you, select the **Recognize non-native accents for this language** check box.

4. Prepare your microphone:

   - If you have a headset microphone, put it on and adjust the microphone so that it's directly in front of your mouth, with two to three finger-widths of space between your lips and the microphone.

   - If you have a freestanding microphone, position it so that it is in front of you when you're facing the computer screen.

   - Close the door and turn off or remove any loud things from the area.

5. In the **Microphone** section of the **Speech** pane, click the **Get started** button to start the Set Up Your Mic wizard. The wizard indicates the microphone it's monitoring. Ensure that this is the microphone you're using.

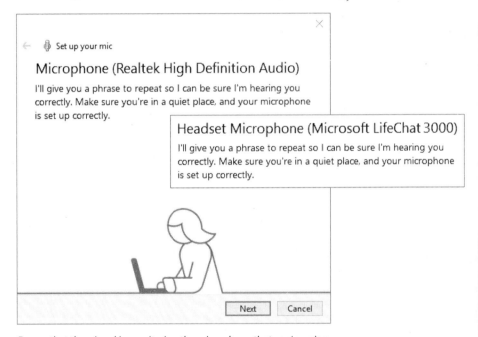

Ensure that the wizard is monitoring the microphone that you're using

> ✓ **TIP** If the wizard indicates a microphone other than the one you want to use, you need to change the default microphone. For information about setting a microphone as the default, see "Set up audio devices" in Chapter 6, "Manage peripheral devices."

6. After you confirm the microphone, click **Next** on the first page of the wizard. The wizard provides a sentence for you to speak.

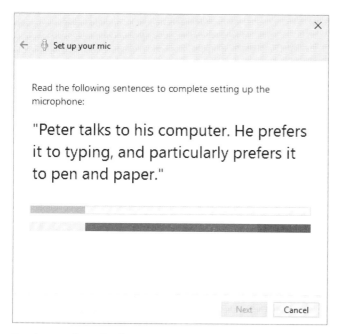

Speak naturally to give the computer a realistic sampling of your voice

7. Begin speaking in the voice that you will normally use when dictating text, giving verbal commands, or speaking to Cortana. When the wizard has a sufficient sample to properly adjust the microphone levels, the **Next** button becomes active.

8. Click the **Next** button, and then click **Finish** to complete and exit the wizard.

> **TIP** Additional speech configuration tools are available from the Speech Recognition page of Control Panel. If you intend to dictate content into an app that supports it, it's worthwhile to invest time in the speech tutorial and the speech recognition voice training. If you use a good microphone and enunciate properly, speech recognition can work pretty well. It won't outpace a fast, accurate typist, but if you are a "hunt and peck" typist, this might help you churn out your next novel.

To display additional speech configuration tools

1. Do either of the following:

   - Display Control Panel in Category view. Click the **Ease of Access** category, and then click **Speech Recognition**.

   - Display Control Panel in Large Icons view or Small Icons view, and then click **Speech recognition**.

To change the voice and speed of the computer's text-to-speech narrator

1. Display the **Speech** settings pane.

2. In the **Text-to-speech** area, click the **Voice** list to display the currently available voices.

Text-to-speech

Change the default voice for apps

Voice

Microsoft Zira Mobile

Microsoft Mark Mobile

Speed

Preview voice

Available voices might change over time or by language

3. In the **Voice** list, click the voice you want to set as the default.

4. On the **Speed** slider, set the speed you think you'll be comfortable with. (The slider represents speeds from very slow on the left to very fast on the right.)

5. Set your speakers to a comfortable level, and then click the **Preview voice** button.

6. Adjust your settings as necessary until the preview voice clip is at a speed you can understand.

To turn off the Getting To Know You feature

1. Do either of the following to display the **Speech, inking, & typing** privacy settings pane:

   - Display the **Speech** settings pane. In the **Related settings** area, click the **Speech, inking, & typing privacy settings** link.

   - In the **Settings** window, click **Privacy**, and then click **Speech, inking, & typing**.

2. Read the feature description and be certain that you don't want to use the dictation or Cortana features. (You can still use the Ease Of Access Speech-to-Text app.)

Getting to know you

Windows and Cortana can get to know your voice and writing to make better suggestions for you. We'll collect info like contacts, recent calendar events, speech and handwriting patterns, and typing history.

Turning this off also turns off dictation and Cortana and clears what this device knows about you.

Stop getting to know me

If you have privacy concerns, you can stop Cortana from learning about you

3. Click the **Stop getting to know me** button.

Customize device display settings

Windows 10 was designed to run on a diverse array of devices, on displays of many different sizes, shapes, and orientations.

When you purchase a computer monitor, all-in-one computer, laptop computer, or handheld device, one of the things you consider is its size, or display area, which is measured like a television screen: diagonally in inches. As important as the physical size, though, is the screen resolution the monitor supports, which is measured in pixels and is expressed as the number of pixels wide by the number of pixels high. Pixels are the individual dots that make up the picture displayed on your screen. Each pixel displays one color; depending on your screen resolution, the images shown on the screen might consist of from 500,000 to several million individual dots of color.

When personal computers first became popular, most computer monitors were capable of displaying only 640 pixels horizontally and 480 pixels vertically (a screen resolution of 640 × 480). Nearly all screen displays now support a screen resolution of no less than 1024 × 768 pixels, and some commercially available screens support a resolution of 3840 × 2160 pixels (or perhaps by the time this book is published, even higher). In effect, as the screen resolution increases, the size of each pixel decreases, and more information can be shown in the same display area. In other words, as the screen resolution increases, so does the amount of information that is shown on the screen—but all of the information appears smaller.

> ✓ **TIP** The maximum resolution is the highest resolution supported by your monitor or the highest resolution supported by the graphics card installed in your computer, whichever is lower.

Most computer systems provide a choice of at least two screen resolutions, but you might have many more choices. Some people prefer to work at a lower screen resolution so that everything on the screen appears larger; others prefer to fit as much information on the screen as they possibly can. Recent statistics indicate that more than 95 percent of Internet users have their screen resolution set to 1024 × 768 or greater. At the time of this writing, the most widely used screen resolution worldwide is 1366 × 768 pixels.

Originally, most monitors had a 4:3 aspect ratio, with the screen 4 units wide and 3 units high. These 4:3 displays are now referred to as *standard displays*. Many monitors now have *widescreen displays* intended to improve the experience of viewing movies on the computer by displaying them at a 16:9 aspect ratio, which is also the standard for high-definition television and ultra-high-definition television. These resolutions might be available on your computer regardless of the native aspect ratio of your actual monitor. The popular 1366 × 768 computer screen resolution is a widescreen display.

> ✓ **TIP** To guarantee clear display of the official Windows 10 desktop background, Microsoft provides nine high-resolution versions of it at different vertically and horizontally oriented sizes. These files are available from the C:\Windows\Web folder.

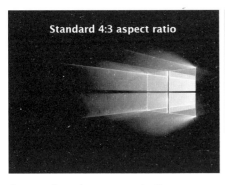
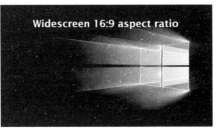

A comparison of screen aspect ratios

In earlier versions of Windows, the screen resolution settings were easily accessible. In Windows 10, the screen resolution is an "advanced" display setting—probably because most people like to set it and forget it. You can modify the screen resolution from the Advanced Display Settings pane.

⚙ **ADVANCED DISPLAY SETTINGS**

1

Identify   Detect

Resolution

1920 × 1080 (Recommended)   ∨

Apply   Cancel

Screen resolution capabilities are hardware specific

Windows 10 offers a different option for increasing the size of user interface elements. Instead of changing the size of everything on the screen (by changing the screen resolution), you can change the size at which Windows displays user interface elements. The default setting is 100%, and you can increase the size in 25-percent increments.

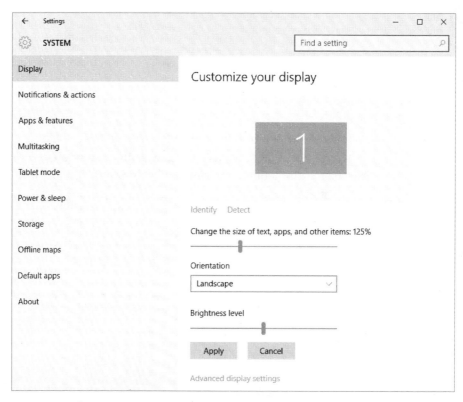

The maximum increase depends on the screen size and resolution

Alternatively, you can increase the text size of only specific user interface elements, such as titles or tooltips, so they're easier to read.

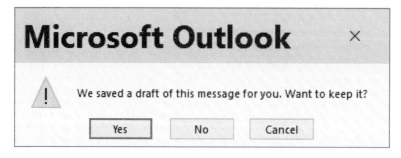

Change the text size or weight

You can temporarily magnify part or all of your on-screen content by using the Magnifier tool. For information about Magnifier, see "Configure Windows accessibility features" in Chapter 10, "Manage power and access options."

 SEE ALSO For information about configuring your computer to display content on multiple monitors, see "Display your desktop on multiple screens" in Chapter 6, "Manage peripheral devices."

Most smaller handheld devices are designed to support the rotation of on-screen content as the device rotates, but this capability isn't generally built in to laptop computers or desktop monitors. If you have a setup that supports the rotation of a monitor or device, you can easily configure Windows 10 to change the orientation of on-screen content. The default orientation is Landscape (with the screen wider than it is high). Other options include Portrait, flipped Landscape, and flipped Portrait.

To display the Display settings pane

1. Do either of the following:

    - Open the **Settings** window. Click **System**, and then click **Display**.

    - Right-click an empty area of the desktop, and then click **Display settings**.

To change the size of user interface elements

1. Display the **Display** settings pane.

2. In the **Change the size of text, apps, and other items** section, drag or click next to the slider to increase or decrease the setting in 25-percent increments.

3. At the bottom of the pane, click the **Apply** button to change the size of many on-screen elements.

4. To complete the process, sign out of Windows and then sign back in.

    TIP It is possible to set a custom scaling level, but this is not recommended. If you're interested in this, click the Advanced Sizing Of Text And Other Items link in the Advanced Display Settings pane, and then in the descriptive paragraph, click the Set A Custom Scaling Level link.

To change the text size for specific user interface elements

1. Do one of the following to open the Display window of Control Panel:

   - At the bottom of the **Advanced display settings** pane, click the **Advanced sizing of text and other items** link.

   - In Category view of Control Panel, click **Appearance and Personalization**, and then click **Display**.

   - In Large Icons view or Small Icons view of Control Panel, click the **Display** icon.

2. In the **Change only the text size** area of the window, click the leftmost list to display the interface elements you can change the text size for.

You can set the text size for specific types of user interface elements

3. Click the element you want to change. Then in the right list, click a font size from **6** through **24** points.

4. If you want to emphasize the interface text even more, select the **Bold** check box. Then click **Apply** to apply the changes.

 IMPORTANT Windows displays a *Please wait* screen while it applies the changes. The process can be somewhat lengthy (about 15 seconds).

To change the orientation of on-screen content

1. In the **Display** settings pane, click the **Orientation** list, and then click **Landscape**, **Portrait**, **Landscape (flipped)**, or **Portrait (flipped)**.

2. Click **Apply** to temporarily change the screen orientation. Windows displays a Keep These Display Changes? message box.

3. If you like the new screen orientation, click **Keep changes**. Otherwise, click **Revert** to return to the previous orientation.

> **TIP** If you don't like the changes and eye-hand coordination in the unfamiliar orientation makes it difficult to click Revert, relax for about 10 seconds and the display will automatically revert to the previous state.

To change the screen brightness

1. In the **Display** settings pane, drag the **Brightness level** slider, or click on either side of the slider, to adjust the screen brightness to a percentage of the maximum level configured for your screen.

   The brightness changes immediately, so you can slowly move the slider until the screen is exactly as bright as you want it in your current lighting conditions.

Or

1. Display the Action Pane and expand the **Quick action** section. Click the **Brightness** icon to adjust the screen brightness to the next multiple of 25 percent and then in 25-percent increments.

> **TIP** Screen brightness is also part of the Power Options that are still set in Control Panel. ,

To change the screen resolution

1. At the bottom of the **Display** settings pane, click the **Advanced display settings** link. The Advanced Display Settings pane shows a preview of the monitors connected to your computer. Each monitor is represented by a box.

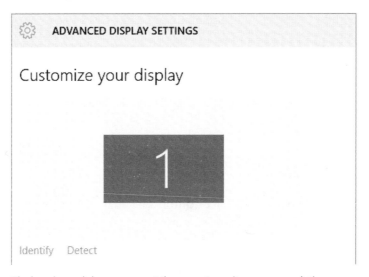

The box size and shape represent the current monitor screen resolution

> ✓ **TIP** When you have multiple monitors connected to your computer, the preview displays each monitor in relation to the others. For information about working with multiple monitors, see "Display your desktop on multiple screens" in Chapter 6, "Manage peripheral devices."

2. In the **Advanced display settings** pane, click the **Resolution** list to display the screen resolutions that are supported by the computer graphics card and the monitor.

> ✓ **TIP** When you change the screen resolution, try to choose one that has the same aspect ratio as your actual monitor. If *(Recommended)* appears after a screen resolution, this will be the largest screen resolution at the native aspect ratio. You might be able to discern the aspect ratio visually from the preview boxes; if not, you can do the math to identify the aspect ratio.

Resolution
1920 × 1080 (Recommended)
1680 × 1050
1600 × 900
1440 × 900
1280 × 1024
1280 × 720
1024 × 768
800 × 600

The available resolutions depend on your graphics card and monitor

3. In the list, click the screen resolution you want. The monitor representation in the preview area updates to reflect the new setting.

4. If you like the preview, click **Apply** to temporarily apply the setting. Windows displays a Keep These Display Changes? message box.

5. If you like the new screen resolution, click **Keep changes**. Otherwise, click **Revert** to return to the previous orientation.

Skills review

In this chapter, you learned how to:

- Manage date and time settings
- Manage regional and language settings
- Manage speech settings
- Customize device display settings

Practice tasks

No practice files are necessary to complete the practice tasks in this chapter.

Manage date and time settings

Perform the following tasks:

1. From the taskbar, experiment with different methods of displaying the current time and date.

2. Display the calendar, and from there display the **Date & time** settings pane.

3. Change the time zone to another, and notice that the clock immediately changes. Examine other content on your computer that has time stamps, such as email messages, and determine how the time zone change affects that content. Then set the time zone to the one you're in.

4. Configure Windows to display date and time information for a second time zone. Choose a time zone that is far away from your own, preferably on the other side of the date line. Then experiment with the different methods of displaying the secondary clock.

5. Configure Windows to display the clocks that you want to have available.

Manage regional and language settings

Display the Region & Language settings pane, and then perform the following tasks:

1. Check that the correct country or region is specified for local content.

2. If you want to, install an additional system language. If the language requires a language pack, install the language pack.

3. If you install an additional language, notice that the language button appears in the notification area of the taskbar. Click the button to display the keyboard language options. Experiment with the other keyboard if you want, to try to locate keys that enter different characters than those shown on your keyboard.

4. Experiment with any other features that are discussed in the "Manage regional and language settings" topic that you're interested in. When you finish, configure the settings on your computer for the way you want to work.

Manage speech settings

Display the Speech settings pane, and then perform the following tasks:

1. Preview the voices that are available for the computer's text-to-speech narrator. Choose the voice you like best, and then adjust its speed so you can best understand it.

2. Complete the process of configuring the computer to recognize your speaking voice.

3. Display the additional speech configuration tools. If you're interested in more precisely configuring the computer for speech recognition, complete at least one of the configuration processes.

Customize device display settings

Display the Display settings pane, and then perform the following tasks:

1. Experiment with the **Change the size of text, apps, and other items** slider to determine the largest possible magnification you can apply to your display by using this feature. If you want to, apply the **125%** setting, and then sign out and back in to your computer to get the full effect of the setting.

2. Adjust the screen brightness to suit your current working environment.

3. Display the **Advanced display settings** pane, and click the **Resolution** list to display the screen resolution options supported by your computer system. If you want to, temporarily apply a different screen resolution and examine the effect. If you find another screen resolution that you prefer, keep it.

4. Open the **Display** window of Control Panel. Display the **Change only the text size** list. If you want to, complete the process to change the text size for one or more user interface elements.

Manage power and access options

Your power settings determine how long your computer will sit idle before reducing power consumption by turning off the screen or going into sleep mode. You can manage these settings independently or as part of a power plan.

When your computer comes out of sleep mode (and between computing sessions), Windows displays the lock screen. By default, the lock screen displays the current time, date, network connection status and battery charge (for devices running on battery power). However, it can be configured to display much more information, including status updates from up to eight apps. It can also double as an electronic picture frame, and display a slide show of pictures stored in multiple folders on your computer and in the cloud.

Microsoft takes accessibility seriously, and this is apparent in the company's early and continued commitment to the Windows Ease of Access features that provide alternative methods for information input and output. Anyone can use these features to enhance their computing experience.

This chapter guides you through procedures related to configuring power options for desktop and portable computers, customizing the lock screen, and configuring Windows accessibility features.

In this chapter

- Configure power options
- Customize the lock screen
- Configure Windows accessibility features

Practice files

For this chapter, use the practice files from the Win10SBS\Ch10 folder. For practice file download instructions, see the introduction.

Configure power options

Reducing power consumption is obviously of higher priority if your device is running on battery power. On battery-powered devices, such as laptop computers, you can configure settings that are in effect when the device is plugged in and other settings that are in effect when the device runs on battery power.

The screen brightness can have a significant effect on the length of time a battery charge powers a computer. You can manage the screen brightness as part of a power plan, or adjust it independently at any time. (For example, if you're working in a dark room, a brighter screen can cause more eyestrain than a dimmer screen.)

Each Windows 10 computer has a set of built-in power plans that define three settings:

- When to turn off the display
- When to put the computer to sleep
- How bright to make the display

The built-in power plans vary based on the computer type and manufacturer, but usually include the following:

- **Power Saver** This power plan prioritizes power conservation over performance. The screen is less bright and computer processes turn off earlier.

- **High Performance** This power plan prioritizes the user experience over power conservation. The screen is brighter and processes turn off after a longer idle time.

- **Balanced** This power plan is less power efficient than High Performance and has higher performance values than Power Saver.

You can choose a preconfigured power plan, modify individual elements of a power plan, or even create your own. Creating a custom plan is similar to editing an existing plan, but you name and save it so you can easily apply it at any time. If you decide you no longer need a custom power plan, you can delete it.

To change the screen brightness without affecting the power management settings

1. Display the Action Pane by doing either of the following:

   • Near the right end of the taskbar, click the Action Pane icon.

   • Press **Win+A**.

2. If all the setting buttons aren't visible at the bottom of the **Action Pane**, click **Expand** to display them. The Brightness button has a sun in its upper-left corner.

Setting buttons vary by system

3. Click the **Brightness** button to cycle through screen brightness settings.

Or

1. Open the **Settings** window. Click **System**, and then click **Display**.

2. In the **Display** settings pane, move the **Brightness level** slider to adjust the screen brightness. Changes are effective immediately; it isn't necessary to click Apply.

To configure the power management settings

1. Open the **Settings** window. Click **System**, and then click **Power & sleep**. The Power & Sleep pane displays the current length of inactive time you want the computer to wait before it turns off the screen and then goes to sleep.

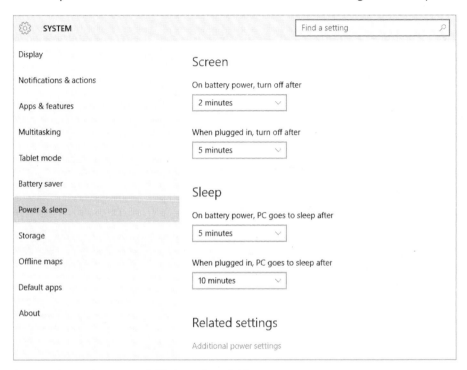

⚙ SYSTEM		Find a setting 🔍
Display	**Screen**	
Notifications & actions	On battery power, turn off after	
Apps & features	2 minutes ⌄	
Multitasking	When plugged in, turn off after	
Tablet mode	5 minutes ⌄	
Battery saver	**Sleep**	
Power & sleep	On battery power, PC goes to sleep after	
Storage	5 minutes ⌄	
Offline maps	When plugged in, PC goes to sleep after	
Default apps	10 minutes ⌄	
About	**Related settings**	
	Additional power settings	

Separate time options are available for each available power source

2. In the **Screen** section of the **Power & sleep** pane, click each available list, and then click a time from **1 minute** to **5 hours**, or **Never**, to indicate the period of inactivity after which you want the screen to turn off (but the computer to continue running).

 TIP It might be necessary to move the cursor away from the list to display its scroll bar.

3. In the **Sleep** section of the **Power & sleep** pane, click each available list, and then click a time from **1 minute** to **5 hours**, or **Never**, to indicate the period of inactivity after which you want the computer to enter Sleep mode.

> **TIP** The Sleep timeout must be equal to or greater than the Screen timeout. Setting the Sleep value to less time than the Screen value lowers the Screen value to match; setting the Screen value to more time than the Sleep value raises the Sleep value to match.

The power setting changes take effect immediately.

To choose a standard power-management plan

1. Display the **Power & sleep** settings pane.

2. In the **Related settings** section of the pane, click **Additional power settings** to open the Power Options window of Control Panel.

3. If **Show additional plans** appears below the plan descriptions, click it to display hidden power plans.

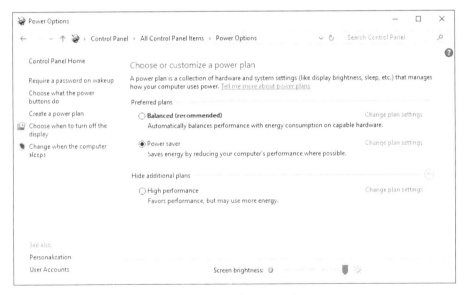

The available power plans vary by computer manufacturer and type

4. To compare plan settings, click the **Change plan settings** link to the right of each plan name, peruse the settings, and then click the **Back** button to return to the Power Options window.

5. In the **Power Options** window, click the preconfigured power option you want.

To modify an existing power plan

1. Open the **Power Options** window of Control Panel.

2. Click **Change plan settings** to the right of the plan that you want to modify, to open the Edit Plan Settings window for the plan.

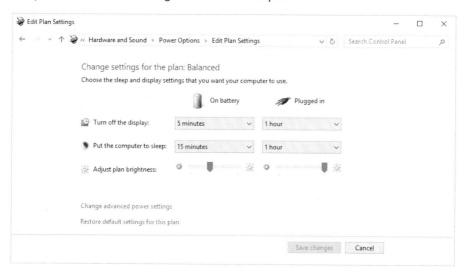

Desktop computers have only the Plugged In settings

3. For each available power source, do the following:

   - To the right of **Turn off the display**, select a time from **1 minute** to **5 hours**, or **Never**, to indicate the period of inactivity after which you want to turn off the screen when the computer is running on that power source.

   - To the right of **Put the computer to sleep**, select a time from **1 minute** to **5 hours**, or **Never**, to indicate the period of inactivity after which you want the computer to enter Sleep mode when it is running on that power source.

   - To the right of **Adjust plan brightness**, move the slider to indicate how bright you want the screen to be when the computer is running on that power source.

4. In the **Edit Plan Settings** window, click **Save change**s to apply your changes to the power plan and return to the Power Options window. If you modified the currently active plan, changes to the brightness are immediately apparent.

> ✓ **TIP** If you decide you don't like the screen brightness you set, you can change it at the bottom of the Power Options window. The change will be applied to the current plan and automatically saved with it.

To create a custom power plan

1. Open the **Power Options** window of Control Panel.

2. In the left pane, click **Create a power plan** to open the Create a Power Plan window.

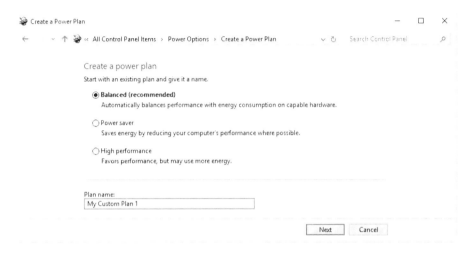

Custom plans are based on existing plans

3. Select one of the default plans as the starting point for your new plan, and provide a name for it. Then click **Next** to display the Edit Plan Settings window.

4. For each available power source, do the following:

   - To the right of **Turn off the display**, select a time from **1 minute** to **5 hours**, or **Never**, to indicate the period of inactivity after which you want to turn off the screen when the computer is running on that power source.

   - To the right of **Put the computer to sleep**, select a time from **1 minute** to **5 hours**, or **Never**, to indicate the period of inactivity after which you want the computer to enter Sleep mode when it is running on that power source.

   - To the right of **Adjust plan brightness**, move the slider to indicate how bright you want the screen to be when the computer is running on that power source.

5. In the **Edit Plan Settings** window, click **Create** to create the custom power plan and return to the Power Options window.

To edit advanced settings of an existing power plan

1. Open the **Power Options** window of Control Panel.

2. Click **Change plan settings** to the right of the plan that you want to modify.

3. At the bottom of the **Edit Plan Settings** window, click **Change advanced power settings** to open the Power Options dialog box.

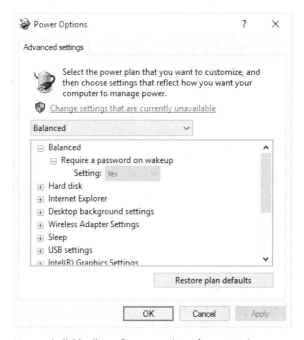

You can individually configure a variety of power options

4. If the plan shown at the top of the **Power Options** dialog box is not the one you want to modify, click the current plan and then, in the list, click the plan you want to customize.

5. Scroll through the available settings and click the expand button (+) to expand any category of interest.

6. If the settings you want to change are disabled (dimmed), you can click the **Change settings that are currently unavailable** link above the list and provide administrator permission, if necessary, to make the changes.

7. If you change settings, click **Apply** or **OK** to apply the changes.

To reset a power plan to its defaults

1. Open the **Power Options** window of Control Panel.

2. Click **Change plan settings** to the right of the plan that you want to restore.

3. At the bottom of the **Edit Plan Settings** window, click the **Restore default settings for this plan** link, and then click **Yes** in the **Power Options** message box that opens.

To delete a custom power plan

1. Open the **Power Options** window of Control Panel.

2. Apply any power plan other than the one you want to delete.

3. Click **Change plan settings** to the right of the plan that you want to delete.

4. At the bottom of the **Edit Plan Settings** window, click the **Delete this plan** link, and then click **OK** in the **Power Options** message box that opens.

 TIP You can delete only custom power plans. You can't delete built-in power plans.

System power settings

Windows 10 has default behaviors for entering sleep mode, waking up, and shutting down. If you find that these defaults aren't working for you, you can change the options. (Changes require approval from an Administrator account.)

There are three sets of settings that you can change:

- **Shutdown action triggers** These settings are related to the Power and Sleep buttons (the physical buttons) on your computer. Not all computers have Sleep buttons, but many do; they're usually located on the keyboard and labeled with something that indicates sleep such as "zzz" or a moon. On a laptop, you can also specify what happens when you close the lid. The following table describes the shutdown actions that can occur when you press the Power or Sleep button, or close the laptop lid.

Shutdown action	Power button	Sleep button	Close the lid
Do nothing	Y	Y	Y
Turn off the display	Y	Y	Not optional
Sleep	Y	Default	Y
Hibernate	Y	Y	Y
Shut down	Default	N	Y

- **Password requirement** By default, when your computer comes out of sleep mode, Windows displays the lock screen. Users whose accounts are protected by passwords must enter their passwords to sign in. You can turn off this requirement.

- **Shutdown settings** This category is a bit of a catchall. You can control whether the Power menu includes the Sleep and Hibernate commands, and whether the user account menu includes the Lock command.

In general, if things are working well for you, it's best to leave them as they are. But if you do want to make changes, you can do so from the System Settings page of Control Panel. In Category view, click Hardware and Sound, and then in the Power Options group, click Change What The Power Buttons Do. Most of the options are unavailable to change until you click Change Settings That Are Currently Unavailable and provide Administrator account credentials.

Make your battery last longer

The Battery Saver feature is new for Windows 10 and available only on battery-powered devices (such as laptop computers). Battery Saver conserves battery power (and thereby extends battery life) by regulating background activity and hardware settings. Windows automatically turns the Battery Saver feature on when the battery charge falls below 20%, but you also have the option of turning it on whenever the device is running on battery power.

To display current battery life information, open the Settings window, click System, and then click Battery Saver.

TIP The Battery Saver pane is visible only on battery-powered devices.

Battery life remaining:
71%

Estimated time remaining:

3 hours 30 minutes

Battery use

Battery life estimates and Battery Saver options

To turn on Battery Saver, display the Battery Saver pane, and then set the Battery Saver Is Currently toggle button to On.

To modify the battery charge level at which Battery Saver turns on, or the actions permitted while Battery Saver is running, display the Battery Saver pane, click the Battery Saver Settings link, and then configure the settings.

☑ Turn battery saver on automatically if my battery falls below:

15%

☑ Allow push notifications from any app while in battery saver
☑ Lower screen brightness while in battery saver

You can opt to permit push notifications and allow specific apps to send data

435

Customize the lock screen

By default, the lock screen is displayed when you start or lock your computer, and when the computer comes out of sleep mode.

The lock screen has three primary purposes:

- Display information from selected apps when the computer session isn't active.

- Display a single photo, or one or more folders of photos. (Windows 10 can display photos from multiple folders.)

- Deter accidental sign-in on a touch device.

For most of us, the lock screen is just a short pause on the way to the sign-in screen, but it can double as an electronic picture frame, and you can also display some useful information on it.

The lock screen always displays the date, the time, and the network icon. If your device operates on battery power, then the lock screen also displays the battery icon so you can see the remaining charge at a glance.

Set the lock screen background

On a clean installation of Windows 10, the lock screen is configured to display one of the Windows 10 theme images. You can choose any photo or a slideshow of photos that are contained in one or more folders. The latter option displays more than a simple slideshow; it displays from one to five images at a time and mixes photos from the selected folders.

If your computer is running Windows 10 Home, you also have options to display the following:

- A Windows Spotlight lock screen background featuring beautiful bing.com images and information about Windows 10

- Windows tips and tricks

 TIP It is possible to disable the lock screen by editing the registry or Group Policies, but these activities shouldn't be undertaken lightly and are beyond the scope of a *Step by Step* book.

To display one image on the lock screen

1. Open the **Settings** window.

2. Click **Personalization**, and then click **Lock screen**. The Preview section of the Lock Screen settings pane displays your current lock screen background.

   If the current background is a single picture, the pane shows thumbnails of other recent picture backgrounds (or background options from the current theme) for quick selection. If the background is a slideshow, the pane shows the folders that contain the slideshow photos.

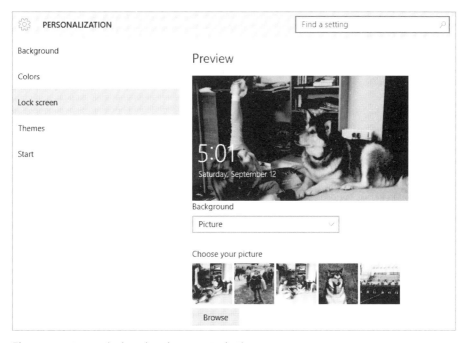

The pane content varies based on the current selection

3. In the **Lock screen** pane, click the **Background** list, and then click **Picture**.

4. Select the background picture by doing either of the following:

   - If the **Choose your picture** section includes a thumbnail of the picture you want to use, click the thumbnail.

   - If the **Choose your picture section** doesn't show the picture you want to use, click the **Browse** button. In the **Open** dialog box, browse to the picture you want to use, and then click the **Choose picture** button.

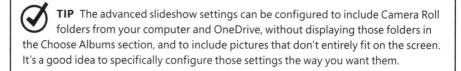 **TIP** The pretty pictures provided with Windows 10 are stored in C:\Windows \Web\Screen and also provided as part of the Windows 10 theme. You can download similar artwork from *windows.microsoft.com/en-US/windows/wallpaper*.

Your selection is shown in the Preview section. If the picture you select doesn't have the same aspect ratio as the screen, Windows fills the screen with the picture, which might cut off part of what you want to see.

5. Press **Win+L** to lock the computer and verify that the background looks the way you want it.

Or

1. Start the Photos app.

2. Locate the photo that you want to display on the lock screen, and open it for editing.

3. At the right end of the **Photos** menu bar, click the **See more** button (...), and then click **Set as lock screen**.

To display a series of images on the lock screen

1. Identify one or more folders that contain pictures you want to display as a slideshow. If you want to use only some of the photos from each folder, create a new folder and copy the photos to it.

2. Display the **Lock screen** settings pane.

3. In the **Background** list, click **Slideshow**. The Choose Albums For Your Slideshow section displays your Pictures folder or any folders that were previously selected for a slideshow.

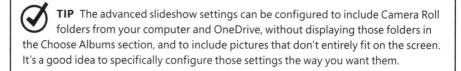 **TIP** The advanced slideshow settings can be configured to include Camera Roll folders from your computer and OneDrive, without displaying those folders in the Choose Albums section, and to include pictures that don't entirely fit on the screen. It's a good idea to specifically configure those settings the way you want them.

4. Do either of the following:

   • To add a folder to the slideshow album, click the **Add a folder** button, browse to the folder you want to add, select the folder, and then click the **Choose this folder** button.

   • To remove a folder from the slideshow album, click the folder to display its controls, and then click the **Remove** button.

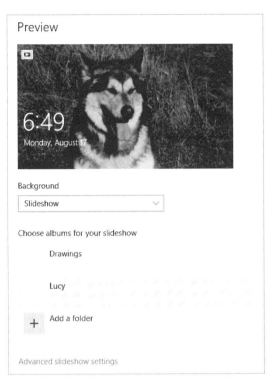

Preview

6:49
Monday, August 17

Background

Slideshow

Choose albums for your slideshow

Drawings

Lucy

 Add a folder

Advanced slideshow settings

Set up a slideshow to display on your lock screen

To display the Windows Spotlight lock screen

> ⚠ **IMPORTANT** At the time of this writing, Windows Spotlight is available in Windows 10 Home, but not in Windows 10 Pro.

1. Display the **Lock screen** settings pane.

2. In the **Background** list, click **Windows spotlight**. A preview of the current Spotlight background appears at the top of the Lock Screen pane.

> ✓ **TIP** On the Windows Spotlight lock screen, you can vote for the backgrounds you like, and Windows 10 will select future backgrounds that reflect your preferences. To vote for or against a background, click *Like What You See?* and then click *I like it!* or *Not a fan.*

To display tips and tricks on the lock screen

 IMPORTANT At the time of this writing, lock screen fun facts are available in Windows 10 Home and not in Windows 10 Pro.

1. Configure the lock screen to display a picture or slideshow.

2. On the **Lock screen** settings pane, below the **Choose your picture** or **Choose an album** section, set the **Get fun facts, tips, tricks, and more on your lock screen** toggle button to **On**.

To configure advanced slideshow settings

1. Display the **Lock screen** settings pane.

2. Below the **Choose your picture** or **Choose albums** section, click the **Advanced slideshow settings** link to display the **Advanced slideshow settings** pane.

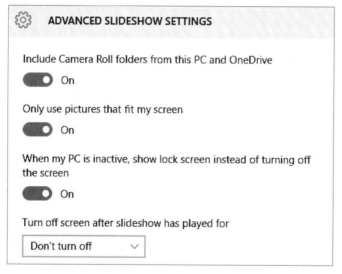

Advanced slideshow settings for the lock screen

3. Configure the advanced settings the way you want them for your slideshow.

Display app status information on the lock screen

In addition to the background photo or photos and the time, date, network, and battery information, you can choose to display detailed status information from one Store app that supports this feature, and quick status information from up to seven Store apps. The additional apps don't display as tiles with the usual live content; they display as an icon with very terse text. The primary purpose of this display is to provide you with quick but basic information about something, such as the number of new emails or an upcoming meeting.

The apps that are available to you depend on the apps that are installed on your computer. Run each app at least once to configure any required settings (for example, to specify the location you want the Weather app to monitor), so it can display updates at the bottom of the lock screen.

To display app information on the lock screen

1. Open the **Settings** window.

2. Click **Personalization**, and then click **Lock screen**. The controls to set lock screen apps are below the background settings.

3. In the **Choose an app to show detailed status** section, click the box to display a list of apps that can display status information on the lock screen.

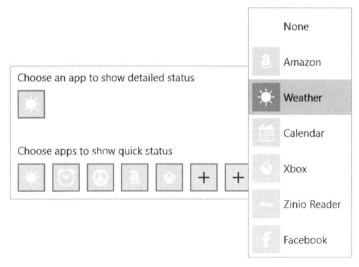

Get information updates directly on your lock screen

4. In the app list, click one app to display detailed status updates on the lock screen.

5. In the **Choose apps to show quick status** section, click any box, and then click an app in the list. Repeat this process to select up to seven apps.

> **TIP** The order of the apps in the list determines the order of status updates on the lock screen. You can choose to leave any of the blocks empty. An empty block is displayed as a gap between the status updates of the surrounding apps.

Configure a screen saver

Screen savers are blank screens or moving images that appear on your screen after some period of inactivity. Originally, screen savers were used to prevent screens from being permanently "imprinted" with a static image that remained on the screen for too long. (This was back in the dark ages of computer history, when monitors fired a stream of electrons at the back of a CRT (cathode ray tube) or plasma screen to create little white dots that combined to display text you could read from the front side of the screen.) Modern monitors are not susceptible to this kind of damage, so screen savers are now primarily for visual entertainment.

The original screen saver was a simple app that made the screen blank after a period of inactivity. It was created by John Socha, and its code was published in the December 1983 issue of the *Softalk* magazine.

Windows 10 has six built-in screen saver options:

- **3D Text** Displays a rotating version of the text you specify. If you don't specify text, it displays "Windows 10."

- **Blank** Clears the screen of content.

- **Bubbles** Displays colorful round bubbles that bounce around the screen.

- **Mystify** Displays colorful repeating lines in geometric and curving patterns.

- **Photos** Displays a slideshow of the files in any folder that you specify. If you don't specify a folder, it displays the content of your Pictures folder.

- **Ribbons** Displays ribbons of color that dance across the screen.

When you select a screen saver, you can preview the effect, set the interval of inactivity before it will be displayed, and specify whether a password is required to stop the screen saver after it is set in motion. For some screen savers, you can set options such as size, motion pattern, and style.

To configure a screen saver, follow these steps:

1. Open the **Settings** window, click **Personalization**, and then click **Lock screen**.

2. At the bottom of the **Lock screen** settings pane, click **Screen saver settings** to open the Screen Saver Settings dialog box.

3. In the **Screen saver** list, click the screen saver you want to use. The dialog box displays a preview of the screen saver.

4. If the screen saver you select has options, the Settings button becomes active. To configure nondefault options, click the **Settings** button and provide the requested information.

5. If you want to preview the screen saver at full size on your screen, click the **Preview** button. The preview ends as soon as you move the mouse or take some similar action.

6. In the **Wait** box, set the number of minutes of inactivity after which you want the screen saver to start.

7. If you want Windows to display the lock screen when the screen saver stops, select the **On resume, display logon screen** check box.

   TIP The term "logon screen" in the Screen Saver Settings dialog box is left over from a previous version of Windows, but refers to the Windows 10 lock screen.

8. In the **Screen Saver Settings** dialog box, click **OK**.

Configure Windows accessibility features

Are the words on the screen too small to read easily? Do you wish the icons were larger? Does it take you a while to locate the insertion point because it is so skinny? Windows 10 has accessibility features that make it easier for you to get information from the computer (output features), and other features that make it easier for you to provide information to the computer (input features).

Windows 10 includes a group of utilities (collectively known as *Ease of Access features*) that are specifically designed to help people interact with the computer by making content easier to access or providing alternative input and output methods. The utilities include the following:

- **Closed captions** Text narrations of audio content that display as videos play.

- **High Contrast** Color schemes that make individual user interface elements stand out on the screen.

   SEE ALSO For information about high-contrast themes, see "Apply and manage themes" in Chapter 2, "Personalize your working environment."

- **Magnifier** A panel that magnifies the screen under the mouse pointer up to nine times. You can move and resize the magnification panel.

- **Narrator** A text-to-speech tool that reads menu commands, dialog box options, and other screen features out loud, telling you what options are available and how to use them. It also reads your keystrokes to you as you type them, and tells you the pointer location on the screen as you move the mouse.

   SEE ALSO For information about using keyboard shortcuts, see Appendix B, "Keyboard shortcuts and touchscreen tips."

You can turn on the High Contrast, Magnifier, Narrator, On-Screen Keyboard, Sticky Keys, or Filter Keys features from the Welcome screen, before you sign in to Windows. When you're signed in to Windows 10, you can manage most of the accessibility features from the Ease Of Access category page of the Settings window.

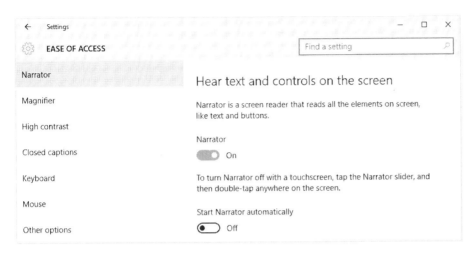

Windows 10 offers several accessibility options

Accessibility features are also still available from the Ease Of Access Center in Control Panel. If you're unsure which features would be helpful to you, you can answer a series of questions, and Windows will recommend accessibility settings based on your answers.

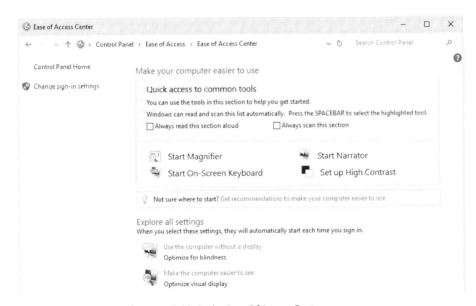

Some of the setting interfaces available in the Ease Of Access Center

When you turn on an accessibility feature, it remains on until you turn it off.

If you sign in to multiple computers by using your Microsoft account credentials, you can configure the accessibility settings on one computer, and then have Windows 10 synchronize the settings across all computers.

 SEE ALSO For information about synchronizing Ease Of Access settings across devices, see "Customize your sign-in options" in Chapter 8, "Manage user accounts and settings."

Many of the accessibility features have keyboard shortcuts, but those aren't of much use when you're working on a device that doesn't have an external keyboard. To simplify the process for users of tablets and other handheld Windows 10 devices, you can configure Windows 10 to launch Magnifier, Narrator, or the On-Screen Keyboard when you press the external Windows button and Volume Up button on those devices.

To display Ease of Access settings

1. To display the Ease Of Access settings category page, open the **Settings** window, and then click **Ease of Access**.

2. To display the Ease Of Access Center, do either of the following:

   - Display Control Panel in category view, click **Ease of Access**, and then click **Ease of Access Center**.

   - Press **Win+U**.

To get accessibility setting recommendations from Windows

1. Display the Ease Of Access Center.

2. Click the **Get recommendations to make your computer easier to use** link.

3. On the **Eyesight**, **Dexterity**, **Hearing**, **Speech**, and **Reasoning** pages, select the check box for each statement that applies to you, and then click **Next**.

4. On the **Recommended settings** page, review the accessibility options that Windows recommended in response to your selections. Select or clear any additional check boxes that you want to, and then click **Apply** or **OK** to apply your changes.

To configure a device hardware shortcut for an accessibility tool

1. Display the Ease Of Access Center.

2. In the **Explore All Settings** section, click **Make touch and tablets easier to use**.

3. In the **Launching common tools** section, click the drop-down list, and then click the accessibility tool that you want to start when you press the Windows button and Volume Up button on your device.

4. In the **Make touch and tablets easier to use** window, click **Apply** or **OK** to implement the change.

High-contrast settings

A high-contrast theme displays text and background colors that might be easier to see and cause less eyestrain. When you apply a high-contrast theme, it affects all the content that you display on your screen. Some content, such as a busy webpage image, is not visible when a high-contrast theme is applied.

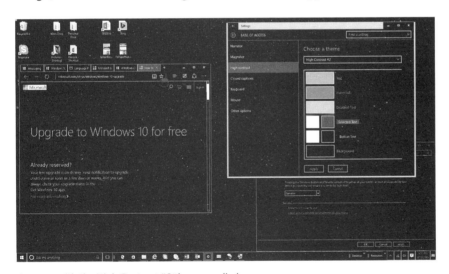

A screen with the High Contrast #2 theme applied

Windows comes with four high-contrast themes, which we introduced in "Apply and manage themes" in Chapter 2, "Personalize your working environment."

It takes Windows a bit longer (about 10 seconds) to apply a high-contrast theme than it does to make other changes. Windows displays a *Please wait* screen while it applies the theme.

To apply a high-contrast theme

1. Do either of the following:

   - Open the **Personalization** window of Control Panel. In the **High Contrast Themes** section of the **Personalization** window, click the high-contrast theme you want to apply.

   - To reapply the most recent high-contrast theme (or to apply High Contrast #1 if you haven't yet applied a high-contrast theme), press **left Alt+left Shift +Print Screen**, and then click **Yes** in the message box that appears.

Or

1. On the **Ease of Access** settings category page, click **High contrast**.

2. In the **High contrast** settings pane, click the box under **Choose a theme**, and then click one of the four high-contrast themes to preview the theme colors that are assigned to the background, text, hyperlinks, disabled text, selected text, and button text.

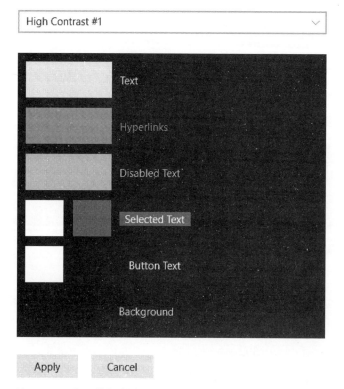

You can preview all the high-contrast themes before you apply one

3. When you identify the theme you want, select that theme in the list, and then click the **Apply** button to apply the theme to the computer.

To revert to a regular contrast theme

1. Do one of the following:

   - Press **left Alt+left Shift+Print Screen**.

   - In the **High Contrast** settings pane, click **None** in the **Choose a theme** list, and then click **Apply**.

   - Open the **Personalization** window of Control Panel, and click the theme you want to apply.

   Windows displays a *Please wait* screen while it applies the theme.

Magnifier settings

You can use the Magnifier tool to make on-screen elements such as text and icons a larger-than-usual size so they're easier to see. When you first turn on Magnifier, it is in full-screen mode and doesn't focus on a specific area of the screen or apply any specific magnification. You must choose a magnification, and you can also choose a view.

Magnifier has three magnification views:

- **Full Screen view** Magnifies the entire screen

- **Lens view** Magnifies a rectangular portion of the screen that is under the cursor

- **Docked view** Magnifies the content that is under the cursor in a separate pane that is docked to one edge of the screen

You can set the size of the Lens and move it around the screen

TIP When you use full-screen mode, click the Views menu and then click Preview Full Screen to locate the cursor or change its location.

When Magnifier is running, you control its settings from the Magnifier window that appears when you click the magnifying glass.

To turn on Magnifier

1. Do one of the following:

    - Press **Win+Plus Sign**.

    - On the **Ease of Access** settings category page, click **Magnifier**. Then in the **Magnifier** settings pane, set the **Magnifier** toggle button to **On**.

    - In the Ease Of Access Center, in the **Quick access to common tools** section, click **Start Magnifier**.

    A magnifying glass that represents the Magnifier window appears on the screen.

    A magnifying glass conceals the Magnifier window

To change the magnified screen area

1. Point to the magnifying glass. When chevrons appear on it, click it to display the Magnifier menu bar.

    The Magnifier commands are available from this menu bar

2. On the **Magnifier** menu bar, click **Views**, and then click **Full Screen**, **Lens**, or **Docked**.

    Or

Press any of the following keyboard shortcuts:

- To display the Full Screen view of Magnifier, press **Ctrl+Alt+F**.

- To display the Lens view of Magnifier, press **Ctrl+Alt+L**.

- To display the Docked view of Magnifier, press **Ctrl+Alt+D**.

To change the level of magnification

1. Turn on Magnifier, and then do either of the following:

   - Press **Win+Plus Sign** or **Windows logo key+Minus Sign**.

   - On the **Magnifier** menu bar, click the **Plus Sign** (+) or **Minus Sign** (-).

   The magnification changes in the increments that are set in the Magnifier Options dialog box.

To configure Magnifier options

1. On the **Magnifier** menu bar, click the **Options** button to open the Magnifier Options dialog box.

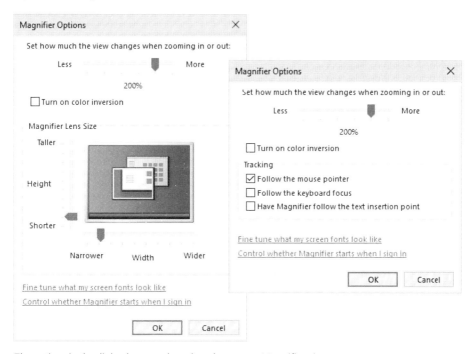

The options in the dialog box vary based on the current Magnifier view

2. Do any of the following:

   - Set the increments of magnification on the slider within a range from 25 percent to 400 percent.

   - To invert the colors within the magnified area, select the **Turn on color inversion** check box.

   - If Magnifier is currently in Lens view, set the Magnifier Lens size to a height and width that are a proportion of the screen size.

   - If Magnifier is currently in Full Screen or Docked view, select the tracking option you want.

3. Click **OK** to close the dialog box and apply the changes.

Or

1. In the **Magnifier** settings pane, set any of the following toggle buttons:

   - To invert the colors within the magnified area, set the **Invert colors** toggle button to **On**.

   - In the **Tracking** section of the pane, set the tracking options you want.

To invert the colors of the magnified area to their color spectrum opposites

1. Do either of the following:

   - Open the **Magnifier Options** dialog box, select the **Turn on color inversion** check box, and then click **OK**.

   - In the **Magnifier** settings pane, set the **Invert colors** toggle button to **On**.

To turn off Magnifier

1. Do either of the following:

   - Press **Win+Esc**.

   - In the **Magnifier** settings pane, set the **Magnifier** toggle button to **Off**.

Narrator and Audio Description settings

Windows 10 includes two utilities that can provide descriptions of visual content: Narrator and Audio Descriptions.

Narrator reads out loud the labels, descriptions, and instructions for on-screen elements. For example, when you select a category in the Settings window, Narrator might tell you the name of the category, how many category options there are, and that you can double-click to open the category. You can select from multiple Narrator voices and adjust the speed of the voice to match your listening speed. You can also specify the interface items that you want Narrator to identify for you.

For those people who sign in to multiple computers with Microsoft accounts, and synchronize settings across those computers, here's a warning: turning on Narrator on one computer turns on Narrator on all the computers, and you'll have to turn it off individually on each computer. This might be exactly what you want, but be prepared, if you're signed in to four separate computers around the house, that things can get a bit noisy. If you want to turn on Narrator (or any of the Ease Of Access tools) on only one computer, turn off the synchronization of Ease Of Access settings on that computer first.

 SEE ALSO For more information about synchronizing settings among computers, see "Customize your sign-in options" in Chapter 8, "Manage user accounts and settings."

Audio Descriptions are spoken descriptions of video content that are provided with the video. In the television and movie industries, these supplemental audio tracks (also referred to as *video descriptions*) are often provided with special versions of films that are called Descriptive Video Service (DVS) versions. Sometimes the audio is provided by professional voiceover performers reading scripted descriptions of the film activity, and other times it's simply a recording of the actors and director watching the film and talking about it.

In Windows 10, you can turn on the Audio Description feature, and if a video has an audio description, it will play with the video. No additional configuration is possible.

To turn on Narrator

1. On the **Ease of Access** settings category page, click **Narrator**.

2. In the **Narrator** settings pane, set the **Narrator** toggle button to **On**.

3. In the Ease Of Access Center, click the **Make the computer easier to see** link. Then in the **Hear text and descriptions read aloud** section, select the **Turn on Narrator** check box. A blue box appears on the screen. Narrator reads the content that is in the box.

4. In the **Voice** section of the **Narrator** pane, select the voice that you want to represent Narrator. Then set the voice speed and pitch.

> 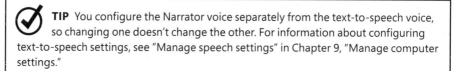 **TIP** You configure the Narrator voice separately from the text-to-speech voice, so changing one doesn't change the other. For information about configuring text-to-speech settings, see "Manage speech settings" in Chapter 9, "Manage computer settings."

Or

1. In the Ease Of Access Center, in the **Quick access to common tools** section, click **Start Narrator**.

To configure audio narration options

1. Display the **Narrator** settings pane, and scroll to the **Sounds you hear** section.

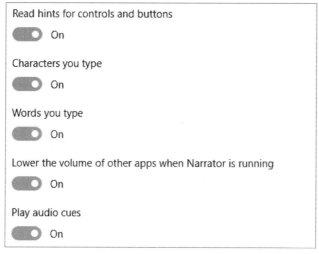

Read hints for controls and buttons
On

Characters you type
On

Words you type
On

Lower the volume of other apps when Narrator is running
On

Play audio cues
On

You control which elements Narrator reads aloud

2. Set the toggle button to **On** for the features you want Narrator to read aloud.

To configure visual narration options

1. Display the **Narrator** settings pane, and scroll to the **Cursor and keys** section.

Make the cursor, insertion point, and touch keyboard easier to access

2. Set the toggle button to **On** for the features you want Narrator to display.

To turn on Audio Description

1. In the Ease Of Access Center, click the **Make the computer easier to see** link.

2. In the **Hear text and descriptions read aloud** section, select the **Turn on Audio Description** check box. Then click **Apply** or **OK** to apply the change.

Keyboard and mouse settings

The traditional method of entering text into an app or other computer interface is by typing it on an external keyboard. However, mobility problems can make typing difficult. Windows 10 includes a variety of tools to help with entering text, including the following:

- **Filter Keys** Causes Windows to ignore brief or repeated keystrokes, or slows the repeat rate.

- **Mouse Keys** Enables you to move the cursor around the screen by pressing the arrow keys on the numeric keypad.

- **On-Screen Keyboard** Displays a visual representation of a keyboard on which you can tap individual keys by using your finger, tablet pen, or other pointing device.

- **Speech Recognition** Allows you to control Windows, control running apps, and dictate text by speaking into a microphone.

SEE ALSO For information about speech recognition, see "Manage speech settings" in Chapter 9, "Manage computer settings."

- **Sticky Keys** Makes it easier to use the keyboard with one hand by making the Ctrl, Shift, and Alt keys "stick down" until you press the next key.

- **Toggle Keys** Sounds an audio signal when you press the Caps Lock, Num Lock, or Scroll Lock key. A high-pitched sound plays when the keys are activated, and a low-pitched sound plays when the keys are deactivated.

The mouse is an integral part of most desktop computer experiences. By default, the mouse pointer is represented by a small arrow that moves around the screen as quickly as you move the mouse, and sometimes fades out of sight when the mouse is still. It can be difficult not only to find the pointer, but also to track its progress across the screen. If you're working in a screen-presenting situation—for example, sharing your screen in an online meeting, or presenting content on a large screen in a conference room, it is even more difficult for your audience members to follow the mouse movements because they aren't controlling the mouse.

You can simplify things for yourself and for other people by enlarging the pointer and changing its color. If you have difficulty moving the mouse, you can opt to control it by using the numeric keypad.

In addition to these Ease of Access features, you can configure other useful mouse features such as "mouse trails" that can be very helpful. For information about keyboard and mouse configuration options that aren't related to the Ease of Access features, see Chapter 6, "Manage peripheral devices."

To turn on keyboard accessibility features

1. In the **Settings** window, click **Ease of Access**, and then click **Keyboard**.

2. In the **Keyboard** settings pane, set the toggle button to **On** for any of the following options:

   - On-Screen Keyboard

   - Sticky Keys

   - Toggle Keys

   - Filter Keys

> **TIP** You can also display a taskbar icon for the on-screen keyboard by right-clicking an empty area in the taskbar and clicking Show Touch Keyboard Button. You can then click that icon to display the keyboard when you need it.

3. In the **Other Settings** section of the **Keyboard** pane, set the toggle buttons that control accessibility options for keyboard shortcuts.

Options in the Other Settings section of the Keyboard settings pane

To configure mouse accessibility features

1. In the **Settings** window, click **Ease of Access**, and then click **Mouse**.

2. In the **Mouse** settings pane, do the following to immediately implement the changes:

   - Click the pointer size you want.

   - Click the pointer color you want.

Pointer size and color options

3. To turn on Mouse Keys, set the **Use numeric keypad to move mouse around the screen** toggle button to **On**.

4. When Mouse Keys is turned on, set the **Hold down Ctrl to speed up and Shift to slow down** and **Use mouse keys when Num Lock is on** options to **On** or **Off**.

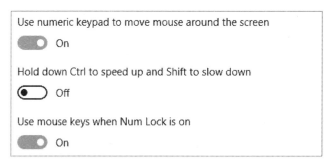

The Mouse Keys options for ease of access

Skills review

In this chapter, you learned how to:

- Configure power options
- Customize the lock screen
- Configure Windows accessibility features

Practice tasks

The practice files for these tasks are located in the Win10SBS\Ch10 folder.

Configure power options

Perform the following tasks:

1. Display the Action Pane, and then cycle through your brightness changes.

2. Display the **Power & sleep** settings pane, and configure the screen and sleep times as you want them. If your computer is running on battery power, configure the settings for when the computer is plugged in and when it is running on battery power.

3. Open the **Power Options** window of Control Panel. If **Show additional plans** appears near the bottom of the window, click it to display any hidden power-management plans.

4. Display the settings for each plan on your computer, and consider which is best for you.

5. Modify a standard power plan. Then reset the plan to its defaults.

6. If none of the power-management plans fits your needs, create a custom plan. Otherwise, apply a standard plan.

Customize the lock screen

 TIP If you don't download the practice files, use any folder of your own pictures to complete this practice task.

Display the Lock Screen setting window, and then perform the following tasks:

1. Configure the lock screen to display a slideshow of the pictures from the practice file folder.

2. Lock your computer and observe the slideshow. Notice that the picture layout changes from a single photo to multiple photos.

3. Unlock your computer, and then display the advanced slideshow settings. Turn on the option to display photos from the Camera Roll folders on your computer and on OneDrive. Then lock your computer and note any changes from the previous lock screen slideshow.

4. Unlock your computer, and then configure the lock screen to display any one image from the practice file folder. If the **Lock screen** settings pane includes the option to display tips and tricks, select that option.

5. Lock your computer and observe the lock screen.

6. Unlock your computer. If the lock screen background options include Windows Spotlight, select that as the lock screen background.

7. Select one app to display detailed information on the lock screen, and at least one app to display quick status information. If you haven't yet done so, start and configure each of the selected apps. Then lock your computer and observe the lock screen. Take note of the app information at the bottom of the screen. If you have the option to do so, indicate whether you like or dislike the current Windows Spotlight background.

8. Unlock your computer, and then configure the lock screen to display the information you want.

Configure Windows accessibility features

Display the Ease Of Access settings pane, and then perform the following tasks:

1. Complete the **Get recommendations to make your computer easier to use** wizard to familiarize yourself with the situations in which you might benefit from using the various accessibility tools.

2. Locate a webpage that contains text and graphic elements, and display it in your default Internet browser.

3. Apply a high contrast theme. Look for differences in the user interface elements and in the webpage content.

4. Start Narrator, and then configure Narrator to use the voice and speech cadence that you prefer.

5. Display the webpage, the **Start** screen, the **Settings** window, any category page, and then any apps or files you want, to gain experience with the information Narrator provides. (Wait each time as Narrator provides you with information.)

 IMPORTANT To click a button when Narrator is on, you must first click once to read the description, and then twice to invoke the click event.

6. Exit Narrator, and return to the Ease Of Access Center.

7. Start Magnifier, and experiment with using it to view different screens and documents. Then exit Magnifier.

8. Display the touch keyboard, and experiment with navigating around Windows and entering text without using an external keyboard. Then close the touch keyboard.

9. Display the Ease Of Access Center, and explore other settings that interest you. Click the links, and try out these features:

   • Turn on **Sticky Keys**, and experiment with using it to enter text that contains capital letters.

   • Turn on **Mouse Keys**, and practice using it to move the cursor around on the screen.

   • Turn on **Filter Keys**, and try using it with an app of your choice.

10. Exit any running accessibility tools.

Work more efficiently

Several features that are new or improved in Windows 10 are designed to help you do things faster and more efficiently—or in some cases to do them for you.

The most exciting of these features is Cortana. Touted as "your personal assistant," Cortana can monitor your online activity and provide helpful reminders. Cortana interacts with Bing Search to locate information, and also enables you to conduct searches and perform tasks on your computer by giving verbal commands.

The new Action Center is a central location for reviewing notifications. It also contains action buttons that provide shortcuts to settings that you might access most often. Another interesting development is virtual desktops, which provide a way for multitaskers to organize apps in separate views of the desktop. This isn't a feature that all Windows 10 users will use, but it's certainly handy for people who want to compartmentalize tasks.

Two other topics we discuss in this chapter are configuring your settings so that files always open in the app you want them to, and finding helpful information in Task Manager.

This chapter guides you through procedures related to configuring Quick Action buttons, getting assistance from Cortana, searching your computer and the web, specifying default apps, organizing apps on multiple desktops, and managing system tasks.

In this chapter

- Configure Quick Action buttons
- Get assistance from Cortana
- Search your computer and the web
- Specify default apps
- Organize apps on multiple desktops
- Manage system tasks

Practice files

No practice files are necessary to complete the practice tasks in this chapter.

Configure Quick Action buttons

Windows 8.1 and earlier versions of Windows had a Control Panel window called the Action Center, in which you could review current security and maintenance settings, and any issues that required action. It was available from the notification area of the taskbar, and it was represented by a white pennant that would change to alert you when something required your attention.

Other than the name and position of the taskbar button, the Windows 10 Action Center bears almost no resemblance to its predecessor. In Windows 10, the Action Center is a full height pane that slides out from the right side of your screen when you click an icon on the taskbar. After Windows displays notifications about recent events on your computer, such as incoming email messages, security and maintenance alerts, and updates, those notifications are available from the Action Center for your review.

In addition to notifications, the Action Center also displays several rows of Quick Action command tiles at the bottom of the panel. The top row is always visible when the panel is open; you can expand or collapse the remaining rows.

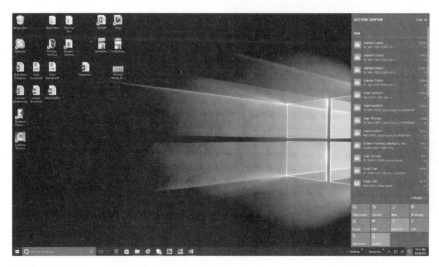

The Action Center on the Windows desktop

In Chapter 1, "Get started using Windows 10," we reviewed procedures for previewing, opening, and removing messages in the Action Center. In Chapter 2, "Personalize your working environment," we reviewed procedures for managing the color and transparency of the Action Center pane. In Chapter 4, "Work with apps and notifications," we reviewed procedures for configuring app notifications that appear in the Action Center, and for temporarily turning off notifications by turning on Quiet Hours.

In this topic, we discuss the action buttons available at the bottom of the Action Center pane. By default, this section is collapsed to display only four buttons.

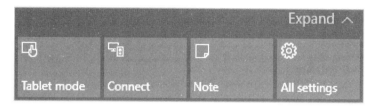

The four Quick Action buttons are always available

These four buttons are the *Quick Action buttons*. You can choose which of the action buttons are designated as Quick Action buttons (and are available when the other action buttons are hidden).

When expanded, the section contains about a dozen buttons. The specific buttons vary based on the functions that are available on your computer or device.

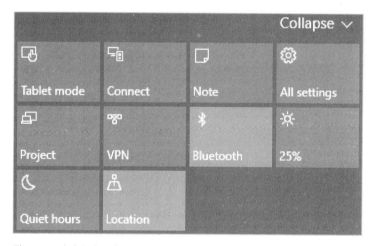

The expanded Actions button area

The action buttons provide quick access to the following Windows 10 tools and settings:

- **Airplane mode** Available only on portable computers and tablets, airplane mode turns off all wireless connections from your device, including Wi-Fi, Bluetooth, and cellular data if you have that service. The action button turns this feature on or off.

- **All settings** Opens the Settings window.

465

- **Battery Saver** Available only on battery-powered computers and devices, Battery Saver is a feature introduced in Windows 10 that reduces background activity to extend the time the device can run on the battery charge. You can turn Battery Saver on at any time; Windows turns it on automatically when the battery charge drops below 20% or the setting you specify. The action button turns this feature on or off.

- **Bluetooth** Turns the Bluetooth connection on or off.

- **Connect** Searches for wireless display and audio devices (including those that support Miracast and WiDi connections).

- **Location** Available only on devices with built-in GPS, this button turns location services on or off. You can configure location settings from the Privacy page of the Settings window.

- **Note** Starts Microsoft OneNote and displays the Quick Notes section.

- **Project** Controls the display of desktop content on multiple screens. You can choose from PC Screen Only, Duplicate, Extend, and Second Screen Only.

- **Quiet hours** Turns on or off the Quiet Hours feature, which temporarily disables sound and banner notifications.

- **Rotation lock** Available only on mobile devices, Rotation lock permits or prevents screen rotation when a mobile Windows 10 device is physically rotated.

- **Screen Brightness** (labeled with a sun) Cycles through 25%, 50%, 75%, and 100% screen brightness settings.

- **Tablet mode** Available only on touchscreen devices, Tablet mode makes the device interface more touch-friendly by enlarging user interface elements and hiding taskbar buttons. You can configure Tablet mode settings from the System page of the Settings window.

- **VPN** Starts a virtual private network (VPN) connection or walks you through the configuration of a connection if one doesn't already exist.

- **WiFi** Available only on portable computers and devices. Turns the wireless network connection on and off.

Buttons that represent features that are simply on or off are a different color (when the feature is turned on) from those that open apps or configure settings.

> ⊙ **SEE ALSO** For more information about the Settings window, see "Explore computer settings" in Chapter 1, "Get started using Windows 10." For more information about the Quiet Hours feature, see "Manage app notifications" in Chapter 4, "Work with apps and notifications." For more information about the screen brightness, see "Customize device display settings" in Chapter 9, "Manage computer settings" and "Configure power options" in Chapter 10, "Manage power and access options." For more information about Battery Saver, see the sidebar "Make your battery last longer," also in Chapter 10.

A final thing to note about the Action Center is that you can hide its taskbar icon if you want to free up space on your taskbar (or always use the keyboard shortcut). The Action Center is always available regardless of whether the taskbar icon is visible.

To display the Action Center pane

1. Do any of the following:

   • In the notification area of the taskbar, click the **Action Center** icon.

   The Action Center icon is filled when new notifications are available

   • Press **Win+A**.

   • On a touchscreen device, swipe in from the right edge of the screen.

To display all available action buttons

1. Display the **Action Center** pane.

2. At the bottom of the pane, click **Expand**.

To designate the Quick Action buttons

1. Open the **Settings** window.

2. In the **Settings** window, click **System**, and then click **Notifications & actions**.

3. In the **Quick actions** section of the **Notifications & actions** pane, below **Choose your quick actions**, click one of the four Quick Action buttons to select that button position and display a list of the action buttons available on your computer. The Quick Action button that is currently in the selected position is highlighted in the list.

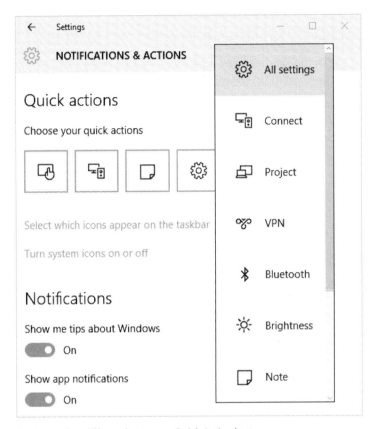

Designate four different buttons as Quick Action buttons

4. In the list, click the button that you want to display in the selected position.

> ✓ **TIP** If you click a button that is already designated as a Quick Action button, that button changes to the next in the list. Each action button appears only once in the Action Center.

5. Repeat the previous step for the other three positions.

To display or hide the Action Center taskbar icon

1. In the **Settings** window, click **System**, and then click **Notifications & actions**.

2. In the **Quick actions** section of the **Notifications & actions** pane, click **Turn system icons on or off**.

3. Set the **Action Center** toggle button to **On** to display the taskbar icon, or **Off** to hide it.

Get assistance from Cortana

We introduced Cortana in the sidebar "Hey, Cortana!" in Chapter 1, "Get started using Windows 10." If you've been using Windows 10 for a while, you might have already experimented with using Cortana as a verbal interface to your computer. It's a technique that's very convenient, and after you become accustomed to using it, you'll probably find a lot of uses for it.

At the time of this writing, Cortana is available in the following countries or regions and languages.

Country/region	Language
China	Chinese (Simplified)
France	French
Germany	German
Italy	Italian
Spain	Spanish
United Kingdom	English (United Kingdom)
United States	English (United States)

To use Cortana, your computer or device must be configured so that the country or region, device language, and speech language match as shown in the table.

> **TIP** When Cortana isn't available, you can still use the taskbar search feature, which works in all locations and languages. For more information about taskbar search, see "Search your computer and the web" later in this chapter.

Initialize Cortana

Until you perform the initial setup tasks for Cortana, the taskbar search box contains the words *Search the web and Windows*. After you set up Cortana, the search box text changes to *Ask me anything* to indicate that you're asking Cortana rather than simply conducting a search.

Setting up Cortana is a simple process of allowing it to collect personal information and providing a name for Cortana to address you by. (In case you've been wondering, Cortana's name is pronounced "Cor-tonn-uh" rather than "Cor-tann-uh." But after you train it to recognize your voice, it responds to your preferred pronunciation.)

To initially set up Cortana

1. Click in the search box. Cortana introduces itself and provides information to help you decide whether you want to complete the configuration process. You have the option of clicking Not Interested to dismiss the setup prompt.

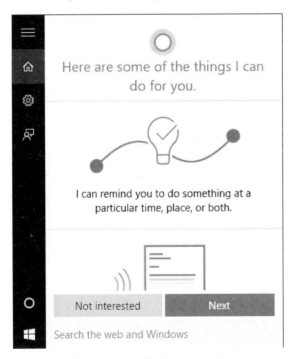

Cortana provides examples of the information it can give you

> **TIP** If you quit the setup process, you can complete the configuration at a later time by clicking in the search box, clicking the Settings button, and then in the Settings pane, setting the Cortana Can Give You Suggestions, Ideas, Reminders, Alerts And More toggle button to On.

2. To continue, click **Next**. Then read the description of the information collected for use by Cortana, and click **I agree**.

Before we get started, I'll need some info.

To let Cortana do her best work, Microsoft collects and uses information including your location and location history, contacts, voice input, searching history, calendar details, content and communication history from messages and apps, and other information on your device. In Microsoft Edge, Cortana collects and uses your browsing history. You can always tinker with what Cortana remembers in the Notebook, disable Cortana in Microsoft Edge, or turn Cortana off entirely.

Privacy Statement

Great! Now what would you like me to call you?

Gorgeous

You can keep it simple by using your name, or have some fun with it

3. Give Cortana a name or nickname to address you by, and then click **Next**.

That's all the personal information you have to provide to get started. Cortana gives you a short introduction to the information it can provide and where it stores information, and you're off and running!

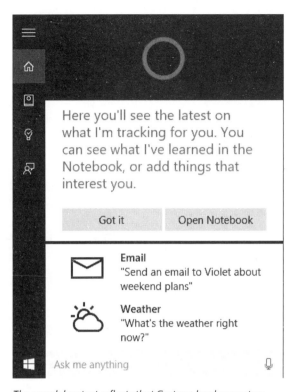

The search box text reflects that Cortana has been set up

To configure Cortana to respond to verbal cuing

1. If you plan to use an external microphone or headset, connect it to the computer and set it as the default recording device.

 SEE ALSO For information about configuring a microphone in Windows 10, see "Set up audio devices" in Chapter 6, "Manage peripheral devices."

2. Click the search box to display the Cortana menu controls on the left side of the search pane.

3. Click the **Notebook** button, or click the menu button to expand the Cortana menu, and then click **Notebook** to display the menus from which you can set your preferences.

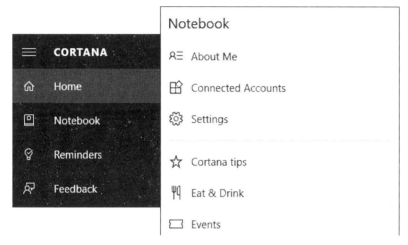

Cortana can suggest local restaurants and events

4. Click **Settings** to display the Settings pane.

5. Near the top of the **Settings** pane, set the **Hey Cortana** toggle button to **On**.

6. If you want to train Cortana to recognize and respond specifically to your voice, do the following:

    *   In the **Respond best** section of the **Settings** pane, click the **Learn my voice** button to start the Cortana-specific voice recognition wizard, which takes you through a quick six-phrase exercise.

    *   When you're ready to start speaking the phrases, click the **Start** button. Cortana prompts you to speak the first phrase. When it understands you, it moves to the next phrase.

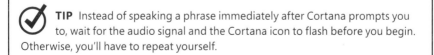

> **TIP** Instead of speaking a phrase immediately after Cortana prompts you to, wait for the audio signal and the Cortana icon to flash before you begin. Otherwise, you'll have to repeat yourself.

Cortana listens to you only after you say, "Hey, Cortana"

7. When you finish, close the Cortana pane, and then speak the cue **Hey Cortana** to test that it activates the search box.

Configure Cortana settings

The Notebook is Cortana's central information portal and also where you configure your Cortana settings.

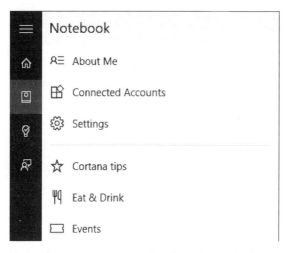

You configure your Cortana settings from the Notebook

Two of the first things you might want to do after setting up Cortana are:

- Configure Cortana for audio input.
- Review and modify the information Cortana tracks for you.

The Cortana Notebook is divided into two sections; the top section contains these three menus on which you configure your personal information:

- **About Me** Change the name or nickname by which Cortana addresses you, and save favorite locations (such as home and work) that Cortana can use when providing information.
- **Connected Accounts** Connect Cortana to your Office 365 account.
- **Settings** Turn on or off suggestions, verbal cuing, information tracking, and taskbar "tidbits;" manage the information Cortana has stored about you and the Bing SafeSearch settings; and access the Windows 10 privacy settings.

The bottom section contains the information categories described in the following table. Each category pane contains options for configuring Cortana to track information in that category.

Category	Options
Cortana tips	On/off: Tip cards
Eat & Drink	On/off: Eat & drink cards, Top recommendations from Foursquare, Restaurant recommendations Set: Price range, Ambience, How often you like to eat out, Distance, Cuisine preference
Events	On/off: Event cards
Finance	On/off: Finance cards Set: Stocks you're tracking
Getting around	On/off: Traffic, time, and route notifications On/off when driving: Traffic updates to my calendar events, Notify me when it's time to go to my calendar events, Traffic updates to my favorite places, Notify me when it's time to go to work or head home On/off when using public transit: Transit updates to my calendar events, Notify me when it's time to go to my calendar events, Transit updates to my favorite places, Notify me when it's time to go to work or head home, Notify me when the last ride is leaving Set: Your preferences for getting around

Category	Options
Meetings & reminders	On/off: Meeting & reminder cards & notifications, Meeting prep, Daily timeline, Related documents, Show reminders on Cortana home
Movies & TV	On/off: Movie & TV cards, Get showtimes for nearby movie theaters, See the latest movie trailers
News	On/off: News cards, Local news - Stories happening near you, Headline news - Today's top stories, Recommended stories - news based on your interests, News topic cards, News category cards, Popular now - Stories people are searching for Set: News categories you're tracking, News topics you're tracking
Packages	On/off: Package tracking cards Set: Packages you're tracking
Sports	On/off: All sports cards & notifications, Score updates for your team, Show upcoming games and matches Set: Teams you're tracking
Travel	On/off: Travel cards & notifications, Flights, Trip Plan
Weather	On/off: Weather cards & notifications, Nearby Forecast, Notify me when there are weather incidents, Forecast for your cities Set: Units, Cities you're tracking

 IMPORTANT When you change an option, you must click Save at the bottom of the category pane to save your change.

One of the fun and useful features of Cortana is that you can give commands verbally. You can click the microphone on the right end of the search box to turn on listening, or you can configure Cortana to listen for the verbal cue "Hey, Cortana." When you provide verbal input to Cortana, the search box displays the detected input; then evaluates and refines it to match logical searches or commands. The input and recalculation is displayed in the search box. It's quite interesting to watch the logical revision of the perceived input.

The Cortana input interface can be hidden, or hidden on the taskbar in one of two ways: as the Cortana icon, or as the search box. When in the form of a search box, the

Cortana icon at the left end indicates that Cortana is configured, and a microphone icon at the right end indicates that Cortana is configured to accept audio input.

Cortana icon   Microphone

The Cortana icon is two nested circles that animate when you interact with Cortana

To configure your Cortana information preferences

1. Click the search box to display the Cortana menu controls, and then click the **Notebook** button.

2. In the bottom section of the **Notebook** pane, click the category you want to configure.

3. In the category pane, set each toggle button to **On** or **Off**. When individual settings are available, click the setting name or **Add** link as appropriate, and then provide the requested information.

   Most options permit only one choice, but some options permit multiple choices.

You can choose multiple options for some settings, such as Cuisine Preference

4. If you make changes in a category, click the **Save** button at the bottom of the category pane before leaving the pane.

5. Click the **Back** arrow in the upper-left corner of the pane to return to the Notebook, where you can select a different category.

To display or hide Cortana on the taskbar

1. Right-click a blank area of the taskbar or the taskbar search box.

2. On the shortcut menu, click **Cortana**, and then click **Hidden**, **Show Cortana icon**, or **Show search box**.

Add reminders

Cortana can remind you about upcoming appointments and travel plans it finds in your electronic information, but you can also set specific reminders in Cortana. This is particularly convenient if you have Cortana not only on your computers, but also on your smartphone, so you can get reminders wherever you are.

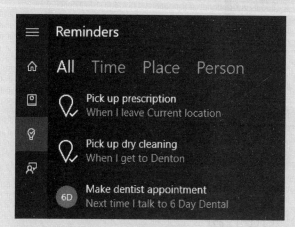

If you use Cortana on a smartphone, it can provide reminders based on your location

You can link each reminder to a specific time, place, or person, and then filter the reminders by that property. To link a reminder to a person, the person must be in your contact list.

You add reminders from the Reminders pane of Cortana, or you can simply say "Hey, Cortana," and then ask Cortana to set a reminder. Cortana interprets your request in the form of a reminder.

Cortana interprets your request in reminder format

Cortana prompts you for any missing information, and then asks you to approve the reminder. You can say *Yes* or click Remind to set the reminder, say *No* or click Cancel to cancel the reminder, or edit the reminder information in the pane and then complete the process.

Search your computer and the web

The technology that supports rapid searching through massive amounts of information has improved tremendously over the past few years. We can probably thank cloud computing and the proliferation of massive data centers for this technology, which has worked its way down to the personal computer level.

In Chapter 1, "Get started using Windows 10," we reviewed procedures for searching for settings from the Settings window search box. In Chapter 3, "Manage folders and files," we reviewed procedures for searching for files from the File Explorer search box. Both of these processes search the content on your computer (or the storage location you're displaying in File Explorer). To speed up these search processes, Windows indexes information on your computer hard drive, and complex processes in the Microsoft cloud index information in your OneDrive storage folders. You can refine the indexing parameters to include or exclude specific storage locations.

Search storage locations and the web

When you're searching for a broader range of information, you can do so from the taskbar search box (with and without Cortana enabled). Windows 10 uses the Bing search engine to quickly locate items on your computer, in connected storage locations, and across the web.

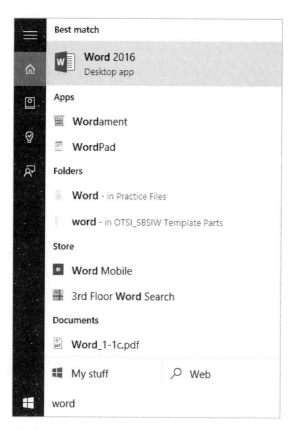

Windows searches your computer, connected storage locations, and the web, and sorts the results by category

> **TIP** To quickly move the cursor to the taskbar search box without opening the Start screen, press Win+S.

In the search results, click any category heading to display only results in that category. Categories include Apps, Documents, Folders, Music, Photos, Settings, Store, Videos, and Web. (You can't filter by the Best Match heading.) When your search locates the item, app, or information you want, click the search result to open, start, or display it.

You can quickly refine the search results to display only search results in local and connected storage locations by clicking the My Stuff button (above the search box).

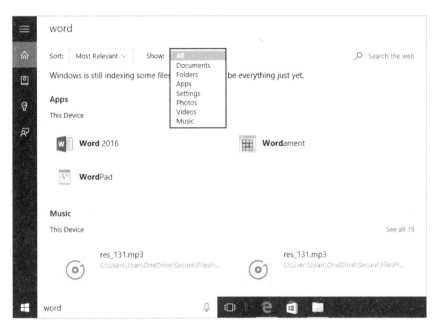

The search term is in the upper-left corner

In the My Stuff search results, you can sort the content in order of relevance (which works best with multiword searches) or date, and you can filter the results by category.

If you're looking for online search results, such as you'd get from searching directly in a web browser, click the Web button (above the search box) to display Bing web search results in your default browser.

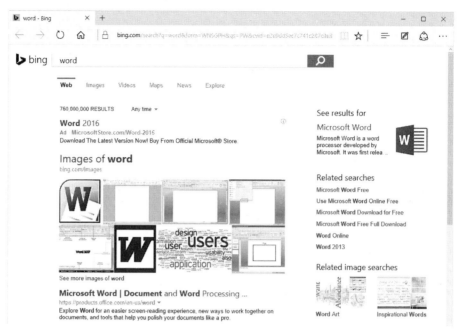

Save time by searching the web from the search box

To search for anything

1. Do any of the following:

    *   Click the taskbar search box, and then enter the search term.

    *   If Cortana is enabled, click the microphone icon in the search box, and then speak the search term.

    *   If Cortana is configured for voice cuing, say **Hey, Cortana** followed by your search request.

> ✓ **TIP** When speaking a search term, you can quickly filter contents by specifying parameters such as file type and contents. For example, "Find PowerPoint presentations on my computer that contain Contoso and Sales." The search results include a snapshot of the content that includes your specified search terms.

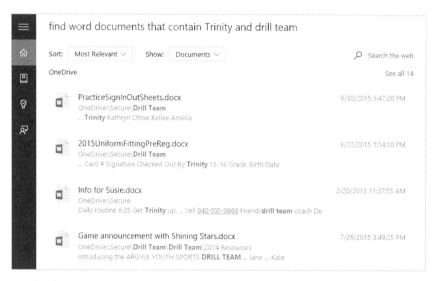

Results of a verbal search

To filter search results

1. In the search results pane, do any of the following:

   - To display only device configuration tools, click the **Settings** category heading.

   - To display only apps that are installed on your computer, click the **Apps** category heading.

   - To display only Store apps that aren't installed on your computer, click the **Store** category heading.

   - To display only a specific category of files, click the **Documents**, **Folders**, **Music**, **Photos**, or **Videos** category heading.

   - To display only search results located in local and connected storage locations, click the **My stuff** button (above the search box).

   - To display only Bing web search results, click the **Web** category heading or the **Web** button (above the search box).

Or

1. In the **My stuff** search results, click the **Show** list, and then click **Documents**, **Folders**, **Apps**, **Settings**, **Photos**, **Videos**, or **Music**.

To sort local search results

1. In the **My stuff** search results, click the **Sort** list, and then click **Most Relevant** or **Most Recent**.

Manage Bing content filters

If you're getting search results that you find offensive, you can configure the Bing SafeSearch settings to control the level of "adult content" that is filtered from or allowed through in search results.

To configure the Bing SafeSearch settings

1. Click the taskbar search box, and then do either of the following to display the Settings pane:

   • If Cortana is enabled, click the **Notebook** icon and then click **Settings**.

   • If Cortana isn't enabled, click the **Settings** icon.

2. Near the bottom of the **Settings** pane, click **Bing SafeSearch settings** to display the Bing Settings page in your default browser. The SafeSearch section of the Settings page has three options for filtering content.

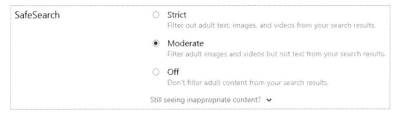

Choose your level of filtering

3. Click **Strict** to filter out text, images, and video that are flagged as "adult content" from your web searches; **Moderate** to filter out images and video, but not text; or **Off** to not filter out adult content. Then at the bottom of the page, click **Save**.

Manage File Explorer search processes

Searching is often the fastest way to locate a file or settings pane on your computer. This is primarily because you're searching the index rather than all the available content and metadata.

The search engine is fast, but you can improve the efficiency of your search by applying a bit of logic and forethought. Here are some hints to help you rapidly locate the files you need:

- The search index includes all the common locations in which users store files. If you want to improve the search time in other locations, either add them to the indexed locations, or add them to Libraries, which is automatically included in the index.

- When searching in File Explorer, select a specific folder in which to start your search, or restrict the search to likely locations, such as Libraries.

- If a simple search from the File Explorer window doesn't locate the item you are looking for, you can perform more advanced searches in the Search Results folder. Your search criteria can include the date a file was created, its size, part of its name or title, its author, and any tags you might have listed as properties of the file.

 SEE ALSO For information about file properties, see "Work with folder and file properties" in Chapter 3, "Manage folders and files."

If search processes don't return all the pertinent results, or return old results that no longer lead to the correct location, you might need to do a bit of maintenance work. You can change some basic search parameters, and adjust the indexing options and the locations that are being indexed to increase the efficiency of your searches.

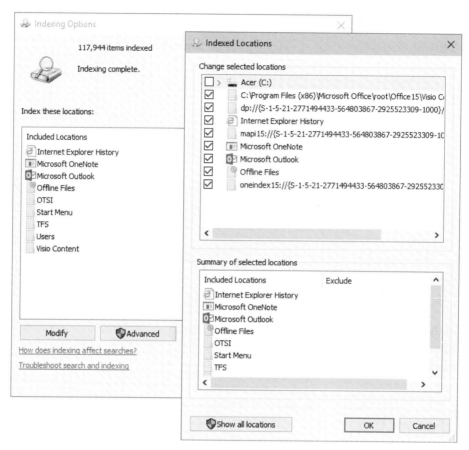

Include locations where you frequently store files

From the Advanced Options dialog box, you can also do the following things, which require administrator permission:

- Include encrypted files in the index.

- Add a type of file to the index.

- Change the indexing level for a type of file.

- Change the location of the index file.

- Restore the default settings.

- Rebuild the index file from scratch.

If you continue to have trouble, you can run the indexing troubleshooter to look for problems and recommend solutions.

To filter File Explorer search results

1. Perform a search.

2. On the **Search** tool tab, click one of the following:

   - **Kind** In the list that appears, click the appropriate kind if it is listed.

   - **Other Properties** Click one of the options: Name is a good choice if you know part of the name. If you are sure about the start of the name, enter that. If you are sure only that some characters are somewhere in the name, enter ~= and the characters. For example, if the search term is *name:~=dog*, the search will return all files with the letters "dog" anywhere in the name.

   - **Date Modified and Size** You can specify parameters for either of these options, if you know that information.

To set File Explorer search options

1. In File Explorer, at the right end of the **View** tab, click **Options**.

2. In the **Folder Options** dialog box, click the **Search** tab. There are only a few options here, but their settings can impact the time required to perform a search in File Explorer.

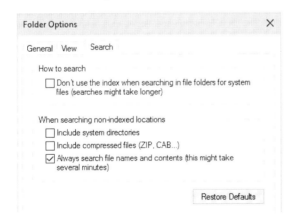

Options for indexed and nonindexed locations

3. Make any changes you want, and then click **OK**.

To change the locations that are being indexed

1. Perform a search.

2. On the **Search** tool tab, in the **Options** group, click the **Advanced options** button, and then click **Change indexed locations**.

3. In the **Indexing Options** dialog box, add or exclude specific folders. Then click **Close**.

To change advanced indexing options

1. Perform a search.

2. On the **Search** tool tab, in the **Options** group, click the **Advanced options** button, and then click **Change indexed locations**.

3. In the **Indexing Options** dialog box, click the **Advanced** button.

4. In the **Advanced Options** dialog box, configure the options on the **Index Settings** and **File Types** tabs.

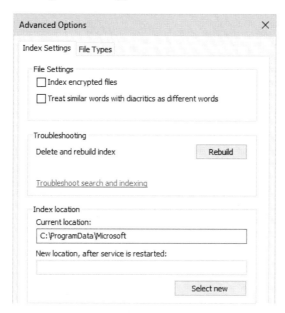

Change advanced indexing options

5. Click **OK** and then **Close** to return to File Explorer.

To rebuild the index

1. Perform a search.

2. On the **Search** tool tab, in the **Options** group, click the **Advanced options** button, and then click **Change indexed locations**.

3. In the **Indexing Options** dialog box, click the **Advanced** button.

4. In the **Advanced Options** dialog box, click the **Rebuild** button. Then in the **Rebuild Index** message box, click **OK**.

> ⚠ **IMPORTANT** Rebuilding the index can take quite a while. You might want to put it off until a time when you don't need the full attention of your computer for a few hours.

Specify default apps

When you open a file by using any of the standard methods, Windows opens it in the default app for that type of file (as specified by the file name extension). The default app might be set when you install an app, or you can set it in Windows independently of the app.

When displaying files in File Explorer, the default app is often apparent from the icon that is associated with the file.

Large Icons view of files in File Explorer

If you uninstall the app that is set as the default for a file type, or don't have an app that associates itself with that file type, Windows will prompt you to choose the app you want to use to open the file. You can select an installed app, or install an app from the Store.

> **TIP** In some cases, you have the option of browsing to an app executable file. This option is necessary only if the app hasn't provided a list of file extensions it can associate, or there is a problem that prevents Windows from detecting the app/file type association.

A clean installation of Windows 10 automatically sets a lot of defaults for you. When it comes to setting default apps, if Microsoft has an app that will open a type or class of file, it generally assigns that as the default app.

During an upgrade from an earlier version of Windows, Windows 10 might leave the defaults as you previously set them or, if there is a change in the apps (for example, the change from Internet Explorer to Edge as the default Microsoft browser) it might change them.

Windows 10 provides several ways for you to change these default settings. You can match category to apps, apps to file types, or file types to apps. As with many Windows configuration processes, there are simple and complicated ways of going about this that provide varying levels of control.

The simplest method for assigning default apps is by category. In the Default Apps pane, you can choose a default email app, map app, music player, photo viewer, video player, and web browser.

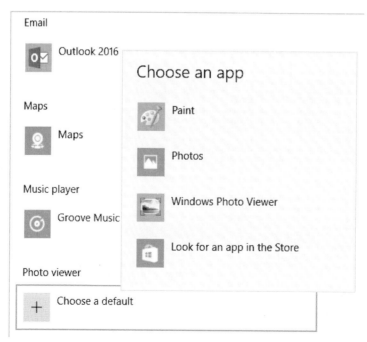

Choose an installed app, or display a list of Store apps that you can install

Each of the categories is associated with a specific set of file types, but you don't interact with those directly.

Another way you can assign default apps is by file type. The Choose Default Apps By File Type pane displays a long list of file extensions, and you can set the default app for each. The list is not based on the files that are installed on your computer—you might never encounter some of these file types. This method is useful if you set the default app for a category—for example, a photo viewer—and then want to specify a different default app for only one type of photo file.

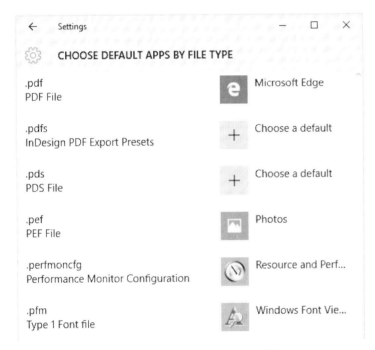

It isn't necessary to assign a default app to every type of file

The Choose Default Apps By File Type list is sorted alphabetically by file extension. You can't sort it by default app (which might be somewhat useful).

Another way to assign default apps is by protocol. Protocols aren't something that most of us think about frequently (if at all), but the word might be familiar to you from *Hypertext Transfer Protocol*, the full name of the HTTP protocol that is used to connect to most websites. The Choose Default Apps By Protocol pane displays a long list of protocols. Unlike the file extension list, each protocol is assigned to a default app.

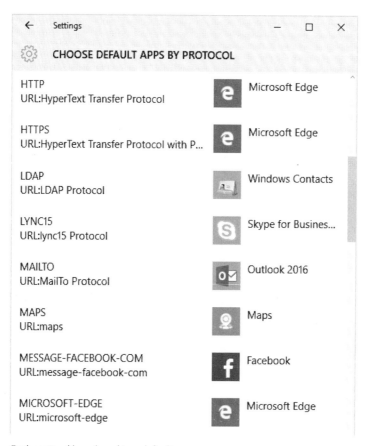

Each protocol is assigned to a default app

From the protocol list, you can assign default apps to different protocols that are associated with the same general kind of file. This creates a relationship between the protocol and the app in the Windows Registry. A file type is also associated with a protocol. So when you double-click a file, Windows can get the file protocol and then locate the default app in the registry.

Another way to assign a default app is when you're opening a file. You can specify a non-default app to open the file with, and at that time, you can also specify whether to set the non-default app as the default for that type of file. Using this method, you're setting default apps for files that you definitely work with.

There is one additional way to assign default apps, which is by selecting the file types and protocols for an app. You do this from the Set Default Programs window of Control Panel.

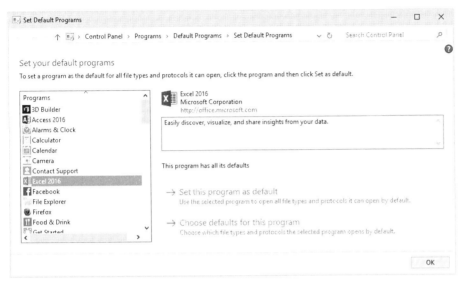

Set an app as the default for some or all of the files it can open

To open a file in the default app

1. In File Explorer, do any of the following:

    -   Double-click the file.

    -   Right-click the file, and then click **Open**.

    -   Click the file. Then on the **Home** tab, in the **Open** group, click the **Open** button.

To open a file in an app other than the default app

1. In File Explorer, do either of the following:

    -   Right-click the file, click **Open with...**, and then click the app you want.

    -   Click the file. On the **Home** tab, in the **Open** group, click the **Open** arrow, and then in the list, click the app you want.

Or

1. Start the app.

2. From within the app, browse to and open the file.

To specify the default app for a type of file

1. In File Explorer, right-click the file, and then click **Open with...** to display a list of apps that can open the file.

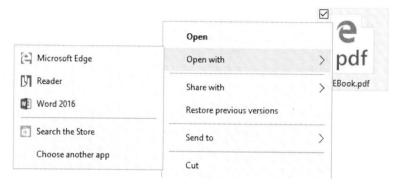

The available file types depend on the apps installed on your computer

> ⚠️ **IMPORTANT** At the time of this writing, some file types display the shortcut menu in the blue and white format shown after the next step. We show you both formats in this procedure so you're not surprised to see one or the other.

2. Click **Choose another app** to display additional options. If the app you want to use isn't on the list, click **More apps** to expand the list.

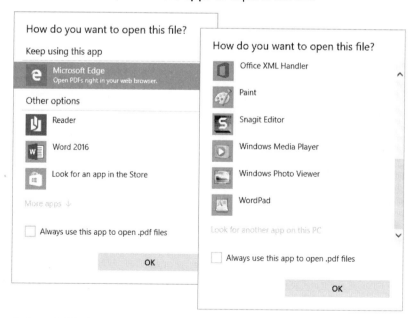

At the end of the More Apps list, you have the option to browse to an app

3. Click the app you want to use to open the selected type of file.

4. Select the **Always use this app to open ... files** check box (the label includes the file extension of the file you're opening), and then click **OK** to open the file and set the default app for the file type.

To specify the default app for a type of file

1. Open the **Settings** window, click **System**, and then click **Default apps**.

2. At the bottom of the pane, click **Choose default apps by file type** to display a long list of file type extensions.

3. Locate the extension for the type of file that you want to change the default app for.

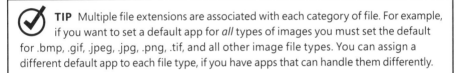

> **TIP** Multiple file extensions are associated with each category of file. For example, if you want to set a default app for *all* types of images you must set the default for .bmp, .gif, .jpeg, .jpg, .png, .tif, and all other image file types. You can assign a different default app to each file type, if you have apps that can handle them differently.

4. Click the icon to the right of the extension, and then do either of the following:

   - Click the installed app that you want to use.

   - Click **Look for an app in the Store** to open the Store and display a list of apps that can open a file of that type. Install an app from the Store, and then return to the **Choose default apps by file type** pane and select that app as the default for the file type.

To specify the default app for a category

1. Display the **Default apps** pane.

2. In the **Default apps** pane, click each task, and then do either of the following:

   - Click the installed app that you want to use.

   - Click **Look for an app in the Store** to open the Store and display a list of apps that can open a typical file of that type. Install an app from the Store, and then return to the **Default apps** pane and select that app as the default for the category.

To choose default apps by protocol

1. Display the **Default apps** pane. At the bottom of the pane, click **Choose default apps by protocol** to display the protocol list.

2. Locate the protocol that you want to change the default app for.

3. Click the current default app, and then do either of the following:

   - Click the installed app that you want to use.

   - Click **Look for an app in the Store** to open the Store and display a list of apps that can handle that protocol. Install an app from the Store, and then return to the **Choose default apps by protocol** pane and select that app as the default for the protocol.

To set the file types and protocols for a specific app

1. Display the **Default apps** pane. At the bottom of the pane, click **Set defaults by app** to open the Set Default Programs window of Control Panel.

2. In the **Programs** list, click the app for which you want to specify file types and protocols.

3. In the right pane, do either of the following:

   - Click **Set this program as default** to assign it as the default app for all file types and protocols that it can open.

   - Click **Choose defaults for this program** to open the Set Associations For A Program window displaying the file types and protocols that the selected app can handle.

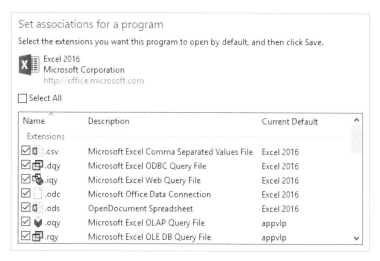

Choose specific file types and protocols

4. Select the check boxes for the file types and protocols you want the app to handle, and clear the check boxes for those you don't want to change from the current defaults. Then click **Save** to set the associations and return to the Set Default Programs window.

5. In the **Set Default Programs** window, click **OK** to complete the process.

Organize apps on multiple desktops

Virtual desktops are a new feature in Windows 10, one of those features that you can't quite imagine how you're going to use until you take the plunge. A virtual desktop is a bit like a second monitor, or a second computer: it's a location in which you can put some of the apps or files you're working on to keep your workspace organized. A basic example would be having a work-centric desktop on which you're running Outlook and Word, and a personal desktop on which you're monitoring Facebook and Twitter. If you frequently work with a dozen app windows open at one time, organizing them on virtual desktops can be a great way of decluttering and helping you to focus on only one set of apps and tasks at a time.

You can create and manage virtual desktops from Task view of the Windows 10 desktop or by using keyboard shortcuts. The original desktop is number 1. When you add more desktops they are numbered consecutively.

Manage apps on multiple desktops

After you create a desktop, you can drag open apps to it, or open new apps directly on that desktop. You can display or work on only one virtual desktop at a time, but it's easy to switch between them from Task view, or more quickly by using a keyboard shortcut.

Each desktop has a taskbar. Each taskbar displays the same pinned apps, but only those apps that are active on the current desktop have active buttons on that desktop taskbar.

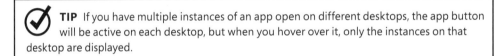
TIP If you have multiple instances of an app open on different desktops, the app button will be active on each desktop, but when you hover over it, only the instances on that desktop are displayed.

You open a file or start an app on a virtual desktop by using the same methods you use on the standard desktop. You can't have the same instance of an app (for example, the same file) open on more than one desktop, but you can move an app instance to another desktop.

You can run multiple instances of some apps (such as the Internet Explorer, Google Chrome, and Microsoft Word desktop apps) on the same desktop or on multiple desktops. From the taskbar on each desktop, you can display thumbnails of the app instances running on that desktop.

The Store apps we tried support only one instance, whether on one desktop or on multiple desktops. If you try to open one of these apps on a different virtual desktop, Windows switches to the desktop where the app is already running.

When you finish working on a desktop, you can close it to free up system resources. If you close a desktop that contains open applications, those applications are moved to the desktop immediately to its left.

To display desktops in Task view

1. Do any of the following:

   - On the taskbar, to the right of the search box, click the **Task view** button.

   - Press **Win+Tab**.

   - On a touchscreen device, swipe in from the left edge of the screen.

   The desktops are shown at the bottom of the screen.

To create a virtual desktop

1. Do either of the following:

   - Display the Task view of your desktop and then, in the lower-right corner of the screen, click **New desktop**.

   - Press **Win+Ctrl+D**.

   Windows creates a new virtual desktop to the right of the existing desktops, numbered with the next sequential number. The new desktop becomes the active desktop.

To move between desktops

1. Do either of the following:

   - Display the Task view of your desktop and then, at the bottom of the screen, click the desktop you want to move to.

   - Press **Win+Ctrl+Right Arrow** or **Win+Ctrl+Left Arrow** to move to the next desktop in the direction of the arrow.

To open a new instance of a running app

1. Press **Win+Shift**+click the taskbar button.

To move an app to a different desktop

1. Display the Task view of your desktop. The available desktops are at the bottom of the screen.

2. Point to (hover over) the desktop that contains the app you want to move, to display each app that is open on that desktop in the app thumbnail area of Task view.

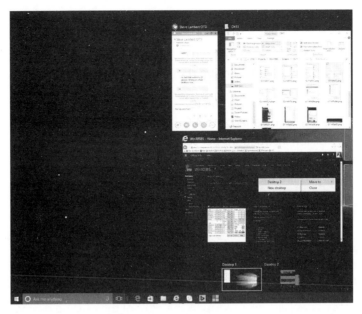

Moving apps among desktops

3. Do either of the following:

- Right-click the thumbnail of the app you want to move. Click **Move to**, and then click the desktop you want to move the app to.

> **TIP** One of the Move To options is New Desktop. You can create a new desktop and move an app to it at the same time by clicking that option.

- Drag the thumbnail (not the title above it) to the destination desktop.

To close the current desktop

1. Press **Win+Ctrl+F4**.

To close selected desktops

1. Display the Task view of your desktop.

2. Point to the desktop that you want to close. When a Close button (X) appears in the upper-right corner of the desktop tile, click it.

> **TIP** To quickly move all open windows and running apps to one desktop, display Task view and then close all open virtual desktops other than Desktop 1.

Monitor system tasks

Windows 10 and the apps and services that run on it constantly perform an amazingly complex dance that is set to the rather boring rhythm of your computer's clock.

Every computer has a central processing unit (CPU) and every CPU has a clock speed, which is generally in the 1 GHz (gigahertz) to 4 GHz range. In very basic terms, a 2 GHz CPU can carry out two billion instructions per second. That seems like a lot of instructions, until you realize that an extremely simple task, such as typing one letter into a Word document, might require thousands of instructions. CPU speed isn't the only factor in assessing the power and efficiency of your computer, but it is one of them, and one of those that you can monitor in Task Manager.

One way to monitor the real-time flow of activities on your computer is by using Task Manager. Task Manager has two views: Fewer Details and More Details. Fewer Details view displays a list of the apps that are currently running on your computer.

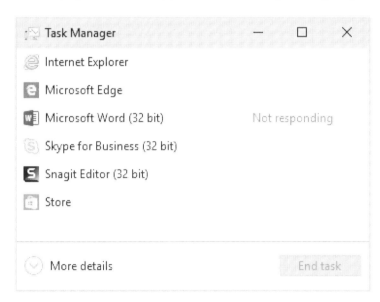

If an app is having trouble, Task Manager indicates that here

More Details view displays a list of all the apps and the background processes that are running on your computer with statistics on how much computer resources the apps and processes are using. Computer resource statistics include CPU, memory, disk, and network usage.

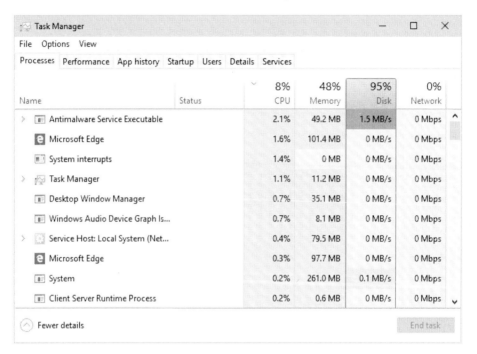

More Details view updates constantly to sort apps and processes by resource usage

Task Manager remembers the last view you used, and opens again in that same view.

> **SEE ALSO** For information about apps that start automatically, and working on the Startup tab of Task Manager, see "Manage app startup" in Chapter 4, "Work with apps and notifications."

To start Task Manager

1. Do any of the following:

   - Right-click an empty area of the taskbar, and then click **Task Manager**.

   - Press **Ctrl+Shift+Esc**.

   - Press **Ctrl+Alt+Del** and then, in the list, click **Task Manager**.

 TIP To quit an unresponsive app, click the app and then click the End Task button in the lower-right corner of the window.

To switch between Fewer Details view and More Details view

1. Open **Task Manager**, and then do either of the following:

   - If Task Manager displays only a list of the currently running apps, Task Manager is displaying Fewer Details view. Click **More details** at the bottom of the pane to switch views.

   - If Task Manager displays apps and background processes and multiple tabs, Task Manager is displaying More Details view. Click **Fewer details** at the bottom of the pane to switch views.

To display active and nonresponsive apps

1. Open **Task Manager** in Fewer Details view. Non-responsive apps are labeled *Not responding*.

To display active and nonresponsive apps and processes

1. Open **Task Manager** in More Details view, and then click the **Processes** tab to display all running processes. Non-responsive apps and processes are labeled *Not responding*.

To sort processes by resource usage

1. Open **Task Manager** in More Details view.

2. On the **Processes** tab, click the **CPU**, **Memory**, **Disk**, or **Network** heading to sort the apps and processes by the data in that column. Click the same heading again to reverse the direction of the sort.

To display performance information

1. Open **Task Manager** in More Details view, and then click the **Performance** tab.

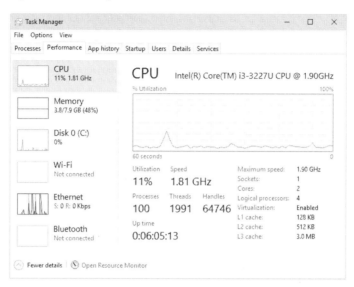

Real-time and historical performance data is available

To identify resource-intensive apps and processes

1. Open **Task Manager** in More Details view, and then click the **App History** tab.

2. At the bottom of the tab, click **Open Resource Monitor**.

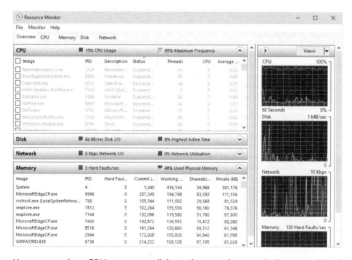

You can analyze CPU, memory, disk, and network usage in Resource Monitor

To display resource usage information

1. Open **Task Manager** in More Details view, and then click the **App History** tab.

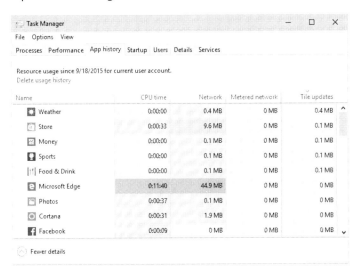

Review resource usage over the past two weeks

To manage services

1. Open **Task Manager** in More Details view, and then click the **Services** tab.

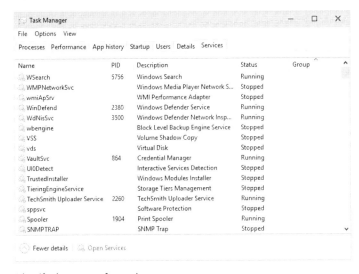

Identify the status of a service

TIP To open the Services management console in which you can manage services, click the Open Services link at the bottom of the tab.

Skills review

In this chapter, you learned how to:

- Configure Quick Action buttons
- Get assistance from Cortana
- Search your computer and the web
- Specify default apps
- Organize apps on multiple desktops
- Monitor system tasks

Practice tasks

No practice files are necessary to complete the practice tasks in this chapter.

Configure Quick Action buttons

Perform the following tasks:

1. Display the **Action Center** pane, and identify the Quick Action buttons.

2. Expand the action button area to display all the available action buttons. Review the action buttons that are available on your computer and consider which you might use. Notice whether any buttons are a different color, and identify what that means.

3. Click the **All settings** action button to open the Settings window. Click **System**, and then click **Notifications & actions**.

4. In the **Notifications & actions** pane, select the four action buttons that you will most frequently use, and assign these to the four Quick Action button positions.

5. Open the **Action Center** pane, collapse the action button area, and ensure that the Quick Action buttons you selected are visible.

Get assistance from Cortana

If your computer supports Cortana and you want to use it, perform the following tasks:

1. If you haven't already done so, turn on Cortana, agree to the collection of information, and provide your name.

2. Configure Cortana to respond to verbal cuing. Then experiment with giving Cortana commands, such as " Hey, Cortana. Start Word," and asking questions, such as " Hey, Cortana. What's the weather?"

3. Configure your Cortana information preferences. Then review the information shown in the default Cortana pane.

4. Experiment with the different ways Cortana can be represented on the taskbar and choose the one you like best.

Search your computer and the web

Perform the following tasks:

1. From the taskbar search box, search for a word, simple phrase, or your first name (anything that will generate a lot of search results).

2. Scroll the search results pane, and notice the types of results the search returned. Click any category heading to display only the results in that category.

3. Perform another search. In the search results pane, click **My stuff** to limit the results to only those on your computer.

4. From the **Show** list, filter the results to display only one type of file. Then display the remaining search results in order by date.

5. Display the Bing **SafeSearch** settings. Notice the other settings that you can configure from the page.

6. Start File Explorer, and open the **Indexing Options** dialog box. Notice the number of indexed items and the locations that are included. If you store files in a location that isn't being indexed, modify the options to include that location. Then close the dialog box.

Specify default apps

Start File Explorer, and then perform the following tasks:

1. Locate a file of a type that you frequently work with.

2. Display the list of apps that you can use to open the file.

3. Display apps from the Store that you could install and use to open the file.

4. If you want to, change the default app for the file.

5. Display the **Default apps** pane, and review the options for setting default apps by category, by file type, and by protocol. If you want to, change the default apps to suit your preferences.

Organize apps on multiple desktops

Perform the following tasks:

1. Display the Task view of your desktop, and then create a virtual desktop.

2. On Desktop 2, start two apps that aren't already running.

3. Switch between the two desktops, and notice any signs of items on the other desktop.

4. Move one of the apps from Desktop 2 to Desktop 1, and confirm that the app is open on Desktop 1.

5. Close Desktop 2, and confirm that the remaining app from that desktop moved to Desktop 1.

6. Close any apps that you aren't using.

Monitor system tasks

Perform the following tasks:

1. Open **Task Manager**. Notice the information that is available in Fewer Details view.

2. Switch to More Details view, and do the following:

   - Display each tab, and review the information that is available on the tab.

   - Notice how the information changes as your computer performs background processes.

   - Consider how and when the information will be useful to you.

3. When you finish reviewing the information, close **Task Manager**.

Protect your computer and data

For many people, their computers and other "smart" devices have become an integral part of their lives. Even if you aren't totally dependent on them, the failure of one or more of them would be at least inconvenient.

The power of modern laptops and tablets means that you can carry your information with you and easily access it for work or play. But mobile devices are more susceptible to being lost or stolen than the clunky desktop you abandoned, and if that happens, you could lose valuable information, and it might be misused by others.

This chapter provides information about a variety of methods that Windows 10 offers to protect your computer and the data on it, to recover that data if something bad happens to the computer, and to prevent others from accessing your data if your computer is stolen.

This chapter guides you through procedures related to configuring update options, configuring privacy settings, restoring computer functionality, backing up data to OneDrive, backing up data by using File History, and backing up and restoring your system.

In this chapter

- Configure update options
- Configure privacy settings
- Restore computer functionality
- Back up data to OneDrive
- Back up data by using File History
- Back up and restore your system

Practice files

No practice files are necessary to complete the practice tasks in this chapter.

Configure update options

The code behind operating systems is usually in a constant state of change. This might be to offer new functionality, or to resolve internal or external issues. External issues include threats from new viruses or the need to improve or create drivers for the devices that you can connect to your computer.

Unlike previous versions of Windows, Windows 10 automatically checks for and installs updates to ensure that the security measures on your computer are current. Depending on the advanced option settings, if updates are available for Windows, the computer will either quietly install them while you aren't using it, or ask you to initiate the installation.

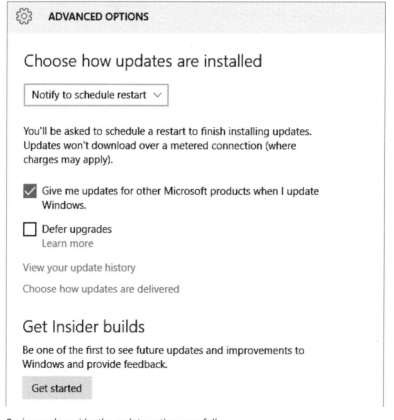

Review and consider the update options carefully

You can configure the following advanced options for Windows Update:

- **How updates are installed** The choices are Automatic and Notify To Schedule Restart. In either case, updates will be downloaded and installed, but you have the option of choosing when to restart your computer if a restart is necessary.

  If you choose the first option, your computer will automatically restart after the installation. If you choose the second option, the computer installs the updates, but you will be asked to schedule the restart.

- **What products you get updates for** In addition to updating operating system files and drivers, you can update other Microsoft products and featured apps through Windows Update. It's a good idea to select this option because many apps and utilities don't automatically update.

- **How soon you get upgrades** Some Windows 10 editions, including Professional, Enterprise, and Education (but not Home), allow you to defer upgrades to your computer. When you defer upgrades, new Windows features won't be downloaded or installed for several months after they're available. Deferring upgrades doesn't defer security updates, but it will prevent you from getting the latest Windows features as soon as they're available.

- **How updates are delivered** This is a new and interesting feature for Windows 10. If you have several Windows 10 computers on your network, and you enable this option, one computer does the download, caches the files on the network, and then sends the files to the other computers. This can substantially reduce the bandwidth you consume each month.

  There is also an option to allow your local computers to pass updates to and from known computers on your local network and unknown computers through the Internet. This is the default update distribution model for Windows 10 Home and Windows 10 Professional. (The Enterprise and Education editions of Windows 10 are configured to pass updates to and from local network computers only.) This process helps to distribute security updates faster, but can increase your bandwidth usage. If you want more information about this, you can click the Learn More link.

- **Get Insider Builds** You can sign up with the Windows Insider program to receive preview builds of upcoming Windows 10 versions. These builds have been tested by the product team, but they have not been released to the general public yet.

You'll have earlier access to new features, but you might also have to deal with issues in those features. Microsoft suggests that you do not install a preview build on a computer that is critical to your happiness or business. If something is drastically wrong with the preview build, you might end up having to reformat and reinstall Windows from scratch.

 IMPORTANT If you decide to get Insider builds, be sure to read the topic "Back up and restore your system" later in this chapter.

Windows chooses a time to install updates when you likely won't be online. You can check for new updates at any time and install available updates earlier if you want to.

To display the Windows Update status

1. In the **Settings** window, click **Update & security**, and then click **Windows Update**.

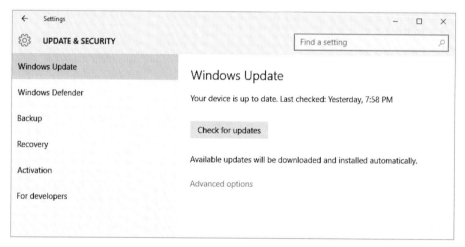

Windows Update status

The right pane displays either an Install Now button or a Check For Updates button. If the Install Now button is present, updates are available to install.

To check for updates

1. In the **Windows Update** pane, click the **Check for updates** button.

To install available updates

1. In the **Windows Update** pane, click the **Install now** button.

To configure update installation options

1. In the **Windows Update** pane, click the **Advanced options** link.

2. In the **Advanced Options** pane, do any of the following:

    - From the **Choose how updates are installed** list, select **Automatic (recommended)** or **Notify to schedule restart**.

    - Select or clear the **Give me updates for other Microsoft products when I update Windows** check box.

    - If available, select or clear the **Defer upgrades** check box.

    - Click the **Choose how updates are delivered** link, and set the **Updates from more than one place** toggle button to **On** or **Off**.

To get Windows Insider builds

1. In the **Windows Update** pane, click the **Advanced options** link.

2. In the **Get Insider builds** section, click the **Get started** button.

> 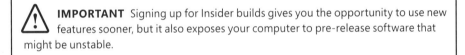 **IMPORTANT** Signing up for Insider builds gives you the opportunity to use new features sooner, but it also exposes your computer to pre-release software that might be unstable.

Configure privacy settings

Privacy, or at least some illusion of privacy, is important to most people. When you use a computer regularly, much of your life takes place inside that box. The operating system, the apps you use, and the sites you visit all have access to bits of information about you. Windows 10 privacy settings can limit how much of that information the apps and devices that are connected to your computer can see, and, to some extent, what the apps and devices can use that information for.

Much of the emphasis of the privacy settings is on how Microsoft and other companies can use any information they gather to present you with advertising that is theoretically more pertinent to your lifestyle than random advertising might be. From that point of view, because you are going to be presented with ads anyway, it seems like a benefit to have those ads more accurately related to your interests.

In the end, it is up to you to consider the benefits, or lack thereof, in sharing your information.

> **TIP** The placement of ads on websites provides a way to defray the expense of offering you free information. If the site is actually useful to you and the ads aren't too distracting, then this might be acceptable. But a lot of sites show up in web searches that exist only to barrage people with ads. Your browser can block pop-up ads, but it can't automatically block inline ads. If you are tired of waiting for these ads to load before you can start scrolling through the page, search the Internet for "remove ads from your browser" and peruse the results. Some of the options are pretty amazing.

In Windows 10, you can configure settings for 13 categories of information. Each category contains a link to the Microsoft online privacy statement, which is about 50 pages long, and some categories have links to one or more additional online topics.

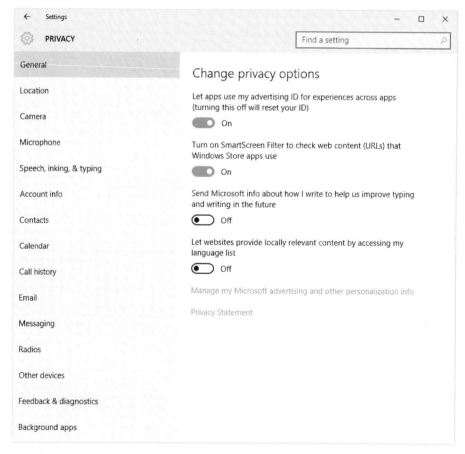

Take the time to review and configure the Privacy settings

We won't go into a lot of detail about all of these privacy settings. Instead, we will take you on a quick tour and leave it up to you to explore those areas that interest you. Sharing some of this information can be beneficial to you, and most is not harmful. Here is a bit of information that might be helpful:

- Your *advertising ID* is a unique ID that is connected to the email address you use to sign in to Windows 10. If you use a Microsoft account to sign in to OneDrive, Office 365, email, and other computers, Microsoft will accumulate information from all sources of these under this one ID.

- Although Windows provides an option to turn SmartScreen Filter on or off, SmartScreen Filter is a security tool, so think carefully about turning it off. You can also turn it on and off in Microsoft Edge, but the two toggle buttons are independent, so you can have it off in one and on in the other.

- Many settings refer to apps that might use your information.

  Windows 10 preinstalls a lot of apps that you might never use. You can turn off the ability for the app to access your data in the settings, but if you don't want to use the app at all, it is better to uninstall it.

   TIP This works only for apps that came from the App Store. If the app is part of Windows, such as Mail or Maps, then you can't uninstall it.

- After you click a privacy category, there is generally a pause as Windows scans your installed apps to identify those that might need access to this category. Windows then lists these below the heading Choose Apps That Can... use or access the feature. If no apps are listed, then no currently installed apps need the feature in this category.

  Only Store apps appear in this list; desktop apps don't. So you could, for example, turn off camera access for the OneNote or Skype Store app, but not for the corresponding desktop app.

Choose apps that can use your location

Acer Crystal Eye	⬤◯	Off
App connector	⬤◯	Off
Cortana Location history must be on for Cortana to work	◯⬤	On
Craigslist+ Pro	◯⬤	On
Facebook	⬤◯	Off
Geofenced!	◯⬤	On

Many apps want to use your information

- Some location features, such as geofencing, are applicable only if you have installed apps that use them.

- Speech, inking, & typing include features that allow Windows and Cortana to "get to know you better." If you plan to use Cortana, don't turn off Getting To Know You.

Additional settings that are related to privacy and advertising in Microsoft products are available at *choice.microsoft.com/en-us/opt-out*. That page also includes links to more information about how Microsoft might use your information.

If you use your computer to manage your life, especially if that computer is portable, leaving many of the privacy settings enabled makes sense. It is useful to you if your computer (and Cortana) know where you are and which meetings you have scheduled and who you are exchanging email with. And sharing information about typing, voice recognition, and other activities with Microsoft can certainly help them improve Windows and their apps in the future. Give some thought to what is useful to you to share, and what isn't.

To manage privacy settings

1. In the **Settings** window, click **Privacy**.

2. Review the options in each pane. Consider how each might impact you.

3. Click the toggle buttons for each option you want to turn off or on.

Restore computer functionality

Modern computers are reasonably robust, but the only absolute guarantee you can expect from any hardware device is that if you continue to use it long enough, it will fail.

Computer software tends to be updated frequently, in an effort to improve its operation, introduce new features, or increase security. But every update is also an opportunity for a little bug to creep in and cause problems.

The Internet is a wonderful resource, but it also exposes your computer to viruses, hackers, and other potentially harmful things.

A serious hardware failure might leave you stranded at a critical point in a work project, or unable to access information you need from the Internet.

Set and use restore points

If your computer starts performing poorly, especially if that happens just after performing updates or perhaps downloading something that installed obnoxious adware that you can't seem to get rid of, you can restore Windows to an earlier point in time, called a *restore point*. Doing this doesn't change your personal files, but it might remove recently installed apps and drivers (which could be a good thing if they are the cause of the problem).

System restore points are automatically added before significant changes are made, but if you are about to do something that makes you a bit nervous, it doesn't hurt to set one manually.

You create restore points from the System Protection tab of the System Properties dialog box.

 TIP You generally need to create a restore point for only your system drive.

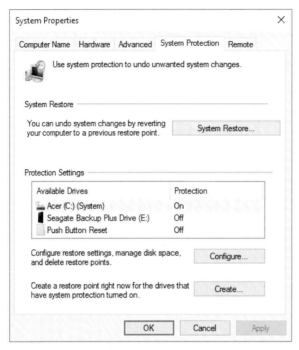

Set a system restore point

When you want to restore your computer to an earlier restore point, you open the System Properties dialog box and display the System Protection tab. From there, you click the System Restore button to start the System Restore wizard.

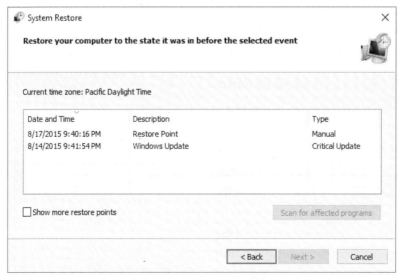

The System Restore wizard shows the last few restore points

Only the last few restore points are displayed. You can select the Show More Restore Points check box to see more, if there are any.

To create a restore point

1. Open **File Explorer**.

2. In the left pane, right-click **This PC**, and then click **System protection** to open the **System Properties** dialog box with the **System Protection** tab displayed.

3. In the **Protection Setting** group, click the **Create...** button to display the **Create a restore point** dialog box.

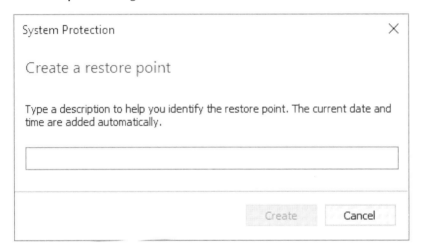

Enter a meaningful description to help you choose a restore point later

4. Enter a description, and then click the **Create** button. Windows adds the current date and time, creates the restore point, and informs you after it is done.

To restore your computer to a saved restore point

1. Open the **System Properties** dialog box with the **System Protection** tab displayed.

2. In the **System Restore** group, click the **System Restore...** button to start the **System Restore** wizard. Read the introduction message, and then click **Next** to display the **Restore your computer to the state it was in before the selected event** dialog box.

3. Click a restore point from the list, or, if the restore point you want to use isn't listed, click the **Show more restore points** check box, and then select a restore point.

4. Click the **Scan for affected programs** button to have the wizard search and display a list of programs and drivers that will be affected. Make a note of any programs or drivers you might need to reinstall after you restore your computer. Click the **Close** button to return to the wizard.

5. Click **Next** to restore your computer to the selected restore point.

Refresh or reset your computer

The ability to refresh or reset your computer was first introduced with Windows 8, and has proven to be a good recovery path that requires less effort than wiping your computer, reinstalling Windows and all your apps, and recovering all your data.

Refreshing your computer is a more serious action than restoring to a saved restore point; it is a bit like upgrading to a fresh version of Windows 10. Here's what happens when you refresh your computer:

■ You keep your personal files (stored in your My Documents folder).

■ Your computer settings are reset to the defaults.

■ Your Store apps remain installed, and your desktop apps are uninstalled. Desktop apps that were installed by the computer manufacturer might be reinstalled. A list of the removed apps is saved as a file on your desktop.

Resetting your computer reinstalls Windows and deletes all apps that weren't included in the original installation. This is a drastic action. If you plan to continue using this computer, you will want to back up all files to another location and make sure you have setup files for any desktop apps you will want to reinstall.

Your computer should restart and then take a while (10 minutes to several hours, depending on various things) to complete the reset. After the reset is done, you will need to re-create your account and reinstall any missing apps.

If you're experiencing problems with your computer, first try restoring it. If that doesn't solve the problem, you can escalate to refreshing the computer, and then to resetting it.

To refresh your computer

1. In the **Settings** window, click **Update & security**, and then click **Recovery**.

2. In the **Reset this PC** section, click **Get started** to display your reset options.

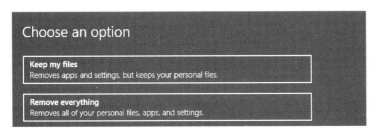

Choose to refresh or reset your computer

3. Click **Keep my files** to display a list of the apps that will be uninstalled.

The list is also saved in a file on your desktop

4. Click **Next**. If you upgraded to Windows 10 within the past 30 days, the wizard might warn you that refreshing your computer will prevent you from being able to roll back to the previous version of Windows.

5. Click **Next**, and then click **Reset**.

Your computer should restart and then take a while (10 minutes to several hours, depending on various things) to complete the refresh.

To reset your computer

1. In the **Settings** window, click **Update & security**, and then click **Recovery**.

2. In the **Reset this PC** section, click **Get started** to display your reset options.

3. Click **Remove everything**, and then click **Next**. If you upgraded to Windows 10 within the past 30 days, the wizard might warn you that resetting your computer will prevent you from being able to roll back to the previous version of Windows.

4. Click **Next**, and then click **Reset**.

Back up data to OneDrive

Although we would like to believe that every "new and improved" computer will be the last one we need, the reality is that your computer will eventually crash or break, or get stolen or left at an international airport (and you'll never get that one back).

If you maintain a fresh backup of your data and have a system recovery drive, you are going to recover from a disaster a lot faster and with less data loss than someone who isn't prepared.

Your computer, operating system, and apps are important, but they can be replaced with a little money. The personal files that are on your computer—the documents you have written, pictures you have taken, and other data—are much harder to replace. They might be worth many times the cost of a new computer. It is ironic that backing up data is so easy, and that so few people do it consistently.

OneDrive is free online storage that comes with your Microsoft account. If you have a Microsoft account, and use it to sign in to your computer, a link to your OneDrive cloud storage is automatically created in C:\Users\[your account]\OneDrive.

TIP At the time of this writing, Microsoft is providing 15 GB of free OneDrive storage with your Microsoft account, or 1 terabyte (TB) for Office 365 subscribers. But Microsoft offers various ways to accumulate more storage. Go to *onedrive.live.com/about* and click Plans to see the available plans for your location.

A shortcut to your OneDrive folder is available from the File Explorer Navigation pane, so you have easy access to it.

OneDrive is more than just a storage location; it is a storage location you can use to synchronize access to your files from every computer you sign in to with your Microsoft account, and from which you can share files with other people.

You can also sign in to your OneDrive web account and from there connect to the hard drive of any other Windows 10 computer that you sign in to with the same account, and that has OneDrive set up properly.

You can connect to your OneDrive cloud account by opening your browser and going to *onedrive.live.com*. You sign in to OneDrive by using your Microsoft account credentials.

 TIP You can quickly go to your OneDrive account by right-clicking the OneDrive icon in the taskbar icons group, and then clicking Go To OneDrive.com.

From here you can view and share the files that are backed up to OneDrive from the computers you sign in to by using your Microsoft account.

Every computer you sign in to with your Microsoft account credentials should automatically display your OneDrive folder in File Explorer and keep the files synchronized with those on your other devices.

You can also access your files on OneDrive from pretty much any other device, including Windows, Android, Mac OSX, iOS, Windows Phone, and Xbox systems. All you have to do is download the OneDrive app (or OneDrive for Business if you have an account of that type) from the appropriate app store.

If you work on multiple computers, you can store all your files on OneDrive so that you have access to the most up-to-date versions from any computer. If you store files locally on computers, OneDrive can help you to access those files, if you need to, by using the Fetch feature. Fetching files is a method of remotely accessing a Windows 10 computer from another computer by using your OneDrive account. You must enable the fetching of files on the computer that you intend to access remotely, and the computer must be turned on and connected to the Internet.

To store files on OneDrive

1. Drag, or copy and paste, files from other locations on your hard drive to your OneDrive folder in File Explorer.

    You can place your original working files, such as Microsoft Word documents, on OneDrive, and access and edit them there. Or you might want to work on your files elsewhere on your hard drive and drop a copy in OneDrive occasionally.

To manage OneDrive settings

1. In the notification area of the taskbar, click the **Show hidden icons** button, and then right-click the **OneDrive** icon.

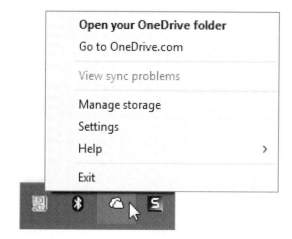

Right-click notification icons to display options

2. On the OneDrive shortcut menu, click **Settings** to open the Microsoft OneDrive dialog box.

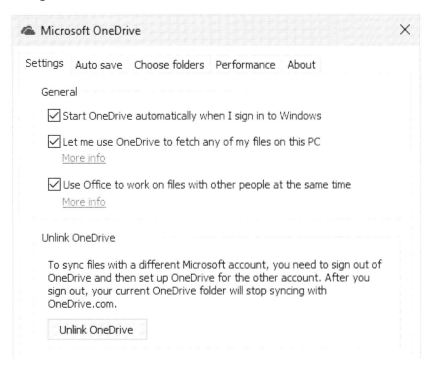

Configure OneDrive settings for your computer

To enable the fetching of files from a computer

1. Open the **Microsoft OneDrive** dialog box.

2. On the **Settings** tab, select the **Let me use OneDrive to fetch any of my files on this PC** check box.

3. Click **OK** to close the dialog box.

4. Exit and then restart the OneDrive app by following these steps:

    a. In the notification icon area, right-click the **OneDrive** icon, and then click **Exit**.

    b. On the **Start** menu, click **All Apps**, scroll or jump to the **OneDrive** entry, and click it.

To specify the folders you want to synchronize to a computer

1. Open the **Microsoft OneDrive** dialog box.

2. On the **Choose folders** tab, click the **Choose folders** button to display a list of the folders on your OneDrive site, the amount of data that is stored in each folder, and the amount of storage space that is available on your computer.

3. In the folder list, select the check boxes for the folders you want to synchronize with the computer, and clear the check boxes for the folders you don't want to synchronize. As you change your selections, OneDrive keeps track of the storage space requirements.

You can selectively synchronize files to save space

4. Click **OK** in each of the open dialog boxes to implement your changes.

> ✓ **TIP** You configure folder synchronization independently on each computer that you connect to OneDrive, and you can make different selections on different computers. For example, you might want to synchronize your Pictures folder on your personal laptop and not on your work computer.

To access OneDrive storage options

1. In the notification area of the taskbar, click the **Show hidden icons** button, right-click the **OneDrive** icon, and then click **Manage storage** to display the storage options page of your OneDrive account.

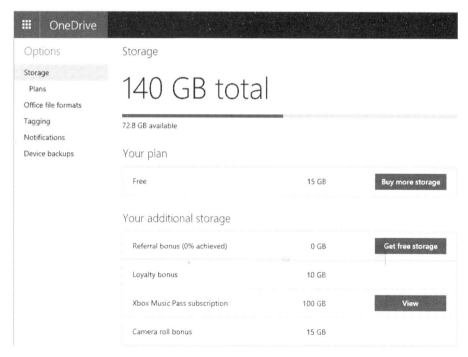

Many Microsoft programs provide additional OneDrive storage

2. From this page, you can display the storage you have with your Microsoft account and with any other programs you participate in. You can also purchase additional storage.

To fetch files remotely

1. In the notification area of the taskbar, click the **Show hidden icons** button, right-click the **OneDrive** icon, and then click **Go to OneDrive.com** to display the home page of your OneDrive account.

2. In the left pane, expand the **PCs** menu, and then click the name of the computer you want to connect to. Enter your credentials if prompted to do so.

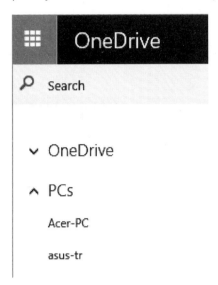

Fetching files from a remote PC by using OneDrive

3. After the folders of that computer are displayed, navigate to the file you need, right-click it, and click Download.

It is a good idea to go through this process a few times at home, to become familiar with the process when you aren't under pressure.

Back up data by using File History

If you use your Microsoft account to log in to Windows 10, you can take advantage of OneDrive to back up files to the cloud and share them among your computers. But it is also nice to have an offline backup that maintains versions and allows you to restore earlier versions. The File History feature in File Manager will help you with this task.

File History can automatically back up each version of files that are in your libraries, contacts, favorites, and on your desktop. If you have files or folders elsewhere that you want backed up, you can move them into one of your existing libraries or create a new library. If you have a OneDrive account that is associated with your login, it is technically included under your Users account, so it is also included in the File History backup.

To activate File History

1. In the **Settings** window, click **Update & security**, and then click **Backup** to display the File History controls. The first time you work with File History, the pane displays an Add A Drive button.

2. To begin using File History, click **Add a drive**. Windows searches your computer and displays a list of the drives that you can back up files to by using File History.

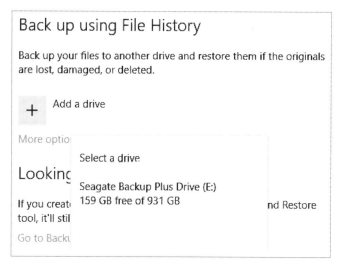

You must have access to a suitable backup drive

3. Click the drive you want to use for backups. After you select a drive, the Add A Drive button changes to a toggle button that is set to On.

4. In the **Backup** pane, click the **More options** link to display the backup frequency and scope settings.

5. In the **Backup options** pane, review the **Back up these folders** list. If you want to exclude any of these folders from the backup, click the folder, and then click **Remove**.

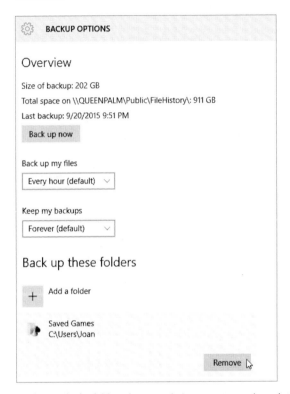

Back up only the folders that contain important or unique data

6. To add a folder to the **Back up these folders** list, click the **Add a folder** button. In the **Select Folder** dialog box, browse to and select the folder, and then click **Choose this folder**.

> 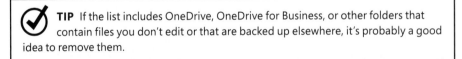 **TIP** If the list includes OneDrive, OneDrive for Business, or other folders that contain files you don't edit or that are backed up elsewhere, it's probably a good idea to remove them.

7. If you want to specifically exclude a folder (for example, a subfolder) from the backup, scroll to the **Exclude these folders** section near the bottom of the **Backup options** pane, and click the **Add a folder** button. In the **Select Folder** dialog box, browse to and select the folder, and then click **Choose this folder**.

8. At the top of the **Backup options** pane, click the **Back up my files** list, and then click a frequency between **Every 10 minutes** and **Daily**.

9. Click the **Keep my backups** list, and then click a retention period from **1 month** to **Forever**, or click **Until space is needed** to have File History manage the retention period based on available storage space.

10. To start using File History, click **Back up now**.

 TIP You can also set up and manage File History from Control Panel. There are a few advanced settings there that are not yet available in Settings.

To view versions of a file that has been backed up

1. In File Explorer, browse to and select a file you have previously backed up.

2. On the **Home** tab, in the **Open** group, click **History**.

A file viewer displays the most recently backed up version of the file. The day, date, and time of the file version and the number of versions are displayed at the top of the window.

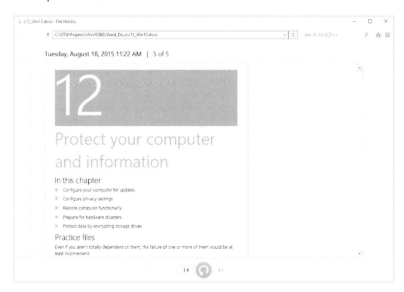

You can navigate through the file backup in the File History viewer

3. You can do any of the following:

- Click the **Restore** button (the circular arrow in the green circle) to restore that version of the file to its original location.

- Click the **Previous version** or **Next version** button (to the left and right of the Restore button) to display a different version of the file.

To manage file versions

1. In File Explorer, select a file you have previously backed up. Then right-click the file, click **Restore previous versions** to open the file's Properties dialog box, and then click the **Previous Versions** tab.

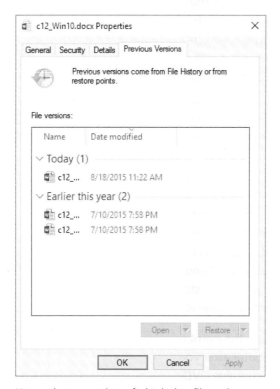

You can browse versions of a backed up file, and open or restore any specific version

2. Click a file version to enable the Open and Restore buttons.

3. Do any of the following:

- Click the **Open** button to open a read-only version of the file in its default app.

- In the **Open** list, click **Open in File History** to display the versions in the File History viewer.

- Click the **Restore** button to restore the selected version to the file's original location.

- In the **Restore** list, click **Restore To** to select a different location.

Back up and restore your system

You can back up an entire drive (or drives) to a system image that contains all operating system and user files, configuration information, and apps. The system image includes everything required to restore the drive to the state you capture in the image. This is a complete restoration to the imaging point, unlike the restorations provided by File History, restore points, or Reset Your PC, which bring back specific portions of the information that is stored on your hard drive. If you create a system image just before your hard drive crashes, you can install a new hard drive, restore that image, and be ready to work with all your apps and data that you saved with that image.

> ⚠ **IMPORTANT** Because a system image is generally needed only if the hard drive crashes and you can't boot up, its usefulness depends on having the image files available on some form of external media. If the old hard drive is still functional, you can restore the system image to that hard drive to return it to the state it was in at the imaging point. If the hard drive no longer functions, it might not be practical to install a new hard drive and restore the image to it. You should consult an expert.

You might choose to create periodic system images to ensure that you have a recent one available. When you do, the first image you create is a complete image of the drive, and each subsequent image stores only the changes from the previous image. Because of this layered storage model, it is possible to restore the most recent image or an earlier one. In this way, restoring to a system image is similar to restoring to a restore point.

Backup images safeguard your data in the event of system failure, but you need to be able to start up (boot) your computer after you wipe the hard drive clean. You can start up your computer from a bootable DVD that contains installation files. You might have received a DVD from your computer manufacturer when you bought the computer. If you didn't, you will need to create some kind of boot media. Windows 10 allows you to create a bootable USB recovery drive.

You can quickly and easily create a recovery drive that you can use to boot up and troubleshoot problems with your computer. The recovery information is stored on a USB drive. The USB drive must have a capacity of at least 8 GB, although it might require as much as 16 GB or 32 GB. Windows will scan your computer at the beginning of the imaging process and tell you how large a drive you need. The drive doesn't have to be blank, but the process of creating the boot image reformats the drive and deletes its contents, so be sure to back up anything you want that is on the drive.

> ⚠ **IMPORTANT** A bootable recovery drive has to be created in the same operating system type (32-bit or 64-bit) that you will boot into later. Ideally you will create it on the same operating system you have backed up.

If you ever actually need to restore from a system image, the process will depend on whether your computer can still boot into Windows.

- If the computer can boot into Windows, follow the process described in "To restore a system image from within Windows 10," later in this topic.

- If the computer can't boot from the hard drive and you created a USB recovery drive as described in the procedure "To create a bootable USB recovery drive," you should be able to boot from that; however, the process takes a bit of effort and varies based on the specific computer.

- If the computer can't boot into Windows at all, follow the process described in "To boot from a recovery drive or disc," later in this topic.

> ✓ **TIP** If you are using a wireless or USB keyboard, your ability to get in to the BIOS will depend on the order in which the drivers for it are loaded. After you do get in, touch controls and the mouse most likely will not work.

To create a system image backup

1. Open Control Panel, and then do one of the following:

   - In **Category** view, in the **System and Security** area, click **Backup and Restore**.

   - In **Large Icons** or **Small Icons** view, click **Backup and Restore**.

2. In the left pane, click **Create a system image** to start the Create A System Image wizard. The wizard scans your system for storage devices that meet the requirements.

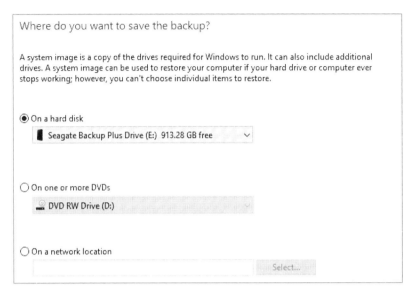

Select the drive where you want to store tne system image

3. Select the location for the image. If you have created previous images, it is best to use the same location, if there is room, so all your images are in one place. Then click **Next** to display the backup settings.

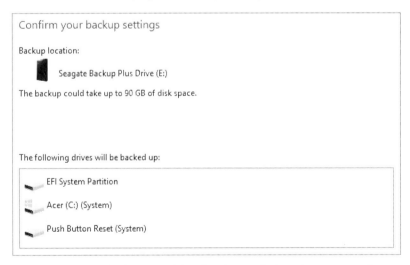

Confirm what will be backed up, and that there is room for it on the storage media

4. Review and confirm the backup settings, and then click **Next** to start the backup. Windows displays a progress bar during the backup process. You can stop the process from the progress bar if you need to.

After the backup is complete, the wizard asks whether you want to create a system repair disc.

 TIP Creating a system repair disc is a good idea. You can boot your computer from it, and it contains Windows system recovery tools that you can use to restore your computer from a system image.

5. Click **Yes**, insert a blank disc in your CD/DVD drive, and then click **Create disc**.

6. After the disc is complete, click **Close** and then click **OK** to finish the process.

 TIP Your first backup will take quite a while. Subsequent ones to the same location take less time.

To restore a system image from within Windows 10

1. Shut down all running apps.

2. Do one of the following to restart your computer in troubleshooting mode:

   - On the **Start** menu, click **Power**. Then hold down the **Shift** key and click **Restart**.

   - In the **Settings** windows, click **Update & security**, click **Recovery**, and then in the **Advanced startup** section, click the **Restart now** button.

3. On the **Choose an option** screen, click **Troubleshoot**.

4. On the **Troubleshoot** screen, click **Advanced options**.

5. On the **Advanced options** screen, click **System Image Recovery**. Your screen will briefly go blank, and then display the message that Windows is preparing System Image Recovery.

6. If the computer is configured with user accounts for more than one Microsoft account, System Image Recovery prompts you to select your account and enter the password.

7. The system locates and displays drives that contain image files. Select the image you want to use, click **Next**, and then continue to the end of the wizard.

To create a bootable USB recovery drive

1. On the taskbar or in the **Settings** window, enter **recovery** in the search box, and then click **Create a recovery drive** in the search results.

2. A User Account Control message box opens. Agree to the request to allow the Recovery Media Creator to make changes to your computer. The Recovery Drive wizard starts.

Create a recovery drive

Even if your PC can't start, you can use a recovery drive to reset it or troubleshoot problems. If you back up system files to this drive, you'll also be able to use it to reinstall Windows.

☐ Back up system files to the recovery drive.

Create a bootable recovery USB drive

If you want to boot from a USB flash drive, clear the **Back up system files to the recovery drive** check box.

3. If you haven't already done so, insert the flash drive into a USB port, wait until it is recognized, and then click **Next**.

Select the USB flash drive

The drive must be able to hold at least 512 MB, and everything on the drive will be deleted.

Available drive(s)
 E:\ (Seagate Backup Plus Drive)
 F:\ (RECOVERY)

Select the USB flash drive

4. If multiple drives are available, select the one you want to use, and then click **Next**.

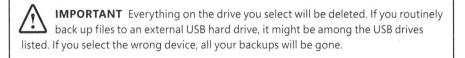

IMPORTANT Everything on the drive you select will be deleted. If you routinely back up files to an external USB hard drive, it might be among the USB drives listed. If you select the wrong device, all your backups will be gone.

5. Read and heed the warning that everything on the drive will be deleted. Make sure this is what you intend to do. Then click **Create** to start the process. A progress bar displays the progress.

6. After the process completes, click **Finish** to close the window.

 TIP You can follow the first few steps in the recovery process to confirm that you can boot from this drive.

To boot from a recovery drive or disc

1. Power your computer all the way down and then turn it back on.

2. If the boot process goes far enough to display the key to press to enter Setup, press it. This may be F8 or Del or some other key.

 IMPORTANT Read the instructions on the screen, read your computer documentation, and search the web for more information before you make any changes in Setup. Making changes that you don't fully understand can cause problems.

3. In the BIOS Setup Utility, press your keyboard arrow keys to select an option such as Boot Options, Boot Order, or something else that includes the word *Boot*.

 IMPORTANT The BIOS Setup Utility varies by computer make and model, so instructions are necessarily a bit vague. Basic instructions are usually included on the BIOS setup screen. If you have problems, search the web for information specific to your computer.

4. In the **Boot Priority Order** section (or something similar), select **1st Boot Device** and press **Enter** to display a list of devices.

5. Select **Removable Device** or **CD&DVD**, depending on what you want to boot from, and then press **Enter**.

 IMPORTANT Depending on your hardware and BIOS, there might be other changes. It is best to read your computer manual or search for information about that model.

6. After making the changes, Press **F10** to save and exit.

7. Your computer should now boot from the USB drive and display the Options screen that appears in step 1 of the procedure "To restore a system image from within Windows 10." Follow those directions from this point forward.

Skills review

In this chapter, you learned how to:

- Configure update options
- Configure privacy settings
- Restore computer functionality
- Back up data to OneDrive
- Back up data by using File History
- Back up and restore your system

Two-factor authentication

For the past several years, Microsoft has offered two-step identity verification as a method of protecting access to sensitive information that is associated with your Microsoft account.

If you try to sign in to your account from an unknown computer, or access sensitive information, such as advanced security settings, you are asked to verify your identity. You could initially do this by entering a key that was sent to you by email, phone, or text. More recently Microsoft has added the ability to verify your identity by using a smartphone authentication app.

If you are using the app, when you try to access a webpage that requires verification, your smartphone beeps, and when you sign in to the app, it displays, the security key and an Accept button. Tap the button and you are done.

If you are in a location where cellular access is not available, you can use the app to generate a key that you can then enter in the webpage that is requesting verification.

Starting with Windows 10, Microsoft is offering the same verification process for use when logging into your computer and other devices. If you choose to enable this on a device, each time you sign in you will need to use one of the verification methods to complete the action.

This might seem like an unnecessary complication for a desktop computer in a secure location (though in reality there are very few such locations), but it seems like a really good idea for laptops and tablets that sometimes seem to wander off on their own.

Along with the verification methods that have been available for a while, Microsoft is planning to accept biometric information, such as facial recognition or a scanned fingerprint or eye, to access your Windows device. This option is managed by the biometric login feature, Windows Hello.

Unfortunately, this technology is dependent on hardware that few people have at the time of this writing. You can check the current status of this service and find lists of compatible hardware by searching for Windows 10 Hello.

Practice tasks

No practice files are necessary to complete the practice tasks in this chapter.

Configure update options

Perform the following tasks:

1. Display the **Windows Update** pane.

2. Check for updates, or, if there are updates waiting, install them.

3. Display the update installation options, and configure the settings the way you want them.

Configure privacy settings

Perform the following tasks:

1. Display the **Privacy** page of the **Settings** window.

2. Review the settings on each pane. Consider the implications of sharing that information, and configure the settings the way you want them.

Restore computer functionality

Perform the following tasks:

1. Create a restore point.

2. In the **Settings** windows, click **Update & security**, click **Recovery**, and then in the **Advanced startup** section, click the **Restart now** button to display the Troubleshooting screen. Investigate the options that are available from this screen so you're familiar with them if you need them in the future.

3. In the **Settings** window, click **Update & Security**, and then click **Recovery**. Explore the options to refresh or reset your computer, but do not complete the process.

Back up data to OneDrive

Perform the following tasks:

1. In the notification area of the taskbar, click the **Show hidden icons** button, and locate the **OneDrive** icon.

2. From the **OneDrive** shortcut menu, open the **Microsoft OneDrive** dialog box. Display each tab in turn, and consider the available options.

3. Review the folders that are synchronized to this computer, and configure OneDrive to synchronize only the folders you want.

4. If you work on multiple computers and want to be able to fetch files from this computer, enable that feature. (Don't forget to exit and restart the OneDrive app.)

5. Open OneDrive from the notification icon, and review the site options, which change from time to time and might be different from those shown in this book.

Back up data by using File History

Perform the following tasks:

1. Display the **File History** pane.

2. If File History has not yet been configured, scan your computer system for a storage drive. If File History locates a suitable drive, do the following:

   a. Add the storage drive to File History.

   b. Display the File History options. Review the list of folders that File History backs up. Modify the list as necessary to include the folders that you want to back up, and exclude folders that you don't want to back up.

   c. Set the backup frequency, and specify how long you want to keep each version.

   d. Start the File History backup process.

3. If File History has been configured, do the following:

    a. Display the File History options. Review the list of folders that File History backs up, and modify the list as necessary.

    b. Review the backup frequency and the length of time File History retains each version. Modify these as necessary.

    c. Open one of the folders that File History backs up, and display a previous version of a file.

Back up and restore your system

There are no practice tasks for this topic.

Appendix A

Install or upgrade to Windows 10

Microsoft has generously offered free upgrades from the Home and Professional editions of Windows 7 with Service Pack 1 (SP1) and Windows 8.1 to the same editions of Windows 10. At the time of this writing, the free upgrade offer is valid for one year from the official Windows 10 release date of July 29, 2015. More information about the upgrade offer is available at *www.microsoft.com/en-us/windows/windows-10-upgrade*.

If your computer is running a licensed copy of Windows 7 SP1 or Windows 8.1 with all the available system updates installed, you should receive an invitation to upgrade through Windows Update.

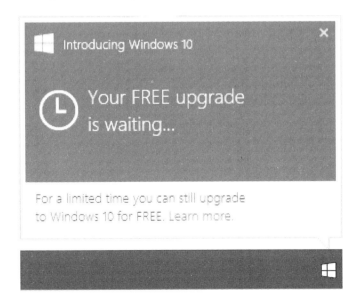

A friendly invitation to upgrade

There are four editions of Windows 10: Windows 10 Home and Windows 10 Pro for the consumer market, Windows 10 Enterprise for volume licensing clients, and Windows 10 Education for schools. The following table shows the free upgrade paths for consumers.

Free upgrade to Windows 10 Home	Free upgrade to Windows 10 Pro
Windows 7 Starter	Windows 7 Professional
Windows 7 Home Basic	Windows 7 Ultimate
Windows 7 Home Premium	Windows 8.1 Pro
Windows 8.1	Windows 8.1 Pro for Students

> **TIP** The free upgrade through the standard consumer offer is not available for computers running Windows 7 Enterprise, Windows 8.1 Enterprise, or Windows RT. Enterprise customers upgrade through their licensing programs, and there is currently no RT version of Windows 10.

The Windows 10 operating system upgrade process is the simplest we've seen in our decades of working with computers. Something certainly can go wrong with any upgrade process, so we offer the information in this appendix to help you ensure that you and your computer are properly prepared.

Where to get Windows 10

As previously stated, Windows 10 is available for the first year as a free upgrade from consumer versions of Windows 7 or Windows 8.1. The Windows Update tool manages the upgrade process. The official Windows 10 Upgrade site at *www.microsoft.com/en-us /windows/windows-10-upgrade* provides a lot of information about the upgrade requirements and process, and has links to additional resources.

If your computer qualifies for the online upgrade but you don't want to use that process, you can create your own installation drive or disc on a USB flash drive or DVD by using the media creation tool that is available from *windows.microsoft.com/en-us /windows-10/media-creation-tool-install*. If you choose this path, be sure to read the instructions carefully before you start, because you have to follow specific steps to upgrade without providing a product key.

> ⚠ **IMPORTANT** If you're accustomed to reformatting your computer and starting fresh with each new version of Windows, be aware that the free upgrade to Windows 10 won't work for that purpose; the computer must already be running a licensed copy of Windows 7 or Windows 8.1.

If your computer isn't eligible for the free upgrade, or if the free upgrade offer has expired, you can buy Windows 10 from the online Microsoft Store at *www.microsoftstore.com*, a physical Microsoft store, or the usual retail outlets.

System requirements

You can upgrade to Windows 10 from Windows XP or Windows Vista if your computer meets these minimum system requirements:

- Processor: 1 gigahertz (GHz) or faster processor
- RAM: 1 gigabyte (GB) for a 32-bit system or 2 GB for a 64-bit system
- Hard disk space: 16 GB for a 32-bit system or 20 GB for a 64-bit system
- Graphics card: DirectX 9 or later with a WDDM 1.0 driver
- Display: 800 × 600

Prepare for the update

If your computer qualifies for the free upgrade and has all necessary updates installed, you should receive an invitation to Get Windows 10 during a normal update. The invitation adds a white Windows 10 icon to the notification area of your taskbar, and pops up a notification from time to time to remind you. If you receive this invitation, then you know your computer meets the basic minimum requirements for installing Windows 10.

The notification area with displaying the white Get Windows 10 icon

If this icon is already in the notification area, you can skip forward to the "Reserve your copy of Windows 10" section, later in this topic.

If the Get Windows 10 icon doesn't appear in the notification area, then there are a few things you can do to remove obstacles so it will appear.

Prepare your computer

If your computer is only a few years old, it should meet the basic hardware requirements provided earlier in this appendix.

Here are some things you should do before you begin the update process:

- Confirm that your computer is running Windows 7 SP1 or Windows 8.1.

  If it is running Windows 8, you must first update the operating system to Windows 8.1 and bring the system files up to date by installing all available Windows updates. This can take several hours and several restarts and is much more arduous than the actual upgrade to Windows 10.

  If your computer has been offline for a while, you might not be able to initiate an update from Windows 8 to Windows 8.1 through the Windows Update tool. If this happens, you can manually initiate the update from the Microsoft Download Center.

- Confirm that the operating system has been properly activated.

- Confirm that all available updates are installed. Specifically check for updates KB3035583 and KB2952664 for Windows 7 or KB3035583 and KB2976978 for Windows 8.1. They should be among the last installed.

- Record your current software product keys.

> **TIP** You don't need the product keys for the upgrade; but if something goes wrong, and you have to reinstall the operating system or your apps, it is good to have a list of keys. There are many free utilities, such as ProduKey, that can retrieve the keys of installed software from your system.

It's also a good idea to clean your hard drive and registry, create a disk image, and back up important files to an external hard drive or to an online storage drive. There are free utilities, such as CCleaner, that will help with most of this.

To determine the current operating system edition

1. Open Windows Explorer or File Explorer.

2. Right-click the icon for your computer, and then click **Properties** to open the System window of Control Panel.

    > **TIP** The computer icon might be named This PC, My PC, or Computer, but it should resemble a computer monitor.

    Information about the edition of Windows that is running on your computer is displayed at the top of the window.

    View basic information about your computer

    Windows edition

    Windows 8.1 Pro

    © 2013 Microsoft Corporation. All rights reserved.

    Get more features with a new edition of Windows

Information about the currently installed edition of Windows

To determine whether your current operating system has been activated

1. In Windows Explorer or File Explorer, right-click your computer icon, and then click **Properties** to open the System window.

2. Scroll to the **Windows activation** section at the bottom of the **System** window. If Windows has been activated, the section contains the phrase *Windows is activated.*

    If Windows is not activated, there might be a button that you can click to start the activation process. You will probably need the Windows product key that should have come with your computer, or with the Windows operating system if you purchased it separately from your computer hardware.

> **TIP** The Windows product key is a set of five five-character blocks. It is usually printed on some of the documentation that comes with a new computer, or provided in the box or by email when you purchase an operating system upgrade. If you can't find the key, there are many free apps that can retrieve it for you. We tested half a dozen of these, and ProduKey from NirSoft.net retrieved both the OEM key and the end user key.

To check for necessary updates

1. Start **Windows Update**. In the left pane, click **Check for updates**.

2. If there are pending updates, install them.

   Or

   If there are no pending updates, click **View update history and check for failed updates**.

   The upgrade to Windows 10 is initiated by the following updates: KB3035583 and KB2952664 for Windows 7 and KB3035583 and KB2976978 for Windows 8.1. If you don't see the white Windows icon in your tray, check your update history for the appropriate updates.

> ✅ **TIP** If the Get Windows 10 icon doesn't appear on your taskbar and your updates are current, there might be some other problem. Microsoft offers some possible causes and solutions at *support.microsoft.com/en-us/kb/3081048*.

To manually initiate an update from Windows 8 to Windows 8.1

1. Start your web browser and go to the Microsoft Download Center at *www.microsoft.com/en-us/download*.

2. Do either of the following:

   - If you have a 32-bit computer, search for update ID **42327**.

   - If you have a 64-bit computer search for update **42335**.

3. Click the **Download** button on the page to start.

Reserve your copy of Windows 10

After the Get Windows 10 icon appears in your notification area, clicking it opens an app that includes a button you must click to reserve your free upgrade. After you reserve your upgrade, you have the option of providing an email address to receive a confirmation email message. The email message includes links to additional information.

Whether or not you provide an email address, Windows Update will inform you when the upgrade is ready for your computer to install, and you can start or postpone the upgrade. The upgrade might not be available immediately because of the volume of computers that it's going to. According to the email message, it could be "days or even weeks" until you receive it.

To reserve Windows 10

1. After the **Get Windows 10 icon** appears in the notification area of your taskbar, click the icon to start the Get Windows 10 app.

2. Click **Reserve your free upgrade**.

3. If you want to receive a confirmation message, provide your email address, and then click **Send confirmation**.

To confirm that your computer is compatible with Windows 10

1. In the notification area of the taskbar, click the **Get Windows 10** icon to start the Get Windows 10 app.

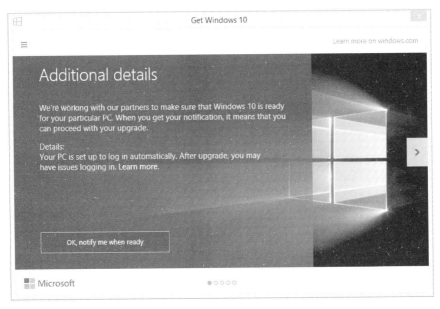

Get Windows 10 app

2. In the upper-left corner of the window, click the menu button (labeled with three horizontal lines).

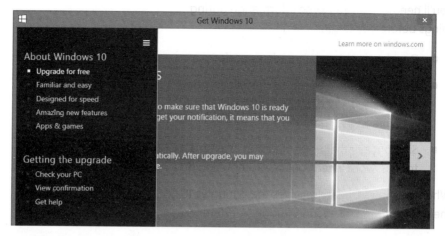

The Get Windows 10 menu

3. In the **Getting the upgrade** section of the menu, click **Check your PC** to begin an examination of your computer against the requirements. When the process completes, the app informs you whether your computer meets the requirements.

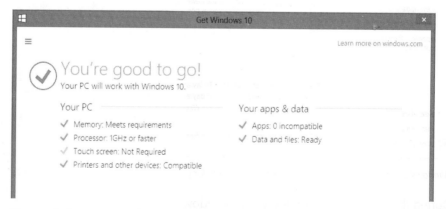

The app displays an approval message or provides information about incompatibilities

If there is a problem (such as outdated device drivers or an installed printer that Windows 10 doesn't support), you can correct the issues and the run the Check Your PC process again.

Perform the update

You'll need to provide some information during the update process. Consider these things before you begin:

- Decide whether to upgrade or perform a clean installation.

- If you're performing a clean installation, decide which account (a local computer account or a Microsoft account) you want to configure as the first administrator account on the computer.

- Sign out all other users, and sign in as an administrator, or provide an administrator password when you are prompted to do so during the installation process.

When Windows Update receives the Windows 10 upgrade notice, an alert appears in the notification area and in Windows Update.

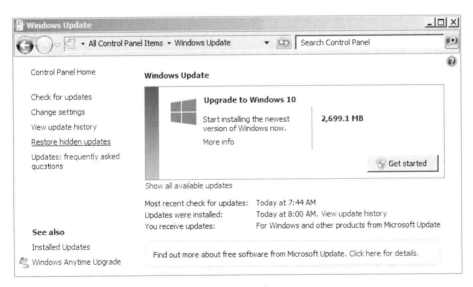

Windows Update informs you that the upgrade is ready for you

During the upgrade from Windows 7 or Windows 8.1, the Windows activation server validates your original product key and generates a Windows 10 license certificate (Microsoft calls it a "digital entitlement") that it stores with your installation ID and the version you just activated (Home or Pro). Because of this, you can reformat your computer and reinstall Windows 10 without re-entering the key.

Your computer will restart multiple times during the upgrade process, which takes a couple of hours but doesn't require any additional input from you. The screen displays the percentage of completion and other information during the process.

To perform the installation

1. In Windows Update, click **Get Started**. The download is about 2.7 GB.

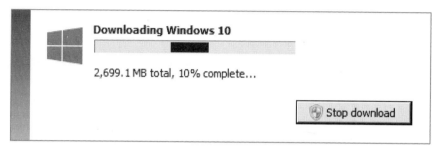

Windows Update keeps you apprised of the progress

2. When the download and preparation are complete, Windows Update displays the license terms.

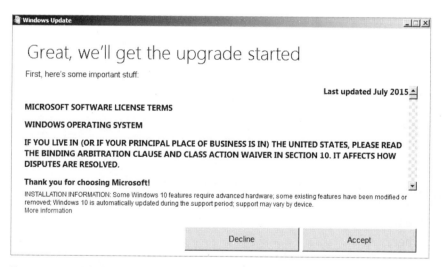

You must accept the license terms to continue

3. Click **Accept** to accept the license terms and continue.

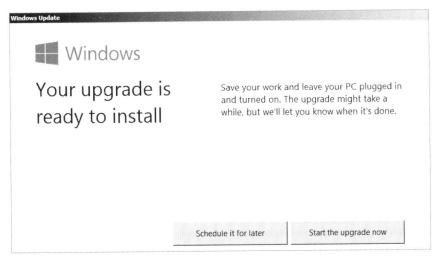

You can choose to schedule the upgrade for later or start it immediately

4. Click **Start the upgrade now**. That's it. The exciting part is done. Window Update will restart the computer and begin the installation process.

> **TIP** It is important to maintain the security of your computer. If your computer has a third-party antimalware program installed on it, Windows Update checks its status during the upgrade process and if it isn't currently active, uninstalls it. Windows 10 includes an updated version of Windows Defender that is getting pretty good reviews and doesn't require you to purchase or subscribe to anything. Windows Defender automatically turns off if you enable a different antimalware app.

After the update

After the final restart, you will be prompted to sign in with the account you were using when you started the update.

The first time you sign in to Windows 10, it goes through a process of configuring your user account. While doing so, the screen cycles repeatedly through a series of colors, and displays messages such as "Sit back and relax" or "This is taking longer than usual," until it finishes. This process can take a few minutes but is somewhat mesmerizing and again, doesn't require any input from you.

To finish the update to Windows 10

1. Provide your password, and then press **Enter** or click **Next**.

    You can choose to use express settings to complete the configuration process, or to customize the settings. If you choose the custom settings option, you can turn off some of the default privacy settings, but you can also change those settings later after you're familiar with Windows 10.

    > **SEE ALSO** For more information about privacy settings, see "Configure privacy settings" in Chapter 12, "Protect your computer and data."

2. Select **Use express settings**. Windows displays your desktop, and you can start exploring the new Start screen, Start menu, and taskbar features.

    Or

    Select **Use custom settings**, and then review and turn on or off several pages of settings. When you finish, Windows displays your desktop.

    For information about what to do after you sign in and how to do it, read this book.

    > ✓ **TIP** If you try Windows 10 and truly don't like it, you have one month from the upgrade date during which you can revert to your previous version of Windows. To do so, open the Settings window, click Update & Security, click Recovery, and then in the Go Back To An Earlier Build section, click the Get Started button.

Appendix B

Keyboard shortcuts and touchscreen tips

The standard method of working with content on a Windows computer is to click the relevant commands. You can perform some tasks faster by pressing specific key combinations or, on a touchscreen device, by using specific gestures.

Keyboard shortcuts

Keyboard shortcuts provide a quick way to perform actions on the computer without taking your hands off the keyboard. Many keyboard shortcuts have become commonplace over the years, to the extent that they perform the same function in apps from almost any publisher. For example, Ctrl+C, Ctrl+X, and Ctrl+V will copy, cut, and paste in many apps.

To differentiate keyboard shortcuts that control Windows from keyboard shortcuts that are specific to apps, many Windows keyboard shortcuts include the Windows logo key, which is located near the lower-left corner of the keyboard and labeled with the Windows icon. (Some keyboards have two Windows logo keys, one on each side of the spacebar.) The appearance of the icon varies based on the version of Windows that was active when the keyboard was manufactured.

Windows logo key variations

The simplest Windows 10 keyboard shortcut is to simply press and release the Windows logo key to display or hide the Start screen.

 TIP Because we refer to the Windows logo key a lot in this appendix, we've abbreviated the key name in multi-key keyboard shortcuts to *Win*.

Most keyboard shortcuts require that you hold down one key and then press another key. These keyboard shortcuts are presented in the form *Win+C*. Some keyboard shortcuts combine three keys; these are presented in the form *Win+Shift+M*. When invoking a three-key shortcut, press and hold the first key, press and hold the second key, press the third key, and then release all three.

New in Windows 10

Most of the Windows 10 shortcuts are the same as those in previous versions of Windows, but there are a few new keyboard shortcuts that simplify interactions with features that are new or different in Windows 10. If you're familiar with the older shortcuts and just want the new ones, they are:

- **Win+A** Open the Action Center

- **Win+S** Open search

- **Win+C** Open Cortana in listening mode

- **Win+Tab** Open Task view

- **Win+Ctrl+D** Add a virtual desktop

- **Win+Ctrl+Right Arrow** Switch between virtual desktops you've created on the right

- **Win+Ctrl+Left Arrow** Switch between virtual desktops you've created on the left

- **Win+Ctrl+F4** Close the virtual desktop you're using

Windows keyboard shortcuts

The following table includes all the keyboard shortcuts we could validate in Windows 10 at the time of this writing. Some of these keyboard shortcuts are valid only when the Windows user interface is active (not in individual apps).

To do this	Press
Display or hide the Start screen	Windows logo key
Open the Action Center	Win+A
Move the focus to the notification area	Win+B
Open or close the Cortana Listening mode window	Win+C
Display or hide the desktop	Win+D
Create a new virtual desktop	Win+Ctrl+D
Open the Quick Access folder in File Explorer	Win+E
Open the Find Computers dialog box (in which you search for domain-joined computers)	Win+Ctrl+F
Open the Game bar (from which you capture screen shots and record video clips in games)	Win+G
Open the Share pane (in which you share the active item by using apps that support the Share function)	Win+H
Open the Settings window	Win+I
Open the Connect pane (in which you connect to wireless display and audio devices)	Win+K
Lock the computer	Win+L
Minimize all app windows (but not system windows)	Win+M
Restore minimized windows	Win+Shift+M
On a mobile device, lock the device orientation	Win+O

To do this	Press
Open the Project pane and then cycle through presentation display modes	Win+P
Activate the taskbar search box	Win+Q
Open the Run dialog box	Win+R
Activate the taskbar search box	Win+S
Cycle through taskbar buttons from left to right	Win+T
Cycle through taskbar buttons from right to left	Win+Shift+T
Open the Ease of Access Center	Win+U
Display the Quick Link menu	Win+X
Show available commands in an app when in full-screen mode	Win+Z
Switch to or start the app that is in the taskbar position indicated by the number	Win+*number* (1–0)
Start a new instance of a pinned or running app	Win+Shift+*taskbar icon*
Start a new instance of the app that is in the taskbar position indicated by the number, if that app supports multiple instances	Win+Shift+*number* (1–0)
Start a new instance of a pinned or running app as an administrator	Win+Ctrl+Shift+*taskbar icon*
Start a new instance of the app that is in the taskbar position indicated by the number, if that app supports multiple instances, as an administrator	Win+Ctrl+Shift+*number* (1–0)
Switch to the last active window of the app that is in the taskbar position indicated by the number	Win+Ctrl+*number* (1–0)
Open the jump list of the app that is in the taskbar position indicated by the number	Win+Alt+*number* (1–0)
Capture an image of the current screen and save the image in the Pictures\Screenshots folder	Win+Print Screen
Display the System panel (of Control Panel)	Win+Pause/Break

To do this	Press
Display the Task view of all open windows	Win+Tab
Switch to the next input language and keyboard (on devices configured for multiple languages or keyboards)	Win+Spacebar
Switch to the previous input language and keyboard (on devices configured for multiple languages or keyboards)	Win+Shift+Spacebar
Display or hide Narrator	Win+Enter
Magnify the screen by using Magnifier	Win+Plus Sign
Decrease the screen magnification when Magnifier is running	Win+Minus Sign
Exit Magnifier	Win+Esc
Maximize a non-snapped window, or Snap a half-screen window to the upper corner	Win+Up Arrow
Restore a non-snapped window, or Snap a half-screen window to the lower corner	Win+Down Arrow
Move a window through the left, center, and right of each screen, or Move a quarter-screen window to another corner	Win+Left Arrow Win+Right Arrow
Move an open window to a different screen	Win+Shift+Right Arrow Win+Shift+Left Arrow
Minimize or restore all windows other than the active window	Win+Home
Search for Windows 10 help	Win+F1
Temporarily make all windows transparent	Win+Comma
Close the current virtual desktop	Win+Ctrl+F4
Switch to the next virtual desktop	Win+Ctrl+Left Arrow Win+Ctrl+Right Arrow

General keyboard shortcuts

The following shortcuts are applicable in multiple interfaces that might include system windows, app windows, File Explorer, dialog boxes, and panes.

To do this	Press
Cycle through thumbnails of open apps	Alt+Tab
Close the current app	Alt+F4
Select all content	Ctrl+A
Copy	Ctrl+C
Switch to the search box or Address bar	Ctrl+E
Open a new browser window	Ctrl+N
Create a new folder in File Explorer	Ctrl+Shift+N
Refresh a browser window	Ctrl+R
Paste	Ctrl+V
Close the current app window	Ctrl+W
Cut	Ctrl+X
Redo	Ctrl+Y
Undo	Ctrl+Z
Close the current file or active browser tab	Ctrl+F4
Select multiple noncontiguous items	Ctrl+click
Select contiguous items	Ctrl+Shift+click
Open Task Manager	Ctrl+Shift+Esc
Capture an image of the current screen and save the image in short-term memory	Print Screen

Touchscreen tips

Many computers, tablets, and phones have touchscreen interfaces, and some computer keyboards have touchpads that allow many of the same types of interactions as touchscreens.

The following table describes some specific terms that we use when describing interactions with a touchscreen.

Term	Action	Mouse equivalent
Tap	Touch your finger to the screen one time and then lift it	Click
Double-tap	Quickly tap the screen twice in the same location	Double-click
Flick	Touch your finger to the screen and quickly move it in a specific direction as you lift it	None
Press and hold	Touch the screen and wait for about one second	Right-click
Pinch	Touch the screen with two fingers and then move the fingers toward each other	None
Stretch	Touch the screen with two fingers and then move the fingers away from each other	None
Slide	Drag your finger or the stylus on the screen	None
Swipe	Briefly drag your finger across an item	None

On a touch device, you can set the permitted time and distance between taps for the double-tap action, and the minimum and maximum length of hold that performs a right-click equivalent. You configure these settings in the Pen And Touch dialog box.

You can use the gestures described in the following table to manage Windows 10 user interface elements on a screen that supports 10-point touch. Other touchscreen gestures might be available on your device, depending on the hardware and drivers.

Action	Touchscreen gesture
Display the Task view of all open windows	Swipe from the left of the screen
Display the Action Center	Swipe from the right edge of the screen
Display the taskbar when it is hidden	Tap or swipe the inside edge of the screen where the taskbar is docked

You can use the gestures described in the following table to move around on the screen.

Action	Touchscreen gesture
Scroll	Swipe up, down, left, or right
Scroll quickly	Flick up, down, left, or right, and then tap to stop scrolling
Zoom in	Stretch two fingers apart
Zoom out	Pinch two fingers together

You can use the gestures described in the following table to work with text content.

Action	Touchscreen gesture
Select a word	Double-tap the word
Select a paragraph	Triple-tap the paragraph
Expand or contract a selection	Drag the selection handles

Glossary

absolute path A path that defines the exact position of a file or folder on a computer or network. See also *path*; *relative path*.

Action Center The Windows 10 Action Center maintains a running list of system notifications that you can review and take action on, if necessary. It also includes Quick Action buttons that provide access to common Windows 10 features. Differs from the Control Panel Action Center that was in previous versions of Windows.

activation The process of validating software with the manufacturer. Activation confirms the genuine status of a product and that the product key has not been compromised. It establishes a relationship between the software's product key and a specific installation of that software on a device.

active window The window in which a user is currently working or directing input.

Address bar In File Explorer, a text box at the top of the window, under the title bar, containing the navigation path to the current folder. Clicking the arrow after each folder name displays a list of its subfolders. In Edge and Internet Explorer, a text box containing the web address of the currently displayed webpage.

Administrator account A type of Windows user account with access to all system files and settings, and with permission to perform all operations. Every computer must have at least one Administrator account. This account type is not recommended for daily use. See also *Standard User account*; *user account*.

app See *desktop app*; *Universal Windows app*.

app icon See *icon*.

aspect ratio The ratio of the width of an image, screen, or other visual element to its height.

background In a graphical user interface such as Windows, a pattern or picture that can be applied to various screen elements, such as the desktop or lock screen. Other elements, such as text, icons, and apps, are displayed on top of this background.

bandwidth The rate of data transfer, in bits per second.

bitmap (.bmp) A patent-free digital image file format that does not support transparency. A bitmap image consists of pixels in a grid. Each pixel is a specific color; the colors within the color palette are governed by the specific bitmap format. Common formats include Monochrome Bitmap, 16 Color Bitmap, 256 Color Bitmap, and 24-bit Bitmap.

blog Short for *web log*. An online journal or news/opinion column. Contributors post entries consisting of text, graphics, or video clips. When permitted by the blog owner, readers can post comments responding to the entries or to other people's comments. Blogs are often used to publish personal or company information in an informal way.

.bmp See *bitmap*.

broadband connection A high-speed Internet connection such as those provided by DSL or cable modem services. Broadband connections typically transfer data at 256 kilobytes per second (KBps) or faster.

browse To search for a folder or file by navigating through the hierarchical storage structure of a computer. Alternatively, to search for information on the web by following links between webpages.

browser See *web browser.*

byte A unit of measurement for data; a byte typically holds a single character, such as a letter, digit, or punctuation mark. Some single characters can take up more than 1 byte.

central processing unit (CPU) The main circuit chip in a computer. It performs most of the calculations necessary to run the computer. Also called a *processor.*

click To point to an interface element and then press the primary mouse button one time.

command An instruction you give to a computer or app.

Compatibility view In Internet Explorer, a feature that displays a website as though you were using an earlier version of the web browser. Compatibility view was first introduced with Internet Explorer 8. Edge doesn't currently include a Compatibility view, but does include a link to open the current site in Internet Explorer.

compress To reduce the size of a set of data, such as a file or group of files, inside a compressed folder that can be stored in less space or transmitted with less bandwidth.

compressed folder A folder containing files whose contents have been compressed. Also called a *zip file.*

Content pane In File Explorer, the pane that displays files and folders stored in the currently selected folder or storage device. See also *Details pane; Navigation pane; Preview pane.*

Control Panel A Windows app that contains items through which you can control system-level features of the computer and perform related tasks, including hardware and software setup and configuration.

CPU See *central processing unit.*

credentials Information that provides proof of identification that is used to gain access to local and network resources. Examples of credentials are user names and passwords, smart cards, and certificates.

cursor The on-screen image that moves around the screen when you move your mouse. Also called a *pointer* or *mouse pointer.*

desktop The work area on a computer screen, on which you can arrange windows, icons, and shortcuts to apps, folders, and data files. The contents of the Desktop folder of your user profile appear on the desktop. You can control the appearance of the desktop by changing the theme or the desktop background.

desktop app An application that is designed to run in the Windows desktop environment.

desktop computer A computer designed for use at one location. A typical desktop computer system includes the computer case containing the actual computer components, a monitor, a keyboard, a mouse, and speakers. See also *device.*

desktop shortcut See *shortcut.*

Details pane In File Explorer, the pane that displays details about the folder or selected items. See also *Content pane; Navigation pane; Preview pane.*

device A piece of equipment, such as a laptop, tablet, or smartphone, that is running an operating system. See also *desktop computer.*

device driver See *driver.*

dialog box A window that appears when you give a command that requires additional information. Also used to provide information or feedback about progress.

digital signature An electronic signature that is composed of a secret code and a private key. Digital signatures are used to help verify file authenticity. Also called a *digital ID.*

Disk Cleanup Reduces the number of unnecessary files on your drives, which can help your computer run faster. It can delete temporary files and system files, empty the Recycle Bin, and remove a variety of other items that you might no longer need.

Disk Defragmenter See *Optimize Drives*.

domain In Windows, a logical (rather than physical) group of resources—computers, servers, and other hardware devices—on a network, that is centrally administered through Windows Server. On the Internet, a name used as the base of website addresses and email addresses that identifies the entity owning the address.

double-click To point to an interface element and press the primary mouse button two times in rapid succession.

drag To move an item on the screen by pointing to it, holding down the primary mouse button, and then moving the mouse.

driver An app that enables Windows to communicate with a software app or hardware device (such as a printer, mouse, or keyboard) that is attached to your computer. Every device needs a driver in order for it to work. Many drivers, such as the keyboard driver, are built into Windows.

dynamic Changing in response to external factors.

Edge A Microsoft web browser released with Windows 10 that includes built-in features such as Inking, Reading view, Sharing, and Cortana integration.

Ethernet A system for exchanging data between computers on a local area network by using coaxial, fiber optic, or twisted-pair cables.

executable file A computer file that starts an app, such as a word processor, game, or Windows utility. Executable files can often be identified by the file name extension *.exe*.

expansion card A printed circuit board that, when inserted into an expansion slot of a computer, provides additional functionality. There are many types of expansion cards, including audio cards, modems, network cards, security device cards, TV tuner cards, video cards, and video processing expansion cards.

expansion slot A socket on a computer's motherboard, designed to establish the electrical contact between the electronics on an expansion card and on the motherboard. Many form factors (physical dimensions) and standards for expansion slots are available. An expansion slot accepts only expansion cards of the same form factor.

Extensible Markup Language (XML) A text markup language, similar to HTML, used to define the structure of data independently of its formatting so that the data can be used for multiple purposes and by multiple apps.

extension See *file name extension*.

external peripheral A peripheral device installed by connecting it to a port from outside the computer. Examples are a monitor, keyboard, mouse, and speakers. See also *internal peripheral*; *peripheral device*.

Favorites bar In Edge or Internet Explorer, a toolbar located below the Address bar that provides buttons for storing web locations for easy future access, obtaining add-ons, and accessing sites that match your browsing history.

File Explorer A utility that enables the user to locate and open files and folders.

File History Windows 10 offers two approaches to file history. One, available in File Manager, can maintain a version history of files you edit. The other, available through Settings > Update and Restore, can automatically back up selected folders to an external hard drive. Both allow you to recover damaged or deleted files.

Glossary

file name extension Characters appended to the name of a file by the app that created it and separated from the file name by a period. Some file name extensions identify the app that can open the file, such as .xlsx for Microsoft Excel workbooks; and some represent formats that more than one app can work with, such as .jpg graphic files.

file recovery Reconstructing or restoring lost or unreadable files on your hard drive.

filter To display only items that match specified criteria.

flash drive See *USB flash drive*.

flick A quick, straight stroke of a finger or pen on a screen. A flick is recognized as a gesture, and interpreted as a navigation or an editing command.

Flip A feature you can use to quickly preview all open windows without clicking the taskbar. Press Alt+Tab to invoke Flip, and then to move between previews. To display the previewed window, release both keys.

folder A named storage area on a computer or device containing files and other folders. Folders are used to organize information electronically, the same way actual folders in a filing cabinet do.

frame The outer border of a window.

gadget A type of app designed to display information on the desktop. Gadgets were popular in Windows Vista and Windows 7, but have been discontinued in Windows 10 because they were vulnerable to malicious attacks.

GB See *gigabyte*.

Gbps Gigabits per second; a unit of data transfer equal to 1,000 Mbps (megabits per second).

gesture A quick movement of a finger or pen on a screen that the computer interprets as a command, rather than as a mouse movement, writing, or drawing.

gigabyte (GB) 1,024 megabytes of data storage; often interpreted as approximately 1 billion bytes.

.gif See *Graphics Interchange Format*.

glyph A graphical representation of either a character, a part of a character, or a sequence of characters.

graphical user interface (GUI) A user interface that incorporates visual elements such as a desktop, icons, and menus, so that you can perform operations by interacting with the visual interface rather than by typing commands.

Graphics Interchange Format (.gif) A digital image file format developed by CompuServe that is used for transmitting raster images on the Internet. An image in this format may contain up to 256 colors, including a transparent color. The size of the file depends on the number of colors actually used.

Guest account A built-in Windows user account that allows limited use of the computer. When logged on to a computer with the Guest account, a user can't install software or hardware, change settings, or create a password. The Guest account is turned off (unavailable) by default; you can turn it on from the User Accounts window of Control Panel.

GUI See *graphical user interface*.

hardware Physical items such as computers and monitors. See also *software*.

Hibernate mode A shut-down option similar to Sleep mode, except that it saves any open files and the state of any running apps on your hard disk instead of in memory and then completely turns off the computer. When you turn on your computer to resume working, Windows retrieves information from the hard disk and restores your previous computing session.

home page In Edge and Internet Explorer, the page or pages that open automatically when you start your web browser, and that open when you click the Home button. For websites, the first page displayed when you connect to a site.

homegroup A password-protected connection among a group of computers through which you can share files and printers. A homegroup can exist only on a private network. A private network doesn't require a homegroup, and it is not necessary to join a homegroup to use the private network.

homegroup member A computer that is joined to a homegroup.

hotspot A public place (such as a coffee shop, airport, or hotel) with a wireless network that you can use to connect to the Internet.

HTML See *Hypertext Markup Language.*

hub A device used to connect multiple devices of one type. See also network hub and USB hub.

hyperlink A link from a text, graphic, audio, or video element to a target location in the same document, another document, or a webpage.

Hypertext Markup Language (HTML) A text markup language used to create documents for the web. HTML defines the structure and layout of a web document by using a variety of tags and attributes.

icon A visual representation of an app, folder, file, or other object or function.

IM See *instant messaging.*

Information bar A bar that appears to notify you that there is a security issue or that a pop-up window has been blocked. You can click the bar to display a menu of actions appropriate to the situation.

information technology (IT) The development, installation, and implementation of computer systems and applications.

InPrivate Browsing A browsing mode available in Edge and Internet Explorer that opens a separate browser window in which the places you visit are not tracked. The pages and sites do not appear on the History tab, and temporary files and cookies are not saved on your computer.

Input device A peripheral device whose purpose is to allow the user to provide input to a computer system. Examples of input devices are keyboards, mice, joysticks, and styluses.

insertion point The point where you can insert text or graphics. It usually appears as a blinking vertical line.

instant messaging (IM) A real-time electronic communication system that you can use to "chat" and interact in other ways with other people by typing in a window on your computer screen.

interface See *user interface.*

internal peripheral A device installed inside the computer's case, such as an expansion card, a hard disk drive, or a DVD drive. See also *external peripheral; peripheral device.*

Internet Explorer A Microsoft web browser that ships with Windows 10 and is available from the Windows Accessories folder of the All Apps menu.

Internet Protocol (IP) address An address that identifies a computer that is connected to the Internet or a network. There are two types of IP addresses: IP version 4 (IPv4) and IP version 6 (IPv6). An IPv4 address usually consists of four groups of numbers separated by periods, such as 192.200.44.69. An IPv6 address has eight groups of hexadecimal characters (the numbers 0–9 and the letters A–H) separated by colons—for example, 3ffe:ffff:0000:2f3b:02aa:00ff:fe28:9c5a.

Internet service provider (ISP) A company that provides Internet access to individuals or companies. An ISP provides the connection information necessary for users to access the Internet through the ISP's computers. An ISP typically charges a monthly or hourly connection fee.

IP address See *Internet Protocol address.*

ISP See *Internet service provider.*

IT See *information technology.*

JPEG (.jpg) file format A digital image file format designed for compressing either full-color or gray-scale still images. It works well on photographs, naturalistic artwork, and similar material. Images saved in this format have .jpg or .jpeg file extensions.

jump list A feature of Windows that provides right-click access from taskbar app buttons to the documents, pictures, songs, or websites a user frequently accesses.

KB See *kilobyte*.

Kbps Kilobits per second; a unit of data transfer equal to 1,000 bits per second or 125 bytes per second.

keyword A word or phrase assigned to a file or webpage so that it can be located in searches for that word or phrase. See also *tag*.

kilobyte (KB) 1,024 bytes of data storage. In reference to data transfer rates, 1,000 bytes.

laptop A term for a portable computer, referring to the fact that portable computers are small enough to set on your lap. Also called a *notebook* or *portable computer*.

library A virtual folder that isn't physically present on the hard disk but that displays the contents of multiple folders as though the files were stored together in one location.

local Located on or attached to your computer.

local account An account you can use to sign in to a computer. A local account is not connected to a Microsoft account and isn't tracked beyond the scope of the computer it exists on.

local printer A printer that is directly connected to one of the ports on a computer. See also *network printer*; *remote printer*; *shared printer*.

lock To make your Windows desktop inaccessible to other people. Most effective when your user account is protected by a password.

lock screen The screen that appears when a user locks the computer.

Magnifier A display utility that makes the computer screen more readable by people who have low vision by creating a separate window that displays a magnified portion of the screen.

mail server A computer that stores email messages.

malware Software designed to deliberately harm your computer. For example, viruses, worms, and Trojan horses are malware. Also called *malicious software*.

map a drive To assign an available drive letter to a specific computer or shared folder; usually a folder located on another computer on the network. This is commonly done to create a constant connection to a network share but can also be used to maintain a connection to an Internet location.

maximize To increase the size of a window so that it completely fills the screen. A maximized window cannot be moved or resized by dragging its frame.

MB See *megabyte*.

Mbps Megabits per second; a unit of data transfer equal to 1,000 Kbps (kilobits per second).

media Materials on which data is recorded or stored, such as CDs, DVDs, or USB flash drives.

megabyte (MB) 1,024 kilobytes or 1,048,576 bytes of data storage; often interpreted as approximately 1 million bytes. In reference to data transfer rates, 1,000 kilobytes.

menu A list from which you can give an instruction by clicking a command.

menu bar A toolbar from which you can access menus of commands.

metadata Descriptive information, including keywords and properties, about a file or webpage. Title, subject, author, and size are examples of a file's metadata.

minimize To reduce a window to a button on the taskbar.

Miracast A wireless technology your computer can use to project your screen to TVs, projectors, and streaming media players that also support Miracast. You can use this to share what you're doing on your computer, present a slide show, or even play your favorite game on a larger screen.

modem A device that allows computer information to be transmitted and received over a telephone line or through a broadband service such as cable or DSL.

multi-monitor The use of more than one monitor or other display device to increase the working surface for a single computer system.

multi-touch gesture An extension of the conventional touch input feature to support gestures involving multiple fingers touching the computer or device screen at the same time.

Narrator A feature that audibly reads the text on the screen aloud and describes some events to users.

navigate To move around in a document.

Navigation pane In File Explorer, the left pane of a folder window. It displays favorite links, libraries, and an expandable list of drives and folders. See also *Content pane*; *Details pane*; *Preview pane*.

network In Windows, a group of computers connected to each other through a wired or wireless connection. A network may be as small as two computers connected directly to each other or as large as the Internet.

network adapter An expansion card or other device used to provide network access to a computer or other device, such as a printer. Mediates between the computer and physical media, such as cabling, over which transmissions travel.

Network and Sharing Center A Control Panel window from which users can get real-time status information about their network, and also make changes to settings.

network discovery A network setting that affects whether your computer can find other computers and devices on the network and whether other computers on the network can find your computer.

network domain A network whose security and settings are centrally administered through Windows Server computer and user accounts.

network drive A shared folder or drive on your network that you assign a drive letter to so that it appears in the Computer window as a named drive.

network hub A device used to connect computers on a network. The computers are connected to the hub with cables. The hub sends information received from one computer to all other computers on the network.

network printer A printer that is connected directly to a network through a wired (Ethernet) or wireless network connection, or through a print server or printer hub. See also *local printer*; *remote printer*; *shared printer*.

network profile Information about a specific network connection, such as the network name, type, and settings.

network router A hardware device connecting computers on a network or connecting multiple networks (for example, connecting a LAN to an ISP).

network share A shared folder on a computer on your network (not your local computer).

notification area The area at the right end of the Windows Taskbar that displays system icons (such as those for the clock, volume, network connection, power, and Action Center) and system and app notification icons. On Windows 10 computers, the user can control the display of both system icons and app notifications in the notification area.

OEM See *original equipment manufacturer*.

offline Not connected to a network or to the Internet. Also used to describe time that you will be away from your computer.

OneDrive The Microsoft online service that lets users access and share documents, photos, and other files from anywhere.

online Connected to a network or to the Internet. Also used to describe time that you will be working on your computer.

on-screen keyboard A keyboard representation on the screen that allows users to type using touch, a stylus, or other input device.

operating system The underlying programs that tell your computer what to do and how to do it. The operating system coordinates interactions among the computer system components, acts as the interface between you and your computer, enables your computer to communicate with other computers and peripheral devices, and interacts with apps installed on your computer.

Optimize Drives A Windows utility that arranges fragmented data so your disks and drives can work more efficiently. Optimize analyzes and optimizes disks and drives on a schedule, but can also be started manually. Optimize is available on the Drive Tools tab when you select your hard drive in File Explorer.

option One of a group of mutually exclusive values for a setting, usually in a dialog box.

option button A standard Windows control that you use to select one of a set of options.

original equipment manufacturer (OEM) A company that assembles a computer from components, brands the computer, and then sells the computer to the public. The OEM might also preinstall an operating system and other software on the computer.

parallel port The input/output connector for a parallel interface device. Some types of printers connect to the computer through a parallel port.

partition A section of space on a physical disk that functions as if it were a separate disk.

password A security measure used to restrict access to user accounts, computer systems, and resources. A password is a unique string of characters that you must provide before access is authorized.

password hint An entry you record when you create or change your password to remind you what the password is. Windows displays the password hint if you enter an incorrect password.

password reset disk A file you create on a flash drive or other removable media to enable you to reset your password if you forget it.

path A sequence of names of drives, directories, or folders, separated by backslashes (\), that leads to a specific file or folder. See also *absolute path*; *relative path*.

peer-to-peer A network, such as a workgroup, where computers and resources are connected directly and are not centrally managed by a server.

peripheral device A device, such as a disk drive, printer, modem, or joystick, that is connected to a computer and is controlled by the computer's microprocessor, but is not necessary to the computer's operation. See also *external peripheral*; *internal peripheral*.

personal folder In Windows, a storage folder created by Windows for each user account and containing subfolders and information that is specific to the user profile, such as Documents and Pictures. The personal folder is labeled with the name used to log on to the computer.

phishing A technique used to trick computer users into revealing personal or financial information. A common online phishing scam starts with an email message that appears to come from a trusted source but actually directs recipients to provide information to a fraudulent website.

picture password A picture-based sign-in method that authenticates a user by checking gestures made on a picture of the user's own choosing.

PID See *product key*.

pin To fix an item, such as a tile, library, movie, game, or app, in a given area of the UI, so it is always accessible in that area (for example, to pin an app to Start or to the taskbar).

PIN A numeric identification code similar to a password that a user can enter to validate his or her credentials.

pinned taskbar button A button representing an app, which appears permanently at the left end of the taskbar. A button that is not pinned appears only when its app is running. See also *taskbar button*.

pixel The smallest element used to form an image on a computer monitor. Computer monitors display images by drawing thousands of pixels arranged in columns and rows. Each pixel displays one color. See also *screen resolution*.

plug and play A technology that enables the computer to automatically discover and configure settings for a device connected to the computer through a USB or IEEE 1394 connection.

.png See *Portable Network Graphic*.

point To position the mouse pointer over an element. Also called *hover or mouse-over*.

pointer The on-screen image that moves around the screen when you move your mouse. Also called a *cursor*.

pointing device A device such as a mouse that controls a pointer with which you can select objects displayed on the screen.

pop-up window (pop-up) A small web browser window that opens on top of (or sometimes below) the web browser window when you display a website or click an advertising link.

port An interface through which data is transferred between a computer and other devices, a network, or a direct connection to another computer.

Portable Network Graphic (.png) A digital image file format that uses lossless compression (compression that doesn't lose data) and was created as a patent-free alternative to the .gif file format.

Power button The button near the bottom of the Windows 10 Start menu that provides access to the commands for putting the computer into Sleep mode and shutting down or restarting the computer.

Preview pane In File Explorer, a pane used to show a preview of a file selected in the Content pane. See also *Content pane*; *Details pane*; *Navigation pane*.

primary display In a multiple-monitor system, the monitor that displays the Welcome screen and taskbar. Most app windows appear on the primary display when they first open. See also *secondary display*.

printer driver See *driver*.

private network A network that requires specific credentials for access and is not available to the general public.

product key A unique registration code issued by the manufacturer of an app. The key must be supplied during the setup process to verify that you have a valid license to install and use the app. Also called a *product ID*, *PID*, *registration key*, or *CD key*.

program icon See *icon*.

progress bar or ring An animated visual indicator of the percentage of completion of a process.

property Identifying information about a file, folder, drive, device, or other computer system element. Some properties are supplied automatically and others are supplied by you. For example, the properties of a file include information such as its file name, size, modification date, title, tags, and comments. You can view an item's properties by right-clicking the item in an interface such as File Explorer or Device Manager, and then clicking Properties.

Public folder In Windows, a storage folder system created by Windows and accessible to all user accounts on the computer. Public folders are shared by all user accounts on the computer and can be shared with other network users.

public network A network that permits anyone to connect and does not require specific credentials.

Quick Access Toolbar A customizable toolbar that provides one-click access to commands.

random access memory (RAM) A data storage area a computer uses to run apps and temporarily store current information. Information stored in RAM is erased when the computer is switched off.

ReadyBoost See *Windows ReadyBoost*.

Recycle Bin The folder on your hard disk where Windows temporarily stores files you delete. By default, the Recycle Bin is represented by an icon on the desktop. You can recover deleted files from the Recycle Bin until you empty it.

refresh your PC To reset an operating system by using a method that restores computer settings to the defaults but retains a user's files and settings.

registration key See *product key*.

registry A repository for information about the computer's configuration. The registry stores settings related to the hardware and software installed on the computer. Registry settings are typically updated through the proper install and uninstall procedures and apps. You can manually update the registry, but only experienced users should undertake this task because mistakes can be disastrous.

relative path A path that defines the position of a file or folder in relation to the current location. Relative paths are frequently used in website navigational code. See also *absolute path*; *path*.

Remote Desktop Connection The client software that enables users to connect to a remote computer that has the Remote Desktop feature enabled or to a remote desktop server.

remote printer A printer that is not connected directly to your computer. See also *local printer*; *network printer*; *shared printer*.

removable media Anything used for information storage that is designed to be easily inserted into and removed from a computer or portable device. Common removable media include CD and DVD discs, in addition to removable memory cards.

reset your PC To reset an operating system by using a method that removes all user customizations.

resolution See *screen resolution*.

Restore See *System Restore*.

restore down To return a window from a maximized state to its previous size.

restore point A snapshot of your computer system settings taken by Windows at regular intervals and before any major change, such as installing an app or updating system files. If you experience problems with your system, you can restore it to any saved restore point without undoing changes to your personal files.

ribbon An area in a window in which commands and other controls are displayed in functionally related groups. A ribbon can be divided into multiple views, known as tabs, and every tab can contain multiple groups of controls. Typically, a ribbon appears at the top of a window.

right-click To point to an interface element and press the secondary mouse button one time.

right-drag To move an item on the screen by pointing to its title bar or handle, holding down the secondary mouse button, and then moving the mouse. A shortcut menu displaying possible actions appears when you release the mouse button.

root Short for root folder or root directory. The highest or uppermost level in a hierarchically organized set of information. The root is the folder or directory from which all other folders or directories branch.

router See *network router*.

screen resolution The fineness or coarseness of detail attained by a monitor in producing an image, measured in pixels, expressed as the number of pixels wide by the number of pixels high. See also *pixel*.

screen saver A blank screen, picture, or moving images that Windows displays after a specified period of inactivity. A screen saver can be used to save power or to hide information while you are away from your desk.

ScreenTip Information that appears when you point to an item.

scroll bar A vertical or horizontal bar that you move to change the position of content within a window.

search The process of seeking a particular file or specific data. A search is carried out by an app through comparison or calculation to determine whether a match to some pattern exists or whether some other criteria have been met.

search provider A company that provides a search engine that you can use to find information on the Internet.

search term The term you type in the search box of the taskbar, Settings window, or any File Explorer window. Windows then filters the contents of the available storage locations or of the folder window's Content pane to include only the items that contain the search term.

secondary display In a multiple-monitor system, the monitor onto which you can expand apps so that you can increase your work area. See also *primary display*.

share To make local files or resources available to other users of the same computer or other computers on a network.

shared component A component, such as a DLL file, that is used by multiple apps. When uninstalling an app that uses a shared component, Windows requests confirmation before removing the component.

shared drive A drive that has been made available for other people on a network to access.

shared folder A folder that has been made available for other people on a network to access.

shared printer A printer connected to a computer that has been shared with other computers on a network. See also *local printer*; *network printer*; *remote printer*.

shortcut A link, usually represented by an icon, that opens an app, data file, or device. For example, clicking a shortcut to Microsoft Word starts Word.

shortcut menu A menu displayed when you right-click an object, showing a list of commands relevant to that object.

shut down To initiate the process that closes all your open apps and files, ends your computing session, closes network connections, stops system processes, stops the hard disk, and turns off the computer.

sign in To start a computing session.

sign out To stop your computing session without affecting other users' sessions.

signature See *digital signature*.

single sign-on (SSO) account An account type that permits a user to log on to a system once with a single set of credentials to access multiple applications or services.

Sleep mode A Windows feature that saves any open files and the state of any running apps to memory and then puts your computer into a power-saving state.

SmartScreen An intelligent spam-filtering solution integrated across all Microsoft email platforms.

Snap A Windows feature that enables users to easily display two documents side by side, maximize a single document, and expand a window vertically by simply dragging window borders to the edge of the screen.

Snipping Tool A Windows tool used to capture a screen shot, or snip, of any object on the screen, and then annotate, save, or share the image.

software Apps that you use to do things with hardware. See also *hardware*.

software piracy The illegal reproduction and distribution of software applications.

sound card Hardware that enables audio information and music to be recorded, played back, and heard on a computer.

Sound Recorder The app that facilitates recording voice from a microphone, in addition to saving, editing, playing and sharing recorded audio clips.

spam An unsolicited and typically unwelcome message, often commercial or political in nature, transmitted via the Internet as a mass mailing (sometimes as if from a fictitious user or domain) to a large number of recipients.

speech recognition The ability to interpret vocal commands or convert spoken words into computer-readable text. Speech recognition apps enable you to control an application or enter text by speaking into a microphone, rather than by using a keyboard.

spyware Software that can display advertisements (such as pop-up ads), collect information about you, or change settings on your computer, generally without appropriately obtaining your consent.

Standard User account A type of Windows user account that allows the user to install software and change system settings that do not affect other users or the security of the computer. This account type is recommended for daily use. See also *Administrator account; user account.*

Start menu A list of options displayed when you click the Start button. The Start menu is your central link to all the apps installed on your computer, in addition to all the tasks you can carry out with Windows 10.

Start screen The non-menu view that is displayed when the Start button is clicked. It includes the list of items, such as apps, websites, and other info that a person can specify and customize. You can choose to display it full-screen or partial-screen.

Store See *Windows Store.*

subfolder A folder nested within another folder.

surf the web To browse information on the Internet.

sync To reconcile the differences between files, email, appointments, and other items stored on one computer, device, or in the cloud with versions of the same files on another computer, device, or in the cloud. After the differences are determined, both sets of items are updated.

system cache An area in the computer memory where Windows stores information it might need to access quickly, for the duration of the current computing session.

system disk The hard disk on which the operating system is installed.

system folder A folder created on the system disk that contains files required by Windows 10.

System Restore A tool used to restore your computer to a previous state, if a problem occurs, without losing your personal data files (such as Microsoft Word documents, browsing history, drawings, favorites, or email).

tab In a dialog box, tabs indicate separate pages of settings within the dialog box window; the tab title indicates the nature of the group. You can display the settings by clicking the tab.

tabbed browsing An Internet browser feature that enables you to open and view multiple webpages or files in one window by displaying them on different tabs. You can display a page by clicking its tab, or display a shortcut menu of options for working with a page by right-clicking its tab.

tag In File Explorer, a keyword assigned to a file. See also *keyword*.

tap (touch) A gesture represented by placing a finger or stylus on the screen and then lifting it up.

Task Manager A tool that provides information about apps and processes running on the computer. Using Task Manager, you can end or run apps, end processes, and display a dynamic overview of your computer's performance.

task pane A fixed pane that appears on one side of an app window, containing options related to the completion of a specific task.

taskbar A bar on the desktop that displays buttons you can click to run apps, utilities, and commands, in addition to buttons representing the windows of open apps and files.

taskbar button A button on the taskbar representing an open window, file, or app. See also *pinned taskbar button*.

taskbar search A search box from which you can locate apps, Control Panel items, settings, files, email messages, and web results containing the search string, grouped by category.

theme A set of visual elements and sounds that applies a unified look to the computer user interface. A theme can include a desktop background, screen saver, window colors, and sounds. Some themes might also include icons and mouse pointers.

tile A moveable object on the Start screen that opens apps or other customized content, like pinned websites.

title bar The horizontal area at the top of a window that displays the title of the app or file displayed in the window, in additon to buttons for controlling the display of the window.

toolbar A horizontal or vertical bar that displays buttons representing commands that can be used with the content of the current window. When more commands are available than can fit on the toolbar, a chevron (>>) appears at the right end of the toolbar; clicking the chevron displays the additional commands.

UAC See *User Account Control.*

UNC See *Universal Naming Convention.*

Uniform Resource Locator (URL) An address that uniquely identifies the location of a website or page. A URL is usually preceded by *http://*, as in *http://www.microsoft.com*. URLs are used by web browsers to locate Internet resources.

Universal Naming Convention (UNC) A system for identifying the location on a network of shared resources such as computers, drives, and folders. A UNC address is in the form \\ComputerName \SharedFolder.

Universal Serial Bus (USB) A connection that provides data transfer capabilities and power to a peripheral device. See also *USB hub; USB port.*

Universal Windows app An app that is built by using the Universal Windows Platform (UWP), which was first introduced in Windows 8 as the Windows Runtime. Universal Windows apps should run on any Windows 10 device, from a smartphone to a desktop computer.

upgrade To replace older hardware with newer hardware or an earlier version of an app with the current version.

URL See *Uniform Resource Locator.*

USB See *Universal Serial Bus.*

USB flash drive A portable flash memory card that plugs into a computer's USB port. You can store data on a USB flash drive or use all or part of the available drive space to increase the operating system speed. See also *Windows ReadyBoost*.

USB hub A device used to connect multiple USB devices to a single USB port, or to connect one or more USB devices to USB ports on multiple computers. The latter type of USB hub, called a sharing hub, operates as a switch box to give control of the hub-connected devices to one computer at a time. See also *Universal Serial Bus*; *USB port*.

USB port A connection that provides both power and data transfer capabilities to a hardware device. See also *Universal Serial Bus*; *USB hub*.

user account On a Windows computer, a uniquely named account that allows an individual to gain access to the system and to specific resources and settings. Each user account includes a collection of information that describes the way the computer environment looks and operates for that particular user, in addition to a private folder not accessible by other people using the computer, in which personal documents, pictures, media, and other files can be stored. See also *Administrator account*; *Standard User account*.

user account button The button at the top of the Windows 10 Start menu that provides access to the commands for changing user account settings, locking the computer, or logging off from Windows.

User Account Control (UAC) A Windows security feature that allows or restricts actions by the user and the system to prevent malicious apps from damaging the computer.

user account name A unique name identifying a user account to Windows.

user account picture An image representing a user account. User account pictures are available only for computer-specific user accounts and not on computers that are members of a network domain.

user credentials See *credentials*.

user interface (UI) The portion of an app with which a user interacts. Types of user interfaces include command-line interfaces, menu-driven interfaces, and graphical user interfaces.

video projector A device that projects a video signal from a computer onto a projection screen by using a lens system.

virtual A software system that acts as if it were a hardware system. Examples are virtual folders (called *libraries*) and virtual printers.

virtual desktop A work area on a computer screen that contains different groups of apps or content open and available for different tasks or aspects of your life.

virtual printer An app that "prints" content to a file rather than on paper. When viewed in the file, the content looks as it would if it were printed.

virus Malware that replicates, commonly by infecting other files in the system, thus allowing the execution of the malware code and its propagation when those files are activated.

web An abbreviation of *World Wide Web*. A worldwide network consisting of millions of smaller networks that exchange data.

web browser A software app used to display webpages and to navigate the Internet, for example Edge or Internet Explorer.

web log See *blog*.

webcam A camera for use with a computer to transmit a video picture.

website A group of related webpages that is hosted by an HTTP server on the World Wide Web or an intranet. The pages in a website typically cover one or more topics and are interconnected through hyperlinks.

Welcome screen The screen that appears when you start your computer, containing a link to each active user account.

WEP See *Wired Equivalent Privacy*.

Wi-Di See *Wireless Display (WiDi)*.

Wi-Fi Protected Access (WPA) A security method used by wireless networks. WPA and WPA2 encrypt the information that is sent between computers on a wireless network and authenticate users to help ensure that only authorized people can access the network. WPA2 is more secure than WPA.

wildcard character In a search operation, a keyboard character, such as an asterisk (*), a question mark (?), or a pound sign (#), that represents one or more characters in a search term.

window A frame within which your computer runs an app or displays a folder or file. Several windows can be open simultaneously. Windows can be sized, moved, minimized to a taskbar button, maximized to take up the entire screen, or closed.

Windows Defender Initially provided in earlier versions of Windows as antispyware, it now serves as antivirus software in Windows 10.

Windows Firewall A security feature that is used to set restrictions on what traffic is allowed to enter your network from the Internet.

Windows ReadyBoost A feature introduced in Windows 7 that makes it possible to increase the available system memory by using a USB flash drive as a memory-expansion device. See also *USB flash drive*.

Windows Store The online store where users can learn about and download apps, games, music, and more for Windows devices.

Windows To Go A feature of Windows 10 Enterprise and Windows 10 Education that provides a predefined image of a computer from a USB flash drive instead of installing the image on the computer.

Windows Update A feature through which Windows catalogs your computer's hardware and software components, communicates with the Microsoft Update online database, and identifies any updates that are available for your operating system, software, or hardware drivers.

Wired Equivalent Privacy (WEP) An algorithm-based security protocol designed for use with wireless networks. WEP was the original wireless network security protocol and, although not as secure as the more recent Wi-Fi Protected Access (WPA) protocol, is still an option in most wireless router configurations.

Wireless Display (WiDi) A technology that enables computers to stream videos, music, or other media wirelessly from a computer to a WiDi-enabled device such as a television or projector.

wizard A tool that walks you through the steps necessary to accomplish a particular task.

work network A network to which you connect with the Work Network connection type.

workgroup A peer-to-peer computer network through which computers can share resources, such as files, printers, and Internet connections.

WPA See *Wi-Fi Protected Access*.

XML See *Extensible Markup Language*.

XML Paper Specification (XPS) A digital file format for saving documents. XPS is based on XML, preserves document formatting, and enables file sharing. XPS was developed by Microsoft but is platform-independent and royalty-free.

XPS See *XML Paper Specification*.

zipped folder See *compressed folder*.

Index

Symbols
3D Text screen saver 442

A
About Me menu (Cortana Notebook) 475
absolute path 567
accent colors, desktop 69–72
accepting license terms 556
accessibility features, configuring 444–458
    High Contrast settings 447–449
    keyboard and mouse settings 455–458
    Magnifier settings 449–452
    Narrator and Audio Description
      settings 453–455
accessing
    Microsoft account settings 170
    Store (Windows Store) 164–165
accessory apps 161
accounts
    local 5
    Microsoft 4–5
    Store (Windows Store) 166–170
    user See user accounts
Accounts settings 30
action buttons (Action Center) 465–466
Action Center 17–18, 567
    action buttons 464–468
    app notifications 190
    displaying Action Center pane 467
    managing messages 21
    opening 193
activating built-in Guest accounts 366
activation 567
active apps, displaying 503
active network adapters 294
active windows 567
adapters, networks 294
Add Printer wizard 283–285
adding
    columns, Details view 121
    folders, Start menu 57

folders to libraries 114–115
local user account passwords 374
reminders, Cortana 478–479
Start screen tiles to tile groups 62
storage locations to Quick Access list 128
Address bar 111, 567
Address toolbar (taskbar) 80
administrative permissions, revoking 367
Administrator accounts 346, 348–349, 365, 567
    See also user accounts
administrators
    changing user account properties 353
    creating user accounts 354
Adult user accounts 347
Advanced Options dialog box, File Explorer
    searches 486
advanced searches, File Explorer 485
advanced settings
    Edge 215
    power plans 432–433
Advanced Sharing dialog box 335
Advanced Sharing Settings window (Control
    Panel) 311
advertising ID 517
Airplane Mode action button 465
Alarms & Clock app 157, 387
All Apps menu 152–156
All Settings action button 465
alphabets, language settings and 401
alphabet-specific fonts 403
annotating webpages 208–209
app lists, displaying on Start menu 56
appearance, changing taskbar 73–78
applying themes 84–91
    built-in themes 85
    customization 88–89
    displaying installed theme 89
    Natural Wonders category 86
    panoramic backgrounds 87
    previewing background images 87
    unpacked theme files 88
    Windows website 90

app-management icons, displaying 20
appointments, Cortana reminders 478–479
apps 567
    built-in 157–162
    default 225, 489–497
    displaying active and nonresponsive 503
    files 98
    Get Windows 10 553
    installing Store apps 163–174
    locating and starting 152–156
    Mail 207–208
    managing startup 188–189
    notifications 190–194
    Reading List 207–208
    running as an administrator 156
    shortcuts 175–187
    virtual desktops 497–500
arranging
    desktop icons 186
    windows 40–43
aspect ratio 420, 567
assistance, Cortana *See* Cortana
Audio Description settings 453–455
audio devices 264–271
    managing playback device settings 266–267
    notifications 265
    switching playback devices 266–267
    switching recording devices 268–271
audio notifications (apps), turning off 194
audio output jacks 264
authentication
    two-factor 542
    Welcome screen methods 381
automatic app updates 170

B

backgrounds 567
    desktop 10, 64–68
    lock screen, customizing 436–440
backing up
    computer systems 535–538
    data, using File History 530–535
    drives to system images 535–541
    files to OneDrive 524–528
backup images *See* system images
Balanced power plan 426
bandwidth 567

banners, turning off 194
Battery Saver action button 466
Battery Saver feature 435
behavior, taskbars 78–79
Bing (search engine) 480, 484
biometric identification 376, 542
BIOS, accessing 536
BIOS Setup Utility 540
bitmap (.bmp) 567
Blank screen saver 442
blocking pop-up windows 231–232
blogs 567
Bluetooth action button 466
.bmp (bitmap) 567
boom microphones 265
boot images 536
bootable USB recovery drives
    535, 539–540
booting
    from bootable DVD 535
    from recovery discs 540
    from recovery drives 540
    wiped computers 535
broadband connections 567
browsers 568 *See* web browsers
browsing 568
    apps 165
    history, Edge 211
Bubbles screen saver 442
built-in apps 157–162
built-in Guest accounts, activating 366
built-in power plans 426
built-in speakers 264
built-in themes 85
button options, mice 272–274
bytes 568

C

Calculator app 157
Calendar app 157
Camera app 159
Camera Roll library 100
caret browsing 236–239
cascading windows 41
CCleaner 550
centering images (desktop background) 66
central processing units (CPUs) 568

Change Homegroup Sharing Settings
    wizard 329
Change Icon dialog box 116
changing
    advanced indexing options 488
    authentication methods, Welcome
      screen 381
    computer name 338–339
    default Edge search engine 218–220
    designation of primary screen 259
    display names, family accounts 359–360
    folder icon of a library 116
    folder options 126–128
    folder view 120
    home page (Edge) 215–217
    homegroup passwords 324
    indexed locations 488
    keyboard language 404
    key repeat delay and rate 279–280
    level of magnification, Magnifier tool 451
    Microsoft account passwords 374–375
    mouse button settings 274
    mouse pointer appearance 274–275
    mouse pointer functionality 276–277
    mouse pointer icon 276
    mouse wheel functionality 277–278
    orientation of on-screen content 419
    PIN (personal identification number) 378
    screen brightness 419, 427–428
    screen resolution 420–421
    size or text size of user interface
      elements 417–418
    time zones 392
    User Account Control settings 352
    user account passwords 374–375
    user account pictures 372–373
    user account properties, administrators 353
    Windows display language 404
Character Map app 162
check boxes, displaying (File Explorer) 108
children and online safety 233
Children's Online Privacy Protection Act
    (COPPA) 233
Child user accounts 347, 356–357
choosing default apps 491
clicks 568
Clipboard 132
clocks 395

Close button 37
Closed Captions (Ease Of Access) 444
closing
    current desktop 500
    selected desktops 500
    windows 37–40
cloud storage 524
collapsing folders 111
colors, desktop background 69–72
columns, Details view
    adding, removing, rearranging 121
    resizing 122
Command Prompt utility 162
commands 568
community-created themes 87
Compatibility view 568
completing Windows 10 update 558
component information, displaying 256
Compressed Folder Tools group (tool tabs) 109
compressed folders 130–132, 568
compressing files or folders 130–132, 568
computer configuration, file sharing 328–329
computer functionality, restoring 519–524
    See also restore points
Computer list, Network window 301
Computer Management console 355
computer name, changing 338–339
computer preparation, upgrading to
    Windows 10 550–552
computer settings 385
    accessibility features 444–458
    device displays 413–421
    lock screen 436–441
    power 426–434
    region and language 396–407
    speech 408–413
computer systems, backing up 535–541
Computer tab 109
computing sessions
    ending 44–46
    starting 4–9
configuring
    accessibility features 444–458
    audio narration options 454
    Bing SafeSearch settings 484
    browser security settings 228–232
    computers, file sharing 328–329
    Cortana settings 472–478

configuring *(continued)*
    language options 402–403
    network connection security 305–311
    power options 426–434
    privacy settings 515–519
    Quick Action buttons 464–468
    Reading view settings 223
    screen savers 442–443
    setting synchronization 381–382
    settings, Control Panel 32–33
    settings, Settings window 29–31
    Start menu 52–57
    Start screen 52–57
    system icons 187
    taskbar 73–84
    visual narration options 455
    voice recognition 409–411
    Windows Hello 378–379
Connect action button 466
Connect pane 261
Connected Accounts menu (Cortana
    Notebook) 475
connecting
    local accounts to Microsoft accounts 369
    to networks 294–300
connection icons 295
connections
    expanding capacity 250–251
    printers 280–287
content
    configuring Start menu 55–57
    Edge tabs 217
    searching 20
    Start menu 23
    tiles, Start screen 59
content filters, Bing 484
Content pane (File Explorer) 105, 568
Content view 120
control levels, UAC (User Account Control) 351
Control Panel 27, 568
    configuring settings 32–33
    displaying home page 34
    Ease Of Access Center 445
    Speech Recognition page 411
Coordinated Universal Time 386
COPPA (Children's Online Privacy Protection
    Act) 233

copying files and folders 132–134
Cortana 18–19, 469–479
    adding reminders 478–479
    configuring settings 472–478
    countries and regions 469
    displaying/hiding 478
    initializing 470–474
    privacy settings 518
    set up 470–472
Cortana Tips information-tracking options
    (Cortana) 475
CPUs (central processing units) 568
credentials 568
Current View group (View tab) 108
cursors 568
custom power plans 431–433
Customize tab, Properties dialog box 139
customizing
    device display settings 413–421
    Edge content 217
    lock screen 436–441
    sign-in options 375–382
    themes 88–90
    tiles, Start screen 60

D

data
    backing up using File History 530–535
    transfer information, displaying 304
    usage by apps, displaying 304–305
Date & Time settings 388–389
date and time
    changing formats 393–394
    changing time zones 392
    displaying multiple clocks 395
    displaying secondary clocks 395
    manually setting 389
    synchronizing with Internet time
        servers 390–391
    taskbar 17
default apps
    managing 225
    specifying 489–497
default Edge search engine, changing 218–220
default notification settings 191
default settings, Start screen 53

Defender updates 228
deleting
    custom power plans 433
    folders and files 135–137
    homegroups 325
    saved information, Edge 222
    user accounts 361–362, 364–365
Descriptive Video Service (DVS) 453
desktop 9–11, 568
    accent colors 69–72
    displaying on multiple screens 256–262
    moving between computers 499
    Recycle Bin 11
desktop apps 568
    configuring icons 187
    defined 152
    icon organization 181–183
    running as an administrator 156
    shortcuts 181–186
    utilities 161
desktop backgrounds 10, 64–68
desktop computers 568
Desktop toolbar (taskbar) 81
Details pane (File Explorer) 105, 108, 568
Details view (File Explorer) 119
device display settings 413–421
    orientation of on-screen content 419
    screen brightness 419
    screen resolution 420–421
    user interface elements, size 417
    user interface elements, text size 418
device drivers 251, 568
Device Manager window 254
devices 568
Devices settings
    contents 252
    features 30
    Printers & Scanners pane 280
Devices And Printers window 280
dialog boxes 568
digital entitlement 555
digital signatures 568
disabling
    network adapters 314
    toolbars, InPrivate browsing
      sessions 235–236
    user accounts 360–361, 364

disconnecting
    peripheral devices 286–287
    wired networks 299
    wireless networks 299–300
Disk Cleanup 569
Disk Defragmenter 569
display names, family accounts 359–360
display options, File Explorer
    changing folder options 126–128
    different views of folders/files 118–122
    displaying/hiding panes 117–118
    group folder content 122–124
    sort and filter folder content 124–126
display settings 413–421
    orientation on-screen content 419
    screen brightness 419
    screen resolution 420–421
    size, user interface elements 417
    text size, user interface elements 418
Display settings, displaying the pane 258, 417
displaying
    action buttons 467
    Action Center pane 467
    Action Center taskbar icon 468
    active and nonresponsive apps 503
    All Apps menu 155
    app lists, Start menu 56
    app status information, lock screen 440–441
    app-management icons 20
    browsing history, Edge 211
    categories of settings 34
    Control Panel home page 34
    Cortana 478
    current date and time 388–389
    Date & Time settings 389
    desktop background images 67
    desktop icons 186
    desktop on multiple screens 256–262
    desktops in Task view 499
    device information 255–256
    Display settings 258, 417
    Ease Of Access settings 446
    favorites list, Edge 211
    file downloads, Edge 211
    File Explorer panes 117–118
    folder content, as icons 120
    folder content, File Explorer 111
    Folder Options dialog box 128

displaying *(continued)*
  hardware, software, and component
    information 256
  homegroup passwords 321
  information about networks and
    connections 300–305
  installed themes 89
  jump lists 57
  libraries, Navigation pane 113
  live content, app tiles 177
  More Actions menu 215
  multiple clocks 395
  notifications 21
  printer status 286
  Properties dialog boxes, files and folders 141
  purchased apps/games 173
  Quick Link menu 34
  reading list, Edge 211
  recent messages 21
  recent files 26
  Region & Language settings 398
  secondary clocks 395
  Settings window 255
  sites in Compatibility view 237–238
  speech recognition tools 411
  Speech settings 409
  Start menu 26
  Start screen 26
  status of network adapters 304
  taskbar buttons 78
  taskbar shortcut menu 75
  taskbar toolbars 80–84
  Task View button 78
  thumbnails 20
  user account controls 26
  websites, Edge 203–206
DLLs (dynamic-link libraries) 98
Docked view (Magnifier tool) 449
Documents library 100, 112
domain name (website addresses) 226
domains 569
double-clicking 569
downloading practice files xii–xiii
Downloads And Updates page 172, 174
dragging
  defined 569
  windows 42
drivers 251, 569

drives, sharing 334–337
DVI monitor ports 250
DVS (Descriptive Video Service) 453
dynamic, defined 569
dynamic-link libraries (DLLs) 98

E
Ease Of Access features 444
  displaying settings 446
  synchronizing settings 376
Ease Of Access settings 31
Easy Access menu, Home tab 107
Eat & Drink information-tracking options
  (Cortana) 475
ebook edition xv
Edge 202, 569
  changing default search engine 218–220
  configuring Reading view settings 223
  configuring security settings 228–232
  customizing content 217
  deleting saved information 222
  displaying browsing history 211
  displaying favorites list 211
  displaying file downloads 211
  displaying reading list 211
  displaying websites 203–206
  finding, saving, and sharing
    information 207–214
  importing Favorites lists to 224
  managing passwords 220–221
  managing settings 214–224
  pinning site to Start screen 212–213
  printing webpages 213–214
  reading articles 212
  saving passwords 220–221
  saving webpages to favorites list 211
  troubleshooting browsing issues 235–238
Edit Plan Settings window 430
editing advanced settings, power plans 432–433
emulating different browsers 236
enabling
  disabled user accounts 361, 364
  network adapters 314–315
ending computing sessions 44–46
errors, reporting xv
Ethernet 569
Ethernet ports 250, 294

Events information-tracking options
   (Cortana) 475
executable files 98, 569
expanding
   connection capacity 250–251
   folders 111
   portable computers, peripheral devices 263
expansion cards 250, 569
expansion slots 569
extending displays 257
Extensible Markup Language (XML) 569
external devices 249
   audio 264–271
   disconnecting from computer 286–287
   displaying desktop on multiple
      screens 256–262
   installation 251
   internal 250
   keyboard management 278–280
   locating device information 252–256
   mice 271–278
   portable computers and 263
   printers 280–287
   terminology 250–251
external Ethernet ports 294
external hard disk drives 104
external peripheral devices 569
external removable storage devices 104
Extra Large Icons view (File Explorer) 119
extracting files, compressed folders 131–132

F

Family & Other Users settings 353–354
Family Safety 356–357
family user accounts 349–350
   creating 357–359
   Family Safety 356–357
   managing 359–362
Favorites bar 569
Favorites lists
   displaying 211
   importing to Edge 224
   saving webpages to 211
Federal Trade Commission, children and online
      safety 233
feedback xv

fetching files to OneDrive
   enabling 527
   from remote computers 530
Fewer Details view (Task Manager) 501, 503
File And Printer Sharing settings, network
      security profiles 305
file downloads, Edge 211
File Explorer 102, 569
   Content pane 105, 568
   Details pane 105, 568
   display options 117–128
   Homegroup node (Navigation pane) 102
   Libraries folder 112–117
   Libraries node (Navigation pane) 102
   Navigation And Search bar 111–113
   Navigation pane 104, 573
   Network node (Navigation pane) 102
   Preview pane 105, 575
   Quick Access node (Navigation pane) 102
   ribbon command interface 104–108
   searches 143–144
   searching 485–489
   starting 111
   This PC node (Navigation pane) 102, 104
   window layout 104–105
File History 569
   activating 531–533
   backing up data 530–531
   backups 113
   displaying 107
   viewing previous versions 533–534
File menu (File Explorer) 105
file name extensions 227, 570
file name extensions, displaying (File
      Explorer) 108
File Sharing Connections settings, network
      security profiles 305
file shortcut menus, jump lists 179
file storage folders 103
files
   backing up 530–531
   compressing 130–132
   created by apps 98
   created by you 98
   creating and renaming 129–130
   deleting/recovering 135–137
   display options, File Explorer 117–128
   displaying recent files 26

files *(continued)*
    File Explorer *See* File Explorer
    grouping 124
    managing versions 534–535
    moving/copying 132–134
    opening in default apps 493
    optimizing folders for 115
    properties 138–142
    recovery 570
    removing groupings 124
    removing personal information 142
    searches 142–144
    sharing network files 326–337
    sorting 125
    updating 35–36
    viewing backed up versions 533–534
filling images (desktop background) 66
Filter Keys (Ease Of Access) 455
filtering
    File Explorer search results 487
    folder content 124–126
    taskbar search results 483–484
filters 570
    applying 126
    Bing 484
Finance information-tracking options
    (Cortana) 475
finding
    information (web browsers) 207–214
    text on a webpage 208
fingerprint authentication 376–379
finishing Windows 10 update 558
fitting images (desktop background) 66
flash drives 570
flicking
    defined 570
    touchscreen interaction 565
Flip feature 570
Flowers theme 85
folder content
    displaying 111
    filtering 124–126
folder name (website addresses) 227
Folder Options dialog box 127–128
folders 98, 570
    adding to libraries 114–115
    adding to Start menu 57
    All Apps menu 155

    changing icon of a library 116
    changing options 126–128
    changing view 120
    compressing 130–132
    creating and renaming 129–130
    deleting/recovering 135–137
    display options, File Explorer 117–128
    File Explorer *See* File Explorer
    grouping content 122–124
    libraries 100–101
    moving/copying 132–134
    optimizing for a file type 115
    Program Files 98
    properties 138–142
    Public 99
    removing from a library 117
    removing from Start menu 57
    searches 142–144
    Users 99
    Windows 99
Food & Drink app 160
form entries, Edge 220–221
formats, date and time settings 393–394
frames 570
freestanding microphones 265
Full Screen view (Magnifier tool) 449
full-screen configuration, Start screen 52

G

gadgets 570
GB (gigabyte) 130, 570
General tab
    Folder Options dialog box 127
    Properties dialog box 138
geofencing 518
gestures (touchscreen tips) 566
Get Windows 10 app 553
Get Windows 10 icon 549
Getting Around information-tracking options
    (Cortana) 475
Getting To Know You feature, turning off 413
gigabyte (GB) 130, 570
glyphs 570
GMT (Greenwich Mean Time) 386
graphical user interface (GUI) 570
Graphics Interchange Format (.gif) 570
Greenwich Mean Time (GMT) 386

Groove Music app 158
Group By menu, View tab 123
group folder content, File Explorer 122–124
grouping files 124
Guest accounts 365–366, 570
GUI (graphical user interface) 570

H

handwriting recognition, language-specific
    features 403
hardware 570
HDMI ports 250
headphone jacks 264
headset microphones 265
Health & Fitness app 160
height, taskbars 77–78
Hibernate mode 570
hidden items, displaying (File Explorer) 108
hiding
    Action Center taskbar icon 468
    Cortana 478
    desktop icons 186
    File Explorer panes 117–118
    jump lists 57
    libraries 113, 117
    live content, app tiles 177
    Start menu app lists 56
    taskbar 79
    Task View button 78
    windows 21, 37–40
High Contrast (Ease Of Access) 444, 447–449
High Performance power plan 426
high-contrast themes 85
home pages 215–217, 570
Home tab (File Explorer) 106–107
HomeGroup troubleshooter 325
HomeGroup window
    Control Panel 319–320
    File Explorer 319
homegroup connections 316–325
HomeGroup connection settings, network
    security profiles 305, 308
homegroup members 571
Homegroup node (File Explorer) 102
homegroups 571
    changing passwords 324
    connecting to resources 323

creating 320–321
deleting 325
discarding password requirements 321–322
disconnecting all computers 323
displaying password 321
joining computers to 322–323
removing computers from 324–325
resources 329–330
sharing folders/libraries 330–332
hotspots 571
HTML (Hypertext Markup Language) 571
HTTP (Hypertext Transfer Protocol) 226
HTTPS protocol 226
hubs 250, 571
hyperlinks 571
Hypertext Markup Language (HTML) 571
Hypertext Transfer Protocol (HTTP) 226

I

ICANN (the Internet Corporation for Assigned
    Names and Numbers) 226
Icon views (File Explorer) 119
icons 571
identity verification 542
IEEE 1394 ports 250
IM (instant messaging) 571
images
    background, themes 87
    desktop background 65–68
    Natural Wonders themes 86
    panoramic backgrounds, themes 87
imaging point 535
importing Favorites lists, Edge 224
index, search 485
    changing advanced indexing options 488
    changing locations being indexed 488
    rebuilding 489
information apps 160
Information bar 571
information management apps 157–158
information technology (IT) 571
information-analysis tools, Cortana 18–19
initializing Cortana 470–474
inline ads, blocking 517
InPrivate Browsing 234–235, 571
Input devices 571
insertion points 571

Insider Builds 513
Install The Printer Driver page (Add Printer
     wizard) 284
installing
     additional system languages 399–400
     Language Interface Packs 401
     peripheral devices 251
     plug-and-play printers 281–282
     Store apps 163–174
     supplemental font features 403
     updates 513–515
     Windows 10 547–558
instant messaging (IM) 571
internal hard disk drives 104
internal peripheral devices 250, 571
internal removable storage drives 104
International Atomic Time 386
Internet browsers *See* web browsers
Internet connections, network connections
     versus 296
Internet Corporation for Assigned Names and
     Numbers (ICANN) 226
Internet Explorer 158, 571
Internet Protocol (IP) addresses 226, 571
Internet service provider (ISP) 571
Internet time servers 386, 390–392
IP (Internet Protocol) addresses 226, 571
ISP (Internet service provider) 571
IT (information technology) 571

J

.jpg (JPEG) file format 572
jump lists 25, 572
     displaying 57
     file shortcut menus 179
     hiding 57

K

KB (kilobyte) 572
Kbps 572
keyboard language, changing 404
keyboard management
     changing key repeat delay and rate 279–280
     configuring text input settings 279
     settings 455–458
     shortcuts 559–564

Keyboard Properties dialog box 279
keywords 572
kilobyte (KB) 572

L

Language Interface Packs 396, 401
language preferences, synchronizing 376
language settings 396–407
     changing Windows display language 404
     configuring options 402–403
     installing additional system
          languages 399–400
laptop computers 572
Large Icons view (File Explorer) 119
layout options (File Explorer) 108
Lens view (Magnifier tool) 449
levels of control, UAC (User Account
     Control) 351
libraries 100–101, 572
     adding folders to 114–115
     changing folder icon 116
     creating 113
     displaying/hiding 113
     File Explorer *See* File Explorer
     hiding 117
     removing folders from 117
Libraries node (File Explorer) 102, 112–117
license certificates 555
limiting system notifications 194
Links toolbar (taskbar) 80–81
List view (File Explorer) 119
live information apps 160
local accounts 5, 346–347, 572
     connecting to Microsoft accounts 369
     creating 363
     passwords 371–372, 374
     pictures 369–371
     switching to, from a Microsoft account 368
local printers 282–285, 572
locating
     apps 152–156
     peripheral device information 252–256
Location action button 466
location-specific language variations 396
lock screen 6–8
     customizing 436–441
     defined 572

locking, defined 572
locking computer 24, 44–45
logo key 559

M

Magnifier tool 444, 572
    changing magnification level 451
    configuring settings 449–452
    magnification views 449
    turning off 452
    turning on 450
Mail app 157, 207–208
mail servers 572
malicious sites, SmartScreen Filter 229–230
malware 228, 572
managing
    audio playback device settings 266–267
    default apps 225
    Edge passwords and form entries 220–221
    Edge settings 214–224
    File Explorer searches 485–489
    hard disk drives 110
    networks 110
    printer connections 280–287
    printer settings 286
    tile groups 62–63
    user accounts 353–369
    Windows 20–21
manual installation, local printers 282–285
manually setting date and time 389
mapping a drive 572
Maps app 158
Math Input Panel 161
maximizing windows 37, 39, 572
MB (megabyte) 572
media 572
Media Devices list (Network window) 301
media management apps 158–159
Media streaming settings, network security
    profiles 305
Medium Icons view (File Explorer) 119
Meetings & Reminders information-tracking
    options (Cortana) 476
megabyte (MB) 572
memory expansion using ReadyBoost 253
menu bar 572

menus 572
    All Apps 152–156
    Store account 167
metadata 572
Microphone Setup wizard 269
microphones 265
    Cortana verbal cues 476–477
    USB-connected 264
Microsoft accounts 4–5
    accessing settings 170
    connecting to local accounts 369
    identity verification 542
    passwords 371–372, 374–375
    pictures 369–371, 373
    registering 368
    switching to a local account 368
Microsoft Edge See Edge
Microsoft Family Safety 356–357
Minimize button 37
minimizing windows 39, 573
Miracast 256, 573
modems 573
Money app 160
monitoring system tasks 501–506
monitors, displaying desktop on multiple
    screens 256–262
More Actions menu (Edge)
    displaying 215
    managing Edge settings 214
More Details view (Task Manager) 501, 503
Most Used apps, Start menu 24–25, 55
mouse accessibility features 455–458
Mouse Keys (Ease Of Access) 455
mouse management 271–278
    button and wheel options 272–273
    button settings 274
    pointer appearance 274–275
    pointer functionality 276–277
    pointer icons 276
    wheel functionality 277–278
mouse ports 250
Movies & TV app 158
Movies & TV information-tracking options
    (Cortana) 476
moving
    apps to different desktops 499–500
    between desktops 499
    files and folders 132–134

moving *(continued)*
taskbar 77
taskbar buttons 181
tile groups, Start screen 63
tiles, Start screen 60–61
windows 40–43
multiple display devices 256–262
Multiple Displays settings 76, 259
multiple monitors 573
multiport hubs 250
multistep procedural instructions xiv
multi-touch gesture 573
Music app 158
Music library 100
Music Tools group (tool tabs) 109
My Library (Store) 171
My Stuff search results 481
Mystify screen saver 442

N

name of computer, changing 338–339
naming Start screen tile groups 62–63
Narrator (Ease Of Access) 444
configuring settings 453–455
defined 573
turning on 454
National Institute of Standards and Technology
(NIST) 391
Natural Wonders category, themes 86
Navigation And Search bar (File Explorer) 111–113
navigation, defined 573
Navigation pane (File Explorer) 104, 111, 573
Navigation pane options 108
Network & Internet settings 30
network adapters 294, 573
disabling 314
displaying status 304
enabling 314–315
Network And Sharing Center 296, 302–304, 573
network connections
configuring security 305–311
connecting to networks 294–300
displaying information about
networks 300–305
sharing files 326–337
troubleshooting 312–316
versus Internet connections 296

network discovery 297, 573
settings, network security profiles 305
turning on 298–299
Network Discovery And File Sharing message
box 298
network domains 573
network drives 573
network hubs 573
Network Infrastructure list, Network
window 301
network interface cards 294
Network node (File Explorer) 102
network printers 281, 573
network profiles 573
network routers 573
network share 573
Network Usage settings 303
Network window 300–301, 303
networks 573
News app 160
News information-tracking options
(Cortana) 476
NIST (National Institute of Standards and
Technology) 391
non-family user accounts 362–365
nonresponsive apps, displaying 503
Note action button 466
Notebook, configuring Cortana
settings 474–478
Notepad 161
notification area 16–17
notifications
apps 190–194
audio devices 265
displaying 21
Notifications & Actions settings 190
Notifications icon 16–17

O

OEM (original equipment manufacturer) 574
offline 573
OneDrive 524, 574
accessing storage options 529
backing up files to 526
connecting 525
fetching files 527, 530
managing settings 526

shortcut to 524
storage size 524
storing files 526
synchronizing folders 528–529
online 574
online safety for children 233
on-screen content, orientation 419
On-Screen Keyboard (Ease Of Access) 455, 574
opening
    Action Center 193
    Computer Management console 355
    default app files 493
    HomeGroup window, Control Panel 319–320
    HomeGroup window, File Explorer 319
    Settings window 34
    Taskbar and Start Menu Properties dialog
        box 76
Open menu (Home tab) 107
operating systems 551, 574
optical character recognition, language-specific
        features 403
Optimize Drives 574
option buttons 574
options 574
Options button, touchscreen tile
        management 176
Options command 108
orientation, on-screen content 419
original equipment manufacturer (OEM) 574
Other Devices list, Network window 301

P

Packages information-tracking options
        (Cortana) 476
page name (website addresses) 227
Paint app 161
panoramic images, themes 87
parallel ports 250, 574
partial-screen configuration, Start screen 52
partitions 574
password reset disks 574
password hints 574
Password-protected sharing settings, network
        security profiles 305
passwords 574
    homegroups 321, 321–322, 324
    local accounts 374

Microsoft accounts 374–375
picture 375, 380
saving and managing (Edge) 220–221
synchronizing 376
system power settings 434
user accounts 353, 371–372
pasting items from the Clipboard 134
paths 574
Peek function 79
peer-to-peer networks 574
peer-to-peer wireless connection, Miracast 256
performance, Task Manager 504
performing upgrade to Windows 10 555–558
peripheral devices 249, 574
    audio 264–271
    disconnecting from computer 286–287
    displaying desktop on multiple
        screens 256–262
    external 250
    installation 251
    internal 250
    keyboard management 278–280
    locating device information 252–256
    mice 271–278
    portable computers and 263
    printers 280–287
    terminology 250–251
permission levels, sharing files 326–327
permissions
    revoking administrator permissions 367
    user accounts 348–349, 366–367
Permissions dialog box 337
personal files 98
personal folders 99, 574
personal identification number (PIN) 375
    changing 378
    creating 377–378
personal information, removing from files 142
Personalization settings 30
phishing 229–230, 574
photos
    as desktop backgrounds 65
    Microsoft accounts 373
    user accounts 369–373
Photos app 159
Photos screen saver 442
picture passwords 375, 380, 574
Picture Tools group (tool tabs) 109

pictures
   as desktop backgrounds 65
   Microsoft accounts 373
   user accounts 353, 369–373
Pictures library 100
PIN (personal identification number) 375
   changing 378
   creating 377–378
   defined 575
pinching (touchscreen interaction) 565
pinned taskbar buttons 575
pinning, defined 575
pinning apps
   to the desktop 181–186
   to the Start screen 175–177
   to the taskbar 180–181
pinning files to a jump list 179
pinning folders
   to a jump list 179
   to the Quick Access list 107
pinning websites to the Start screen 212–213
pixels 575
Playback tab (Sound dialog box) 266
plug-and-play devices 251, 281–282, 575
.png (Portable Network Graphic) 575
pointers (mice) 575
   changing how pointer works 276–277
   changing individual icon 276
   changing looks 274–275
pointing devices 575
pointing (mouse) 575
pop-up windows
   blocking 231–232
   defined 575
portable computers, peripheral devices and 263
Portable Network Graphic (.png) 575
ports 250, 575
Power button 575
power options, configuring 426–434
   Battery Saver feature 435
   changing screen brightness 427–428
   editing advanced settings 432–433
   password requirements 434
   power management settings 428–429
   resetting power plan to defaults 433
   shutdown settings and triggers 434

power plans
   creating custom 431
   deleting custom 433
   modifying 430
   standard 429
Power Saver power plan 426
PowerShell *See* Windows PowerShell
practice files, downloading xii–xiii
preparing for upgrade to Windows 10 549–554
Preview pane (File Explorer) 105, 108, 575
Previous Versions tab, Properties dialog box 139
prices, Store apps 165
primary displays 257, 259, 575
printer connections 280–287
   displaying printer status 286
   managing printer settings 286
   manual installation of local printers 282–285
   network printers 281
   plug-and-play printers 281–282
   virtual printers 288
printer ports, parallel 250
printer sharing 285
Printers & Scanners settings 280
Printers list
   in the Add Printer wizard 284
   in the Network window 301
printing webpages 213
privacy, browsers 233–235
privacy settings 31
   advertising ID 517
   categories 516–517
   configuring 515–519
   Cortana 518
   managing 519
   SmartScreen Filter 517
private networks 309, 575
processes, sorting by resource usage 503–504
product keys 575
productivity apps 157–158
profiles, users 347–348
programs *See* apps; desktop apps; Store apps
progress bars 575
Project action button 466
properties 575
   files and folders 138–142
   Recycle Bin 137

Properties dialog box
  files 140
  folders 138–139
protocol (website addresses) 226
PS/2 keyboard ports 250
Public Folder Sharing settings, network security
    profiles 305
Public folders 99, 576
Public network profile 307
public networks 309, 576
putting computer to sleep 44–45

Q

Quick Access list 128
Quick Access node (File Explorer) 102
Quick Access Toolbar 576
Quick Action buttons, configuring 464–468
Quick Link menu 13, 34
Quiet Hours 193
Quiet Hours action button 466

R

random access memory (RAM) 576
Read permission 326
reading articles, Edge reading list 212
reading list, Edge
  displaying 211
  reading articles 212
Reading List app 207–208, 210
Reading view settings (Edge), configuring 223
Read-only attribute 138
Read/Write permission 326
ReadyBoost 253, 576
rearranging columns, Details view 121
rebuilding search index 489
Recently Added apps (Start menu) 24–25, 55
Recently Opened Items setting 55
recording devices, switching between 268–271
Recording tab (Sound dialog box) 268
recovering folders and files 135–137
recovery drives
  bootable USB 535–536, 539–540
  booting from 540–541
  creating 535–536
Recycle Bin 11, 135, 137, 576
Recycle Bin Tools group (tool tabs) 110

refining File Explorer searches 144
Refresh button 111
refreshing your PC 522–523, 576
Region & Language settings 398–399
regional settings 396–407
  copying to Windows system screens 407
  date and time formats 405–406
registering Microsoft accounts 368
registration keys 576
registries 576
reinstalling Store apps 171–174
relative paths 576
reminders, Cortana 478–479
Remote Desktop Connection 576
Remote Desktop Connection app 162
remote printers 576
removable media 576
removable storage devices 104
removing
  app shortcuts from desktop 186
  app shortcuts from Start screen 177
  app shortcuts from taskbar 181
  columns, Details view 121
  file groupings 124
  file properties 140–142
  folders, libraries 117
  folders, Start menu 57
  personal information from files 142
  system languages 404
  themes 91
  toolbar from taskbar 84
Rename your PC dialog box 339
renaming
  computer 338–339
  folders and files 129–130
  Start screen tile groups 63
Repeat Delay settings, keyboard 280
Repeat Rate settings, keyboard 280
reporting errors xv
reporting unsafe websites 230
reserving copy of Windows 10 552–554
resetting your PC 522, 524, 576
resizing
  columns, Details view 122
  partial-screen Start screen 54
  tiles, Start screen 61
  windows 37–40

resolution 576
resources, homegroups 323, 329–330
restarting computer 44, 46
Restore button 37
restore points 576
    See also computer functionality, restoring
    creating 519, 521
    definition 519
    displaying all 521
restoring
    cascaded, stacked, or side-by-side
      windows 42–43
    computer functionality 519–524
    deleted items 136
    from system images 535–536, 538
    minimized windows 40
    to restore points 520–522
restoring down windows 576
restricting user accounts 367–368
revoking administrative permissions 367
ribbon command interface (File
    Explorer) 104–110
ribbons 576
Ribbons screen saver 442
ribbon tabs 105–108
right-clicking 576
right-drag 576
roots 576
Rotation Lock action button 466
Run As Administrator command, desktop
    apps 156
running
    desktop apps as an administrator 156
    HomeGroup troubleshooter 325
    Troubleshooters 315–316

S

safeguards, user profiles 347–348
Safely Remove Hardware And Eject Media
    icon 287
SafeSearch (Bing), configuring settings 484
safety settings, Microsoft Family Safety 356–357
saved passwords (Edge), managing 221
Saved Pictures library 100
saving
    customized themes 90
    Edge passwords and form entries 220–221

information (web browsers) 207–224
    searches 144
    webpages to Edge favorites list 211
    webpages, to Reading List app 210
Scan app 157
Scanners list (Network window) 301
screen brightness 419
Screen Brightness action button 466
screen brightness, changing 427–428
screen resolution 420–421, 577
Screen Resolution window 260
screen savers 442–443, 577
screen size, configuring Start screen 53–54
ScreenTips 577
scroll action gesture 566
scroll bars 577
search box 13–14, 20
Search box 111
search engines, Edge 218–220
search index 485
    changing advanced indexing options 488
    changing locations being indexed 488
    rebuilding 489
search providers 577
search terms 577
searches 479–489, 577
    Bing content filters 484
    in Edge 207–214
    in File Explorer 485–489
    files and folders 142–144
    filtering results 483–484, 487
    Recycle Bin contents 135
    saving 144
    storage locations 480–484
    web 480–484
secondary clocks, displaying 395
secondary displays 257, 259, 577
security
    blocking pop-up windows 231–232
    browsers, configuring settings 228–232
    browsing privacy 233–235
    configuring network connections 305–311
    Family Safety 356–357
    SmartScreen Filter 229–230, 517
    user profile safeguards 347–348
    wireless networks 310–311
Security tab, Properties dialog box 139
selecting files 132–133

services, Task Manager 505
sessions (computing)
    ending 44–46
    starting 4–9
Set Default Programs window 492–493,
    496–497
set up
    audio devices 264–271
    Cortana 470–472
Set Up Your Mic wizard 410
setting
    accent colors, desktop background 71–72
    default apps 489–497
    desktop background color 68
    desktop background image 66
    File Explorer search options 487
    home page, Edge 215–217
    Microsoft account pictures 373
    mouse button and wheel options 272–273
    user account pictures 372–373
settings
    accessibility features 444–458
    Bing SafeSearch 484
    browser security 228–232
    configuring synchronization 381–382
    Control Panel 32–33
    Cortana 472–478
    desktop background and color 64–68
    device displays 413–421
    displaying categories 34
    Edge 214–224
    lock screen 436–441
    network security profiles 305–309
    power 426–434
    printers 286
    regional and language 396–407
    Settings window 27–34
    speech 408–413
    Store (Windows Store) 166–170
    synchronizing 376
    user accounts 365–369
Settings menu (Cortana Notebook) 475
Settings window 27–34
    Background pane 66–68
    Colors pane 71–72
    configurable features 29–31
    Date & Time pane 388
    Devices page 252

Display pane 258–259
Family & Other Users pane 353–354
Notifications & Actions pane 190
opening 34, 255
Region & Language pane 398–399
Settings window (Store) 167
Share pane (Edge) 207
Share tab (File Explorer) 106
shared components 577
shared drives 577
shared folders 577
shared homegroup resources 329–330
shared printers 577
sharing
    files 577
    information (web browsers) 207–214
    network files 326–337
    printers 285
    webpages 209–210
Sharing tab, Properties dialog box 138
shortcut menus 75, 577
shortcuts 577
    apps 175–187
    keyboard 559–564
    taskbar 15
Show Desktop button 17
Show Hidden Icons button 16
showing hidden items (File Explorer) 108
showing the desktop on only one display 257
shutdown action triggers 434
shutdown settings, configuring 434
shutting down 44, 46, 577
signatures 577
signing in 9, 577
signing out 24, 44–45, 577
sign-in options, user accounts 375–382
single sign-on (SSO) accounts 577
size
    Recycle Bin 137
    Start screen 53–54
    tiles, Start screen 59
    user interface elements 417
Sleep mode 44–45, 577
slideshow
    as desktop background 65
    on lock screen 440
sliding (touchscreen interaction) 565
Small Icons view (File Explorer) 119

smartphone authentication app 542
SmartScreen Filter 229–230, 517, 578
Snap feature 578
snapping windows 41–43
Snipping Tool 161, 578
software 578
    displaying information 256
    piracy 578
solid colors, as desktop background 65
solid-state drives (SSDs) 253
sort order, folder content 124–126
sorting
    files 125
    processes by resource usage 503–504
sound cards 264, 578
Sound dialog box
    Playback tab 266
    Recording tab 268
Sound Recorder 578
spam 578
spanning images (desktop background) 66
speakers, built-in 264
specifying default apps 489–497
    by category 490–491, 495
    by file type 491, 494–495
    by protocol 491–492, 496
    opening a file 492
    Set Default Programs window 492–493,
        496–497
speech recognition 578
    displaying tools 411
    language-specific features 403
    Speech Recognition feature 265, 455
Speech Recognition page (Control Panel) 411
Speech Recognition window 269
speech settings 408–413
    configuring voice recognition 409–411
    displaying Speech pane 409
speed
    network connection 304
    text-to-speech 412–413
spelling
    language-specific features 403
    text input feature 278
Sports app 160
Sports information-tracking options
    (Cortana) 476
spyware 578

SSDs (solid-state drives) 253
SSO (single sign-on) accounts 577
standard libraries 100
standard power-management plans 429
standard ribbon tabs 105–108
Standard User accounts 346, 578
    See also Administrator accounts; user
        accounts
standard Windows notification icons 16
Start button, taskbar 12
Start menu 21–26, 578
    configuring 52–57
    content sections 23
    displaying 26
    jump lists 25
    Most Used section 24–25
    Recently Added section 24–25
    user account information 23–24
Start screen 21–26, 578
    app shortcuts 175–177
    configuring 52–57
    default settings 53
    displaying 26
    full-screen, Start menu open 22
    tile management 58–63
starting
    apps 152–156
    computing sessions 4–9
    File Explorer 111
    InPrivate browsing sessions 234
    Store apps 166
    Task Manager 503
startup apps, management 188–189
Steps Recorder app 162
Sticky Keys tool 456
Sticky Notes app 161
storage locations, searches 480–484
Store (Windows Store) 152
    account menu 167
    managing accounts and settings 166–170
    shopping 163–166
Store apps
    automatic updates 170
    defined 152
    installation 163–174
storing files on OneDrive 526, 529
stretching images (desktop background) 66
stretching (touchscreen interaction) 565

subdomains (website addresses) 227
subfolders 99, 578
supplemental font features, installation 403
support xv
surfing the web 578
swiping (touchscreen interaction) 565
switching users, user accounts 26
switching views (Task Manager) 503
synchronizing
    date and time settings, Internet time
      servers 390–391
    files 578
    OneDrive folders to computers 528–529
    settings 376
system cache 578
system disks 578
system failure, booting from recovery drives 535
system folders 578
system images
    creating backups 535, 536–538
    periodic 535
    restoring from 535, 538
    storing 535, 537
System Information window 255
system languages
    installation 399–400
    removing 404
system repair disc 538
system requirements, upgrading to
    Windows 10 549
System Restore 578
system restore points 519
System settings 30
system tasks, monitoring 501–506

T

tabbed browsing 579
Tablet Mode action button 466
tabs 578
    Edge 217
    ribbon 105–108
    tool 109–111
tags 579
tapping (touchscreen interaction) 565, 579
task management 463
    configuring Quick Action buttons 464–468
    Cortana 469–479

searches 479–489
specifying default apps 489–497
Task Manager 501–506
virtual desktops 497–500
Task Manager 501–506, 579
    displaying performance information 504
    displaying resource usage information 505
    identifying resource-intensive apps 504
    managing services 505
    managing startup processes 188–189
    starting 503
task pane 579
Task view 15
    displaying desktops 499
    managing Windows 20
Task View button 78
taskbar 12–21
    Action Center icon 468
    app shortcuts 178–181
    behavior 78–79
    buttons 579
    changing appearance 73–78
    Cortana 18–19
    date and time information 386
    defined 579
    displaying app window thumbnails 20
    displaying app-management icons 20
    displaying buttons 78
    displaying notifications 21
    displaying buttons 15
    displaying/hiding Task View button 78
    displaying/managing toolbars 80–84
    height 77–78
    hiding 79
    hiding all open windows 21
    managing notifications in the Action
      Center 21
    moving 77
    multiple screens 262
    notification area 16–17
    Quick Link menu 13
    search box 13–14, 579
    searching for content 20
    Start button 12
    Task view 15
    time and date settings 17
Taskbar And Start Menu Properties dialog box,
    opening 76

taskbar toolbars
  Address 80
  Desktop 81
  Links 80
text
  finding on a webpage 208
  prediction, language-specific features 403
  size, user interface elements 418
text input features 278–279
text-to-speech
  changing voice and speed 412–413
  language-specific features 403
  Narrator tool 444
themes 84–91, 579
  applying from Windows website 90
  built-in 85
  customization 88–89
  displaying installed theme 89
  Natural Wonders category 86
  panoramic backgrounds 87
  previewing background images 87
  removing 91
  saving customized themes 90
  synchronizing 376
  unpacked theme files 88
  on Windows website 85
third-party apps 152
This PC node (File Explorer) 102, 104
thumbnails, displaying 20
tile groups, managing 62–63
tiles 579
  adding tiles to tile groups 62
  configuration 58
  moving 60–61
  resizing 61
  size 58–59
  touchscreen management 176
Tiles view 120
tiling images (desktop background) 66
Time & Language settings 31
time servers 386, 390–392
time settings, taskbar 17
time zones 386, 392
title bars 579
TLDs (top-level domains) 226, 228
toast popups 151
Toggle Keys tool 456

tool tabs 109–111
toolbars 80–84, 579
top-level domains (TLDs) 226, 228
touch keyboard 278, 397
touchscreens
  tile management 176
  tips 565–566
Travel information-tracking options
  (Cortana) 476
Troubleshooters 315–316
troubleshooting
  browsing issues 235–238
  network connections 312–316
  using recovery drives 535
turning off
  app notifications 192, 194
  banners and audio notifications 194
  caret browsing 238
  Getting To Know You feature 413
  Magnifier tool 452
  SmartScreen Filter 230
turning on
  app notifications 192
  Audio Description feature 455
  caret browsing 238–239
  keyboard accessibility features 456–457
  Magnifier tool 450
  Narrator tool 454
  network discovery feature 298–299
  SmartScreen Filter 230
two-factor authentication 542
Typing, text input feature 278

U

UAC (User Account Control) 350–352, 580
UI (user interface) 580
UNC (Universal Naming Convention) 579
Uniform Resource Locator (URL) 579
uninstalling Store apps 171–174
Universal Naming Convention (UNC) 579
Universal Serial Bus (USB) 579
Universal Windows apps 579
unpacked theme files 88
Unpin button, touchscreen tile management 176
unread messages, displaying 21
unsafe websites, reporting to Microsoft 230
Update & Security settings 31

updates
    caching 513
    checking for 514
    configuring 513–516
    displaying status 514
    files 35–36
    installing 512, 514
    timing installation 514
    turning off automatic app updates 170
upgrades 513, 579
upgrading to Windows 10 547–558
    manually initiating update 552
    performing the update 555–558
    preparing for the update 549–554
    reserving copy of Windows 10 552–554
    upgrade paths 548
    Windows Update tool 548–549
URL (Uniform Resource Locator) 579
USB (Universal Serial Bus) 579
USB flash drives 580
USB hubs 580
USB ports 250, 580
USB recovery drives 539–540
USB-connected microphones 264
User Account Control (UAC) 350–352, 580
user accounts 580
    Administrator 348–349, 365
    Adult 347
    buttons 580
    Child 347
    creating 354
    defined 346
    displaying controls 26
    family 349–350
    Guest 365
    local 5, 346, 363, 368, 369
    managing 353–369
    Microsoft 4–5, 346, 368–369
    names 580
    passwords 353, 371–372
    permissions 348–349, 366–367
    pictures 353, 369–373, 580
    restricting 367–368
    settings 365–369
    signing out 24
    sign-in options 375–382
    Standard 346, 578
    Start menu settings 23–24
    switching users 24, 26
    UAC (User Account Control) 350–352
    user profiles 347–348
user credentials 580
user interface (UI) 580
user interface elements 417–418
user profiles 347–348
Users folders 99
UTC time 386
utility apps 161

V
verbal cues, Cortana and 472–474, 476–477
verbal searches 483
VGA ports 250
video projectors 580
Videos library 100
View tab (File Explorer) 106
View tab (Folder Options dialog box) 127
viewing
    file history 533–534
    update history 36
virtual desktops 497–500, 580
virtual printers 288, 580
virtual systems 580
viruses 580
voice recognition, configuring 409–411
Voice Recorder app 157
VPN action button 466

W
Weather app 160
Weather information-tracking options
    (Cortana) 476
web browsers 158, 580
    configuring security settings 228–232
    displaying websites in Edge 203–206
    Edge 202
    managing Edge settings 214–224
    privacy 233–235
    synchronizing settings 376
    troubleshooting issues 235–238
web logs 580
web searches 207–214, 480–484
web (World Wide Web) 580
webcams 580

webpages
    annotating 208–209
    finding text 208
    printing 213
    saving to Edge favorites list 211
    saving to Reading List app 210
    sharing 209–210
website addresses, anatomy of 226–227
websites 580
    displaying in Edge 203–206
    pinning to Start screen, Edge 212–213
Welcome screen 7–8, 381, 581
WEP (Wired Equivalent Privacy) 581
wheel options, mice 272–273, 277–278
WiDi (Wi-Fi Direct) technology 256, 260–261
Wi-Fi action button 466
Wi-Fi Direct (WiDi) technology 256, 260–261
Wi-Fi Protected Access (WPA) 581
wildcard characters 581
window layout, File Explorer 104–105
windows 581
    arranging 40–43
    cascading and snapping 41
    closing 37–40
    dragging 42
    hiding 21, 37–40
    managing in Task view 20
    moving 40–43
    resizing 37–40
Windows, upgrading other versions to
    Windows 10 547–558
Windows Journal app 161
Windows Media Player 159
Windows PowerShell 162
Windows PowerShell ISE (Integrated Scripting
    Environment) 162
Windows ReadyBoost 581
Windows Search 142–143
Windows Spotlight lock screen 439
Windows Store See Store (Windows Store)
Windows To Go 581
Windows Update 35–36, 548–549, 581
    See also updates
    configuring 513–516
    displaying status 514
Windows 10 upgrade paths 548
Windows Defender 228, 581
Windows DVD Player app 159

Windows Fax And Scan app 161
Windows Firewall 581
Windows folders 99
Windows Hello 376–379, 542
Windows Insider builds 513, 515
window-sizing buttons 37
Wired Equivalent Privacy (WEP) 581
wired networks, disconnecting 299
wireless connections, Miracast 256
wireless devices 251
wireless display (WiDi) 581
wireless networks
    connecting to 297–298
    disconnecting 299–300
    security 310–311
wireless screen extensions 260–261
wizards 581
WordPad 161
work networks 581
workgroups 581
World Clock page (Alarms & Clock app) 387
World Wide Web (web) 580
WPA (Wi-Fi Protected Access) 581

X

XML (Extensible Markup Language) 569
XML Paper Specification (XPS) 162, 581
XPS Viewer app 162
XPS (XML Paper Specification) 162, 581

Y

Your Account settings 371–372
Your Apps page (My Library) 171
Your Games page (My Library) 171

Z

zipped folders See compressed folders
zipper, compressed folders 130
zoom gestures 566

About the authors

Joan Lambert has worked closely with Microsoft technologies since 1986, and in the training and certification industry since 1997. As President and CEO of Online Training Solutions, Inc. (OTSI), Joan guides the translation of technical information and requirements into useful, relevant, and measurable resources for people who are seeking certification of their computer skills or who simply want to get things done efficiently.

Joan is the author or coauthor of more than three dozen books about Windows and Office (for Windows, Mac, and iPad), video-based training courses for SharePoint and OneNote, and three generations of Microsoft Office Specialist certification study guides. She provides certification development consulting services to software companies, universities, and certification vendors, and enjoys communicating about the benefits of technology at onsite training events.

Joan is a Microsoft Certified Professional, Microsoft Office Specialist Master (for all Office versions since Office 2007), Microsoft Certified Technology Specialist (for Windows and Windows Server), Microsoft Certified Technology Associate (for Windows), Microsoft Dynamics Specialist, and Microsoft Certified Trainer.

Joan currently lives in a small town in Texas with her simply divine daughter, Trinity; an ever-growing menagerie of dogs, cats, and fish (and the occasional frog, lizard, or vole); and the DeLonghi Gran Dama super-automatic espresso machine that runs the house.

Joan's first publishing collaboration with her father, Steve, was the inclusion of her depiction of *Robots in Love* in one of his earliest books, *Presentation Graphics on the Apple Macintosh*.

Steve Lambert started playing with computers in the mid-1970s. As computers evolved from wire-wrap and solder to consumer products, he evolved from hardware geek to programmer and writer.

Steve has written or co-written more than 20 books on developing technologies, including *Presentation Graphics on the Apple Macintosh*, *Creative Programming in Microsoft Basic*, the CD-ROM *The New Papyrus*, and *Internet Basics: Your Online Access to the Global Electronic Superhighway*. Steve is also the author of *Built by Anhalt*, a biographical exploration into the life and architecture of the famed Seattle architect Fred Anhalt.

Steve has specialized for many years in the conversion of content from one format to another, including projects such as the Microsoft Programmer's Library in 1988 and the conversion of the 25-volume Funk & Wagnalls Encyclopedia for the initial Microsoft Encarta CD-ROM. He has created several content authoring and delivery systems, including those used by the Microsoft Mastering Series, the Quick Course Series, and numerous pubStudio titles that are published by Microsoft and several US government agencies. He is a strong advocate of good template design and of using Microsoft Visual Basic for Applications (VBA) automation to smooth out the conversion, assembly, formatting, and validation of content for delivery via print, ebook, or web.

Steve and Joan's first collaboration

Acknowledgments

As always, we appreciate the time and efforts of Carol Dillingham, Rosemary Caperton, and the team at Microsoft Press—past and present—who made this and so many other books possible.

We are extremely grateful for the support of the many people without whom this book would not exist, particularly these talented members of America's finest publishing team at OTSI:

- **Angela Martin** for thoroughly and efficiently indexing this book so readers can find the information they're looking for

- **Jaime Odell** for proofreading, copyediting support, and late-night "live thesaurus" services

- **Jean Trenary** for creating the production template and laying out the book

- **Jeanne Craver** for processing and pixelating graphics

- **Kathy Krause** for developmental editing, copyediting support, and proofreading the final product

- **Susie Carr** for shepherding the project through to completion, firm but gentle nudging, and indexing support

- **Val Serdy** for thoughtful and thorough copyediting and invaluable assistance with content structuring

OTSI specializes in the design and creation of Microsoft Office, SharePoint, and Windows training solutions and the production of online and printed training resources. For more information about OTSI, visit *www.otsi.com* or follow us on Facebook at *www.facebook.com/Online.Training.Solutions.Inc* for advance information about upcoming training resources and informative tidbits about technology and publishing.

We hope you enjoy this book and find it useful. While working on this book, we were guided by all the feedback submitted by readers of previously published *Windows Step by Step* books. If you find errors or omissions in this book, or feel compelled to say something positive about it, you can use the feedback process outlined in the introduction.

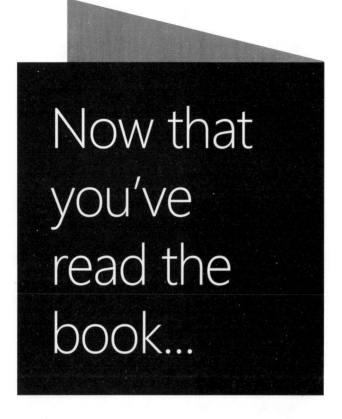

Now that you've read the book...

Tell us what you think!

Was it useful?
Did it teach you what you wanted to learn?
Was there room for improvement?

Let us know at http://aka.ms/tellpress

Your feedback goes directly to the staff at Microsoft Press,
and we read every one of your responses. Thanks in advance!

 Microsoft